SCIENCE AnyTime™

Harcourt Brace & Company

Orlando   Atlanta   Austin   Boston   San Francisco   Chicago   Dallas   New York
Toronto   London

This book is printed on acid-free recycled
content paper, containing
MORE THAN
10% POSTCONSUMER WASTE

Authors

Napoleon A. Bryant, Jr.
Professor Emeritus of Education
Xavier University
Cincinnati, Ohio

Marjorie Slavick Frank
Specialist in Literacy and Language Development
Adjunct Faculty, Hunter, Brooklyn, and
Manhattan Colleges
Brooklyn, New York

Gerald Krockover
Professor of Science Education
School of Mathematics and Science Center
Purdue University
West Lafayette, Indiana

Mozell Lang
Science Specialist
Michigan Department of Education
Lansing, Michigan

Carol J. Valenta
Director of Education
California Museum of Science and Industry
Los Angeles, California

Barry A. Van Deman
Director
International Museum of Surgical Science
Chicago, Illinois

Advisors

Betsy Balzano
Professor
State University of New York
Brockport, New York

Anne R. Biggins
Speech-Language Pathologist
Fairfax County Public Schools
Fairfax, Virginia

Walter Brautigan
State University of New York
Brockport, New York

Gerard F. Consuegra
Director of Curriculum Coordination and
Implementation
Montgomery County Public Schools
Rockville. Maryland

Robert H. Fronk
Head, Science Education Department
Florida Institute of Technology
Melbourne, Florida

Carolyn Gambrel
Learning Disabilities Teacher
Fairfax County Public Schools
Fairfax, Virginia

Joyce E. Haines
Instructor of Humanities
Haskell Indian Nations University
Lawrence, Kansas

Chris Hasegawa
Associate Professor of Teacher Education
California State University
Sacramento, California

Asa Hilliard III
Fuller E. Calloway Professor of Urban Education
Georgia State University
Atlanta, Georgia

V. Daniel Ochs
Professor of Science Education
University of Louisville
Louisville, Kentucky

Donna M. Ogle
Chair, Reading & Language Arts Department
National-Louis University
Evanston, Illinois

Young Pai
Interim Dean, School of Education
University of Missouri
Kansas City, Missouri

Susan Cashman Paterniti
School Board Member
Fort Charlotte, Florida

Barbara S. Pettegrew
Associate Professor
Otterbein College
Westerville, Ohio

Stearns W. Rogers
Professor of Chemistry
McNeese State University
Lake Charles, Louisiana

CONTENTS

Unit A

Weather Watch

Investigating Weather and Climate

Unit B

The Inside Story

Cells and Body Systems

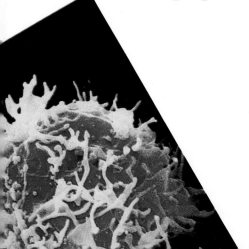

v

Unit C

StarBase Earth

The Solar System and Beyond

Unit D

Cooking with Science

Interactions of Matter and Energy

Unit E

Prairie Dog Tales

Exploring the Grassland Biome

Unit F

Amusement Park

Experiencing Forces and Motion

SCIENCE ANYTIME

Doesn't Calvin have a wonderful imagination? Where do you suppose he gets his ideas? You probably use what you have learned in science class in your everyday life. How does what you learn make your life easier or make the world around you easier to understand? What kinds of questions do you have as you study science? The following pages show an exciting process you will use this year as you study science.

Wonder...

Many science discoveries begin when someone says, "I wonder ..." What do *you* wonder about?

I PLAN

Plan.

Scientists wonder and then plan how they will
find answers to their questions. You too can be a
scientist by planning ways to answer questions
you wonder about. You may do some things with
your class. Other things you may do in a small
group or by yourself. However you work, your
plan will guide you.

Investigate

Finding answers to your **I Wonder** questions will lead you to do investigations. Investigations can be activities, research, reading, talking to experts, using a computer, or watching videos.

Your investigations may answer some of your questions, but they may also lead to new questions.

Reflect

Investigations are not complete until you reflect on what you did and what you learned. When you reflect, you think about something quietly and calmly. Reflecting helps you make sense of the science you are learning.

You will have many opportunities to share your science discoveries with others. By sharing, you will continue to learn about your topic and about communicating to others what you have discovered. As you listen to others share, you will also continue to learn.

Share...

Act.

People who make discoveries often try to use what they have discovered. You may take action this year by setting up a family weather-emergency evacuation plan, drawing up a "Stop the Spread of Colds" poster for your classroom, taking part in a community cleanup day, or becoming a volunteer at a local planetarium.

As you **wonder, plan, investigate, reflect, share,** and **act,** you will be a scientist at work. What an exciting year of science discoveries lies ahead!

WEATHER WATCH

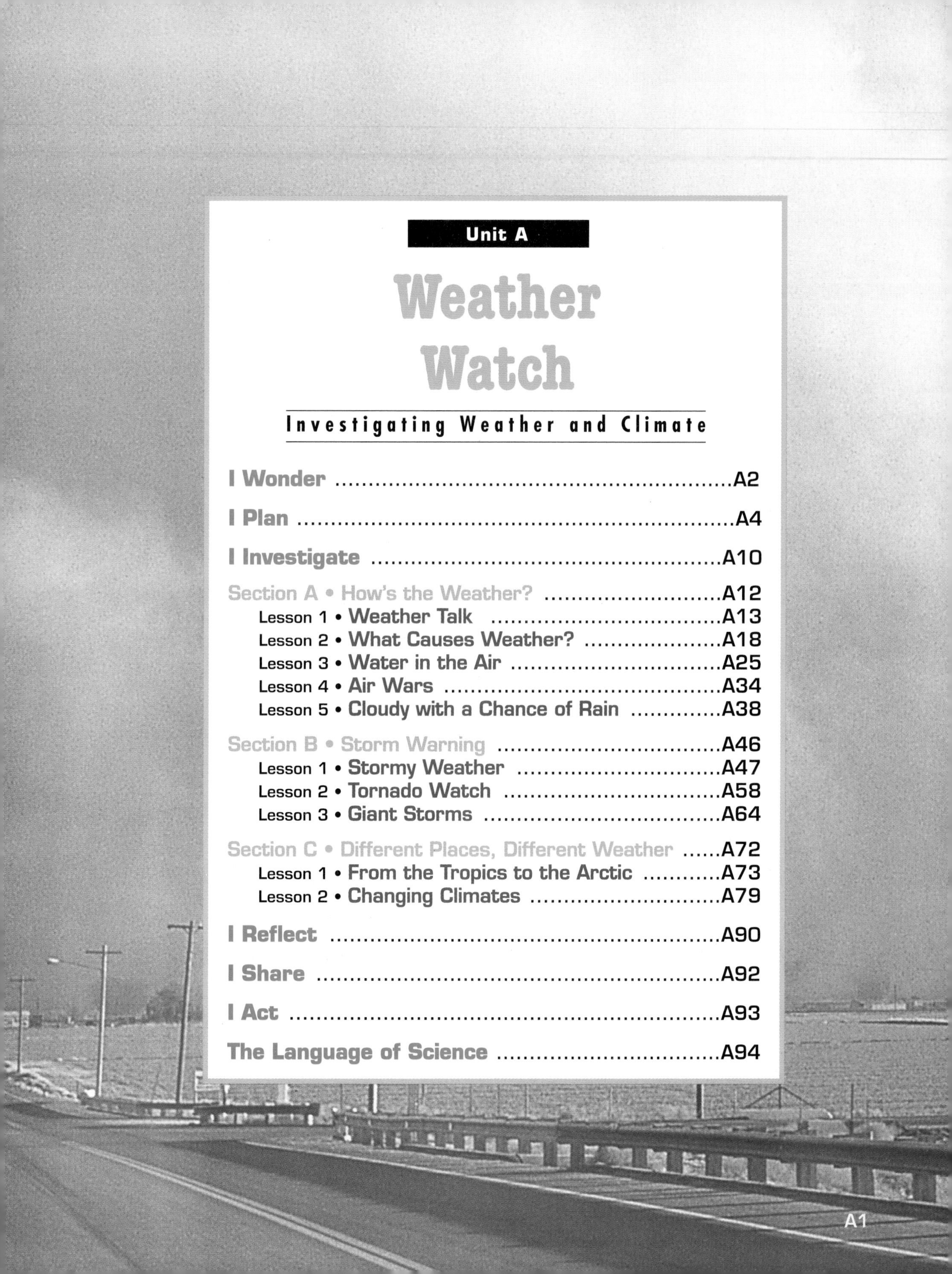

Weather Watch

Investigating Weather and Climate

I WONDER

Science begins with wondering. What do you wonder about when you see storms like those shown?

Work with a partner to make a list of weather questions you may have. Be ready to share your list with the rest of the class.

Approaching storm
Waterspout and lightning

A3

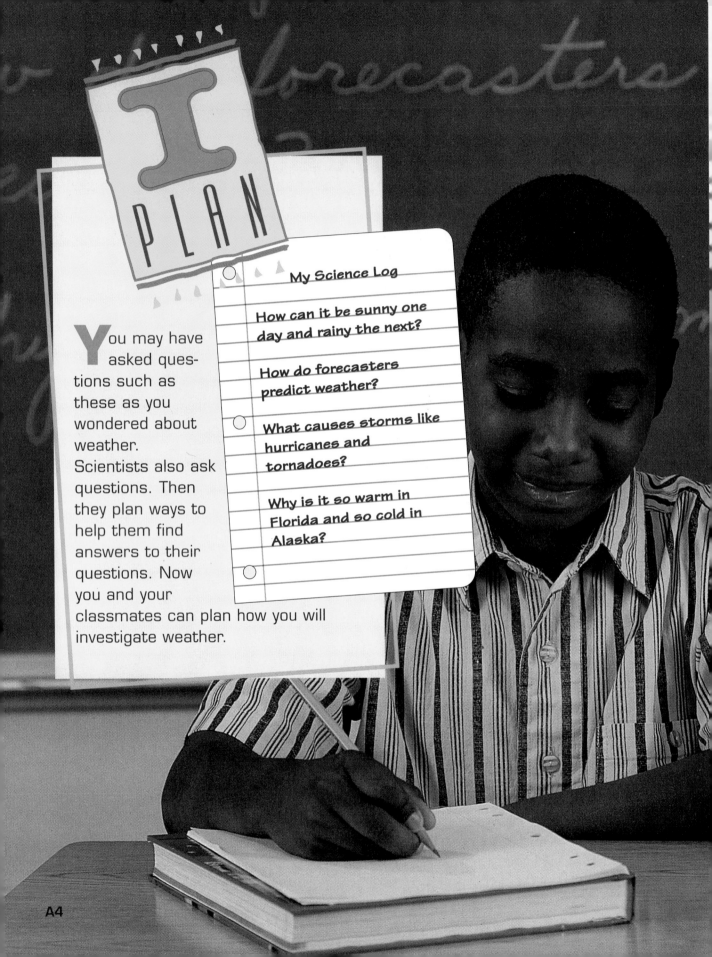

I PLAN

You may have asked questions such as these as you wondered about weather. Scientists also ask questions. Then they plan ways to help them find answers to their questions. Now you and your classmates can plan how you will investigate weather.

My Science Log

How can it be sunny one day and rainy the next?

How do forecasters predict weather?

What causes storms like hurricanes and tornadoes?

Why is it so warm in Florida and so cold in Alaska?

With Your Class

Plan how your class will use the activities and readings from the **I Investigate** part of this unit. Decide what other resources you might use.

On Your Own

There are many ways to learn about weather. Following are some things you can do to explore weather by yourself or with some classmates. Some explorations may take longer to do than others. Look over the suggestions and choose . . .

- Projects to Do
- People to Contact
- Books to Read

PROJECTS TO DO

WEATHER SHOW

Set up a weather station at school. Place a thermometer, a rain gauge, and a barometer on the school grounds or on a windowsill. Check your instruments twice a day and prepare a daily weather report. Use the information gathered from your weather station or a newspaper weather map to predict tomorrow's weather. Then, if your school has closed-circuit TV, present a weather broadcast for the school, or post your daily forecast on a school bulletin board.

SCIENCE FAIR PROJECT

Review the **I Wonder** questions you and your partner asked. One way to find answers to these questions is through a science fair project. Choose one of your questions. Plan a project that will help you answer the question. Discuss your plan with your teacher. With his or her approval, begin work by collecting materials and finding resources. Then carry out your plan.

WEATHER DIORAMA

Choose a weather condition and create a diorama illustrating the condition. You might want to show a bright, sunny day in a park or a rainstorm on a city street. Be creative in your use of materials. For example, you could use dyed cotton balls for storm clouds and shredded plastic wrap for rain.

PEOPLE TO CONTACT

IN PERSON

Almost everyone has a weather story to tell. People might recall a particularly hot summer, a huge snowstorm, or a violent thunderstorm. Talk to relatives, friends, and neighbors. Ask them to recall a weather event and tell how it affected them.

Take notes during your interview and organize your notes so you can share your information in an interesting way.

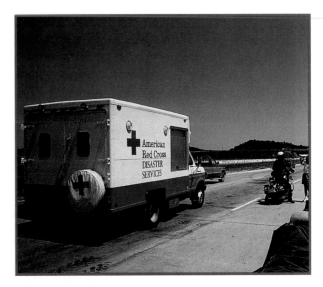

- Federal Emergency Management Agency
- National Guard
- American Red Cross
- Salvation Army

BY TELEPHONE

A weather disaster strikes, and people need help. Answering their calls for help are individual volunteers, government agencies, and many service organizations. What kinds of help do agencies and organizations provide? You can call them to find out. You might try calling one of these groups or organizations, but don't call during an actual emergency.

BY COMPUTER

Use a computer with a modem to connect to on-line services or bulletin boards. You can look for weather news from around the world and talk with others to find out what the weather is like where they live.

Perhaps the computers at your school are connected to Internet, an international network of computers. Internet links computer users in more than 40 countries worldwide. Contact students in several parts of the world. Ask them about any unusual weather they may have had recently.

BOOKS TO READ

Burton and Stanley

by Frank O'Rourke (David R. Godine, 1993). How did two African storks end up on a roof in a small American town? They were blown in by a twister. In this funny, modern tall tale, the storks try to adapt to American bird life although they still long to return home. Read to find out what happens.

Weather

by John Farndon (Dorling Kindersley, 1992). It's been raining cats and dogs—well, not really. But it *has* rained frogs and fish. Fun weather facts and scientific information are highlighted throughout this book. Its lively illustrations add a humorous touch. What different people have believed about weather and how to test for acid rain are just two of the topics you will learn more about.

More Books to Read

Tornadoes

by Stephen Kramer (Carolrhoda, 1992). What color is a tornado? What's the difference between a tornado watch and a tornado warning? This book answers these and many other questions about tornadoes. Photographs, maps, and diagrams illustrate the information about these violent storms. You'll read interesting tornado facts, including how and where tornadoes form.

Hurricane

by Christopher Lampton (Millbrook, 1991). "The first sign is a change in the waves." From this opening sentence, the book goes on to describe the fury and power of hurricanes. You will read how hurricanes form, the destruction they can cause, ways of predicting hurricanes, and safety procedures to follow.

The Crystal Drop

by Monica Hughes (Simon & Schuster, 1993). In this book, the year is 2011. Megan is in charge now. She and her younger brother must leave the dying farm to find a place with water and life. There has been no rain, only the wind. Megan takes her brother and begins a journey toward water and hope. Read about their courageous journey.

Global Warming: Assessing the Greenhouse Threat

by Laurence Pringle (Little, Brown, 1990). Is global warming a threat to the future? Will the polar ice caps melt? You can find out about the possible dangers of global warming by reading this book.

INVESTIGATE

To find answers to their questions, scientists read, think, talk to others, and do experiments. Their investigations often lead to new questions.

In this unit, you will have many chances to think and work like a scientist. How will you find answers to questions you asked?

▶ **OBSERVING** You use your senses of sight, hearing, smell, and touch to observe the world around you. Sometimes you use instruments to extend your senses.

▶ **INTERPRETING DATA** Data is information given to you or information that you gather during activities. When you interpret data, you decide what it means.

▶ **PREDICTING** A prediction is a statement about what you think will happen. To make a prediction, you think about what you've observed before. You also think about how to interpret the data you have.

Are you ready to begin?

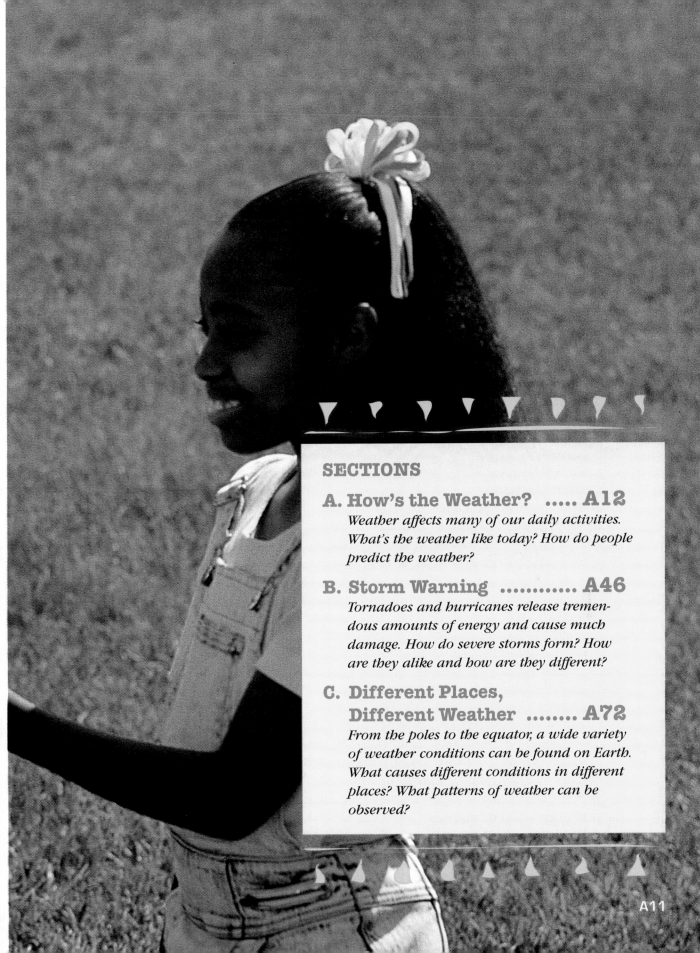

SECTIONS

How's the Weather?

▲ Barometer

Have you ever been awakened by a thunderstorm? The roar of thunder and the clatter of rain may have jolted you awake. Your first thought may have been about the things you had planned to do that day. But weather affects you in many different ways. This section discusses different types of weather and their causes.

What kinds of weather are common in your area? How does the weather affect what you do and when you do it? In your Science Log, identify ways in which the weather affects you and other living things as you work through the investigations that follow.

1 WEATHER TALK

Charles Dudley Warner said, "Everybody talks about the weather, but nobody does anything about it." Some people use weather sayings to predict what the weather will be. Many people read the weather forecasts in their daily newspaper. What's the best way to find out what the weather will be? In the activities that follow, you can decide which are more accurate, weather sayings or modern predictions.

Weather Sayings

You will need: poster board and markers

Choose a weather saying from those listed below. Work with a partner. Using poster board and markers, draw a picture that illustrates one of the sayings. Then, in small groups, decide if each saying represents an accurate way to predict the weather.

Red sky at night, sailor's delight;

Red sky at morning, sailors take warning.

When smoke descends, good weather ends.

Flies will swarm before a storm.

A halo around the moon or sun

Means that rain will surely come.

When the dew is on the grass,

Rain will never come to pass.

When the bees stay near the hive, rain is close by.

Summer fog will scorch a hog.

Ring around the sun, rain before night is done.

Birds gathered on the ground

Means rain will soon come down.

Moss dry, sunny sky;

Moss wet, rain you'll get.

Bubbles in the puddles means it will rain all day.

In the News

Suppose you're watching your favorite TV program, and suddenly you hear *Beep! Beep! Beep! Beep!* A warning about a severe thunderstorm in your area prints across the bottom of the screen. TV and radio stations as well as newspapers provide daily weather reports along with special weather bulletins. The reports tell what the day's weather has been and predict what it will be in the next few days. You can find out just how accurate these predictions are by doing this activity.

MATERIALS

- newspaper weather forecasts
- notebook paper
- graph paper
- colored pencils
- Science Log data sheet

DO THIS

1 Every day for one week, highlight newspaper predictions for high and low temperatures and for precipitation—rain, sleet, or snow. Or, if you prefer, take notes based on TV weather reports.

2 Record the actual temperatures and precipitation for each day.

3 On graph paper, draw a line graph that shows the predicted high and low temperatures in one color and the actual temperatures in another.

4 Make a table that shows whether precipitation did or did not occur as predicted.

THINK AND WRITE

Compare and contrast the predicted and actual weather data you recorded. Write a paragraph telling how alike or how different the predicted and actual temperatures and precipitation were.

. . . SEVERE THUNDERSTORM WARNING

Predicting Weather

People have always tried to predict the weather. As you read the stories about Mario and his grandfather, think about some of the ways that predicting the weather has changed over the years.

 Mario saw his abuelo, or grandfather, reading the newspaper at the kitchen table. "Abuelo," cried Mario excitedly, "want to go to the beach?"

"Maybe tomorrow, Mario," his grandfather answered. "I'm a little stiff today. That arthritis in my hip is giving me trouble again. I guess that means we'll get some rain this afternoon."

Mario eyed his grandfather with a puzzled look. "Abuelo, how does your hip know it's going to rain? The sky looks clear to me."

His grandfather sighed. "I don't know how my hip knows, but the weather forecaster predicted we'd have rain by this afternoon. Remember the drawings you made for a science assignment about the old weather sayings? How many of those sayings are usually true?"

"Some of the sayings might be right sometimes, but not always," Mario answered. "Why did people make up those sayings, Abuelo?" he asked, sitting down at the table. "Some of them are even kind of silly."

"They're not silly at all," replied his grandfather. "Remember, many years ago people didn't have accurate instruments to measure things like temperature and wind speed. Even after weather instruments were invented, there was no TV or radio to get the weather reports to the people.

Those old weather sayings were based on the observations people made before a change in the weather. For example, they remembered what the sky had looked like just before a storm. And as you found out, some sayings really are pretty accurate."

"Well, I still like the weather reports on TV better," said Mario. "Scientists can measure and track all kinds of weather. Remember how we watched The Weather Channel ™ before Hurricane Andrew hit?"

His grandfather leaned back in his chair and folded his arms across his chest. "Sure do, Mario. Even though the storm caused a lot of damage here in South Florida, many lives were saved because of the accuracy of tracking that storm. I guess the modern way is better. But my hip still hurts, so I think we should wait until tomorrow to go to the beach."

THINK ABOUT IT

How does the way we predict weather today differ from the way people predicted weather when Mario's grandfather was young?

Weather Instruments

Predicting the weather today requires complicated instruments that were not available when Mario's grandfather was young. Look at these weather instruments and see if you can figure out how each would be helpful for predicting the weather.

▶ **A barometer measures air pressure.**

▼ **Shipboard weather station**

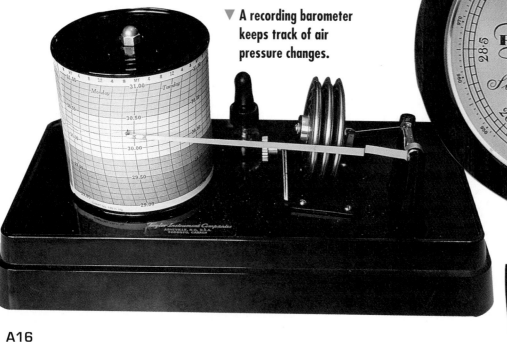

▶ **Home weather stations measure tempurature, air pressure, and humidity**

▼ **A recording barometer keeps track of air pressure changes.**

▶ **Weather balloons record conditions in the upper atmosphere.**

◀ **Antique spiral thermometer**

◀ **Pyrometer for measuring extreme temperatures**

QUICK CHECK

LESSON 1 REVIEW

Think about weather predictions. Which provide more accurate predictions of the weather—traditional weather sayings or modern weather forecasts?

A17

2 WHAT CAUSES WEATHER?

Have you ever thought about what causes weather? Many different factors—such as temperature, moisture, and wind—combine to produce the weather where you live. In the following activities, you will explore the temperature factor and the role of the sun in producing wind.

ACTIVITY

The Sun's Rays

DO THIS

1 On the globe, tape one thermometer on the equator at a point in South America. Tape another thermometer at a location in the central United States. Tape the third thermometer at the North Pole.

2 Record the temperature reading of each thermometer.

3 **CAUTION: Do not touch the hot light bulb.** Set the lamp about 50 cm from the globe, and aim the lamp at the equator. Now turn on the lamp.

4 Predict what will happen to the temperature reading of each thermometer. Check your predictions by recording the temperature reading of each thermometer every 5 minutes for 20 minutes.

THINK AND WRITE

▶ **PREDICTING** Scientists often make predictions based on their observations. What would happen if you moved the thermometer on the United States to a position halfway between the South Pole and the equator? Would the temperature reading change very much? Explain.

A18

The Sun's Energy

Earth's weather starts with the sun. Sunlight provides the energy that produces weather. Even though some parts of the Earth receive more sunlight than other parts, there is weather everywhere on Earth. How much of the sun's energy does it take to produce weather?

Although it was nearly November, the weather in Miami was still hot. Mario sat in front of a big fan, reading a letter from his pen pal in Argentina. "I'm freezing here," Emilio wrote. "It's been raining for three days, and I haven't seen the sun all week."

Mario wasn't suprised. Rio Gallegos, Emilio's hometown, is pretty far south. Mario remembered the science activity he had done in class with the light and the globe. He had taped the thermometer over Rio Gallegos, and it had registered a much lower temperature than the thermometer he had placed over Miami. The teacher had said that energy is needed to make weather, and that energy comes from the sun.

The sun gives off energy in all directions. But the Earth receives only a small portion of that energy. Clouds bounce some of the energy back into space. Water vapor and carbon dioxide in the air take in some more of the energy, warming the air slightly.

Study the diagram. Notice that just over half of the sun's energy reaches the Earth's surface. Most is absorbed, but a little is reflected, or bounced back, into the air. In the next activity, you can see how air is heated.

THINK ABOUT IT

What happens to the sun's energy when it reaches the Earth?

100% incoming solar radiation

5% reflected by surface

25% scattered and reflected by clouds and air

20% absorbed by ozone, clouds and atmosphere

50% absorbed by surface

A19

ACTIVITY

The Sun Heats Water and Land

Have you ever walked barefoot on a sunny day? Did all of the surfaces on which you walked feel the same? In this activity, you will explore how the sun heats different surfaces.

MATERIALS
- 2 cake pans
- water
- dry soil
- 2 ring stands
- string
- 2 thermometers
- gooseneck lamp
- stopwatch
- Science Log data sheet

DO THIS

1. Fill one pan with water and the other with dry soil. Place the pans next to each other. Place a ring stand near each pan.

2. With the string, suspend a thermometer from each ring stand so that it is about 5 cm above the pan. Wait until the temperature readings of the thermometers are the same. Position the lamp so that the light bulb is about 30 cm above the top of the pans.

3. **CAUTION: Do not touch the hot light.** Record the temperatures above the water and above the soil every 2 minutes for a total of 10 minutes.

4. Turn off the lamp and continue to record the temperatures above the water and the soil every 2 minutes for a total of 10 minutes.

THINK AND WRITE

1. When the sun shines, which heats faster, land or water? During the night, which cools more slowly, land or water?

2. What can you infer from this about the heating and cooling of the air over land and water?

Moving Air

You can infer from the last activity that air is heated by the surface below it. If the surface is warm, the air will be warm, and if the surface is cold, the air will be cold. This activity will give you an idea of what happens to warm and cold air.

DO THIS

1 Unfold the paper bags. Tape one end of a piece of string to the bottom of each bag.

2 Tie the free end of one of the strings near one end of the meter stick. Tie the free end of the other string near the opposite end of the meter stick.

3 Tie the third piece of string to the center of the meter stick. Hold the center string, and then slide one of the strings taped to the bags until the bags are balanced.

4 **CAUTION: Be careful not to touch the hot light bulb or look directly at it.** Turn on the lamp and place it under one of the paper bags, with the bulb pointing up. Observe what happens. After 30 seconds, turn off the lamp. Again observe what happens.

THINK AND WRITE

1. What happened to the bag over the lamp? What happened to the bag when the lamp was turned off?

2. Why do you think this happened?

What Makes the Wind?

Mario discovers that a beach is a good place to observe how wind is produced. Think about a windy place near you. Then try to figure out what factors produce wind there.

 At last, Mario and his grandfather make it to the beach on Virginia Key. A cool breeze is blowing in from the Atlantic. It is clear and sunny, a perfect day for kite flying.

Mario has no trouble getting his kite into the air—the breeze is very strong—but it won't fly out over the water. No matter how hard he tries, the kite will fly only over the land. "Abuelo," Mario complains, "why won't my kite fly right? I can't get it to fly over the ocean."

"There's nothing wrong with your kite, Mario," his grandfather answers. "There's a *brisa marina*, a sea breeze, here."

"What do you mean by a sea breeze, Abuelo?" the boy asks.

His grandfather points from the sun to the sand and explains: "The sun heats the land, so the air above it gets warm. Did you notice how much warmer the sand is than the water?"

"Yeah, I did!" the boy replies.

"Well," continues his grandfather, "it's like the science activity you told me you did in school. Remember the one with the paper bags and the warm and cool air? The air over the land gets very warm and light. The air over the water is cooler and heavier. Air moves from where it is heavy to where it is light. The heavy, cool air from the ocean moves under the warm air over the land and pushes it up. All that movement of air is what makes the wind."

"OK," Mario replies, and then asks, "but Abuelo, why did you call this a sea breeze?"

His grandfather smiles at Mario and asks him, "Where is the wind coming from?"

"From the ocean," Mario answers.

"Right," says his grandfather. "A wind is named for the place it comes from. Back in Cuba, there is a wind that blows down from the mountains, because the mountain air is cool and heavy, just like the ocean air. This wind is called *brisa del montes*. There are many names for these **local winds**, depending on where they come from.

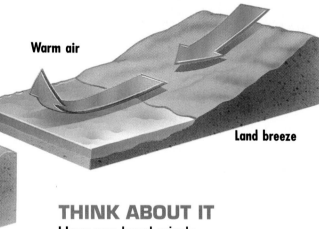

Warm air

Cool air

Sea breeze

Cool air

Warm air

Land breeze

THINK ABOUT IT
How are local winds produced where you live, and what special names do they have?

They Call the Wind . . .

Sometimes in midwinter a warm, dry wind blows down the eastern side of the Rocky Mountains, causing a sudden rise in temperature. The people living there call this wind *chinook*. People around the world have names for local winds. Try to locate the country or region where each of the winds in the list blows.

You will need: Science Log

Working with a partner, read the name and description of each wind. Then use a map to find the country or region where the wind occurs. You may also use dictionaries and other reference sources.

Wind Words

chinook (chih NOOK) — a warm, dry wind that blows down the eastern side of the Rocky Mountains

monsoon (mahn SOON) — a wind that causes wet summers and dry winters

sirocco (suh RAHK oh) — a hot, dust-carrying wind that blows from the Sahara

imbat (im BAHT) — a sea breeze

zonda (ZOHN duh) — a hot, dry wind that blows down the slopes of the Andes Mountains

kapalilua (kah pah lee LOO uh) — a Hawaiian breeze

fumarea (foo muh REE uh) — a wind that stirs up waves in the Adriatic Sea

shamal (shuh MAHL) — a dry, sand-carrying wind

◀ Anemometer, or wind meter

Prevailing Winds

In addition to local winds, such as sea breezes and chinooks, there are places where the wind blows constantly from the same direction. In other places the wind almost never blows. A passing sailboat causes Mario to think about part of a poem his teacher read to the class the day before.

from
THE RIME OF THE
ANCIENT MARINER

by Samuel Taylor Coleridge

Down dropt the breeze, the sails dropt down,
'Twas sad as sad could be;
And we did speak only to break
The silence of the sea!
All in a hot and copper sky,
The bloody Sun, at noon,
Right up above the mast did stand,
No bigger than the Moon.
Day after day, day after day,
We stuck, nor breath, nor motion,
As idle as a painted ship
Upon a painted ocean.

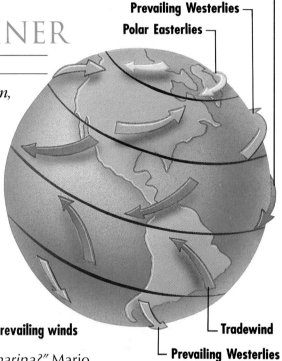

Tradewinds —
Prevailing Westerlies —
Polar Easterlies —
— Tradewind
— Prevailing Westerlies

▶ Earth's prevailing winds

"Abuelo, is there always a *brisa marina*?" Mario asked. "Our teacher read us part of a poem about a ship stranded at sea without a wind. How could that be?"

"Well, Mario," his grandfather replied, "remember when I told you how our ancestors sailed south from Spain to reach the winds that carried them all the way across the ocean to Cuba? These winds are the *trade winds*. They were given this name because they brought the European traders to the Caribbean. To return to Europe, the fleets sailed north to catch the *westerlies*, which quickly sent them east toward home. These winds are part of the Earth's **prevailing winds**, because they always blow from the same direction.

"But near the Equator there is an area where there are no prevailing winds. This area is called the *doldrums*. Perhaps the ship in the poem was in this calm area."

LESSON 2 REVIEW

Earth's weather starts with energy from the sun. In your Science Log, write a short paragraph that describes how the sun produces weather.

3 WATER IN THE AIR

In addition to uneven heating of the air, another factor in producing weather is water. It's easy to see water in rivers, lakes, and oceans. But the air holds water that you cannot see. How can you tell that the air around you contains water? You can find out in the activities that follow.

ACTIVITY

MATERIALS
- plastic cup
- water
- ice
- stirring rod
- Science Log data sheet

Just Dew It!

DO THIS

1. Fill $\frac{2}{3}$ of the cup with water.

2. Place two ice cubes in the cup and stir continuously.

3. Observe what happens.

THINK AND WRITE

1. Where did water form on the cup? Where did this water come from?

2. Look at the picture of the spider web covered with dew. Name some other things that are covered with dew in the early morning.

3. **OBSERVING** Observations are an important part of any scientific investigation. Why did you have to observe the cup so carefully in this activity?

The Water Cycle

The dew that forms on grass is the result of a process called *condensation.* Most water enters the air from the oceans, by a process called *evaporation.* The diagram of the *water cycle* shows these processes, which constantly recycle the Earth's water.

Condensation (clouds)

▼ Dew on flowers

Evaporation

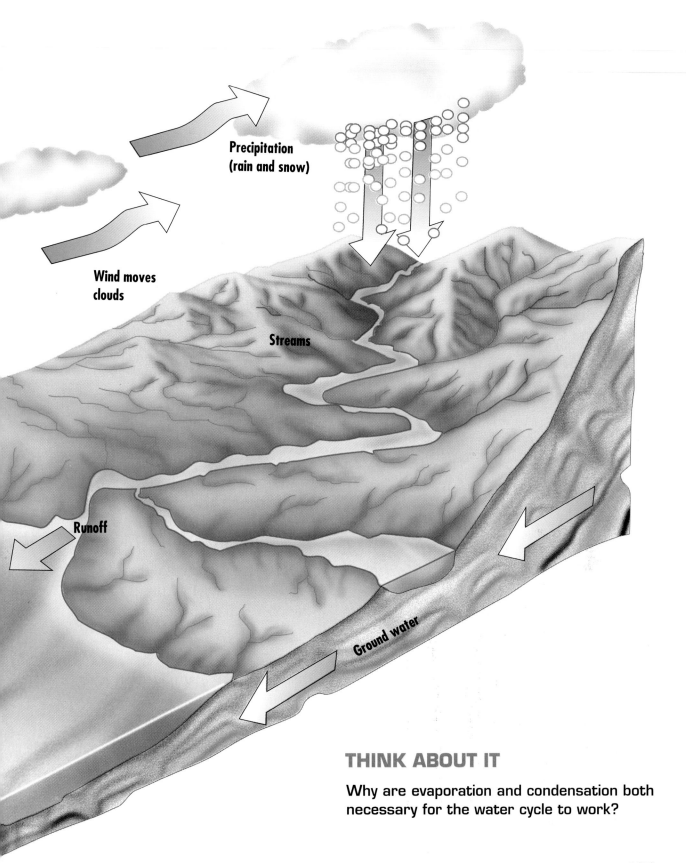

Precipitation
(rain and snow)

Wind moves
clouds

Streams

Runoff

Ground water

THINK ABOUT IT

Why are evaporation and condensation both
necessary for the water cycle to work?

A Foggy Day

Dew isn't the only proof that the air contains water. You have probably seen fog hanging over a mountain valley or rolling in from the sea. Fog is made up of tiny droplets that have condensed from water vapor in the air. But what does the water condense on? This activity might give you some ideas.

MATERIALS
- water
- measuring cup
- 2-L plastic bottle
- drinking straw
- modeling clay
- wooden match
- Science Log data sheet

DO THIS

1 Pour $\frac{1}{2}$ cup of water into the bottle.

2 Put the straw into the mouth of the bottle, and seal around the straw with clay.

3 Blow air into the bottle through the straw without letting any of it escape around your lips. Then, allow the air in the bottle to escape suddenly.

4 Your teacher will light the match, blow out the flame, and drop the smoking match into the bottle through the straw.

5 Once again, blow air into the bottle without letting any escape. Then allow the air in the bottle to escape suddenly.

THINK AND WRITE

1. Describe what you observed both before and after you dropped the smoking match into the bottle.

2. What did the water vapor condense on to make the fog?

Clouds and Precipitation

Mario and his grandfather spent a great day at the beach. But the sunny day slowly turned cloudy, and the thunder rumbled in the distance. Where do clouds come from, and why do some clouds make rain while others don't? Read the poem. Then see if you can answer the poet's questions.

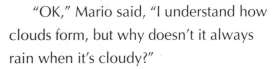

CLOUDS

by **Aileen Fisher**

Wonder where they come from?

Wonder where they go?

Wonder why they're sometimes hanging high
* and sometimes hanging low?*

Wonder what they're made of, and if they weigh a lot?

Wonder if the sky feels bare up there when clouds are not?

 As Mario and his grandfather were walking from the beach to the bus stop, Mario asked, "Abuelo, what makes the different kinds of clouds?"

"Well, Mario," his grandfather answered, "remember when you showed me how you made fog in a bottle? The formation of clouds is very similar. In fact, fog is just a cloud that is close to the ground.

"As warmed air expands and rises, it begins to cool. The water vapor in the air condenses around tiny particles of dust, smoke, or even salt crystals from the ocean. Clouds are different, depending on how high they are, how cool the air is, and how much water vapor there is in the air."

"OK," Mario said, "I understand how clouds form, but why doesn't it always rain when it's cloudy?"

His grandfather answered. "The cloud droplets grow as more and more water vapor condenses from the air. When the droplets get too big to be held up by the rising air, they fall as rain. Up north, in the winter, the clouds may contain tiny crystals of ice, so instead of raining, it snows. Rain and snow are just different kinds of **precipitation,** like they talk about on TV."

THINK ABOUT IT

Why don't all clouds produce rain?

That One Looks Like . . .

Remember when you used to try to find animal shapes or other familiar objects in the clouds? There are many different kinds of clouds, and some can be used to predict the weather.

High above the Earth, wispy clouds often streak the sky. These clouds, made of ice crystals, are called *cirrus clouds.* They are usually seen in fair weather, but they may appear before a storm.

Low, dark clouds close to the Earth sometimes fill the sky. These clouds, called *stratus clouds,* may produce snow or rain.

White, fluffy clouds that remind you of cotton balls may be seen in good weather. But these clouds, called *cumulus clouds,* can produce heavy rain showers or snow showers.

THINK ABOUT IT

How can clouds be used to predict the weather?

▶ **Weather vane**

◀ **Far left:**
  cumulus clouds
Middle:
  cirrus clouds
Near left:
  stratus clouds

You Wouldn't Believe Where I've Been!

Did you know that a drop of rain that falls on you might have fallen on the head of a dinosaur millions of years ago? If a drop of water could talk, here's what it might say:

 "I started in the ocean millions and millions of years ago. I evaporated into the air and later fell as rain on a dinosaur's head. I made my way back into the ocean, where I stayed a long time. Ten thousand years ago, a hurricane picked me up as part of a wave and tossed me high into the air. I traveled miles and miles. Two months later, I came down as snow over North America and became part of a glacier. A warm wind blew across the ice, and I melted and became part of a huge lake. A fish swallowed me, but I passed through the fish and stayed in the lake until the spring of 1993. Then I washed up on a Wisconsin beach and evaporated into the air. I fell as a raindrop on a cornfield in Iowa just as the great floods were beginning. I went swirling down the Mississippi River until I reached the Gulf of Mexico. And that's where I am today."

THINK ABOUT IT

Is the water on Earth today the same water that has always been on Earth? Explain your reasoning.

My Life: The Story of a Water Drop

You will need: Science Log

Write your own story to describe the history of a drop of water. Your story should include at least three separate parts of the water cycle. It should describe where, when, and how the water drop arrives at each stage. When your story is complete, you might want to read it to your classmates.

QUICK CHECK

LESSON 3 REVIEW

❶ Describe three main stages of the water cycle. Where does each stage take place?

❷ How does water in the air affect weather?

4 AIR WARS

Masses of air move slowly across the Earth's surface. As they do, these air masses take on the characteristics of the surfaces beneath them. For example, air moving over a warm surface is warmed, but air moving over a cold surface is cooled. Air moving over water becomes moist, and air moving over land dries out. An *air mass* has almost the same temperature and moisture throughout. As it moves, an air mass causes changes—sometimes dramatic changes—in the weather of an area.

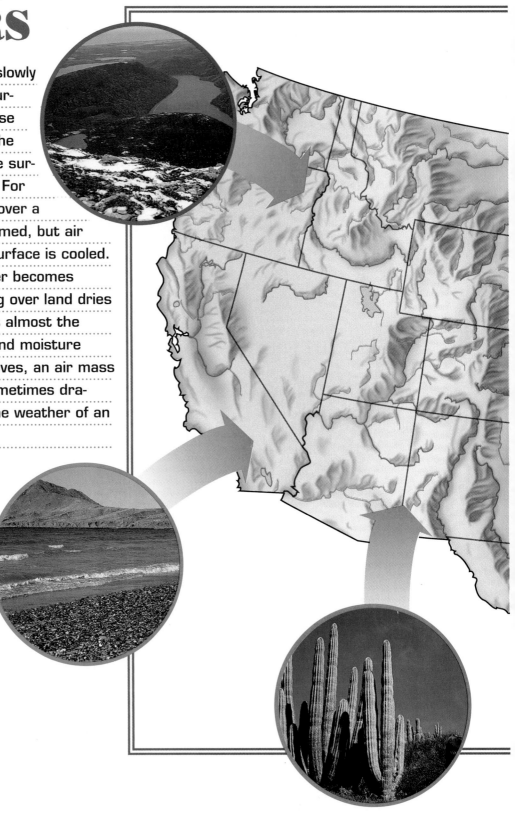

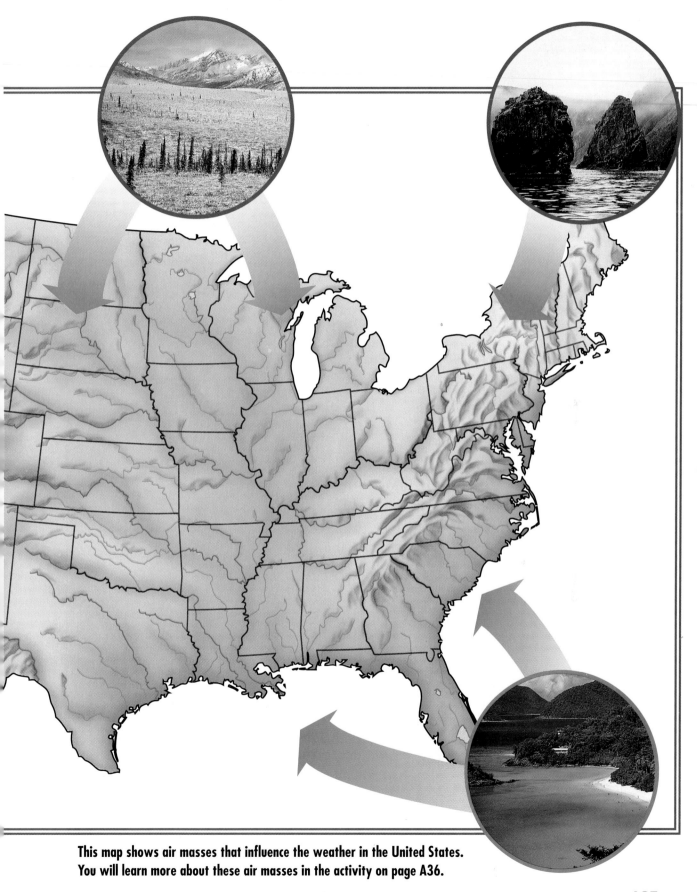

This map shows air masses that influence the weather in the United States.
You will learn more about these air masses in the activity on page A36.

Name That Air Mass

Several types of air masses are responsible for most of the weather in the United States. In this activity, you can explore the characteristics of some of these air masses.

DO THIS

1 On your outline map, add circles and arrows like those as on the map on page A34 and A35.

2 Recall that air masses can be warm or cold and dry or moist. Air masses with these characteristics are shown by photos in the circles.

3 Decide which air masses are cold, and use a blue pencil to color half of each of their circles.

4 Decide which air masses are warm, and use a red pencil to color half of each of their circles.

5 Decide which air masses are dry, and use a brown pencil to color half of each of their circles.

6 Decide which air masses are moist, and use a green pencil to color half of each of their circles.

THINK AND WRITE

Notice that each of the circles now has two colors—one for temperature and one for moisture. Air masses are named for both characteristics. For example, moist, warm air masses are *maritime tropical*; moist, cold air masses are *maritime polar*; dry, warm air masses are *continental tropical*; and dry, cold air masses are *continental polar*. Name each of the air masses on your map by using this system. Then describe where each kind of air mass gets its characteristics.

Air Masses and Fronts

It seems to Mario that it has been hot forever. Summer comes early in Miami, and it lasts well into October. But the TV weather forecaster says that a front is coming and that the temperatures might drop into the 60s by the weekend. Why does the weather sometimes stay the same for so long? What is a front, and how does it affect weather?

When the weather in your area does not change for many days, the chances are good that your area is under a large, slow-moving air mass. When there is a sudden change in the weather, a front has probably just passed through. A **front** is a line, or boundary, that separates air masses. *Front* is a good word to describe the boundary between air masses. As on a battle front in a war, there is often conflict on a weather front, so the weather along a front can sometimes be quite stormy. The forecast for Miami includes the possibility of severe thunderstorms on Friday and then clearing and much cooler on Saturday and Sunday.

Recall that there are different kinds of air masses. The one that is keeping the temperatures so warm in South Florida is a maritime tropical air mass. However, the air mass that is expected to arrive by the weekend is a continental polar air mass. The front, or boundary, that separates these two very different air masses is called a *cold front*. The weather along a cold front often includes thunderstorms with heavy precipitation.

Mario is worried about the weather for his class trip next Tuesday to Miami Metrozoo. He hopes it won't be too cold, because cold weather means the koalas won't be outside. The extended forecast is for a warming trend to begin early in the week. However, that may mean rain along with warmer temperatures. A *warm front* forms when a warm air mass replaces a cold air mass. Precipitation along a warm front is usually steady, but not as heavy as that along a cold front.

Where air masses meet without moving, a *stationary front* forms. Precipitation may occur for many days when a stationary front is in an area.

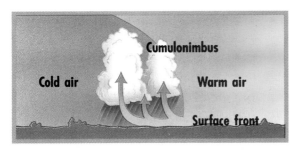

▲ **Cold front**

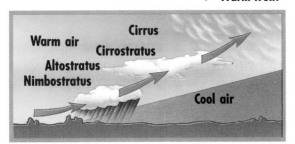

▼ **Warm front**

LESSON 4 REVIEW

Different types of air masses affect the weather in the United States. Which types produce the weather you like best? Explain.

5 CLOUDY WITH A CHANCE OF RAIN

Today is the day of Mario's big class trip. The weekend was clear and cool after the cold front passed, but today it's much warmer. The sky is covered with clouds, and Mario is concerned that the weather will affect today's trip. Knowing what the weather will be helps everyone plan ahead. How will the weather affect what you have planned for today? The following activities can help you predict weather changes.

Falling Barometers

While eating breakfast, Mario turns on the TV. The weather forecaster says the high pressure of the weekend is moving out and the barometer is falling. She predicts rain for this afternoon. Mario confirms the prediction as he notices his grandfather limping again.

 "Hope the rain holds off for your class trip, Mario," his grandfather comments.

"Me too, Abuelo," Mario replies. "I really want to see how the zoo looks since the hurricane damage has been cleaned up. Do you think it will rain this morning?"

"Well, the barometer is falling," his grandfather comments as he looks at the weather data on the TV screen, "but not too fast. I think it might hold off till this afternoon."

"Abuelo, what does it mean when they say 'the barometer is falling'? And what does a barometer measure?"

"A barometer measures the weight of the air. Remember when we talked about warm air being lighter than cold air?" Mario nodded, and his grandfather continued. "A falling barometer means the air is getting lighter—it is rising. Rising air cools, and the water vapor condenses, forming clouds. This often means rain. A rising barometer usually means fair weather— the air is getting heavier and doesn't rise, so there are few clouds. A changing barometer is one of the best ways to predict a change in the weather."

THINK ABOUT IT

For what kind of people would knowing the weather be very important?

Heavy Air

Air surrounds the Earth. Although you cannot see it, air is everywhere. Air is made up of tiny particles called *molecules*, so it has mass. A simple activity can show you that air has mass.

MATERIALS
- balloon
- balance
- balloon pump
- Science Log data sheet

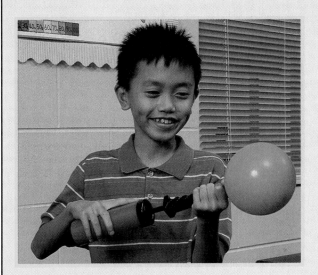

DO THIS

1 Find the mass of the balloon.

2 Fill the balloon by using the balloon pump.

3 Find the mass of the inflated balloon.

THINK AND WRITE

1. What is the difference in mass between the empty balloon and the inflated balloon?

2. What do you think the difference in mass would be if the balloon was inflated more? less?

ACTIVITY

Air Pressure

The pull of gravity on air molecules gives them weight. Because of its weight, air pushes down on the Earth and everything on the Earth's surface. You can see this in the following activity.

DO THIS

1 Fill the bottle with warm water. Be sure the bottle feels warm.

2 Pour the water out quickly, and screw the cap on.

THINK AND WRITE

What happened to the bottle when the warm water was poured out? What caused this to happen?

Air pressure When air is heated, its molecules spread apart. The molecules of cold air are closer together, so warm air takes up more space than cold air. Both warm air and cold air push down on the Earth's surface. However, since molecules of cold air are closer together than molecules of warm air, cold air pushes down with more force than warm air does. The force with which air pushes down on the Earth is called **air pressure.** Air pressure can be measured with a *barometer*.

dial

hand

Air pressure pushes on metal.

chain

spring

airtight box

▲ How a barometer works

A40

Pressure Systems

Is it sunny and warm where you are, or is it cloudy and cold? Is the barometer low and rising, or is it high and steady? The weather conditions in any specific area are called local weather conditions. Local weather conditions change as air masses move across the country. Since warm air masses tend to have lower air pressure than cold air masses, systems of high pressure and systems of low pressure can be identified and tracked as they move. In this activity, you can track some pressure systems.

MATERIALS
- newspaper weather maps for 3 consecutive days
- scissors
- glue
- construction paper
- outline map of the United States
- Science Log data sheet

DO THIS

❶ Cut the national weather map from a newspaper three days in a row. Glue each weather map onto a sheet of construction paper.

❷ On the first weather map you cut out, find a low-pressure system, look for an Ⓛ, and a high-pressure system, look for an Ⓗ. Mark the locations of the pressure systems on the outline map.

❸ Find the same two pressure systems on the second and third newspaper maps. Mark their new locations on your outline map.

THINK AND WRITE

1. In what direction did the weather systems move from the first to the third day?

2. What might cause weather to move in this direction across the United States? Do you think weather always moves in this direction? Explain your answer.

ACTIVITY

Making Weather Predictions

Just as Mario's class was leaving the zoo, it began to rain. The weather forecast was right. How can changing air pressure be used to predict the weather? What other data do weather forecasters use? In this activity, you will use two kinds of data to predict weather.

MATERIALS
- Weather Data table
- Science Log data sheet

DO THIS

1. Record the wind direction and air pressure (barometer reading) from today's newspaper.

2. Use the table to predict tomorrow's weather. Record your predictions.

3. Tomorrow, record the actual weather. Compare it with your prediction.

WEATHER DATA		
Wind Direction	Barometer Reading	Expected Weather
North	28.00 - 28.99; falling	steady rain; cold
	29.00 - 29.99; rising	showers ending; cool
	30.00 - 31.00; steady	clear, fair, and cool
South	28.00 - 28.99; falling	extended rain; cool
	29.00 - 29.99; rising	showers ending; warmer
	30.00 - 31.00; steady	fair and warm
East	28.00 - 28.99; falling	showers and cloudy
	29.00 - 29.99; rising	fair and partly cloudy
	30.00 - 31.00; steady	fair and warm
West	28.00 - 28.99; falling	extended rain; cool
	29.00 - 29.99; rising	rain ending; mostly fair
	30.00 - 31.00; steady	sunny and fair

▲ Weather vane

THINK AND WRITE

1. What kind of weather can be expected when the barometer reading is very high or very low?

2. How accurate was your prediction?

3. Why do you think weather predictions aren't always correct?

4. **PREDICTING** Scientists often predict what they think will happen. Do you think a prediction based on a great amount of data would be more accurate or less accurate than a prediction based on a small amount of data? Explain your reasoning.

TV Weather Forecaster:
Before the Cameras Roll

Newspapers, TV stations, and radio stations provide weather forecasts. A *forecast* is a prediction of future weather. Weather forecasters predict weather in much the same way that scientists perform investigations. They collect data, study the data, and draw conclusions based on the data.

Have you ever wondered what the job of a TV weather forecaster is like? Many people may think it involves pointing to weather maps, satellite images, and radar screens in front of a camera for just a few minutes each day. Some people may think it is glamorous and exciting to be a TV personality. But what you see on TV is just a small part of the job of a weather forecaster.

You know that weather is produced by a combination of many factors. Accurate forecasting of weather requires information on temperature, air pressure, wind speed and direction, and moisture in the air. A weather forecaster uses many sources to gather data and prepare information for a forecast. He or she uses national weather observations, satellite images, and radar data to understand weather patterns.

Forecasters also monitor local conditions right up to the moment of a broadcast. The weather forecaster wants updated information and graphics in order to provide people with an accurate forecast. All of the information has to be arranged and organized by the TV weather forecaster.

The amount of time allowed for a weather forecast is usually limited. Once the camera goes on, the forecast takes just a few minutes and then it's over. What you don't see is all the preparation that goes into the report beforehand.

THINK ABOUT IT

Why must weather forecasters be good scientists, too?

COLD   WARM   ST.

"Now Here's the Weather"

It's your turn "in front of the camera." You are going to use everything you have learned about weather conditions and forecasting to write, edit, and produce your own five-minute weather show.

You will need: Science Log

In your Science Log, write a script that reports the weather conditions for today. Title your script "Today's Weather." You can use a local newspaper weather report for the data you need.

Then study the weather map from the same newspaper. Use the map to predict the local weather for the next day. Write a script for the forecast, titled "Tomorrow's Weather," in your Science Log.

Read your report and your forecast to your classmates. You can even make maps and charts to help you illustrate your "show."

LESSON 5 REVIEW

Think about weather changes and the kind of weather you enjoy most. Describe what it might be like if you lived where the weather *never* changed.

✓ DOUBLE CHECK

SECTION A REVIEW

1. How do the sun's rays affect the Earth's weather?

2. Using the terms *evaporation*, *condensation*, and *precipitation*, describe the water cycle.

3. How are air masses and fronts related? Describe what might happen when a cold air mass and a warm air mass meet.

A45

SECTION B
Storm Warning

▲ Weather satellite

Crashing thunder, streaking lightning, howl-ing wind, driving rain, and pounding hail are all characteristics of thunderstorms. Have you ever wondered why the weather is so violent at times? Thunderstorms, tornadoes, hurricanes, and bliz-zards are all types of storms. This section discusses the causes and effects of these kinds of severe weather.

How do storms form? What makes them so destructive? How do weather forecasters predict and track storms? Keep careful notes in your Science Log as you work through the investigations in this section.

1 STORMY WEATHER

Have you ever watched a puffy, white cumulus cloud grow and grow until it turned into a dark, brooding thunderhead? What causes the formation of storm clouds? The activities and readings that follow will help you find out how thunderstorms form and why they are so dangerous.

MATERIALS
- tracing paper
- spiral pattern
- scissors
- ruler
- string
- tape
- gooseneck lamp
- Science Log data sheet

ACTIVITY

Growing Storm Clouds

DO THIS (CAUTION)

1 Put the tracing paper over the spiral pattern. Trace the circle and the dotted line on the circle.

2 Cut the circle into a spiral by following the dotted line.

3 Tape a piece of string about 15 cm long to what was once the center of the circle.

Bend the neck of the lamp so that the light bulb is facing up.

5 **CAUTION: Do not touch the hot light bulb or look directly at the light.** Turn on the light and, with the string between your fingers, hold the spiral about 10 cm above the light bulb.

THINK AND WRITE

1. What happens to the spiral when it is held over the light bulb?

2. Why do you think this happens?

3. Think about what happens to the spiral. What do you think might happen to a cloud over a warm surface?

Thunderheads

On hot, humid days, cumulus clouds reach high into the air—stretching, spreading, and flattening out at the top. Near the ground, their darkening bases threaten a storm. Thunderheads are the typical thunderstorm clouds. Study the diagrams. They can help you understand how thunderstorms form.

▶ Because of the prevailing winds, thunderheads often have a flattened top.

▲ Warmed, moist air rises. As the rising air cools, water vapor condenses, and cumulus clouds form.

▲ The hot ground causes air to rise faster and higher. The cumulus clouds become larger and taller.

▲ The clouds continue to grow thicker and higher. They can reach 16 km (10 mi) or more into the air. The clouds are now called *cumulonimbus* clouds. *Nimbus* means "rain."

THINK ABOUT IT

Why do cumulonimbus clouds produce thunderstorms?

A48

ACTIVITY

Charge It!

One of the most dramatic characteristics of a thunder-storm is lightning. Have you ever wondered what causes lightning? The following activity can help you find out how lightning is produced.

DO THIS

1 Turn off the classroom lights.

2 Briskly shuffle your feet on the carpet for about a minute.

3 With one finger, touch the doorknob or another metal object. Observe what happens.

MATERIALS
- carpeted floor
- doorknob
- Science Log data sheet

THINK AND WRITE

1. What happened when you touched the doorknob or metal object?

2. Look at the picture of the lightning. In what ways is lightning similar to what you observed?

3. **OBSERVING** Observing is an important scientific process. In this activity you observed a process similar to the process that produces lightning. Discuss what you observed and how you made your observations.

A49

Thunder and Lightning

A loud clap of thunder may make you jump, but you have nothing to fear from it. What do you think about when you hear the rumble of thunder? As you read this Navaho song, think about what the sound of thunder means to the poet and to you. Then write your own poem about thunder.

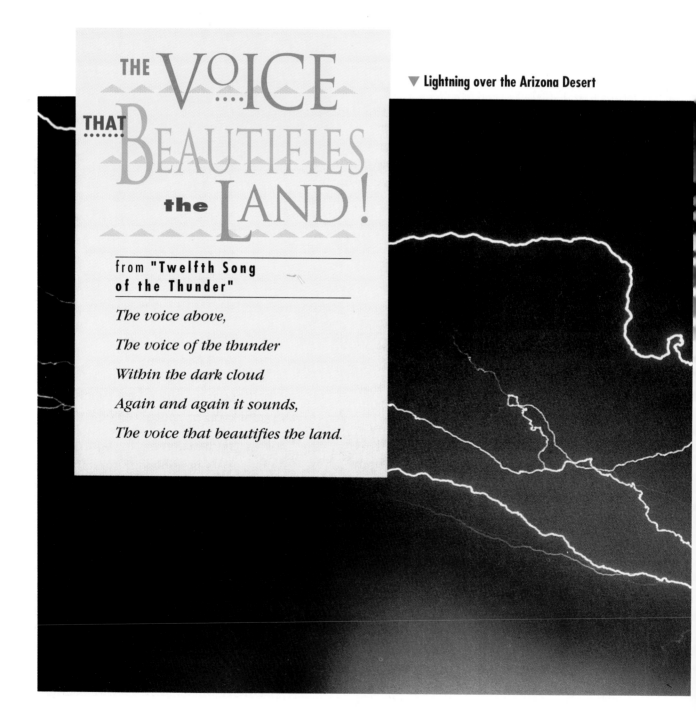

THE VOICE THAT BEAUTIFIES the LAND!

▼ Lightning over the Arizona Desert

from "Twelfth Song of the Thunder"

The voice above,

The voice of the thunder

Within the dark cloud

Again and again it sounds,

The voice that beautifies the land.

Although thunder may startle you, the most dangerous part of a thunderstorm is the lightning. Like the spark you may have observed in the last activity, **lightning** is an electrical spark. But the spark is huge. So huge, in fact, that lightning can destroy electronic equipment, set houses on fire, snap large trees as if they were toothpicks, and kill people.

Lightning can put on a spectacular show, brightening the entire sky, or streaking down in jagged bolts. But every year, more people in the United States are killed and injured by lightning than by all other storms combined.

LIGHTNING

by **Robert Irby**

Now when the weather's hectic,

The sky can turn electric,

And sparks begin to leap
      from cloud to cloud.

Then with a fearful sound,

Some lightning strikes the ground,

And that is when
      the thunder seems so loud.

Don't hide 'neath trees or metal

To wait for storms to settle,

And stay away from places
      that are high.

And when you're getting wetter,

Remember that it's better

To try to stay inside
      all snug and dry!

There's Electricity in the Air

Imagine what it must be like in a thunderhead—all those raindrops being tossed around by the rapidly rising air. As raindrops scrape by each other, the friction between them builds up strong electrical charges—like the electrical charges you build up shuffling your feet on a carpet.

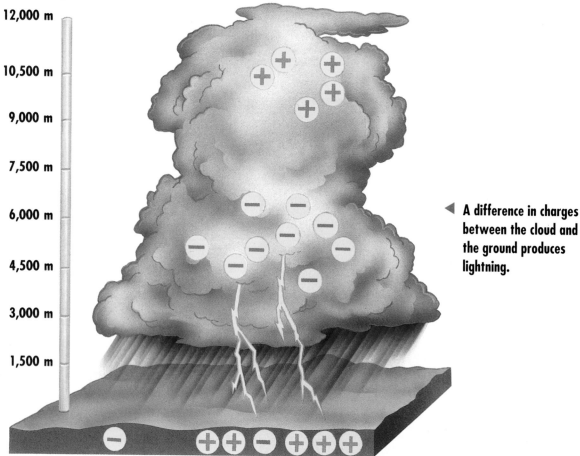

◀ A difference in charges between the cloud and the ground produces lightning.

In a cloud, some of the charges are positive and some are negative. Look at the diagram. Where are most of the cloud's negative charges?

On the ground, negative charges are repelled by negative charges in the cloud. They are replaced by positive charges near the surface. When the difference between the negative charges in the cloud and the positive charges on the ground is great enough, a spark jumps between the cloud and the ground—just as a spark jumped between your finger and the doorknob. This spark from the cloud instantly heats the air, which expands rapidly and collides with cooler air. The collision between the hot air and the cooler air is the thunder you hear.

THINK ABOUT IT

How are thunder and lightning related?

Safe from the Storm

Mario and his classmates are returning home from their trip to Miami Metrozoo. Because of the rain and the traffic, the bus ride seems to take hours. When the bus finally reaches the school, the students jump off and begin walking home. Within minutes the wind picks up and a downpour begins. Lightning flashes all around, and Mario is still a block away from home.

"Hurry, Mario!" his grandfather urges him from the front porch. "Come inside!" Instead, Mario heads for cover under a tree. "Don't stop there!" his grandfather warns. "That's one of the worst places you can be! Hurry, run for the house!"

Out of breath and soaking wet, Mario drops into a chair at the kitchen table. "Abuelo," he complains, "if I had stayed under that tree, I wouldn't be so wet. Why couldn't I stay there?"

"Lightning always takes the shortest path," his grandfather explains, "so it often strikes the tallest thing in an area. If it struck that tree, its electrical charge would travel down the tree and into the ground. If you were under the tree, the charge could travel from the ground through your body."

"Wow!" exclaims Mario. "What other places are dangerous during a thunderstorm?"

"Well, you should never stand in an open place, like the soccer field. You could be hit there, because you would be the tallest thing around. Beaches are dangerous places, too. You should always stay away from water during a thunderstorm. The best place to be is indoors. While you're inside, stay away from windows. Don't use electrical appliances or run water. And use the telephone only in emergencies."

THINK ABOUT IT

Why is a field a bad place to be during a thunderstorm?

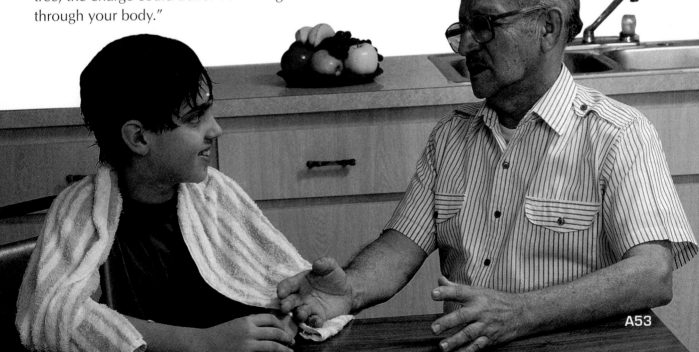

ACTIVITY

How Far Away?

Suppose you're playing ball. It's starting to get cloudy. You see a distant flash, and then a few seconds later you hear the low rumble of thunder. You wonder how far away the storm is. If you live in an area that has thunderstorms, this activity will help you figure out how far away a storm is.

MATERIALS
- stopwatch
- calculator
- Science Log data sheet

DO THIS

❶ Darken the classroom as much as possible.

❷ Start the stopwatch as soon as you see a flash of lightning.

❸ Stop the stopwatch when you hear the thunder.

❹ Multiply the number of seconds by 340 (the number of meters sound travels per second). This gives you the lightning's distance from you in meters.

THINK AND WRITE

1. Suppose the time between seeing the lightning and hearing the thunder is 10 seconds. How far away is the lightning?

2. Suppose a storm is 5,100 m away. How long will it be after you see the lightning before you hear the thunder?

3. Suppose you see lightning and hear thunder at about the same time. Where is the storm?

All Hail!

Have you ever seen hail during a thunderstorm? What is hail, and how does it form? In this activity, you can model the structure of a hailstone.

MATERIALS
- 30-cm piece of string
- modeling clay
- safety goggles
- 2 pots of melted wax of different colors
- plastic knife
- Science Log data sheet

DO THIS

1 Tie a large knot at the end of the string. Then form a ball of clay, about 1 cm in diameter, around the knot.

2 **CAUTION: Put on the safety goggles for this activity. Do not touch the pots or the hot wax.** Dip the ball of clay into one pot of wax. Allow the layer of wax to harden. Then dip the ball into the second pot.

3 Keep adding different colored layers of wax.

4 Use the knife to cut your "hailstone" in half. Examine the layers.

THINK AND WRITE

1. What does your model hailstone look like inside? Why do you think it looks this way?

2. Why did you need the clay ball in the center?

Hail In some thunderstorms, cumulonimbus clouds can reach heights of 16 kilometers (10 miles) or more. At the top of the clouds, the temperature is well below freezing, so raindrops can become hailstones. A hailstone grows as it is tossed up and down within a cloud. Every time a hailstone drops, a new layer of water is added, just as you added a layer of wax to your model. Every time a hailstone rises, the water freezes, just as the wax in your model hardened. When a hailstone is too heavy to be held up by rising air, it falls to the ground.

Floods

In addition to lightning and hail, a thunderstorm has heavy rains that can flood roads and basements and send rivers over their banks. If you live in the Midwest, you may have experienced some of this yourself. As you read the article, think about what you might do in a similar situation.

THE GREAT FLOOD OF 1993

by Barbara Brownell
from *National Geographic World*

Muddy water lapped at his shoulders, and the sky threatened rain. But Jesse Blaise, 12, stood his soggy ground. He was working hard to protect the North Lee County Historic Center in Fort Madison, Iowa, from the great Mississippi River flood of 1993. Shawn Pulis, 14, worked nearby. "Volunteers brought us boatloads of sandbags," he says. "We stacked them around the building."

The volunteers worked around the clock for 13 days. It paid off. The water receded to the riverbed. The building stood. "I was so tired," says Shawn, "but I felt really good."

Jesse and Shawn are among thousands who pitched in to fight one of the worst floods in the United States.

Kids helped make history. "We called for help, and they came right away," says Barbara Hocker, the treasurer of the Fort Madison historic center. "They're largely responsible for saving the building."

▲ Game called on account of rain — a lot of rain

A56

During the fall and winter of 1992, record amounts of snowmelt and rainfall soaked the ground and filled rivers in the Midwest. In June of 1993, heavy rainstorms began to flood the rivers.

A wind pattern called a jet stream combined with other weather forces to increase the storms' energy and hold the storms in place over nine states in the Midwest. For 30 days, rain pelted the area.

> "It's as if another Great Lake had been added to the United States."

The ground became so soaked that it could not absorb any more water. And from the Mississippi and its tributaries, water gushed over towns and farmland alike.

By the end of July a satellite photograph showed a flooded area so large that Vice President Al Gore said, "It's as if another

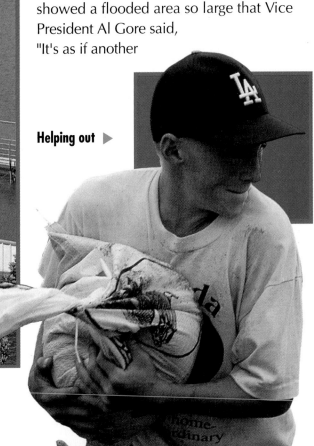

Helping out ▶

Great Lake had been added to the United States."

Most Midwest riverbanks are lined with barriers called levees. But during huge floods levees may not be high enough to contain the water. Or they may leak. Or they may collapse as water pressure builds. In the flood of 1993, all these things happened to many levees.

When some levees gave way, water suddenly flowed out. By August 31,000 people had lost their homes, and more than $11 billion in damage had been done.

In Fort Madison water seeped through the levee and poured over its top. Workers stacked up sandbags to try to stop much of the flow. "We got scared once when the wall sprung a leak," says Shawn. "We blocked it fast."

Money, volunteers, and other support arrived from across the country. Des Moines, Iowa, received a special gift from the people of Florida. When they heard that the city's water supply was contaminated, they remembered Iowa's help after Hurricane Andrew and sent truckloads of drinking water.

LESSON 1 REVIEW

❶ How can you use thunder and lightning to determine how far away a thunderstorm is?

❷ Where is the best place to be during a thunderstorm? Why?

2 TORNADO WATCH

You've probably seen pictures that show the fury of severe storms such as tornadoes. Maybe you've even experienced one of these storms yourself. The following activities and readings can help you understand the causes of violent weather.

Squall Line

Recall from the last section that the boundary between air masses is called a front. The air masses can be quite different on either side of a front. If one air mass is very warm and moist while the other is cold and very dry, a line of extremely severe thunderstorms, called a *squall line*, forms along the front. These thunderstorms can be dangerous.

▼ Tornado damage

The National Weather Service usually issues a severe thunderstorm watch for such a squall line. This watch makes people aware of the likelihood of frequent lightning, strong winds, heavy rain, damaging hail and *tornadoes*.

A tornado watch is often issued with a severe thunderstorm watch. A tornado watch means conditions are right for the development of tornadoes. If a tornado watch is issued, people should be on the lookout for these storms. If a tornado does form, the watch is changed to a tornado warning. A tornado warning means "Take cover!"

THINK ABOUT IT

Why does the National Weather Service issue a severe thunderstorm warning when a squall line develops?

Out of Harm's Way

Mario has a cousin who lives in Tulsa, Oklahoma. Tornado watches are pretty ordinary in Tulsa. However, one day last spring was anything but ordinary. Read Ana's letter to her grandfather. Find out what she did to protect herself. As you read, think about what you would do.

Dear Abuelo,

I'll never forget last evening as long as I live. Mama and I were watching TV when a tornado watch message came on. Not half an hour later, the TV flashed a tornado warning. Then we heard the sirens. A tornado was on the way!

We didn't waste a second. We ran to the basement and hid beneath the workbench. I was really scared. At first everything was quiet, but then we heard a loud roar. It sounded like racing engines or a train. The house shook. Mama and I hugged each other tight.

When it was over, an all-clear blew. My legs were shaking as we climbed the stairs. I didn't know what to expect. Broken glass was everywhere and part of the roof was torn off our house. Mama and I felt lucky, though. We weren't hurt.

My friend Kathy wasn't hurt either. She lives in an apartment building that doesn't have a basement, so she crawled under a desk in her room. But some of our neighbors were hurt and many houses were damaged.

We're staying with friends until our house is fixed. Now I know how you felt after Hurricane Andrew. I can't wait to be back in my own home.

love to all,
Ana

THINK ABOUT IT

What can you do to protect yourself during a tornado?

A C T I V I T Y

Tornado in a Bottle

Why do tornadoes cause so much damage? A tornado is a rapidly spinning storm with very high winds. In this activity, you can observe how a tornado spins.

MATERIALS
- 2 clear plastic soft-drink bottles
- water
- clear dish detergent
- sand
- toothpick
- heavy plastic tape
- Science Log data sheet

DO THIS

1. Fill one bottle with water.

2. Add a small drop of detergent, a pinch of sand, and the toothpick.

3. Tape the mouth of the empty bottle to the mouth of the full bottle. Use a lot of tape, and completely seal the bottles.

4. Hold the bottles over a sink, and turn them so that the full bottle is on top. Observe what happens to the sand, the toothpick, and the detergent bubbles as the water drains from one bottle into the other.

THINK AND WRITE

1. Describe the motion of the water as it drained from one bottle into the other.

2. **OBSERVING** In the activity, you did not have much time to make your observations. When observation time will be short, you need to pay careful attention to what you want to observe. Do you think repeating this activity would help you improve your observations? Explain.

Deadly Twisters

In nature, a tornado starts as a small area of low pressure within a thunderhead. Recall from Section A that low pressure is caused by rising air. As the air within the thunderhead rises, it pulls warm, moist air into the cloud at very high speeds.

The rising air begins to spin, slowly at first, like the water in the bottle in the last activity. The air picks up speed, whirling faster and faster. As moisture in the rising, spinning air condenses, it forms a visible funnel—the shape of all tornadoes.

The funnel dips down from the cloud through the calmer air below it. If it reaches the ground, it races along, leaving a path of almost total destruction.

▼ **Formation of a tornado**

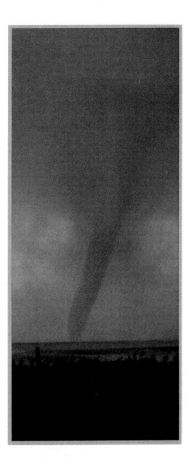

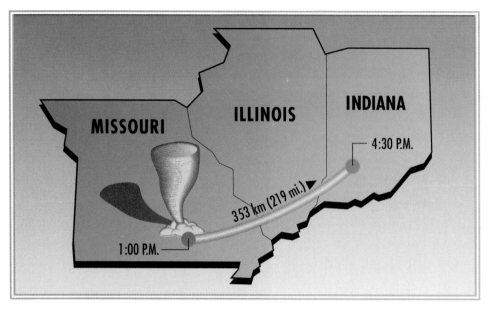

MISSOURI

ILLINOIS

INDIANA

4:30 P.M.

353 km (219 mi.)

1:00 P.M.

◀ Path of Tri-State Tornado

Most tornadoes last less than 20 minutes. But in 1925, a tornado in the Midwest spent more than three hours on the ground. The deadliest tornado in United States history, it roared through Missouri, Illinois, and Indiana. Almost 700 people were killed, and whole towns were smashed to pieces.

Why were so many lives lost in the Tri-State Tornado? People didn't know the storm was coming, so they didn't have time to seek shelter. In 1925, weather forecasters didn't have the equipment to predict the development of tornadoes or TV to broadcast warnings.

Today, forecasters use computers and instruments such as Doppler radar to spot areas where tornadoes are likely to develop. This allows them to issue watches and warnings 20 minutes or more in advance. Early warnings give people more time to seek shelter.

THINK ABOUT IT

Why is it important to issue tornado warnings as early as possible?

▼ Damage from Tri-State Tornado

A C T I V I T Y

Tornado Alley

In the United States, hundreds of tornadoes occur every year. In the following activity, you will map some of the locations where tornadoes have struck in recent years.

DO THIS

1 For each state listed, write the average number of tornadoes per year from the table on the map.

2 Use a red pencil to color all the states that average 25 or more tornadoes per year. Use a yellow pencil to color all the states that average between 10 and 24 tornadoes per year.

AVERAGE NUMBER OF TORNADOES PER YEAR IN EACH STATE							
Alabama	19	Indiana	23	Mississippi	22	Oklahoma	55
Arkansas	18	Iowa	26	Missouri	30	South Dakota	23
Colorado	14	Kansas	46	Nebraska	34	Tennessee	11
Florida	36	Louisiana	19	North Carolina	10	Texas	124
Georgia	21	Michigan	15	North Dakota	15	Wisconsin	17
Illinois	28	Minnesota	17	Ohio	13		

THINK AND WRITE

1. In what part of the United States do most tornadoes occur?

2. Why do you think this part of the United States is called "Tornado Alley"?

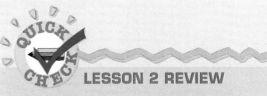

QUICK CHECK

LESSON 2 REVIEW

In your Science Log, describe how tornadoes form. Then explain why most tornadoes in the United States occur in Tornado Alley.

3 GIANT STORMS

As powerful and terrifying as thunderstorms and tornadoes are, they are relatively small storms and therefore affect only small areas. There are, however, giant storms that affect entire regions of the Earth. The following activities and readings will help you understand how these giant storms develop and how they can affect the entire country.

Hurricane Warning!

In August 1992, the most destructive storm ever to affect the United States—Hurricane Andrew—roared across South Florida and eventually hit Louisiana. In the following article, you will read how the *hurricane* affected one family in Miami.

SURVIVING ANDREW, 1992's BIGGEST HURRICANE!

by **Judith E. Rinard**
from *National Geographic World*

LITERATURE

"I couldn't believe it!" says Farrell Dottin, remembering that early morning of August 24, 1992. That's when he met Hurricane Andrew face-to-face. The huge whirling storm ripped through his neighborhood in South Miami, Florida. It blew his home to pieces as he took shelter, terrified, with his parents in a closet.

As Farrell and his mom sift through the wreckage of their house, they find a tattered copy of *World*. "Most of my books and toys were lost or ruined," says Farrell.

"When we went out and looked at what the hurricane had done, I got very scared."

One of the most destructive hurricanes in U.S. history, Andrew slammed into southern Florida about 5 a.m. Packing winds with gusts of up to 175 miles an hour, it tossed up boats, trucks, and airplanes, and flattened entire city blocks. Before it died out Andrew killed 62 people and left hundreds of thousands homeless.

When the storm hit, the Dottins first took refuge in a bathroom. After part of its roof blew off, they fled to a closet alcove. There, with a flashlight, they watched as walls swayed and the main roof began rising upward. The wind popped and shattered glass doors and windows. Then furniture, room doors, and framed pictures all flew by like deadly missiles as the savage wind sucked them out of the house.

"The wind was terrible," says Farrell. "It made a loud whistle, like a train coming down on top of us. Everything was rattling like a rattlesnake. You could feel the house coming apart. I thought we were going to die."

When it was over, the Dottins felt lucky to be alive. Most of their house was destroyed. Outside, the neighborhood looked liked a bombed-out war zone. The family moved in with friends. They plan to rebuild their home but will not stay if another hurricane comes. "We'll go someplace safe," says Farrell.

The hurricane plowed a path through many towns south of Miami. In Cutler Ridge Jessica Mayhew, 10, says her family ran into a bathroom when Andrew hit.

"After it was over, I was so scared I didn't want to come out," she says. "Our house was wrecked. There was water everywhere. I caught fish from our aquarium swimming around in water on the floor. Our street was like a river with water

▲ **Path of destruction**

up to my knees. You couldn't recognize our block. My swing set was smashed by a tree. I lost nearly everything. Even my dog ran off. I was so happy when it came back."

Jessica and her family are living in a camper trailer while their home is being rebuilt. Even Jessica's school was damaged by the hurricane.

"Some of the ceilings collapsed," says Sally James, a teacher at Cutler Ridge Elementary School. "And everything looks ugly and scarred." But, she says, the community is slowly rebuilding and has received an outpouring of food, supplies, and support.

"Our school," she adds, "has been adopted by more than 30 other schools and organizations in different states. They've sent school supplies, money, and letters. Our kids are writing back. It's really lifted our spirits and made us feel closer to other parts of our country."

THINK ABOUT IT

How did people survive Hurricane Andrew in South Florida?

In the Eye of the Storm

After reading about the destruction caused by Andrew, you know that hurricanes are violent storms. But how do these storms form, and what makes them so destructive? Mario asked his teacher about it when school finally started that fall.

Mario and his classmates were still stunned by the damage all around them. Hurricane Andrew had torn many of their homes apart. Friends and neighbors helped each other as well as they could. Mario's friend André was staying with him while André's family looked for a new apartment.

Mario could see firsthand how violent hurricanes were. And he knew that in his grandfather's native Cuba, and in Haiti, where André was from, hurricanes were common. But he still wasn't sure how they formed, or why they moved the way they did. At school one morning, he asked his teacher, "Ms. Baker, how do hurricanes form?"

Ms. Baker thought for a moment and then began to explain. "You all know that hurricanes are very large, powerful storms. They form over warm waters, like the tropical Atlantic, the Caribbean, or the Gulf of Mexico. In these areas, the prevailing winds collide and low-pressure areas, called *tropical depressions,* form.

"Each year some of these depressions develop into tropical storms. A few develop into powerful hurricanes with wind speeds of 120 kilometers (74 miles) per hour or more. Do you remember the diagram of the hurricane that was in the newspaper last month? Let me make a quick sketch of it on the board.

"This diagram shows what a hurricane would look like if it were cut in half from top to bottom. In the middle of the storm is the *eye,* where the air is warm and calm. Some of you may remember how quiet it was when the eye of Andrew passed over us. The eye acts like a big chimney, drawing in warm, moist air. The highest winds and heaviest rains of a hurricane are just outside the eye. The winds near Andrew's eye reached speeds of 250 kilometers (155 miles) per hour."

▼ After the storm

Prevailing wind

Eye

Downdraft

▲ Inside a hurricane

THINK ABOUT IT

How and where do hurricanes form?

Hurricane Tracking

Although Hurricane Andrew was the most destructive hurricane ever to hit the United States, it could have been much worse. Many more people might have been killed or injured if the National Hurricane Center had not carefully tracked the storm and warned the residents of Florida of its danger. But how is a hurricane tracked? In the following activity, you can track the movement of two hurricanes as they head west toward the United States.

MATERIALS
- colored pencils or markers
- outline map of the Atlantic Ocean and Southeastern states
- Science Log data sheet

DO THIS

1 Look at the table. The locations of Hurricane Barry and Hurricane Cassie on different days are given.

2 On the outline map, plot the daily location of Hurricane Barry in red.

3 Use blue to plot the daily location of Hurricane Cassie on the map.

	HURRICANE LOCATION				
	HURRICANE BARRY			HURRICANE CASSIE	
Day	Latitude	Longitude		Latitude	Longitude
1	27° N	79° W		22° N	66° W
2	30° N	77° W		21° N	67° W
3	32° N	79° W		23° N	68° W
4	36° N	71° W		22° N	70° W
5	34° N	69° W		25° N	71° W
6	35° N	67° W		28° N	73° W
7	33° N	70° W		28° N	76° W
8	32° N	73° W		25° N	77° W
9	35° N	71° W		26° N	81° W
10	27° N	87° W			
11	29° N	90° W			
12	32° N	91° W			

HURRICANE ANDREW
23 AUGUST 1992
5 PM EDT
MAX. WIND 150 MPH
923 MB

VERO BEACH

MIAMI

KEY WEST

85

80

THINK AND WRITE

1. Where does each hurricane hit land?

2. Which hurricane has traveled farther?

3. Which hurricane will probably do the most damage? Explain.

4. Why is tracking a hurricane important?

Storm of the Century

Hurricanes affect the coastal regions of the United States from Maine to Texas, as well as extreme Southern California and Hawaii. But inland states have their giant storms, too. In the middle of the country, cold, dry air from Canada often collides with warm, moist air from the Gulf of Mexico. As you continue reading, you will learn that the results are sometimes dramatic.

In March 1993, a *blizzard* buried much of the eastern United States under tons of snow. From Alabama to Maine, snowdrifts of 2 meters (6 feet) or more closed roads and airports. Snow even fell in parts of Florida. Winds of more than 160 kilometers (100 miles) per hour blew down hundred-year-old trees, tore off roofs, and left much of the eastern half of the United States without electricity. High tides forced people along the Atlantic and Gulf coasts to evacuate their homes.

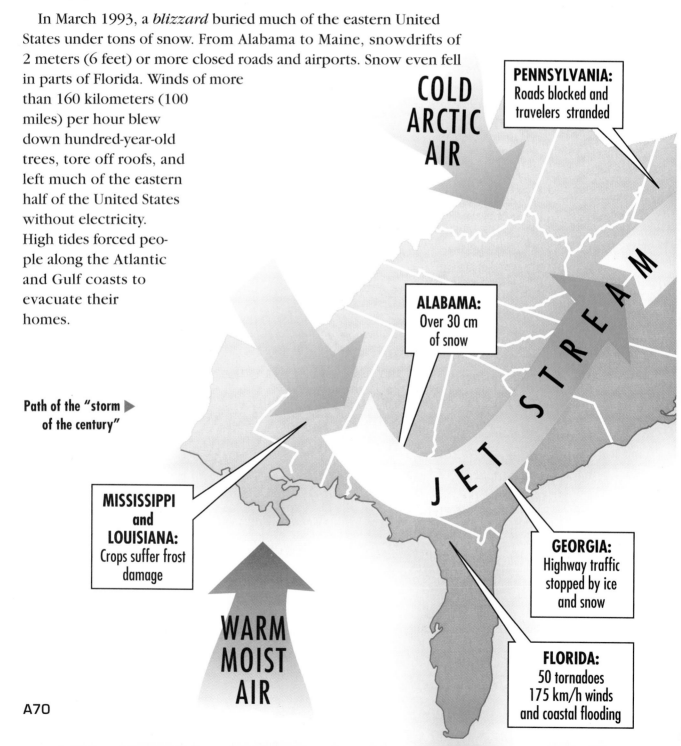

COLD ARCTIC AIR

PENNSYLVANIA:
Roads blocked and travelers stranded

ALABAMA:
Over 30 cm of snow

JET STREAM

Path of the "storm ▶
of the century"

MISSISSIPPI
and
LOUISIANA:
Crops suffer frost damage

GEORGIA:
Highway traffic stopped by ice and snow

WARM MOIST AIR

FLORIDA:
50 tornadoes
175 km/h winds
and coastal flooding

▲ Safe after the storm

This blizzard was one that some people will never forget. For example, some students from Michigan were camping in the Great Smoky Mountains of Tennessee when the storm hit. They were stranded for several days. Happily, the campers were rescued, but others weren't so lucky. Many people were killed during and immediately after the storm.

Whether this was truly the storm of the century, as some people are calling it, is not important. The fact is, blizzards are monster storms, like hurricanes. They can cause deathand destruction if people are not warned and prepared.

Today's forecasters have the tools to understand how these storms develop and how they move. This helps them make more accurate predictions and issue earlier warnings so that people will have more time to prepare. And preparation can save lives.

LESSON 3 REVIEW

❶ Why is it not safe to leave shelter as the eye of a hurricane passes over?

❷ Along what kind of front do you think blizzards form? Explain.

 DOUBLE CHECK

SECTION B REVIEW

1. How are tornadoes and hurricanes alike? How are they different?

2. What characteristics do all severe storms share? Explain why.

Different Places, Different Weather

Think about the weather your area has had over the past few years. Maybe the summers have been hot and rainy, and the winters cold and dry. Perhaps the summers have been warm and dry, and the winters cold and snowy. Whatever the weather, you've probably noticed that year after year the weather patterns remain about the same in your area.

In this section, you will study weather patterns. You will find out what weather patterns there are, where these weather patterns are located, and what factors affect weather patterns. Keep careful notes in your Science Log as you work through the readings and activities.

1 FROM THE TROPICS TO THE ARCTIC

Do you live in a place like Miami, Florida, where the weather is usually warm? Or do you live in a place like Fairbanks, Alaska, where it is usually much colder? More than likely, you live somewhere in between, where the weather is moderate—sometimes it's warm and sometimes it's cold. Wherever you live, many factors combine to produce your area's weather patterns, or *climate.* From the readings and activities that follow, you will learn about some of these factors.

Climate vs. Weather

One way to understand climate better is to compare it with weather. In this activity, you will describe your area's weather and then determine its climate. From your descriptions, you will be able to infer the difference between weather and climate.

You will need: a pencil or pen and your Science Log.

Working in small groups, discuss the kinds of weather your area has had during the past year. Write five sentences in your Science Log that describe your area's weather. Next, discuss what each of the seasons is like in your area. Write two sentences in your Science Log about each season.

After you have described the weather and the seasons, write definitions for *weather* and *climate.* Compare your definitions with those in a dictionary or in The Language of Science on pages A94–A95.

Compare your definations with those in the dictionary

Heading Home

You know that the weather changes from day to day. After you have lived in an area for a while, you probably have an idea of the climate there. How does climate vary in different parts of the United States?

Suppose you've been vacationing in Miami, where the climate is nearly tropical—sunny and warm most of the year. You've been swimming, sailing, and snorkeling all week. But the date is November 29, the last day of your vacation. You're on your way home—to Fairbanks, Alaska.

You are pressed back in your seat as your plane lifts off the runway in Miami. You climb into a sky filled with puffy white clouds. The palm trees along the beach look very small as you turn north and head for Chicago, the first stop on your way home.

The warm, moist air below you looks hazy as the plane climbs. Ships in the Atlantic Ocean look like tiny, white dots. The surrounding ocean still holds the warmth of summer, which makes Florida a wonderful, warm vacation spot in winter.

▼ **Thunderhead**

A74

After 30 minutes of flying, you reach a cruising altitude of 10,000 meters (33,000 feet). But the pilot does not turn off the "fasten seat belt" sign. "We expect a bumpy ride as we try to pick our way through some thunderstorms over Georgia," he says.

Your plane begins to bounce as it skims the clouds below. The thunderstorms mark a boundary between two air masses. To the north is cold, dry air moving in from Canada. Warm, moist air from the Caribbean Sea is hanging over the Southeast. Where they meet, there is a cold front with thunderstorms.

As you look out the window, your plane passes a towering thunderhead. The thunderhead reaches almost 16 kilometers (10 miles) into the sky. It's a good thing your pilot does not fly through the storm. Strong winds, hail, and lightning would threaten the safety of the plane and passengers.

As you continue north, the plane bounces in the rough air. You think about the warm weather in Miami, and wonder how cold it will be in Fairbanks.

THINK ABOUT IT

Why is the climate so different as you travel from the south to the north? Think about the way the sun shines on different parts of the Earth.

Allow Me Some Latitude Here

Scientists use *latitude,* or distance from the equator, to divide the Earth into three main climate zones. The map will help you identify these zones and the characteristics of each.

▼ Earth's climate zones

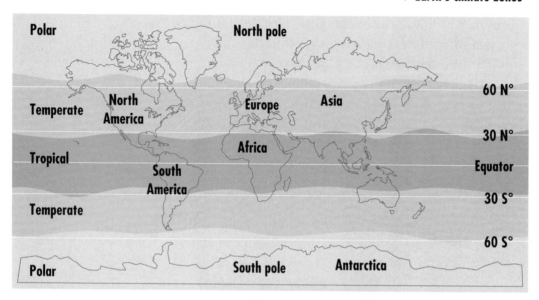

Polar

North pole

60 N°

Temperate

North America

Europe

Asia

30 N°

Africa

Tropical

Equator

South America

Temperate

30 S°

60 S°

Polar

South pole

Antarctica

▲ The two regions of temperate climate are located between the tropical zone and the polar zones. The average temperature for the coldest months is lower than that of the tropical zone. The average temperature for the warmest months is greater than that of the polar zones.

▲ The tropical zone is located near the equator. The average temperature in the coldest month is 18°C (64°F). This is higher than the average temperature of the warmest months in the polar zones.

▲ The two zones of polar climate are located near the poles. In these zones, the warmest months average less than 10°C (50°F).

THINK ABOUT IT

How is climate related to the amount of sunlight a climate zone receives?

Local Climates

"Arrival in Chicago will be at 10:50 A.M. local time," the pilot announces. "The temperature at O'Hare Airport is 0°C (32°F), and it's snowing. Downtown Chicago is 3°C (37°F), with mixed snow and rain. I hope you all brought warm coats with you!" Why is it warmer in the city? This activity can help you understand local variations in climate.

MATERIALS
- 2 thermometers
- Science Log data sheet

DO THIS

1 You should do this activity on a warm, sunny day that's not windy. Find an area of pavement next to a grassy area, such as a sidewalk or driveway.

2 Hold one thermometer over the pavement and the other thermometer over the grassy area. Record the temperature at each location after 10 minutes.

THINK AND WRITE

1. Which thermometer showed the higher temperature? Explain why.

2. City streets, parking lots, sidewalks, and buildings give off heat. Other things in a city also give off heat. Make a list of all the things you can think of in a city that give off heat.

Heat Islands

The temperature difference between O'Hare Airport and downtown Chicago is not surprising. The airport lies far from the city's center. Certain conditions of temperature, moisture, and wind often create local variations in climate. These variations are called *microclimates*.

▼ **Heat island**

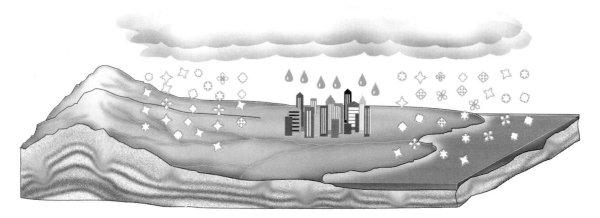

If you have ever been outdoors and walked past an air conditioner in operation, you know how much heat it can give off. Imagine how much heat all the air conditioners in a large city give off in the summer! In winter, when those same buildings are heated, a lot of heat escapes into the air. Cars, trucks, buses, and even people give off heat, too. As a result of all of these heat sources, a city is actually surrounded by a dome of warm air called a *heat island*. A heat island may be 2 to 5 degrees Celsius warmer than the surrounding countryside.

Cities affect climate in other ways as well. For example, the buildings in a city tend to redirect the wind. As a result, wind speeds in large cities may be lower or higher than those in nearby rural areas.

As you approach O'Hare Airport, light snow is falling. The landing is routine, since snowplows have been able to keep the runway clear. Your stay in Chicago is only long enough to let you board another plane. Before you know it, you are climbing above the city, heading for your next stop—Seattle, Washington. You feel lucky that your connection was so easy. Snow often results in travel delays.

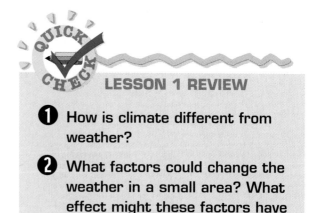

QUICK CHECK

LESSON 1 REVIEW

❶ How is climate different from weather?

❷ What factors could change the weather in a small area? What effect might these factors have on local climate?

2 CHANGING CLIMATES

Latitude is the major factor that determines climate. The farther you get from the equator, the colder the climate gets. But there are factors that can modify, or change, climate. What do you think those factors are? As you read and do the activities that follow, keep a list in your Science Log.

Water and Ice

Think about how water heats up and cools down more slowly than land. How might the nearness to water affect climate?

On takeoff you catch a glimpse of Lake Michigan before your plane enters the clouds. The lake looks dark and angry. You notice that near the lake shore there is no snow on the ground, even though it has been snowing for hours. Why do you think this is so?

The water of the lake, while only about 4.5°C (40°F), keeps the nearby air warm enough to melt the falling snow. Large bodies of water act like heaters in winter and air conditioners in summer. In warm months, they refresh the land with cool breezes. In cold months, they slowly release stored heat, keeping the nearby land slightly warmer than surrounding areas.

▲ **Could this be Chicago during the Ice Age?**

Your flight continues. Below you, the Great Plains of North Dakota and Montana must look like something out of the last Ice Age. Although you can't see much because of the clouds, the newspaper you are reading says a severe winter storm is raging through these states. Another cold front, like the one that produced the thunderstorms over Georgia, is causing a blizzard in this part of the country.

The climate of North America was not always the same as it is now. About 12,000 years ago, a giant glacier covered much of what is now the northern United States. Ahead of the moving glacier, only a few hardy plants grew. Animals such as the arctic fox and the arctic hare lived here. The climate was probably much like the polar zones are now, with the land snow-covered in summer as well as in winter.

Sometimes, in the midst of a blizzard, people worry that the Earth is entering a new Ice Age. After a scorching July, they may be convinced that Earth's climate is getting warmer and drier. The following story will tell you about a dry, dusty time in our history—the Dust Bowl years of the 1930s.

THINK ABOUT IT

How does nearness to water affect climate?

The Dust Bowl

It's the 1930s on the Great Plains. It hasn't rained much for a couple of years. High winds whip the dry, cracked earth into giant dust storms. The Great Plains, stretching from Texas to North Dakota, have become known as the Dust Bowl. What is life like on the plains at this time?

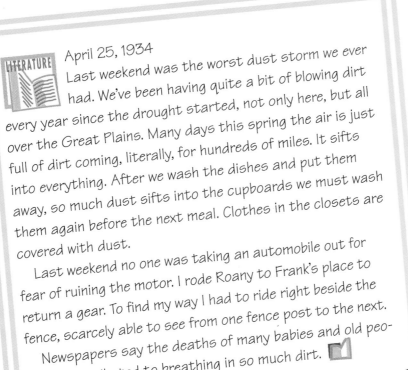

LITERATURE

April 25, 1934

Last weekend was the worst dust storm we ever had. We've been having quite a bit of blowing dirt every year since the drought started, not only here, but all over the Great Plains. Many days this spring the air is just full of dirt coming, literally, for hundreds of miles. It sifts into everything. After we wash the dishes and put them away, so much dust sifts into the cupboards we must wash them again before the next meal. Clothes in the closets are covered with dust.

Last weekend no one was taking an automobile out for fear of ruining the motor. I rode Roany to Frank's place to return a gear. To find my way I had to ride right beside the fence, scarcely able to see from one fence post to the next.

Newspapers say the deaths of many babies and old people are attributed to breathing in so much dirt.

from *Dust Bowl Diary*
by Ann Marie Low

THINK ABOUT IT

How did the drought affect farmers' everyday life?

A81

ACTIVITY

The Greenhouse Effect

Some changes in climate are short-term—like the changes that produced the Dust Bowl. Other changes are long-term. In this activity, you will investigate a process that could produce a long-term change in climate.

DO THIS

1 Place one thermometer in the jar.

2 Put the lid on the jar, and place it in direct sunlight.

3 Place the other thermometer next to the jar.

4 Without opening the jar, read the temperature from both thermometers every 15 minutes for 1 hour. Record the temperatures.

THINK AND WRITE

INTERPRETING DATA Data is information gathered during an activity. How did the temperature inside the jar differ from the temperature outside the jar? Explain any difference.

Greenhouse effect The glass of a greenhouse allows sunlight to pass through and traps heat, just as the jar did. This is known as a *greenhouse effect*. Gases in the air produce a greenhouse effect that keeps the Earth warm. But what if something increases the Earth's greenhouse effect? How would climates change?

Global Warming

Remember that people can produce microclimates, such as those of cities. But human activities can affect more than just micro-climates—they can affect all the climates of Earth.

People use oil, coal, or gas to run factories and operate vehicles. Burning these fuels increases the amount of carbon dioxide in the air. Carbon dioxide in the air traps heat—like the glass in a greenhouse.

Small increases in carbon dioxide are controlled naturally. Green plants use carbon dioxide to make food. So plants slow the increase of carbon dioxide due to burning fuels. However, as more and more forests are cut down to produce the wood and paper people need, the natural control is destroyed. The level of carbon dioxide in the air is increasing. As the carbon dioxide level rises, the greenhouse effect increases. This increased greenhouse effect, called *global warming,* could raise the temperature of climates all over the world.

THINK ABOUT IT

What do you think might happen if polar climates got warmer and stayed warmer?

▲ Pollution over factories and houses

▲ Deforestation after jungle fires

A83

ACTIVITY

Nature's High-Rise

Although human activities can change climate, the effects of Earth's features on climate are much easier to observe. You can model the effects of one of Earth's features in this activity.

DO THIS

1. **CAUTION: Wear gloves when using calcium chloride. Try not to get it on your clothes.** Rub calcium chloride on the construction paper. Be sure you cover all the paper.

2. Fold the paper in half and place it in the aquarium so that it forms a "mountain," as the picture shows. Put a lump of clay on either side of the "mountain" to keep it in place.

3. **CAUTION: Be careful with the hot water.** Fill the cup with hot tap water. Place the cup next to your "mountain."

4. Cover the aquarium with plastic wrap. Observe both sides of the mountain for 5 minutes.

THINK AND WRITE

1. What happened to the "mountain"?

2. Calcium chloride turns dark as it absorbes moisture from the air. Why didn't both sides of the "mountain" look the same?

A84

Mountain Shadows

Sometimes one side of a mountain has a climate that is very different from that of the other side. How do mountains affect climate?

The trip from Chicago to Seattle is a long one. As your plane crosses the Cascade Mountains, the weather seems less severe. There are breaks in the cloud cover, allowing you to see the land below. A few snowcapped peaks rise above the scattered clouds.

As you look down through the clouds, you notice a pattern of tree growth on the mountains below. The western sides of the mountains seem to have more trees than the eastern sides. Why should this be?

As clouds carrying moisture from the Pacific Ocean are forced to rise over the mountains, they dump their rain or snow on the western sides. By the time the clouds reach the eastern sides, they have lost much of their moisture. Little rain falls on the eastern sides of the Cascades, so few trees grow there. This effect is called a rain shadow. The great deserts of North America, which extend from Canada into Mexico, are all produced by the rain-shadow effects of the mountains to their west.

THINK ABOUT IT

How does a rain-shadow effect change climate?

▼ Rain shadow

Dry air

Moist Pacific air

Up Is North

The Ruwenzori (roo ehn ZOR ee) are a small mountain range in the tropical zone of central Africa. As you study the diagram and read about each level, you will discover another way that mountains affect climate.

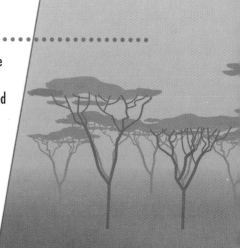

4,267 m
(14,500 ft.)

3,658 m
(12,000 ft.)

2,896 m
(9,500 ft.)

2,285 m
(7,500 ft.)

1,676m
(5,500 ft.)

In the alpine zone, which starts at about 3,700 m (12,000 ft), hardy lichens and mosses survive in the cold temperatures.

The rain forest gives way to bamboo forests between 2,300 m (7,500 ft) and 2,900 m (9,500 ft).

The Ruwenzori Mountains rise from grassy plains called *savannas*. Here elephants feed on tall grasses.

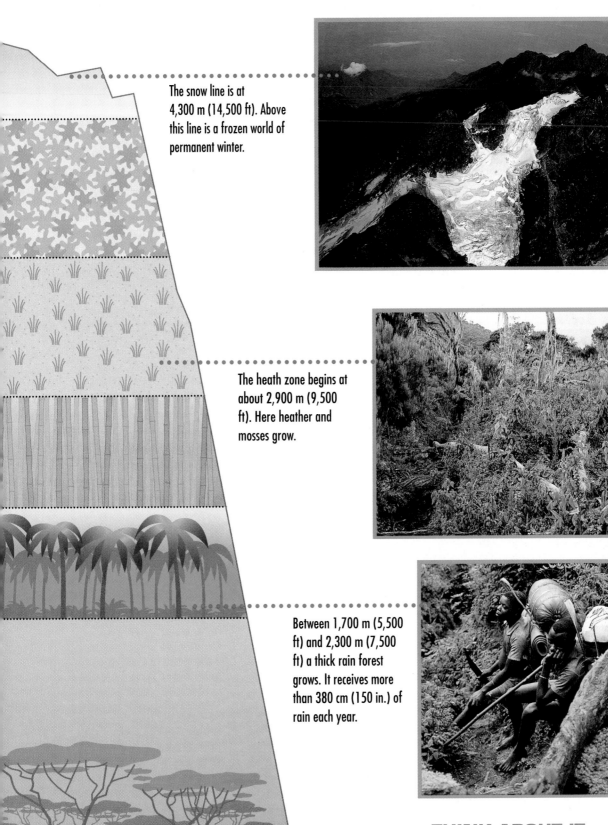

The snow line is at 4,300 m (14,500 ft). Above this line is a frozen world of permanent winter.

The heath zone begins at about 2,900 m (9,500 ft). Here heather and mosses grow.

Between 1,700 m (5,500 ft) and 2,300 m (7,500 ft) a thick rain forest grows. It receives more than 380 cm (150 in.) of rain each year.

THINK ABOUT IT

What does "Up Is North" mean?

Home at Last

Latitude, water, and mountains are all natural factors that affect climate. As you begin the last leg of your trip, see whether you can find one final factor that affects climate.

"The weather in Seattle is partly cloudy and 7°C (45°F)," the pilot reports. "We will be landing in just a few minutes." It is foggy and raining as you descend into Seattle. Although Seattle is farther north than Chicago, snow in Seattle rarely sticks to the ground. Air from the Pacific Ocean warms the area in winter and brings a lot of fog and rain.

After an hour on the ground for refueling, you're off to Fairbanks on the last leg of your journey. Vancouver Island is somewhere below the clouds off to your right. In fact, the entire coast of British Columbia

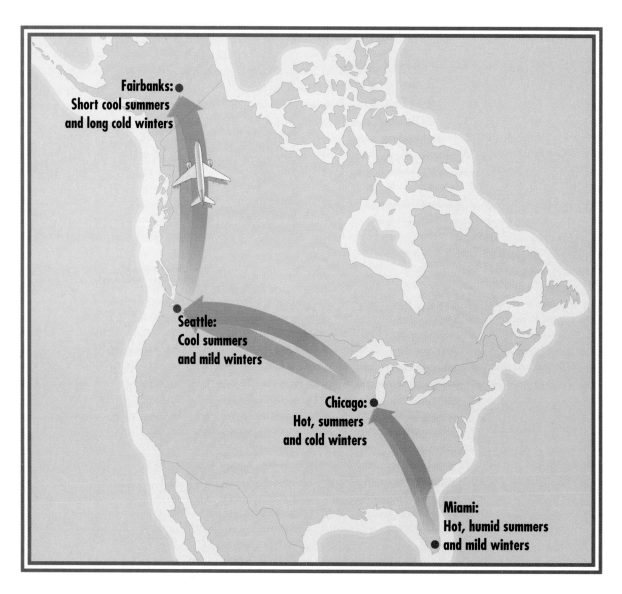

Fairbanks: Short cool summers and long cold winters

Seattle: Cool summers and mild winters

Chicago: Hot, summers and cold winters

Miami: Hot, humid summers and mild winters

is covered with clouds and fog. "Wish we could give you a better view of the coast," the pilot announces. "But things will clear up by the time we cross the coast between Anchorage and Port Valdez."

As promised, the skies clear over the Gulf of Alaska. Port Valdez, the southern end of the Alaska Pipeline, is visible to your right. Huge tankers transport oil from here to refineries in California.

The port at Valdez remains free of ice and fairly warm in winter, considering its northern location. An ocean current brings warm water from near Hawaii into the Gulf of Alaska.

"Ladies and gentlemen, we are on our final approach. We will be landing in just a few minutes. The local time is 6:30 P.M. The weather is clear and the temperature is a nippy –24°C (–10°F). Welcome to Fairbanks, Alaska, gateway to the Arctic!"

You're very tired as the plane lands. In one day you have gone from balmy Miami, to snowy Chicago, to rainy Seattle, to icy Fairbanks. Since you got up this morning, you have experienced four different climates. Look at the diagram as you review your trip.

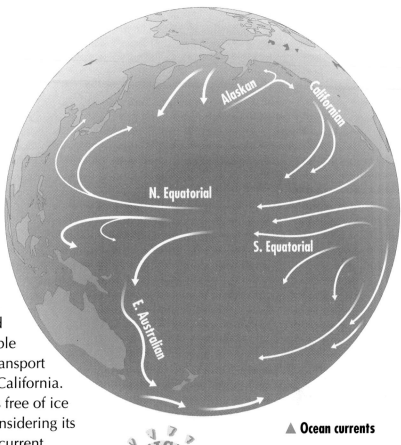

▲ Ocean currents

LESSON 2 REVIEW

❶ Name several natural factors that can change climate.

❷ How might human activity lead to global warming?

 **DOUBLE CHECK**

SECTION B REVIEW

In your Science Log, draw a circle and write the word *climate* in it. Then draw four circles around the first circle, and label them with factors that can affect climate. Be sure to include ways in which people affect climate.

REFLECT

It's time to think about the ideas you have discovered during your investigations. Think, too, about your many accomplishments.

SUMMARIZE

Complete the following in your Science Log.

1. What **I Wonder** questions have you answered in your investigations, and what new questions have you asked?

2. What have you discovered about weather and climate, and how have your ideas changed?

3. Did any of your discoveries surprise you? Explain.

My Weather Prediction

I see a huge cold front in the Midwest. I predict the front will bring thunderstorms to western Pennsylvania tomorrow.

CONNECT IDEAS

1. In the water cycle, what two processes are opposite?

2. Describe the weather that accompanies each kind of front.

3. Why are thunderstorms so dangerous?

4. How have technologies helped forecasters improve their weather predictions?

5. Describe the major factor that determines climate, and name three factors that modify climate.

6. How does weather affect you and your family?

SCIENCE PORTFOLIO

1 Complete your Science Experiences Record.

2 Choose one or two samples of your best work from each section to include in your Science Portfolio.

3 Tell why you chose each sample. Complete A Guide to My Science Portfolio.

I SHARE

Scientists share their discoveries and ideas and learn from one another. How can you share what you've learned?

Decide

▶ what you want to say.

▶ what the best way is to get your message across.

Share

▶ what you did and why.

▶ what worked and what didn't work.

▶ what conclusions you have drawn.

▶ what else you'd like to find out.

Find Out

▶ what classmates liked about what you shared—and why.

▶ what questions your classmates have.

What I Discovered About Tornadoes in WEATHER WATCH

- Thunderheads can produce tornadoes.

- The best place to be if a tornado hits is under a heavy table or desk in a basement.

- Tornadoes can do a lot of damage.

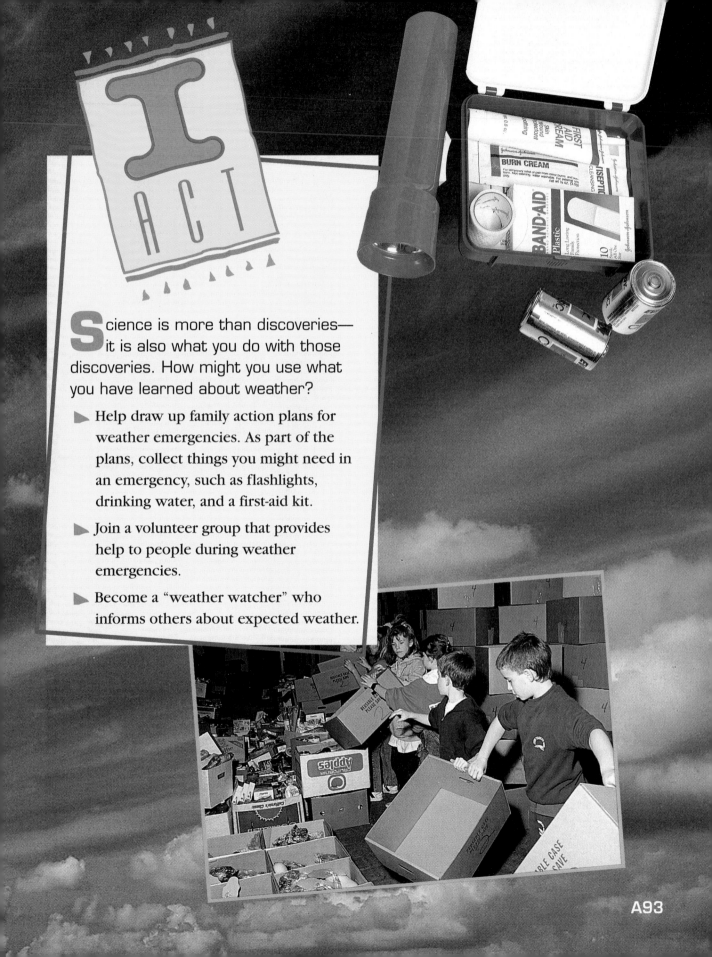

I ACT

Science is more than discoveries— it is also what you do with those discoveries. How might you use what you have learned about weather?

► Help draw up family action plans for weather emergencies. As part of the plans, collect things you might need in an emergency, such as flashlights, drinking water, and a first-aid kit.

► Join a volunteer group that provides help to people during weather emergencies.

► Become a "weather watcher" who informs others about expected weather.

THE LANGUAGE OF SCIENCE

The language of science helps people communicate clearly when they talk about weather. Here are some vocabulary words you can use when you talk about weather with friends, family, and others.

air mass—a large body of air that has nearly the same temperature and moisture throughout. Maritime tropical, maritime polar, continental tropical, and continental polar are the air masses that determine most of the weather in the United States. **(A34)**

air pressure—the force with which air pushes down on the Earth. **(A40)**

barometer – an instrument that measures air pressure. **(A40)**

blizzard—a severe winter snowstorm. **(A70)**

cirrus clouds – high, thin clouds composed of ice crystals. **(A30)**

climate – the average weather conditions over a long period of time. Earth's climates fall into three major types: polar, temperate, and tropical. **(A73)**

▼ Climate

▲ Polar

▲ Temporate

▲ Tropical

cumulonimbus clouds—huge clouds with very high, flattened tops and low, dark bases. Cumulonimbus clouds are also called *thunderheads* because they are the typical clouds of thunderstorms. **(A48)**

cumulus clouds—white, puffy clouds that dot the sky during fair weather. **(A30)**

forecast—a prediction of future weather. **(A44)**

front—a boundary between air masses. A *cold front* is the leading edge of a cold air mass. A *warm front* is the leading edge of a warm air mass. A *stationary front* is the boundary between air masses that are not moving. **(A37)**

▼ **Fronts**

▲ **Cold front**

▲ **Warm front**

global warming—a warming of climates around the world. **(A83)**

greenhouse effect—a process of trapping heat. Carbon dioxide and water vapor in the air trap heat, keeping the Earth warm. **(A82)**

hurricane—a giant tropical storm that can be very destructive because of damaging winds, heavy rains, and high waves. **(A64)**

lightning—a huge electrical spark that jumps between clouds or from a cloud to the ground. **(A51)**

local winds—winds that affect small areas. Sea breezes and mountain breezes are examples of local winds. **(A22)**

microclimate—the climate of a small area. **(A78)**

precipitation—water that falls from clouds in the form of rain, sleet, snow, or hail. **(A29)**

prevailing winds—global winds that blow mainly from one direction. **(A24)**

▲ **Prevailing winds**

squall line—a line of severe thunderstorms that forms along a strong cold front. **(A58)**

stratus clouds—low, dark clouds that cover the sky. **(A30)**

tornado—a small, very severe storm that sometimes forms along squall lines. **(A58)**

water cycle—the process by which all the water on Earth is recycled. **(A26)**

THE INSIDE STORY

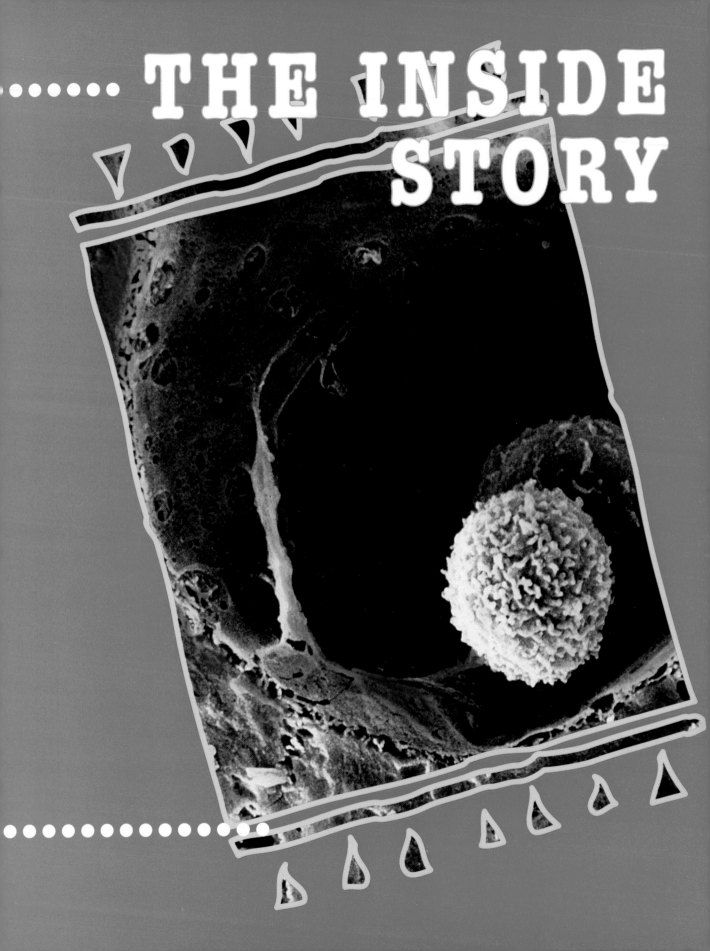

The Inside Story

Cells and Body Systems

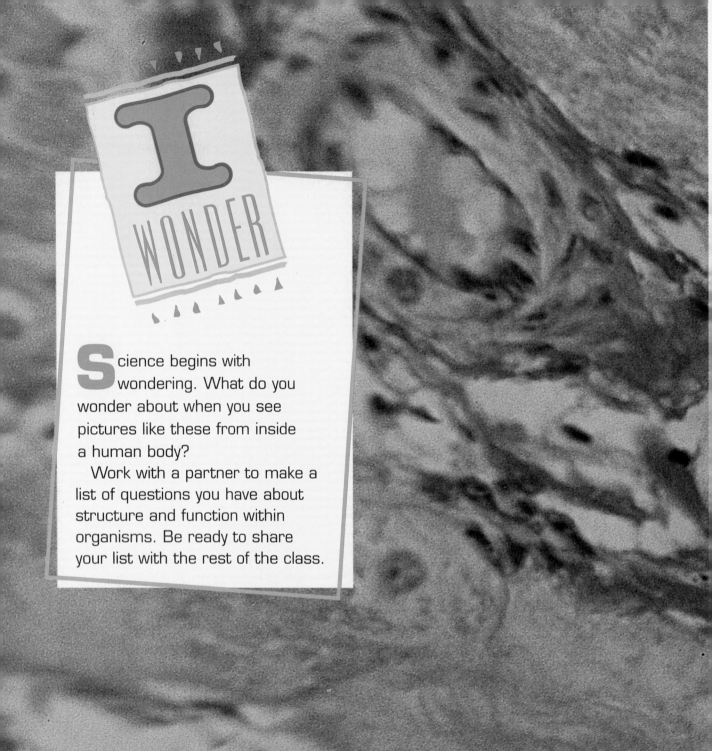

I WONDER

Science begins with wondering. What do you wonder about when you see pictures like these from inside a human body?

Work with a partner to make a list of questions you have about structure and function within organisms. Be ready to share your list with the rest of the class.

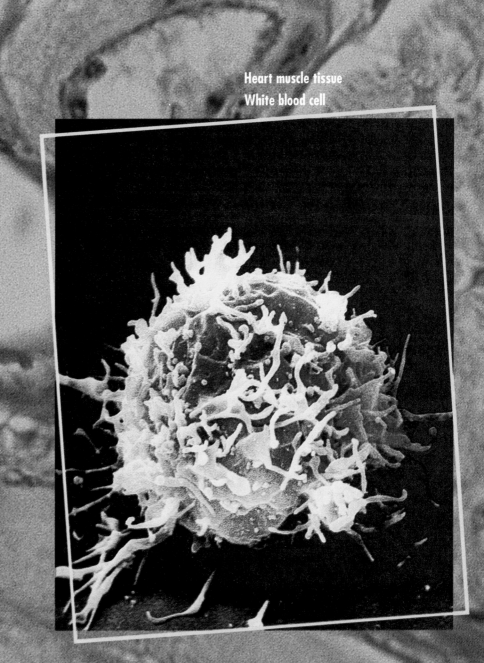

Heart muscle tissue
White blood cell

I PLAN

You may have asked questions like these as you wondered about your body. Scientists also ask questions. Then they plan ways to find answers to their questions. Now you and your classmates can plan how you will investigate structure and function within organisms.

My Science Log

How are all organisms alike? How are they different?

What is the inside of my body like?

How do different body parts work together?

How can I protect myself from disease?

Microorganism

Collect sample

1. Neighborhood

2. ...from sc...

With Your Class

Plan how your class will use the activities and readings from the **I Investigate** part of this unit. Decide what other resources you might use.

On Your Own

There are many ways to learn about organisms. Following are some things you can do to explore the structure and function of organisms by yourself or with some classmates. Some explorations may take longer to do than others. Look over the suggestions and choose...

- **Places to Visit**
- **Projects to Do**
- **Books to Read**

PLACES TO VISIT

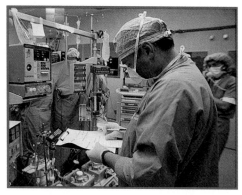

HOSPITAL

Arrange to visit a nearby health clinic or hospital. Ask for a guided tour of the medical and surgical departments, X-ray and other specialized equipment centers, and the lab. Be sure to ask about procedures for patients with highly contagious diseases.

CRIME LAB

In crime labs, experts analyze samples of hair, blood, and other body tissues to help the police identify criminals and victims. A community near you may have a regional crime-lab center. Arrange to visit the center and see the experts at work.

PHARMACY

Ask a pharmacist if you may observe as he or she fills prescriptions. Find out how different medicines are prepared. Ask about the uses of some of the medicines. If a pharmaceutical company is nearby, arrange for a tour to see how medicines are made.

WATER TREATMENT PLANT

At water treatment plants, water is analyzed for the presence of microorganisms that can cause diseases. Visit a water treatment plant near you. Find out how the water is treated to get rid of microorganisms.

PROJECTS TO DO

HEALTH VIDEO

Make a health video for younger students. Ask several classmates to help write a script or perform in the video. Your video should identify ways students can protect themselves and others from diseases caused by microorganisms.

SCIENCE FAIR PROJECT

Review the **I Wonder** questions you and your partner asked. One way to find answers to these questions is by doing a science fair project. Choose one of your questions. Plan a project that would help answer the question. Discuss your plan with your teacher. With his or her approval, begin work by collecting materials and resources. Then carry out your plan.

SYSTEM MODEL

Choose an organ or a system of the human body and make a model of it. For example, you might make a model of the lungs or of the digestive system. Use common materials, such as papier-mâché, modeling clay, paper-towel tubes, or lightweight cardboard, for your model.

MICROORGANISM HUNT

Collect samples of soil, leaves, and water. Be sure to ask permission before taking any samples from someone else's property. Examine your samples under a microscope. Look for microorganisms. Try to identify them. Sketch any microorganisms you see and tell where you found them.

BOOKS TO READ

The Princess in the Pigpen

by Jane Resh Thomas (Clarion Books, 1989). What a place to wake up—a pigpen on a farm in Iowa! That is just the first surprise for Elizabeth, who had been living in England in the year 1600. Join her as she learns about a different world, one with electricity, cars, sneakers, and, best of all, modern medicines. Read this book to find out whether Elizabeth can bring some medicines back to 1600 to save her mother's life.

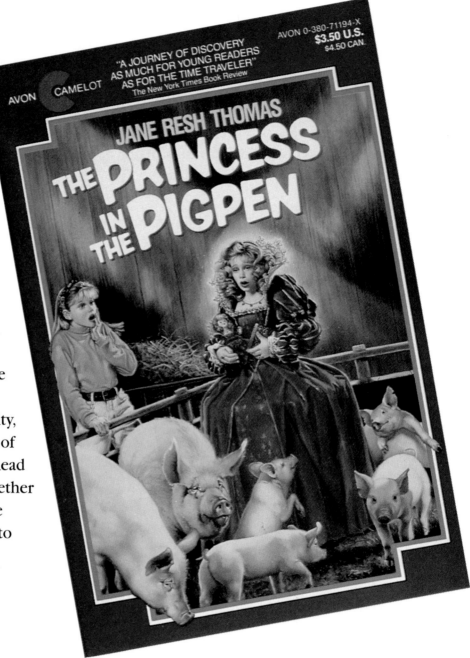

Facing the Future: Choosing Health

by Alan Collinson (Steck-Vaughn, 1991). How do you have a healthy life? This book provides some answers. They include eating right, exercising, and not smoking. But the most important factor is living in a country with good medical resources. That's an important step to a long, healthy life.

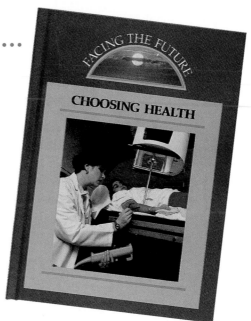

More Books to Read

Atoms and Cells

by Lionel Bender (Gloucester Press, 1990). In this book, you will learn about the microscope, how it works, and what it does. You will see pictures taken through a microscope, showing crystals and atoms. You will see chromosomes pictured 2,000 times larger than they really are so that we can see them. Imagine seeing the smallest parts of yourself 2,000 times larger than normal!

Could You Ever Live Forever?

by David Darling (Dillon Press, 1991). Do you want to live forever? That is a very long time, especially if you keep getting older and older. How would you look? This book will help you find out what happens as your body ages and what we have learned to help us live longer.

Native American Doctor: The Story of Susan LaFlesche Picotte

by Jeri Ferris (Carolrhoda, 1991). Read about Susan LaFlesche, who in 1889 became the first Native American woman to graduate from medical school. Her goal was to help her people, the Omahas. On their behalf, she worked all her life as an advisor and spokesperson to the U.S. government. Her dream was realized two years before her death when a hospital was built for them.

Outside and Inside You

by Sandra Markle (Bradbury Press, 1991). How does your body work? How do you grow and change? This book tells you about different parts of your body and what each part does. The photographs are amazing. Who would have thought we really look like that?

INVESTIGATE

To find answers to their questions, scientists do many things. They read, think, talk to others, and do experiments. Their investigations often lead to new questions.

In this unit you will have many chances to think and work like a scientist. How will you find answers to questions you asked?

▶ COMPARING When you compare objects or events, you look for what they have in common. You also look for differences between them.

▶ CLASSIFYING/ORDERING When you classify objects, you put them into groups according to how they are alike. Ordering is putting things in an order. For example, you might order things from first to last, smallest to largest, or lightest to heaviest.

▶ INFERRING Inferring is using what you have observed to explain what has happened. An observation is something you see or experience. An inference is an explanation of an observation, and it may be right or wrong.

Are you ready to begin?

SECTIONS

SECTION A
Cells

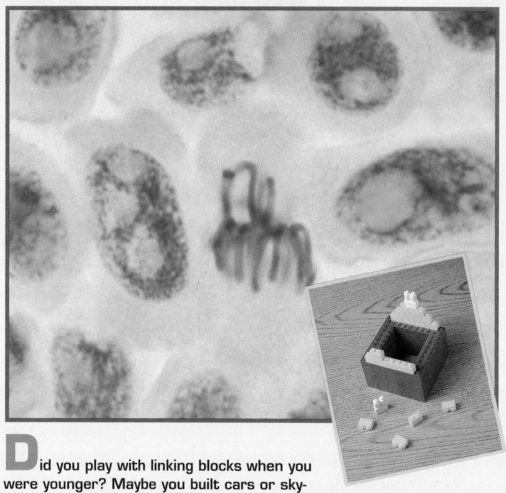

Did you play with linking blocks when you were younger? Maybe you built cars or skyscrapers with your blocks. You probably built many different things. Although they looked different, all of the things you built were made of the same types of blocks.

Now think about plants and animals. Each has many different parts. Yet the parts have the same basic building blocks. All living things on the Earth are made up of the same things—cells. In this section, you will take a closer look at these basic building blocks of living things. Keep careful notes in your Science Log as you work through some of the investigations in this section.

1 THROUGH THE LOOKING GLASS

For a long time, scientists did not have a way to look at very small things. The invention of the microscope changed that. The microscope helped scientists explore a world never before seen. In the activities that follow, you can use a microscope to discover what early scientists first saw inside living things.

ACTIVITY

Take a Closer Look

Do you like onions on your hamburgers? Whether you like onions or not, you probably have never seen inside one. In this activity, you will discover something new about an onion.

MATERIALS
- small piece of onion skin
- microscope slide
- red food coloring
- microscope
- Science Log data sheet

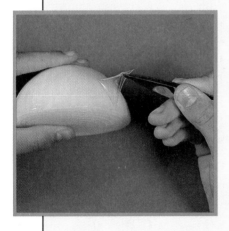

DO THIS

1 Break a piece of onion. Peel off a small piece of "skin," and put it on a microscope slide. Add a drop or two of red food coloring.

2 Place the slide under the microscope and adjust the focus.

3 Sketch what you see.

THINK AND WRITE

1. What did the onion skin look like under the microscope?

2. Do you think other parts of the onion would look the same? Explain.

What Does It Look Like?

Just as you did in the activity, scientists have used microscopes to make discoveries about living things. As you read, think about how exciting some of these discoveries must have been.

Working as a scientist in the 1600s, Robert Hooke spent many hours forming hypotheses, conducting experiments, and drawing conclusions. Yet he couldn't have known that doing something as simple as observing a piece of cork under a microscope would enable him to see something no scientist had ever seen before.

Suppose that you are with Hooke in his lab. He explains to you what he has done:

To Hooke the cork seemed to be divided like the sleeping rooms in a monastery. He decided to call them *cells*, which is what monks' rooms are called. The cork cells that Hooke saw looked very much like the onion you saw in the activity.

I took a good clear piece of cork, and with a penknife sharpened as keen as a razor, I cut a piece of it off and thereby left the surface of it exceedingly smooth. Then, examining the piece very diligently with a microscope, me thought I could perceive it to appear a little porous. These pores, or cells, were not very deep but consisted of a great many little boxes separated out of one long pore. These were the first microscopic pores I ever saw, and perhaps that were ever seen; for I have not met with any writer or person that has made any mention of them before this.

B14

▶ **Hooke's microscope**

Hooke's discovery of cork cells was just the beginning. Scientists wondered whether all living things are made of cells. For scientists it was like putting together the first few pieces of a jigsaw puzzle. But many other pieces were needed before the picture would be complete. For nearly 200 years, scientists continued looking for cells. Some looked at plants, while others studied animals. They shared their information and finally, in the mid-1800s, they had all the pieces they needed to finish the puzzle.

First, scientists discovered that all plants and animals are made up of cells. In fact, all living things—trees, people, dogs, mushrooms, bacteria, and amoebas—are made up of cells.

Second, scientists determined that the cell is the basic, or smallest, unit of structure and function in all living things.

Third, and this was the final piece of the cell puzzle, scientists found out that every cell can reproduce to form new cells. This completed cell puzzle is called the *cell theory.*

▶ All living things are made of cells.

QUICK CHECK

LESSON 1 REVIEW

❶ Why was Hooke's discovery of cells so important?

❷ In your own words, define the word cell.

B15

2 INSIDE A CELL

You have fingers, eyes, ears, and many other parts. Each part does something different. The same is true of cells. They have many parts, and each part does something different. Let's find out what the parts are and what they do.

Fantastic Journey

A good way to observe a cell would be to get inside to see what it looks like. It sounds impossible, but with virtual reality, a kind of interactive video, you *can* travel inside a cell. Put on your gloves and glasses; reach for the door. You are about to begin a fantastic journey through a cell.

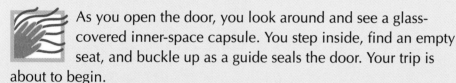 As you open the door, you look around and see a glass-covered inner-space capsule. You step inside, find an empty seat, and buckle up as a guide seals the door. Your trip is about to begin.

Before you know it, a wave of water carries the capsule through the cell membrane. A *cell membrane* surrounds a cell in the same way that your skin covers your body. The cell membrane allows water, oxygen, and other materials to pass into and out of the cell.

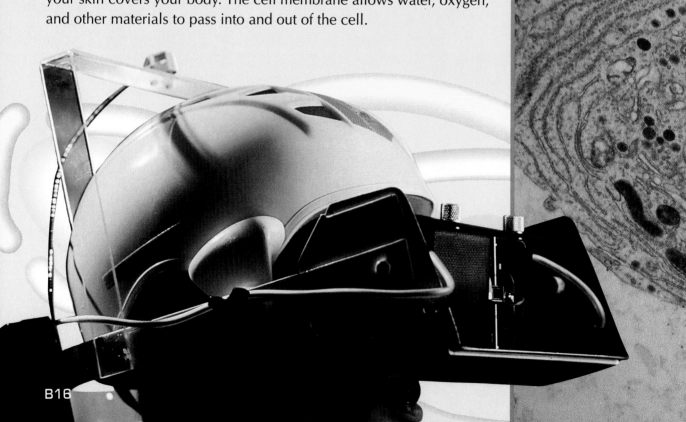

As you enter the cell, something splatters against the capsule. "That's cytoplasm," the guide says. *"Cytoplasm* is the material between the cell's nucleus and the cell membrane." Inside the cytoplasm, you see many structures. But you are most interested in seeing the nucleus. You turn to the guide and ask, "Where is the nucleus?"

Your guide points it out and reminds you that the nucleus is the most important structure in the cell. "The *nucleus* is the cell's command center," she says. "It controls everything that goes on inside the cell."

Within the cytoplasm, you notice some things that look like red beans. You ask about them and learn that they are *mitochondria* (myt oh KAHN dree uh). "Mitochondria are like batteries; they provide the energy the cell needs for all of its functions."

You see many other structures that you can't identify yet. The guide calls them organelles (awr guh NELZ). An *organelle* is any cell structure that has a specific job to do. You've seen several organelles already. For example, the nucleus and mitochondria are organelles. You would like to see more, but your turn with the interactive video is over. You take off the gloves and glasses and decide to take another look at cells through a microscope.

THINK ABOUT IT

Why is the nucleus the most important organelle?

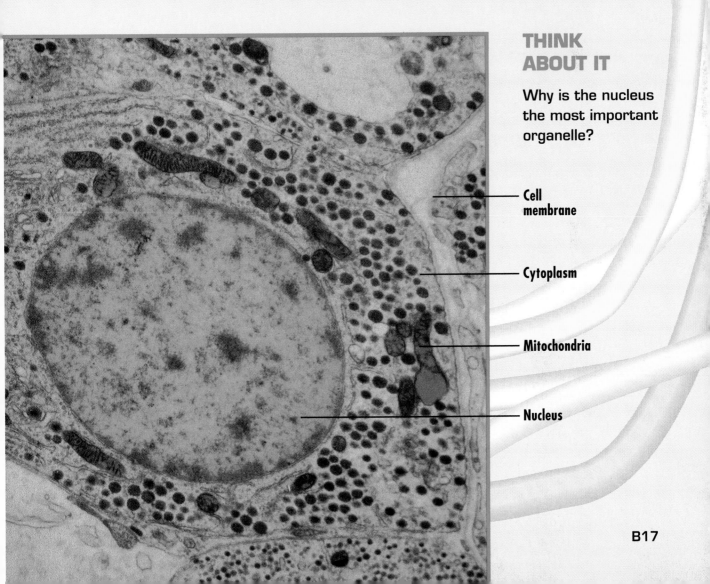

Cell membrane

Cytoplasm

Mitochondria

Nucleus

A C T I V I T Y

How Are They Different?

You know that plants and animals are different, yet both are made of cells. Are their cells alike? In the following activity, you can observe plant and animal cells to find out for yourself.

MATERIALS
- prepared slide of animal cell
- prepared slide of plant cell
- microscope
- Science Log data sheet

DO THIS

❶ Place a prepared slide of an animal cell under the microscope, and adjust the focus.

❷ Sketch what you see. Label any organelles that you can identify.

❸ Place a prepared slide of a plant cell under the microscope, and adjust the focus.

❹ Sketch what you see. Label any organelles that you can identify.

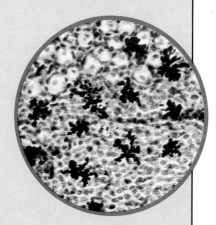

▲ Animal cells

THINK AND WRITE

1. What organelles did you see in the animal cell? in the plant cell?

2. **COMPARING** When you compare objects, you observe what they have in common and what differences they have. Carefully study your diagrams. How is the animal cell different from the plant cell? How is it the same?

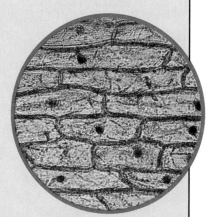

▲ Plant cells

Chloroplasts Plant cells are surrounded by a thick wall as well as by a cell membrane. A cell wall gives a plant cell strength and support. Plant cells also have many green organelles called *chloroplasts*. Chloroplasts are the sites of food production in green plants.

QUICK CHECK

LESSON 2 REVIEW

List all the organelles you have learned about so far, and write a short description of the function of each.

3 IN AND OUT

On your fantastic journey, a wave of water carried your capsule through the cell membrane and into the cell. In this lesson, you will discover how materials really move in and out of cells.

Hot and Sweaty

It was a great game! Your team won the game, and you scored the winning point. As you head for the locker room, your friends are talking excitedly about the game. All you want is some nice, cool water to drink. You get thirsty when you exercise or when it's hot. Why?

You're thirsty because you're sweating. Your body sweats to help keep you cool. Because you lose water when you sweat, you need to replace it. That's why you want that drink of water.

The cells in your body need water. If you don't replace the water you lose by sweating, you might become dehydrated. *Dehydration* means "loss of water." This happens when your body's cells lose more water than they take in. Dehydration can make you very sick. So go for it! Fill up those cells. Drink some cool, refreshing water, and enjoy your victory.

▲ **Your cells need water to avoid dehydration.**

THINK ABOUT IT

Why do you think dehydration makes people sick?

Thirst Quencher

As you gulp water from the fountain, you wonder about those sports drinks you've seen advertised on TV. Do they really get into your body's cells faster than plain water? This activity will help you find out.

MATERIALS
- 2 jars with lids
- measuring cup
- water
- sports drink
- 2 hard-boiled eggs
- marker
- Science Log data sheet

DO THIS

1 Pour 300 mL of water into one jar. Into the other jar, pour 300 mL of a sports drink.

2 Shell the eggs, and place one egg in each jar.

3 Cover the jars. Use the marker to write the contents of each jar on the lid.

4 After 2 hours, remove the eggs from the jars. Measure the amount of liquid remaining in each jar.

THINK AND WRITE

1. Which egg absorbed the most liquid?

2. Do you think sports drinks get into your cells faster than water? Explain.

3. **INFERRING** Scientists often use what they have observed to explain what has happened. In this activity, you observed one egg absorbing more liquid than the other. What could you infer caused that to happen?

Movin', Movin', Movin'

Things are always moving in and out of cells. What causes all this movement? In this activity, you will observe one process that causes materials to move in and out of cells.

DO THIS

1 Fill the glass with water.

2 Put three drops of food coloring into the water.

3 Allow the glass to remain undisturbed for 15 minutes, and then observe.

THINK AND WRITE

1. What happened to the water?

2. Why do you think this happened?

Keep Those Cell Things Movin'

When you're hungry, you eat. When you're thirsty, you drink. Your body's cells need food and drink, too. In the last activity, you saw a process that causes things to move. Read to find out how this process helps move things in and out of cells.

Cells need water, nutrients, and other materials to do their work. They also need to get rid of wastes. One way materials move in and out of cells is through diffusion. *Diffusion* is the movement of material from an area that has a lot of the material to an area that has less of the material. In the last activity, you watched the diffusion of food coloring throughout the water. The food coloring moved from where there was a lot of it—the drops—to where there was less of it—the water.

Just as the food coloring spread, or diffused, throughout the water, materials diffuse into and throughout your cells. When your cells need oxygen, for example, oxygen outside the cells moves through the cell membranes and into the cells. When wastes build up inside cells, they move through the cell membranes to the outside of the cells.

▲ **Diffusion**

Water is something your cells need a lot of. Remember, without water your cells become dehydrated. You help your cells get the water they need whenever you drink something. Water enters cells in a kind of diffusion known as *osmosis.* Osmosis is the diffusion of water across a cell membrane.

Both plant cells and animal cells get the water they need through osmosis. You can see the effects of osmosis by looking at the plants in the photographs. The first picture shows

◀ The plant on the left is wilted; its cells are dehydrated.

▶ The plant on the right is not wilted; its cells are full of water.

a wilted plant. Its cells are dehydrated. When the plant is watered, water moves by osmosis from the soil into the cells of the plant's roots. From the roots, water travels in little tubes through the roots and stems to the leaves. In the leaves, water moves by osmosis from the tubes into cells throughout the leaves. The cells take in water and swell. What happens to the plant?

LESSON 3 REVIEW

❶ Why do you get thirsty when you exercise?

❷ Explain how waste materials, such as carbon dioxide, leave a cell.

❸ Is osmosis different from any other kind of diffusion? Explain.

4 MAKING COPIES

Have you ever used a photocopier? With it you can make an exact
copy of something you wrote or an article you read and give it to
a friend. Cells make copies of themselves, too. You can discover
how they do this by reading and doing the activity.

ACTIVITY

Two for One

Remember the cell theory? According to one
part of the theory, all cells come from other
cells. In the following activity, you will see how
this happens.

MATERIALS
- prepared slides of stages of cell division
- microscope
- Science Log data sheet

DO THIS

❶ Place slide 1 under the microscope, and adjust the
focus. Draw and describe what you see.

❷ Repeat the procedure for slides 2, 3, and 4.

THINK AND WRITE

1. How were the cells you observed the same? How were
they different?

2. What happens to a cell as it divides?

Chromosomes Within the nucleus of a cell are thin
strands called *chromosomes*. Chromosomes contain the
instructions that enable the nucleus to control all the activities of the cell. Before a cell divides, it makes an exact copy
of its chromosomes. During cell division, the chromosomes
and cytoplasm are divided so that each new cell receives a
full set of chromosomes.

Cells, Cells, and More Cells

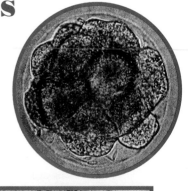

Close your eyes and slowly count to five, or look at a clock with a second hand and watch five seconds tick by. What happened? It's easy to think that nothing happened, but during those few seconds, your body made about 10 million new blood cells! That's right—10 million! Why do you need so many new cells?

What happens to your cells as you grow? Do they enlarge? Not much. As you grow, your body produces new cells. At the same time, many cells get old and die. Others wear away from the surface of your skin. Your body needs to produce more and more cells for growth and as replacements for old cells. New cells are produced through a division process called *mitosis* (my TOH sis).

Through mitosis, a cell makes an exact copy of its chromosomes, and then it divides. Where there was once one cell, there are now two. And two can quickly become four. Your body has several trillion cells, and most are able to make copies of themselves through mitosis.

THINK ABOUT IT

How does a cell "photocopy" itself?

▶ The trillions of cells in your body started from a single cell.

Let's Wrap It Up

Now that you've seen plant and animal cells and read about some important cell functions, let's summarize with a rap about the cell theory, written by a student in Cobb County, Georgia.

CELL THEORY RaP

by Deborah Carver

Listen close to the story I tell:
It's the rapping story of the living cell.
It's a happy tune that's sort of cheery,
About a real tough topic called cell theory.

All animals, plants, and protists too,
Are made of cells with different jobs to do.
They're the basic units of all organisms,
And I hope by now you've got the rhythm.

It all started with one dude named Hooke,
Who at some cork cells took a look.
He used a scope and took his time,
'Cause a cell is small and thinner than a dime.

Say 1, 2, 3, 4,
Are you ready to learn some more?
The animal cell has many parts,
And you must know each one by heart.

Like the farmer man in the dell,
The nucleus controls the cell.
It gives the orders—kind of like a brain,
And it's protected by a nuclear membrane.

Around the cell, you'll find another "skin."
This cellular membrane holds the whole cell in.
But its job isn't simple, there's no doubt,
It lets some particles go in and out.

Now please don't lose your science enthusiasm;
Listen to the story of the cytoplasm.
All around the cell this thick fluid does go,
But in the nucleus it will not flow.

And don't forget those ribosomes—
This is where proteins come from.
These protein factories are so small, you'll agree,
You need an electron microscope to see.

Just when you thought you weren't having any fun,
Along comes endoplasmic reticulum.
These tubelike structures serve as a track,
To carry stuff to the membrane and back.

Now have you ever seen doughnuts without any holes?
In a cell, they're called vacuoles.
They're filled with stuff like H_2O,
And they carry food so the cell can grow.

Last of all, but not the very least,
Mitochondria—mighty cellular beasts.
Since they turn sugars into energy so well,
We call them the powerhouses of the cell.

Now my friend, you know it well,
The unforgettable story of the living cell.

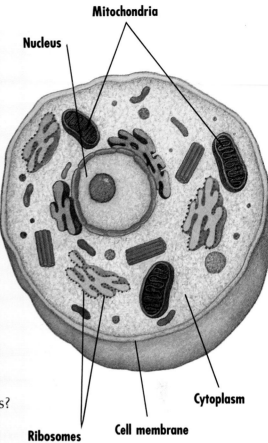

Mitochondria

Nucleus

Cytoplasm

Cell membrane

Ribosomes

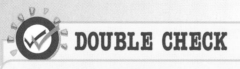

LESSON 4 REVIEW

❶ What happens in the nucleus before a cell divides?

❷ Why is it important that your body has the ability to make new cells?

DOUBLE CHECK

SECTION A REVIEW

1. Why are cells considered the building blocks of living things?

2. How do materials move in and out of cells?

3. Why is it important that cells make exact copies of themselves?

SECTION B
We're Organized

▲ **Muscle cells**

Think about a bicycle for a moment. Bicycles have many different parts, and each part has its own job to do. You wouldn't get very far on a bicycle without wheels. And stopping a bicycle wouldn't be easy if it didn't have brakes. All the parts work together to make a bicycle fun to ride.

Like a bicycle, your body has many different parts. Each part has its own job to do. You already know that the basic units of structure and function in your body are its cells. And like bicycle parts, your body cells are organized into levels of structure and function.

In this section, you will discover how your cells are organized. As you complete the following investigations about body organization, keep careful notes in your Science Log.

1 FROM CELLS TO ORGANISMS

Look around your classroom. How many different living things do you see? Your classmates and teacher are living things. So are any plants or classroom pets you may have. Remember, all these living things are made up of cells. In the activities and readings that follow, you will discover how cells are organized to make up living things.

ACTIVITY

All Alone

Not all living things are as big as those you just counted. Some can be seen only with a microscope. In this activity, you will observe one very small living thing. As you look at it, think about how it is like you and how it is different from you.

DO THIS

1 Place the prepared slide under the microscope and adjust the focus.

2 Sketch the organism.

THINK AND WRITE

1. Describe the organism you observed.

2. How many cells did the organism have?

3. **CLASSIFYING/ORDERING**
   When you classify objects, you put them into groups according to how they are alike. How is this organism different from you?

MATERIALS
- microscope
- prepared slide of amoeba
- Science Log data sheet

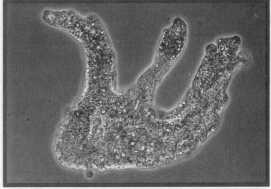

▲ Amoeba

Amoeba The living thing you examined is an amoeba (uh MEE buh). An *amoeba* is a single-celled living thing. Everything it must do to stay alive has to be done by its one and only cell. Like larger, many-celled living things, an amoeba moves, eats, and reproduces itself.

ACTIVITY

Muscle-Bound

You know your body is made up of many cells. But are all the cells alike? In this activity, you will look at muscle cells like those in your own body.

MATERIALS

- microscope
- prepared slides of skeletal muscle, smooth muscle, and heart muscle
- Science Log data sheet

▲ Skeletal-muscle cell

▲ Smooth-muscle cell

▲ Cardiac-muscle cell

DO THIS

① Look at the first slide under the microscope. Sketch what you see, and label your sketch *Skeletal-Muscle Cells.*

② Look at the second slide under the microscope. Sketch what you see, and label your sketch *Smooth-Muscle Cells.*

③ Repeat the procedure for the third slide. Label this sketch *Heart-Muscle Cells.*

THINK AND WRITE

1. How are smooth-muscle cells and skeletal-muscle cells alike? How are they different?

2. Which types of muscle cells look most alike?

3. The muscles in your arm are skeletal muscles. Explain what that means.

Fantastic Journey: Part II

You've seen three different groups of muscle cells. What other cell groups are there? You can find the answer by taking another video tour. Put your virtual reality gloves and glasses back on, climb into the capsule, and buckle up. You're about to take another fantastic journey.

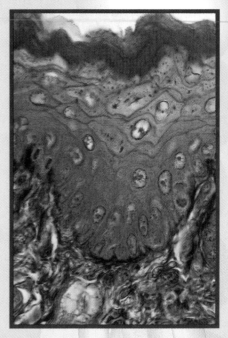

The first thing you come to is a vast field of cells. Cells are everywhere, as far as you can see. You finally figure out that you're looking at human skin cells—millions of them. Your tour guide reminds you that cells are the basic units of structure and function in a living thing. They're also the first of five levels of body organization. You ask your guide what the other levels are. She tells you that you will find out as you continue your journey. Just then your capsule plunges into a long, deep tunnel.

As your capsule clears the tunnel, you begin hovering above another group of cells. They look like the skeletal-muscle cells you observed under the microscope. Your guide asks what you notice about the cells. "They all look alike," you reply.

The guide agrees and continues: "They not only look alike, but they also do the same job. Groups of cells that have the same structure and do the same job are called *tissues.* Tissues are the second level of body organization."

▲ **Skin cells**
▼ **Muscle tissue**

Without warning, the muscle tissue you're looking at seems to shorten and the capsule rocks violently! "Nothing to worry about," the guide explains. "This tissue is in the *biceps,* a muscle at the front of the arm. The owner of this muscle is just bending his arm. For that to happen, the tissue must contract. This shows one of the characteristics of tissues—the cells all work together." All the passengers in the capsule begin bending their arms and feeling their biceps.

The tour moves on. Soon the capsule begins rocking, as if to a musical beat. The beat gets louder and stronger. Now a throbbing structure comes into view. You know immediately where you are—the heart. You recognize the heart-muscle tissue. It's just like the tissue you observed in the activity. You also see tissues that don't look anything like muscle tissue.

Your guide explains that the heart is made up of several different kinds of tissues. "The heart is an organ that pumps blood throughout the body. An *organ* is a group of different kinds of tissues working together to do a specific job. Organs are the third level of body organization."

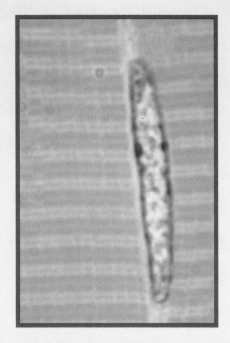

▲ **Muscle tissue—relaxed**

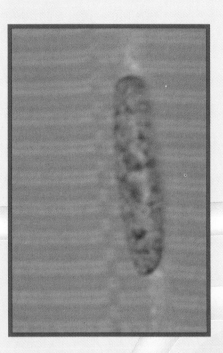

▲ **Muscle tissue—contracted**

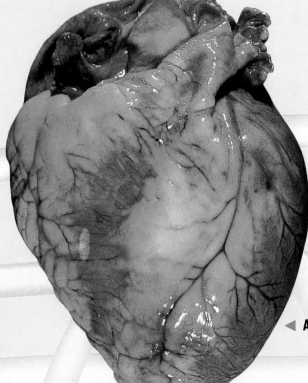

◄ **A human heart**

Before you have time to think about organs, your capsule races into a dark, windy passageway. "We're in a lung—part of the respiratory system," the guide yells over the howling wind. "A *system* is a group of organs working together to do a job. The respiratory system is responsible for breathing. Your body has several major systems. Systems are the fourth level of body organization."

Suddenly there is a loud noise like an explosion, and your capsule is hurtled into bright sunlight. "We must have irritated the owner's lungs, so he coughed us out," the guide explains. "I'm afraid this tour must end immediately."

You're back in your classroom. The video tour is over. But you haven't seen the final level of organization. What is the fifth level? Take a look in a mirror. *You* are an example of the final level. The fifth level of organization is the *organism*, a living thing that carries out all life functions.

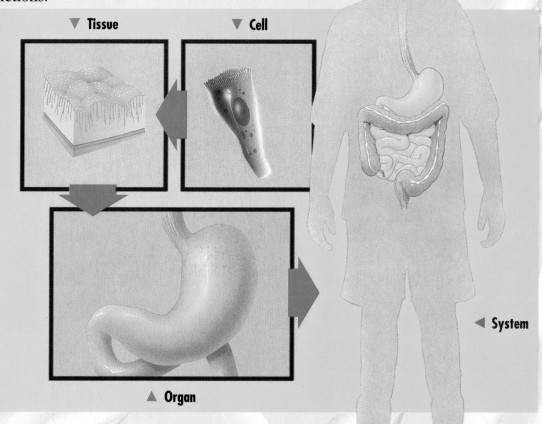

▼ Tissue ▼ Cell

◄ System

▲ Organ

THINK ABOUT IT

How are the five levels of body organization related?

What's That?

Through an imaginary video tour, you were able to see cells, tissues, organs, and systems. One photographer has developed another way to look at these structures. These pages show *his* fantastic voyage.

The Inside Story

A Fantastic Voyage Through the Human Body

by **Beth Chayet** from *3 2 1 Contact*

 LITERATURE

Photographer Lennart Nilsson really knows how to get under your skin. His fantastic photos give close-up looks at the inside of the human body.

To photograph organs, tissues and cells, Nilsson uses a camera with lots of special lenses. To get an even closer look, he connects his camera to a scanning electron microscope. The microscope magnifies objects up to 100,000 times! The image appears on a TV screen, which Nilsson then photographs. The black and white photos are later colored by hand.

Nilsson works with scientists and doctors to get the inside scoop. He photographs body parts that have been preserved for research. Many of the cells are kept in laboratory dishes until he's ready to snap a photo.

Nilsson's photos give people a better understanding of how our body works. Here are just a few of his inside views.

Cleaning House

In each drop of blood are millions of red blood cells. They carry oxygen from the lungs to the rest of the body. After about 120 days, a red blood cell gets worn out and dies.

Magnified 10,000 times, this white blood cell is swallowing an old red blood cell. Luckily, every second, two million new ones are made deep in our bones.

Down Under

This underground cave is really the lining of the large intestine, magnified 400 times. About five feet long and two-and-a-half inches wide, it receives undigested food from the small intestine. The large intestine absorbs water from these pieces of food.

Food takes about 24 hours to pass through the body. It remains the longest in the large intestine, about 14 hours.

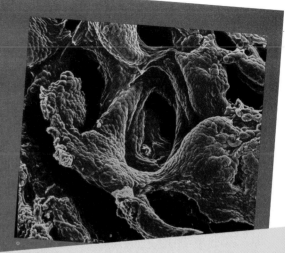

Go with the Flow

No yolk! These yellow globs, magnified 1,000 times, are fat droplets clinging to the wall of a coronary artery.

Arteries are blood vessels that carry blood from the heart to other parts of the body. Eating too many fatty foods can cause fat deposits to collect in arteries. This could block the arteries causing heart problems.

The Whole Tooth

If you don't brush at night, here's what your toothbrush (the bristly stuff at top) has to remove in the morning: plaque. That's the invisible, sticky film that forms on your teeth. In 24 hours, bacteria living in plaque begin to eat away at the surface of teeth and cause cavities.

This tooth (magnified 75 times) was just pulled from a patient's mouth.

Say AHH!

Without them, food would have no taste. They are papillae (say: puh-PIL-ee), little bumps found all over the top of your tongue. They tell your brain when something is sweet, sour, salty or bitter.

More than 10,000 taste buds are in the skin around the base of papillae (here magnified eight times). Each taste bud has about 50 taste cells. They live about a week. But new cells always replace them.

Under Pressure

Sitting between the bones of the spine is a rubbery substance called cartilage. It acts as a shock absorber. It's also on the end of your nose and on the outer part of your ears. The sponge-like bone (left) and cartilage have been magnified five times.

Cartilage keeps these bones from grinding together. Otherwise, the bones would wear away!

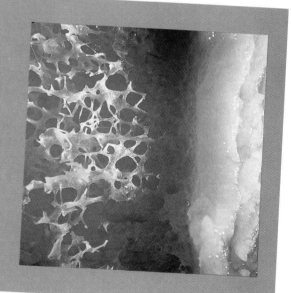

THINK ABOUT IT

How can Nilsson's photographs help people better understand how their bodies work?

A Body of Riddles

Do you enjoy riddles? To summarize this lesson, you will use what you know about levels of organization to write riddles.

You will need: Science Log

Work in small groups. Brainstorm riddles about different levels of organization. Here's one to get you started.

> Riddle: *I am an organ of the human body. If I were a musical instrument, I would provide the beat. What am I?*
>
> Answer: *The heart.*

Try to think of a riddle for each level of organization. Write your best riddles and their answers in your Science Log. Also write the riddles, but not the answers, on a sheet of notebook paper.

Hold a Riddle Challenge by exchanging riddles with other groups and working in your own group to solve the riddles.

QUICK CHECK

LESSON 1 REVIEW

Do all organisms have the same levels of organization? Explain.

A SYSTEMATIC LOOK AT THE BODY

Every life function of your body is the job of a certain system. In the following activities and readings, you will examine one system in detail, and you will identify other body systems.

ACTIVITY

In Transport

In the United States, highways, railroads, and rivers provide ways to transport people and materials from one place to another. In your body, the transportation of materials from one place to another is the job of the circulatory (SUR kyoo luh tawr ee) system. In this activity, you will observe an important part of the circulatory system.

MATERIALS
- prepared slide of blood
- microscope
- Science Log data sheet

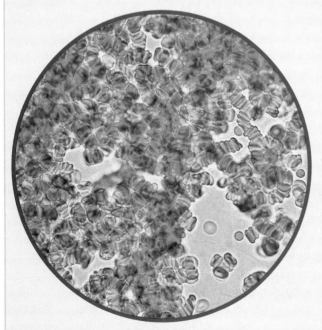

▲ Human blood

DO THIS

❶ Place the prepared slide under the microscope, and adjust the focus.

❷ Sketch what you see.

THINK AND WRITE

Describe the blood cells you observed.

Red-Blooded Tissues

If someone asked you to describe blood, you might say it's a red liquid. From your observations of blood in the last activity, you know that blood is more than that. Read on to find out just what blood is.

Blood is a fluid tissue that moves from place to place. It transports things your body needs, like food and oxygen. Blood is composed of two parts—a liquid part and a solid part.

The solid part of blood is mostly *red blood cells.* Red blood cells are like river barges. Their cargo is oxygen, and they carry it to body cells. The river is *plasma,* the liquid part of blood. Plasma is mostly water, but it contains nutrients and other materials, which it carries to body cells. Plasma also contains waste materials, such as carbon dioxide, which it carries away from body cells.

There are *white blood cells* in plasma, too. Although there are more red blood cells, white blood cells are huge in comparison. White blood cells help protect you from disease and infection. You will learn more about this later.

Plasma also contains *platelets,* which are pieces of white blood cells. These help form a plug to stop the flow of blood when you cut yourself.

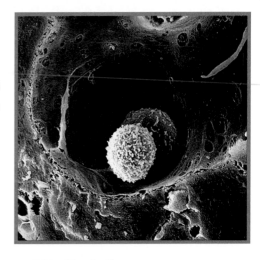

▲ White blood cell

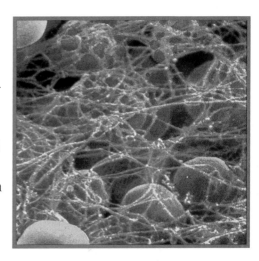

▲ Platelets

THINK ABOUT IT

Why is blood a tissue?

▼ Red blood cells

ACTIVITY

Back in Circulation

You have learned that blood carries food and oxygen to your body cells. But how does it get around your body? You'll find the answer to that question as you do the following activity.

MATERIALS

- cooking baster
- rubber tubing (40–50 cm)
- glass of water
- empty glass
- Science Log data sheet

DO THIS

❶ Attach one end of the tubing to the baster.

❷ Hold the bulb of the baster in one hand, and place the free end of the tubing in the glass of water.

❸ Squeeze and then release the bulb to draw water into the baster.

❹ Place the free end of the tubing in the empty glass. While holding the tubing, use your other hand to squeeze the bulb.

❺ Repeat the procedure several times. Squeeze the bulb hard sometimes and not so hard other times. Record your observations.

THINK AND WRITE

1. What part of the circulatory system does the baster represent? What does the rubber tubing represent? How does the water pulsing through the tubing feel to your fingertips?

2. Work with a partner to design another model to demonstrate how the heart and circulatory system work.

The Beat Goes On

In the last activity, you used a baster to pump water. The harder you squeezed the baster, the more water you pumped. In your body, your heart pumps blood. How does your heart increase the amount of blood it pumps? The following activity will help you find the answer.

MATERIALS
- stopwatch
- Science Log data sheet

DO THIS

1. Work with a partner. Find your partner's pulse by placing your index and middle fingers on the underside of his or her wrist. A person's pulse rate is the same as his or her heartbeat rate.

2. While sitting quietly at your desks, count the number of beats in your partner's pulse in 60 seconds. Record this number and label it *Heartbeat Rate at Rest*.

3. **CAUTION: Obtain your teacher's permission before doing step 3.** Have your partner run in place or do some other exercise for 1 minute. Once again, count the beats in your partner's pulse for 60 seconds. Record this number and label it *Heartbeat Rate After Exercising*.

4. Change places with your partner and repeat steps 1–3.

THINK AND WRITE

1. What was your partner's heartbeat rate before exercise? after exercise?

2. How is heartbeat rate related to the amount of blood the heart pumps in a minute?

3. **COMPARING** When you compare objects or events, you look for what they have in common. In this activity, you and your partner took each other's heartbeat rate. How did your heartbeat rate after exercise compare with your partner's?

Fantastic Voyage:
Part III

You know that blood flows to all parts of your body, but exactly where does blood flow? Let's take another trip into virtual reality to find out. Gloves on, glasses on, buckle up—you know what to do.

This tour begins inside the heart. You're on the left side of the heart, and bright red blood cells are pouring into it. You ask, "Where is all the blood coming from?"

Your guide replies, "It's coming from the lungs, where it has just received lots of oxygen. That's why the blood looks so red. Oxygen is what makes red blood cells look blood-red."

Suddenly the floor opens up. Blood and your capsule drain into another part of the heart. You hear a low sound, sort of a "lub-dub," as the heart muscle contracts and you're pushed into a large tube. The guide calls this an artery. *"Arteries,"* she explains, "are thick-walled, flexible tubes that carry blood away from the heart. Smooth-muscle tissue in the walls of arteries helps control the flow of blood by expanding and contracting. Arteries carry blood to different parts of the body, but they can't pick up or drop off materials that cells need."

You wonder how cells get the materials they need. You get your answer almost immediately.

The movement of the blood is getting slower. You can see that the capsule is being pushed into smaller and smaller tubes. There is very little room between the capsule and the thin walls of the tube you're in now. You soon

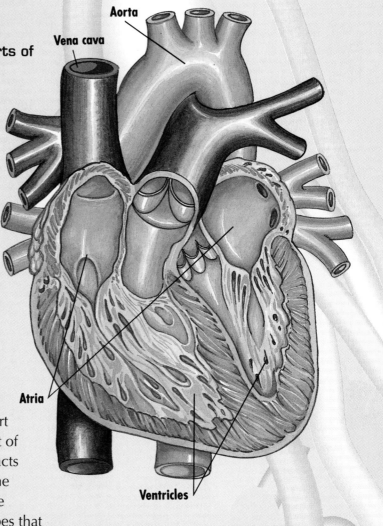

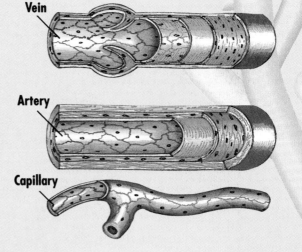

notice that red blood cells are flowing through the tube in single file. Your guide reports, "We are now in a capillary (KAP uh lair ee). A *capillary* is a very narrow blood vessel with thin walls. Capillaries are the smallest blood vessels, and they carry materials to and away from body cells. For example, oxygen carried by red blood cells diffuses through the walls of this capillary and into the surrounding cells. Cell wastes, such as carbon dioxide, diffuse through the walls and into the blood."

The red blood cells in front of you and behind you are now dark red. You ask about the color change, and the guide explains that it is due to the loss of oxygen. These blood cells have done their job and now must return to the heart. Your capsule will follow along.

You enter a series of larger and larger tubes and begin racing toward the heart. As you pass through each tube, a trapdoor closes behind you. Your guide announces, "We are now in the veins. *Veins* are blood vessels that carry blood back to the heart. The trapdoors, called *valves,* keep the blood from flowing in the wrong direction."

Your capsule now enters the right side of the heart. Once again, blood drains into another chamber and is pumped into an artery. This time, you are headed for the lungs. In the lungs, red blood cells drop off carbon dioxide and pick up oxygen. The cells turn bright red. You leave the lungs through veins and head back for the heart. You have now completed a round trip through the circulatory system.

THINK ABOUT IT

Describe how blood circulates through the body.

All Systems Go

You've had quite a ride through the circulatory system. But a visit to any of the body systems would have been exciting. Let's take a look at them all.

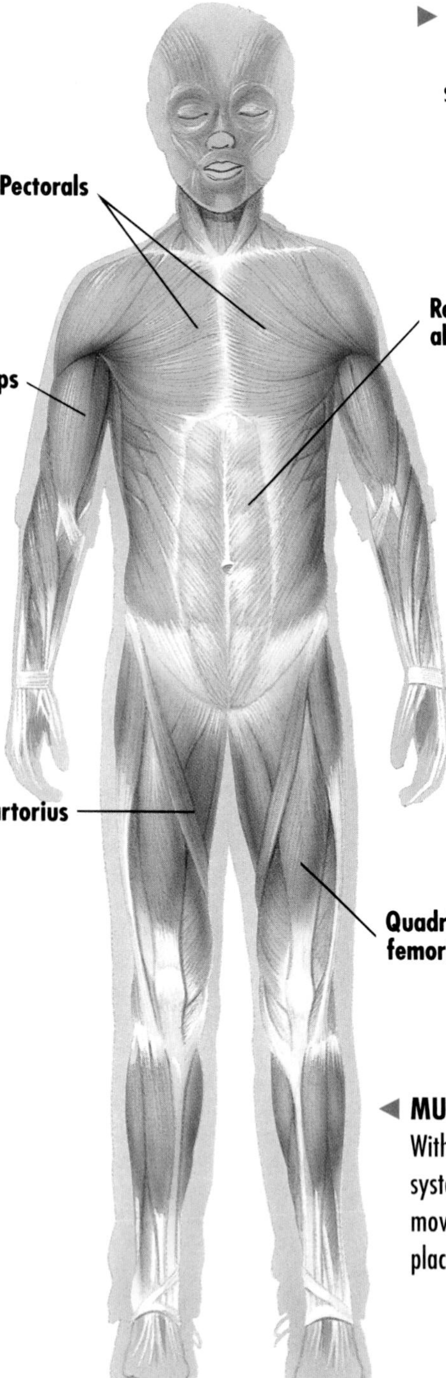

Pectorals

Biceps

Sartorius

Rectus abdominus

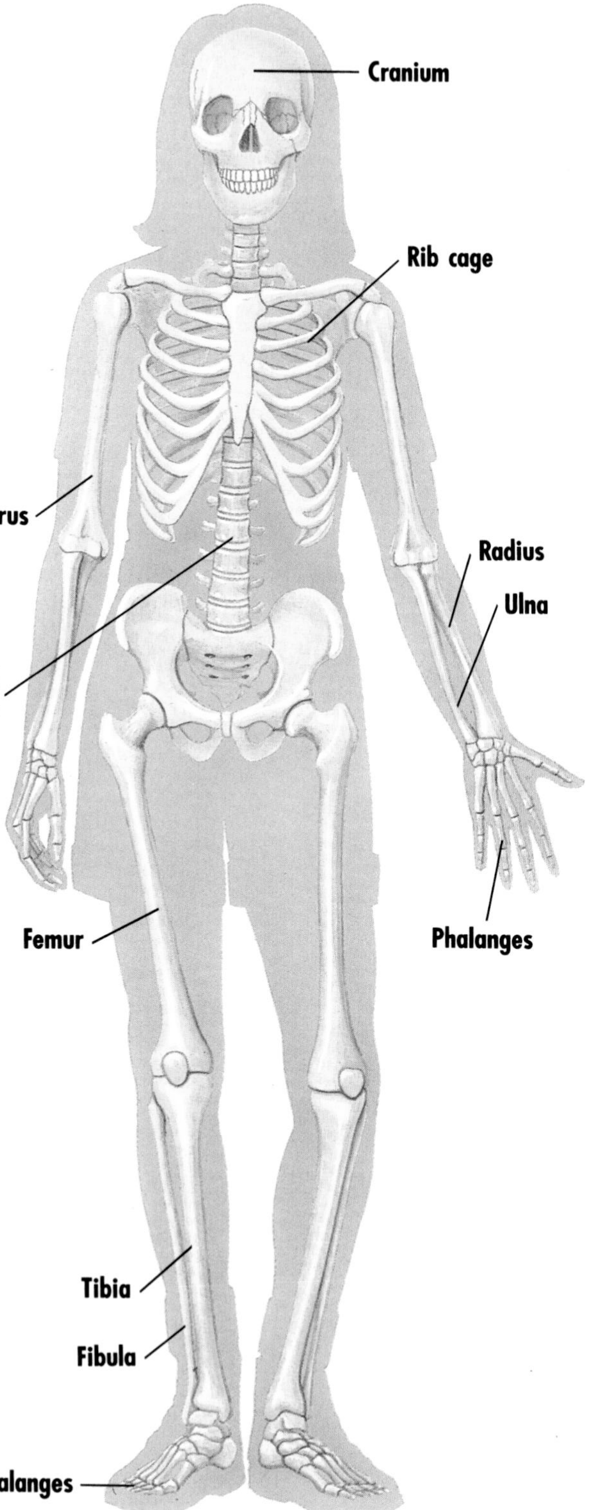

▶ **SKELETAL SYSTEM**
Bones of the skeletal system give your body its shape and provide support. They also protect internal organs.

Quadriceps femoris

◀ **MUSCULAR SYSTEM**
Without the muscular system, you couldn't move from place to place or lift things.

Cranium

Rib cage

Humerus

Radius

Ulna

Vertebral column

Femur

Phalanges

Tibia

Fibula

Phalanges

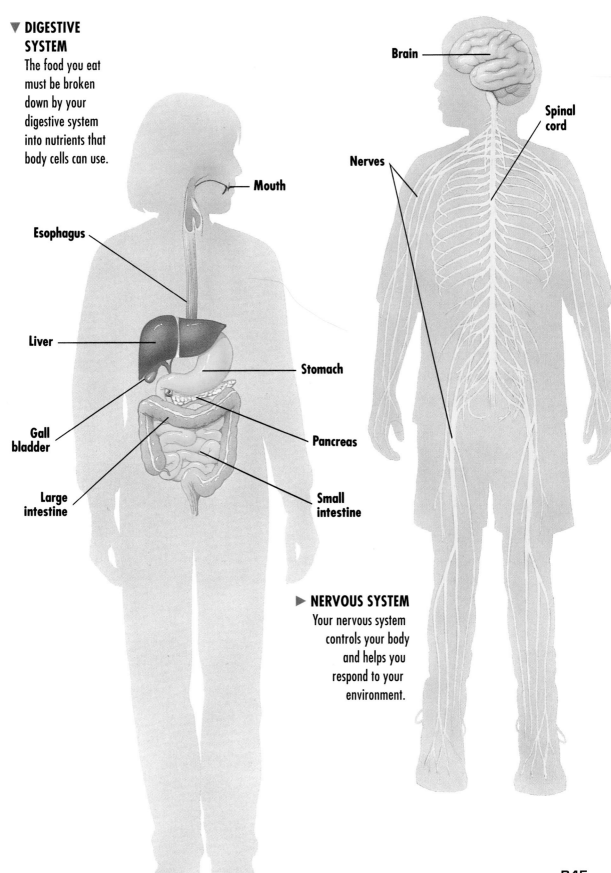

▼ DIGESTIVE SYSTEM
The food you eat must be broken down by your digestive system into nutrients that body cells can use.

Mouth

Esophagus

Liver

Stomach

Gall bladder

Pancreas

Large intestine

Small intestine

Brain

Spinal cord

Nerves

▶ NERVOUS SYSTEM
Your nervous system controls your body and helps you respond to your environment.

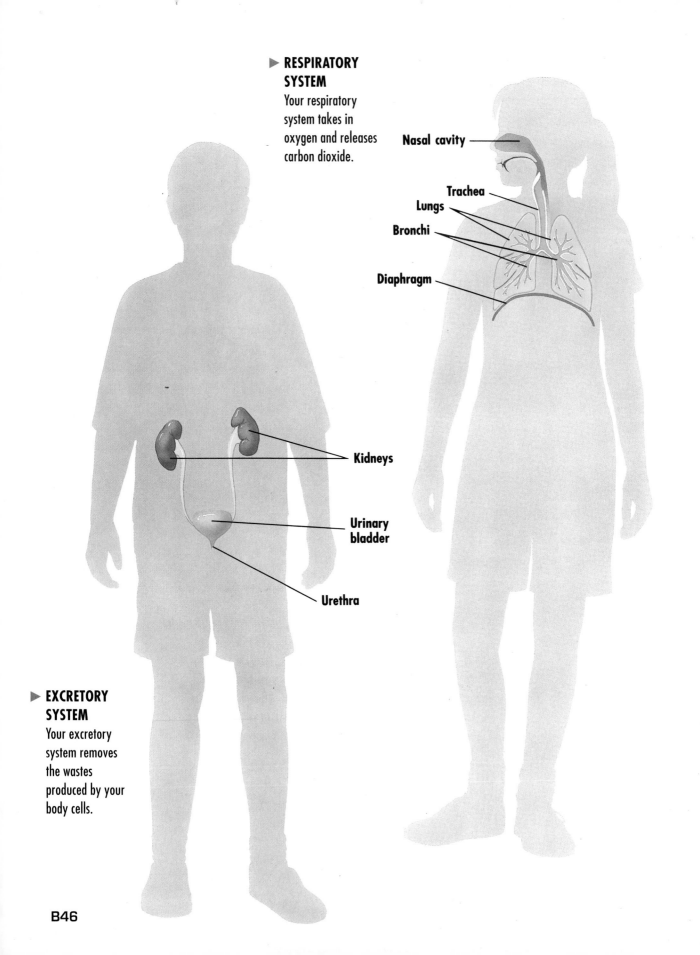

▶ RESPIRATORY SYSTEM
Your respiratory system takes in oxygen and releases carbon dioxide.

Nasal cavity

Trachea

Lungs

Bronchi

Diaphragm

Kidneys

Urinary bladder

Urethra

▶ EXCRETORY SYSTEM
Your excretory system removes the wastes produced by your body cells.

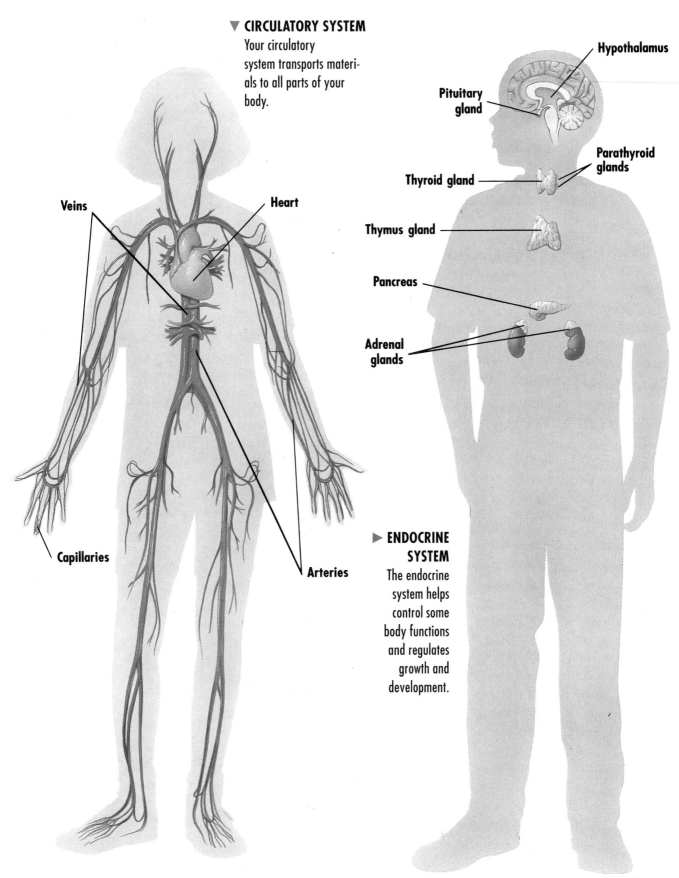

▼ CIRCULATORY SYSTEM

Your circulatory system transports materials to all parts of your body.

Veins

Heart

Capillaries

Arteries

Hypothalamus

Pituitary gland

Thyroid gland

Parathyroid glands

Thymus gland

Pancreas

Adrenal glands

▶ ENDOCRINE SYSTEM

The endocrine system helps control some body functions and regulates growth and development.

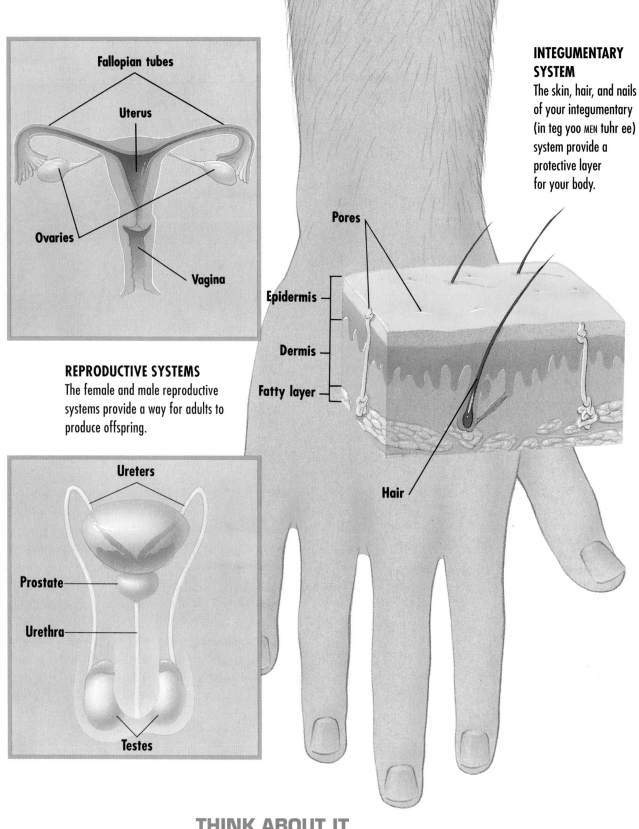

Fallopian tubes

Uterus

Ovaries

Vagina

REPRODUCTIVE SYSTEMS
The female and male reproductive systems provide a way for adults to produce offspring.

Ureters

Prostate

Urethra

Testes

INTEGUMENTARY SYSTEM
The skin, hair, and nails of your integumentary (in teg yoo MEN tuhr ee) system provide a protective layer for your body.

Pores

Epidermis

Dermis

Fatty layer

Hair

THINK ABOUT IT

Select one body system, and briefly describe its function.

All for One

You've seen that your body has ten systems, each with a specific job to do. Can one body system work without the help of the other systems?

You will need: Science Log

Try doing the following as fast as you can, and think about the body systems you are using.

- Smile.
- Close your right eye, and blink your left eye ten times.
- Touch your nose.
- Swallow.
- Breathe deeply.
- Close your left eye, and blink your right eye ten times.
- Clap your hands five times.

What systems did you use to do the first action, smiling? To smile, you needed your muscular and nervous systems. You used these systems and others to do the other actions.

The systems of your body work together. Every system depends on other systems to help it do its job. Your skeleton, for example, has joints so it can move. But it needs muscles to help it move and a brain to tell the muscles what to do. Your cells, tissues, organs, and systems form one working, magnificent organism—you!

LESSON 2 REVIEW

Describe a body activity and explain how it depends on the coordination of serveral organ systems.

 **DOUBLE CHECK**

SECTION B REVIEW

1. Describe the different organs that make up the circulatory system, and tell what each organ does.
2. Give examples of the different levels of organization in one body system.

SECTION C
In Sickness and in Health

▲ Virus

All of us have had minor illnesses at one time or another. Perhaps you've recently had a cold or a sore throat. Maybe you had a fever. Most likely you were sick because tiny, disease-causing organisms entered your body and grew there.

What are these tiny organisms, and how do they get into your body? Once inside, how do they make you sick? How can your body protect you from them? The following investigations will help you answer these questions as well as others you may have about disease. Keep careful notes in your Science Log as you work through these investigations.

1 IT'S INFECTIOUS!

All around you are organisms so tiny that you can't see them without a microscope. Some of these tiny organisms, or *microorganisms,* cause diseases. In this lesson, you will find out how microorganisms enter your body and how they can be passed from one person to another. You will also discover one of the ways to tell if you have been infected by microorganisms.

ACTIVITY

MATERIALS
- tissue paper in various colors
- Science Log data sheet

Pass It On

You probably already know that many microorganisms can infect humans. Microorganisms cause everything from colds and flu to more serious diseases, such as chickenpox. In this activity, you can find out how some microorganisms travel from one person to another.

DO THIS

❶ Tear one color of tissue paper into tiny pieces.

❷ Place some of the pieces in your right hand. Shake hands with a classmate who has pieces of a different color in his or her hand. Repeat the handshaking with several other classmates. Note what happens to the colored pieces of paper.

THINK AND WRITE

1. How is the way the pieces of colored paper spread similar to the way microorganisms might spread?

2. In what other ways do you think microorganisms can spread?

On the Move

Your brother had a cold last week, and now you have one. Could he have given you the cold, and if so, how? Read the following story to find out.

from *Current Health*

 "I feel terrible. My nose is running, my throat is scratchy, and my head hurts! Ah-ah-ah-ah-ah—chooo!" Ashley sneezed right into the phone.

On the other end of the line, her friend Bonnie jerked the phone away. "Don't make *me* sick, too!"

Ashley groaned, "I can't infect you, silly. You're not here!"

"Maybe not. But how did you get sick?"

Ashley glared at her brother. "It's Desmond's fault. I caught a cold from that little germ!"

Desmond hung his head. He felt ill, too. So did the rest of the family, and they all blamed him. "I'm not a germ!" Desmond pouted.

Just then his mom walked into the family room. "No, Desmond, you're not a germ. Ashley is just angry because she's going to miss her ski trip."

"He is a germ," Ashley whined. "He was the first to get sick, and then he passed it on to the rest of us. I learned all about it in health class. Germs are tiny living things called microorganisms. There are many kinds of microorganisms in our world, but only a few kinds make us sick."

Desmond rolled his eyes. He thought he was going to get a boring talk on microorganisms. But then his mom told them something that made them both sit up. "A thousand microorganisms could fit in a line across the eraser of a pencil. There are trillions of them all around, even inside us, Desmond."

"Wow! What's a germ look like?" he asked.

"You," said Ashley, who was still angry.

Mrs. Layton said, "Don't be foolish, Ashley. You can't see microorganisms without a microscope. Some are round balls, some are twisted spirals, while others are straight rods. And under a very powerful microscope, you'd see many strange shapes. Some look like metal screws on top of spider legs."

Desmond tried to imagine tiny shapes swimming inside his body. "I don't see how rods or screws can make me sick."

"I do," said Ashley. "You need to know about the chain of infection."

B52

THE CHAIN OF INFECTION

Mrs. Layton nodded. "In order for anyone to get sick, you need an agent. That would be someone or something that carries the microorganisms. Since you were the first to get sick, Desmond, you were probably the agent. Every once in a while the agent infects someone else. Then that person has the microorganism. He or she becomes an agent and gives it to someone else. It's almost like a game of tag."

Desmond asked, "You mean all you have to do is touch someone when you're sick and then she'll get sick, too?"

"Well, there's more to it than that," Ashley said. "There must have been an agent at your school. Maybe someone sneezed and didn't cover his mouth. You breathed the microorganisms into your lungs. Then you came home and took a sip of my juice. So I got the microorganisms. Then you wrestled your brother and coughed in his face. Then you fed the baby something with your unwashed hands and she got sick. Then you sneezed on the phone just before Dad got a call. That's how he got infected. See, it's all your fault."

Just then the phone rang. Ashley answered it with a big sneeze. Mrs. Layton gave Ashley a tissue. "Or maybe you gave the microorganisms to the others, Ashley."

Ashley grew very quiet. "I'm sorry, Desmond. Maybe you're not the only agent around here."

MODES OF TRANSMISSION

After the phone call, Ashley continued. "There are four ways that most microorganisms are passed from one person to another: by touch or physical contact, through the air, from food, and from insect or animal bites.

"The first, physical contact, is just like a game of tag. Microorganisms pass from one person to another—or from an object to a person. It can happen by sharing clothes or using the same fork or spoon. It can also happen when you cut yourself on something that's not clean. You get an infection.

"Microorganisms are also passed through the air. Like with a sneeze. By breathing in someone else's microorganisms, we can get a cold or the flu. Mr. Cullum, our health teacher, told us that in one sneeze there could be 20,000 microorganisms flying through the air. He also told us that sneezes could fly as far as 15 feet!"

Suddenly, Desmond understood. He smiled for the first time all day. "So if an animal is sick and it bites you, it sends the germs into your body!"

"Exactly," Mrs. Layton agreed.

Ashley yawned and remembered the ski trip. "And that's how you got us all sick, tick."

THINK ABOUT IT

How are microorganisms passed from one person to another?

ACTIVITY

Hot! Hot! Hot!

Mrs. Layton took Desmond's temperature and found that it was 38°C (100.5°F). Desmond had a *fever*, or a body temperature that is higher than normal. When disease-causing microorganisms invade your body, they may cause a fever. In this activity, you will find out what normal body temperature is.

DO THIS

1. On graph paper, draw a horizontal line, and label it *Days*. Number the blocks along the line from 1 to 5. Draw a vertical line, and label it *Degrees Celsius*. Number the blocks along that line from 35°C (95°F) to 40°C (106°F).

2. Place the thermometer strip on your forehead. Leave it there for 2 minutes.

3. Have a classmate read the thermometer.

4. Fill in the correct number of blocks to show your temperature for day 1.

5. Repeat the procedure at the same time every day for four more days.

THINK AND WRITE

1. Study your graph. Describe any variations in your daily temperature.

2. Add the daily temperatures together. Divide the total by 5. You may use a calculator. This is an average of your normal temperature.

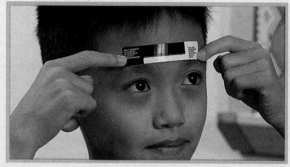

3. **CLASSIFYING/ORDERING**
Classifying is putting similar things in groups and ordering is putting things in an order. In this activity, you kept track of your temperature over several days. What was your highest temperature? lowest temperature? Arrange your temperatures in order.

LESSON 1 REVIEW

1. How would frequent washing of your hands reduce the spread of microorganisms?

2. Describe several ways to stop disease-causing microorganisms from being passed from one person to another.

2 INVISIBLE INVADERS

Every day thousands of microorganisms invade your body. Some of them can make you sick. In this lesson, you will learn about several kinds of microorganisms and how they grow and reproduce on and inside the human body.

Fantastic Journey: Part IV

Several kinds of microorganisms cause diseases—bacteria, fungi, and protozoa. A virtual reality tour can help you find out what they are. Get ready once again to enter the microscopic world.

Your guide seals the capsule door tightly and announces over the intercom, "We're going to visit a world filled with disease-causing microorganisms. However, you have no need to worry, because the microorganisms can't penetrate our inner-space capsule. Ordinarily, microorganisms are so small that they can be seen only with a micro-scope. Here they're as big as our capsule. Hold on, we're approaching a *virus*."

You look out the window and see something that reminds you of a spaceship. You're told that this is a flu virus, one of several kinds going around this season. The guide points out viruses with different shapes—those that cause other dis-eases, such as colds, chickenpox, and polio. She also explains that viruses are very unusual.

◀ Virus

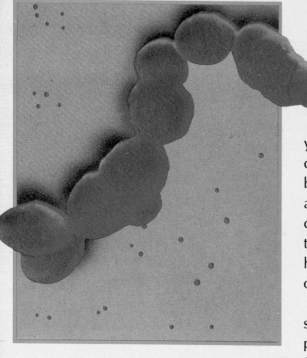

▲ Bacteria

▼ Protozoa

"We often think of viruses as microorganisms, but they really aren't. Remember, you discovered that all organisms are made up of cells. Viruses aren't made up of cells, so they can't be living organisms. They have none of the characteristics of cells—no membrane, nucleus, or cytoplasm. Viruses can reproduce, however, by taking over the cells of a host." You ask what a host is, and the guide explains that a *host* is an organism in or on which another organism lives.

Just then the capsule veers left, traveling next to something that looks like a huge chain of pop beads. "Take a good look," the guide says. "These are *bacteria*. Specifically, they're the bacteria that cause strep throat. Bacteria are true microorganisms. But the cells are very different from the ones you've seen before. For example, bacterial cells have no nucleus."

Suddenly, everything seems darker. A huge blob has plastered itself against the window of the capsule. You recognize the blob immediately and volunteer the information that it looks like the amoeba you saw with the microscope. "Right!" says the guide. "Amoebas belong to a group of microorganisms called *protozoa*, and some protozoa can make you sick."

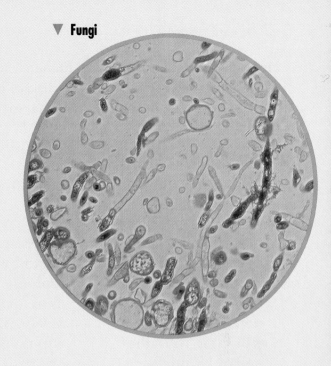

▼ Fungi

The capsule breaks the skin surface, races through a forest of hair covering a muscular leg, then dives into a valley with steep walls. The walls have deep cracks along their sides. "Where are we?" you ask.

"We're between someone's toes," the guide explains, "and this person has a bad case of athlete's foot. See those microorganisms over there? Those are the kind of *fungus* that causes athlete's foot."

"Wait a minute," you protest. "I read that the yeast my mom uses to make bread rise is a kind of fungus, but it doesn't cause disease."

"You're right," says the guide. "Not all microorganisms cause disease. In fact, most microorganisms, like yeast, are helpful."

Once again your tour has ended. You begin to think about all the different kinds of microorganisms you've seen. They seem to be everywhere.

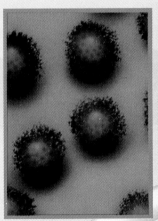 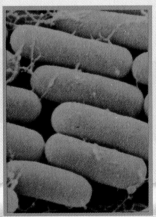  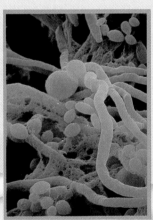

▲ From left: viruses, bacteria, protozoa, and fungi.

THINK ABOUT IT

What four kinds of microorganisms do these photographs show? What are the general characteristics of each?

"Rapid Grow"

Not only are microorganisms found almost everywhere, they also reproduce very quickly. One cell divides into two, two divide into four, four into eight, and so on. How many bacteria can be produced in one day? Try this to find out.

You will need: a calculator

Read each of the following situations. Then determine how many bacteria will be produced.

1. In warm conditions, bacterium A will reproduce every 10 minutes. At that rate, how many bacteria will there be at the end of 1 hour?

2. In cool conditions, bacterium B will reproduce every 90 minutes. At that rate, how many bacteria will there be at the end of 24 hours?

3. In very cold conditions, bacterium C will reproduce every 36 hours. At that rate, how many bacteria will there be at the end of 30 days?

Bacteria reproduce very rapidly, and they are found nearly everywhere on Earth. They live in hot springs and in snowbanks, in the air and in the ground. Most bacteria are harmless. In fact, many are used to make foods you enjoy. Did you know that yogurt is made with bacteria? But many bacteria, like the one that causes strep throat, are harmful. They make you feel sick by producing poisons, or *toxins.*

Remember, the bacteria that cause strep throat are round. Other bacteria may be shaped like spirals or rods. All bacteria have one of these three basic shapes.

▲ Rod-shaped bacterium

▲ Spiral-shaped bacterium

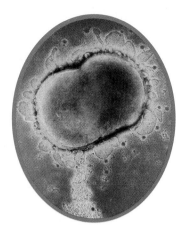

▲ Round bacterium

ACTIVITY

Count Bacteria

Now that you know how quickly bacteria reproduce, imagine trying to count the number of bacteria in your classroom. How would you do it? The following activity will show you how to sample small areas and then to estimate, from those samples, the population of a larger area.

DO THIS

1 Use the marker and ruler to divide the poster board into 12 equal-sized sections. Number each section. Then place the poster board on the floor.

2 Open the bag of beans and pour the beans onto the poster board. Allow the beans to fall freely.

3 Count the number of beans in section 1 of the poster board, and record the number.

4 Repeat step 3 for sections 6, 8, and 11 of the poster board.

5 Add together the numbers you recorded. Then divide the total by 4 and round to the nearest whole number. This is the average number of beans in the sections you sampled.

6 Multiply this number by 12 to estimate the total number of beans on the poster board.

THINK AND WRITE

How could this procedure be used to estimate the number of bacteria on a large area such as your body?

The Cold War

Bacteria reproduce rapidly but not as rapidly as viruses. Continue reading to find out how viruses reproduce and what diseases they cause.

On their own, viruses are about as lively as a rock. They can't eat, move, respond, or reproduce. But once they are inside cells, the story is very different. These tiny invaders completely take over cells, reproduce explosively, and make people very ill.

Recall that viruses are not organisms. They are nonliving pieces of hereditary material. The hereditary material is surrounded by a coat of protein. When a virus enters your body, it attaches itself to a cell and injects its hereditary material into the cell. The invaded cell can't tell the difference between its own hereditary material and the hereditary material of the virus, so the cell begins producing new viruses. Soon the cell has produced so many viruses that it can't hold any more. The cell bursts, and the new viruses look for other cells to invade.

Viruses cause many different illnesses. The colds that Desmond and his family had were due to a virus. Measles, mumps, and flu are also caused by viruses. All of these illnesses produce aching joints and muscles, headaches, and fevers.

THINK ABOUT IT

Describe the process of infection involved with "catching a cold."

▼ Virus invading a host cell.

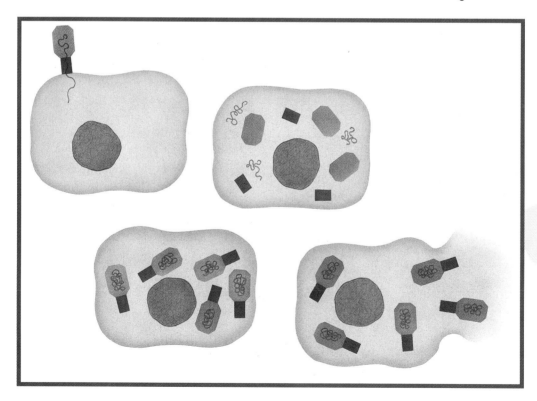

"I Think It's a Virus"

What other diseases are caused by viruses? The following list includes just a few of them. Try to find some others.

You will need: reference sources, Science Log

DISEASES CAUSED BY VIRUSES	
Cold sores	Rabies
Hepatitis	Polio
Mononucleosis	Yellow fever
Chickenpox	AIDS

Choose one of the diseases listed. Find out about the symptoms of the disease. If possible, find out what the virus that causes the disease looks like. Also, find out how the virus is spread. Luckily, not all viruses are spread as easily as the ones that cause colds. Finally, try to discover if there is a treatment or a way to protect yourself from the virus you choose. In your Science Log, write a short report about the disease you investigated. Share your findings with your classmates.

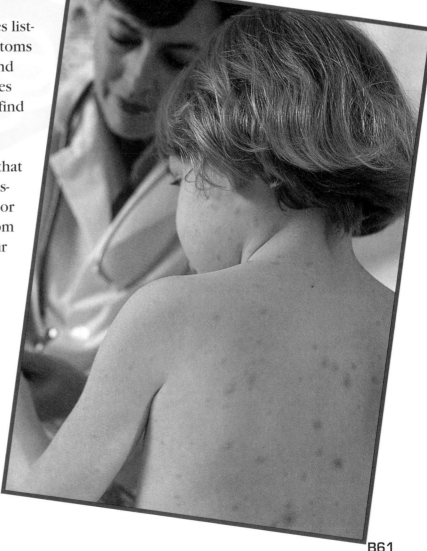

▶ Chickenpox is caused by a virus.

Parasites

Although bacteria and viruses cause most infections, some other microorganisms also cause diseases. Remember the amoeba you observed earlier? Amoebas belong to a group of microorganisms known as protozoa. Although most protozoa are helpful, a few can cause disease. Some fungi also cause diseases. Study these pages to find out more about protozoa and fungi.

◄ Protozoa live in moist places. Some live in damp soil or water environments like the one shown. A few protozoa are *parasites*— that is, they live in animals and plants.

► Unlike bacteria, most protozoa can move from place to place. An amoeba moves by extending part of its cytoplasm forward and then gliding into the extension. One type of amoeba can cause severe diarrhea if it infects the digestive system. This parasite may be found in contaminated food or water.

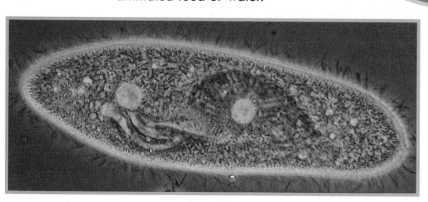

◄ Protozoa like this paramecium have hundreds of short hairlike structures that help them move through water. Most paramecia do not cause diseases.

▼ Although this protozoan cannot move on its own, it can cause malaria in humans. People become infected when they are bitten by a mosquito that is carrying the protozoan.

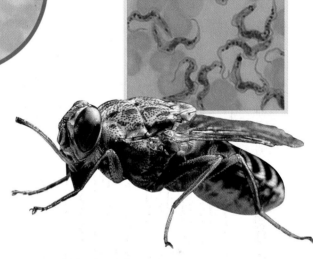

▶ The trypanosome moves by swishing a whiplike structure back and forth. This protozoan causes a disease known as African sleeping sickness, which attacks the nervous system. People are infected by the parasite when bitten by an infected tsetse fly.

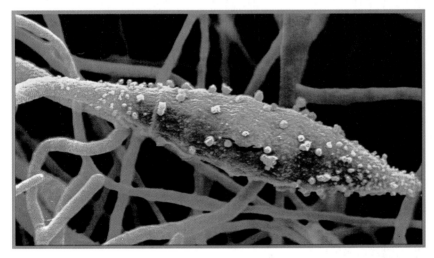

◀ Ringworm is one type of disease caused by fungi. Ringworm and athlete's foot are diseases of the skin. Some fungi attack the lungs or reproductive organs and cause diseases there. Fungi that cause diseases are parasites because they live off the living tissues of other organisms.

THINK ABOUT IT

Describe the effects of protozoa or fungi on the human body.

A Mystery to Solve

Although the microorganisms that cause most infections are well known, there are still mysteries to be solved. For example, Christopher seemed fine one minute and was violently ill the next. Read the following excerpt to find out what happened.

THE PUZZLE

by **Elaine Landau** from *Lyme Disease*

▲ **Bacterium that causes Lyme disease**

LITERATURE

It happened on a sizzling hot August day. Twelve-year-old Christopher stood on a swimming pool diving board in his northern New Jersey town. He paused before div-

ing. Suddenly, a strong bolt of headache pain struck the left side of Christopher's head. It seemed to come from out of nowhere. The young boy later recalled how at one moment he'd felt fine, and then the next, his head throbbed with pain. Christopher broke out in a cold sweat. He felt nauseous and his body ached all over.

At first, Christopher's family and doctor thought he had a bad case of the flu. Yet something else was wrong. Time passed, but Christopher's symptoms remained. His doctor didn't understand why. He couldn't find any medical reason for Christopher's illness.

Christopher tried to continue leading a normal life. He attended school regularly. Christopher enjoyed sports and being outdoors, and he was determined not to give up any of his activities. But several months later, the situation worsened.

Christopher experienced an extremely sharp pain in his right knee. It happened while he was on a backpacking trip with his father and two brothers. The pain was so severe that Christopher could barely walk.

After returning home, Christopher's knee felt even worse. His parents took him to a number of doctors. Unfortunately, no one was able to pinpoint Christopher's baffling ailment. A bone specialist from a nearby city diagnosed Christopher's condition as an inflamed kneecap. The doctor prescribed aspirin for Christopher and had him begin physical therapy.

But nothing seemed to help. Christopher grew weaker, and eventually needed crutches to walk. He often felt tired and his muscles were sore. After a while, Christopher found it difficult to even carry his school books. By now, his right leg was partially paralyzed. At times, Christopher seemed to show improvement. Then, unfortunately, there would be relapses and he'd become extremely ill again.

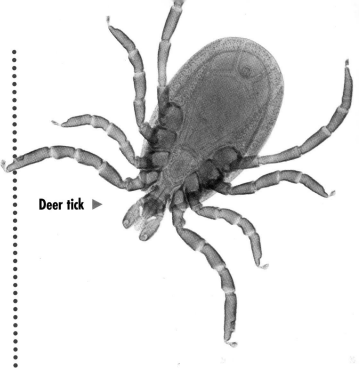

Deer tick ▶

Christopher's family continued to seek the help of different doctors. Finally, after another series of tests, Christopher was correctly diagnosed. Now he was given the proper medication. And after nearly eighteen months of suffering, Christopher's condition began to improve.

The strange illness that had struck Christopher and puzzled so many doctors was Lyme disease.

QUICK CHECK

LESSON 2 REVIEW

❶ Why aren't viruses considered microorganisms?

❷ How are protozoa and bacteria alike? How are they different?

❸ Why are some diseases, such as Lyme disease, so hard to diagnose?

3 ON DEFENSE

With so many disease-causing viruses, bacteria, fungi, and protozoa around, you might think that people wouldn't stand a chance of staying healthy. Fortunately, your body has ways of fighting these microorganisms. Medical science has also developed ways of treating infections and preventing them. In this lesson, you will discover the amazing defenses available to fight disease.

Fantastic Journey:
The Final Chapter

▲ Cilia lining the trachea

Your body is constantly working to prevent invasion by disease-causing microorganisms. A final virtual reality tour will give you a good opportunity to see just how this happens. Let's go!

 Once again your guide seals the capsule door as you adjust your seat belt. "Welcome aboard," she says. "Today we are going to see the human body defend itself against invaders. Our first stop is the respiratory system."

As you cruise down the throat and into the windpipe, or *trachea,* your guide asks you to look around carefully. "What do you see?"she asks.

"The walls of the trachea look wet and sort of shiny," you respond.

"Right," she replies. "The passages of the respiratory system are coated with a sticky substance called *mucus.* Mucus helps trap and kill microorganisms and other debris in the air that you breathe." The guide tells you to observe the tiny hairs that line the passages. "These tiny hairs also trap things, and they move in waves to 'sweep' foreign objects out of your body," she explains.

The capsule roars on through the respiratory system and into the bloodstream. Red blood cells are everywhere around you, but the guide asks you to look for white blood cells. "They're sometimes hard to find because there usually aren't very many of them," she says, "unless there is some sort of infection present."

Off in the distance, you see a giant cell coming toward you. "Look!" you shout. "There's one!"

Everyone looks as your guide explains, "White blood cells are the warriors of your body. These gigantic cells constantly move around, looking for disease-causing microorganisms. Whenever they find one, they swallow it whole!"

The capsule moves on to other parts of the bloodstream. Your guide tells you she is looking for antibodies. "What are antibodies?" you ask.

Your guide answers, *"Antibodies* are proteins that find and destroy specific kinds of microorganisms in the bloodstream." She goes on to explain that some antibodies occur naturally, while others are made when you receive a *vaccination.*

▼ **White blood cell attacking bacteria**

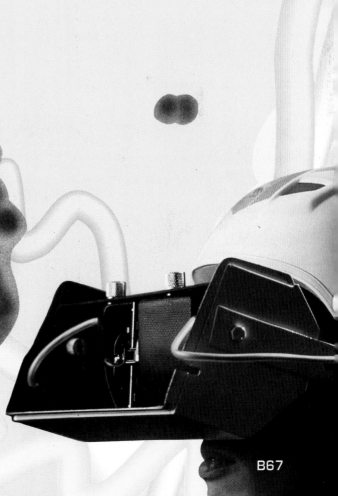

"Antibodies have great 'memories,'" she says, "and some antibodies last a lifetime. For example, if you've ever had measles or received a measles vaccination, the measles antibodies are still moving through your bloodstream searching for any new measles viruses that may have gotten inside you. If they find any, they destroy them."

The inner-space capsule comes to a halt for the last time. It really has been a fantastic journey through the human body. After thinking for a minute, you ask your guide one final question. "Is it true that people probably wouldn't live as long if there weren't antibodies and white blood cells in their bodies?"

"Yes," she says, "as you've seen, the human body is a remarkable organism, but it needs to be protected. Take care of yourself," she calls out as you cross back into the real world. 〽

THINK ABOUT IT

How does the human body protect itself from diseases?

Lucky Shot

Scientists have developed many vaccinations to help your body fight invading microorganisms. Today, medical research is conducted under controlled conditions. In the late 1700s, however, that was not the case. Read on to find out how one doctor made a remarkable discovery about 200 years ago that led to the elimination of a dreaded and often fatal disease—smallpox.

In 1796, Edward Jenner, a doctor in Gloucestershire, England, risked his reputation—and the life of one of his patients—by performing a dangerous experiment.

Jenner made two small scratches on the arm of James Phipps, a healthy eight-year-old boy. Then Jenner took some pus from a cowpox sore on the hand of a local milkmaid and rubbed it into the scratches. Cowpox was a common disease that was easily passed from infected cows to humans. The boy soon developed a sore on his arm, just like the one on the milkmaid's hand. It was a minor infection, and it soon healed completely.

Six weeks later, Jenner took infected matter from a sore of a person with smallpox. At the time, smallpox was one of the most deadly human diseases

▲ **Jenner vaccinating for smallpox**

known. Jenner rubbed the material into new scratches he had made on the boy's arm. The boy should have contracted smallpox in just a few days, but he didn't. Jenner had discovered a safe way of preventing a terrible disease—a vaccination that kept people safe from smallpox for the rest of their lives.

Since then, smallpox has been completely eliminated, and scientists have developed vaccinations against many other diseases. However, their methods are more scientific and don't risk people's health unnecessarily.

THINK ABOUT IT

In your own words, define *vaccination*.

ACTIVITY

Kills Germs on Contact

MATERIALS
• 2 disposable petri dishes of agar
• tape
• antiseptic hand soap
• Science Log data sheet

You could not possibly receive a vaccination against every kind of microorganism you might come in contact with. So another way to prevent infection is to kill microorganisms before they enter your body. In the following activity, you will discover a simple way to kill bacteria before they can cause infection.

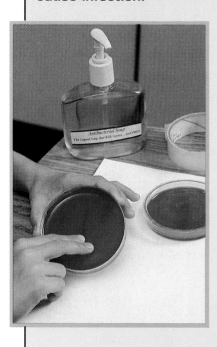

DO THIS

1. Open one of the petri dishes, and gently rub your fingers over the surface of the agar. Close the lid and tape it shut. Write *Dish 1* on the tape with a pen.

2. Wash your hands for a full minute with very warm water and antiseptic soap.

3. Repeat step 1 with the other petri dish. Write *Dish 2* on the tape. Put both dishes in a warm, dark place for two days.

4. **CAUTION: Do not open either of the dishes.** After two days, observe the agar surface of each dish. When you finish making your observations, give the dishes to your teacher for disposal.

THINK AND WRITE

Compare the surface of each dish, and explain any differences you observe.

Antiseptics As you saw in the activity, there are a lot of bacteria on your hands, and they need to be eliminated before they can make you sick. There are many things that can kill bacteria. Extreme heat and ultraviolet radiation from the sun work well but can't be used on your skin. Certain chemicals, called *antiseptics*, also kill bacteria. Many soaps now contain antiseptics. One of the best things you can do to prevent infection is to wash your hands many times a day with one of these soaps.

Helping Out

Antiseptics work well to kill microorganisms on the outside of your body, but they can't be used inside because they are too strong. There are, however, medicines that can be used to help fight infections inside your body. Read to find out how they work.

In the past, moldy meats, cheeses, and breads were used to treat infected wounds. Sometimes they worked, but nobody knew why. Then, in 1928, a British doctor, Sir Alexander Fleming, made a discovery. While trying to grow bacteria in a petri dish, Fleming noticed that some of his dishes were contaminated with fuzzy-looking molds. Many scientists had seen these molds, and they just threw their dishes away and started their experiments again. But not Fleming. He noticed that there weren't any bacteria in the areas where the mold was the thickest. He hypothesized that the mold produced something that kept bacteria from growing.

Fleming's hypothesis was right. The mold produced a chemical that prevented bacteria from grow-ing. Fleming called this chemical *penicillin,* after the name of the mold. Penicillin was the first *antibiotic* discovered.

Since the accidental discovery of penicillin, scientists have developed many kinds of antibiotics, which have helped conquer most diseases caused by bacteria. However, antibiotics don't work against diseases caused by viruses because viruses aren't living organisms. They reproduce only in host cells.

One of the most serious diseases ever discovered—AIDS—is caused by a virus. The best hope for a cure for AIDS is to develop a vaccination to prevent it. But this may take many years. In the meantime, the best way to stop AIDS is to educate people on how to protect themselves from getting the virus. In the following article, you can read about a person who is leading the fight to stop this deadly disease.

THINK ABOUT IT

How are antiseptics and antibiotics different?

Penicillin growing on petri dish ▶

Dr. Helene Gayle:
Public Health Physician

Dr. Helene Gayle provides information to people about how to prevent disease. She is a public health physician who believes that the more people know about AIDS and how it spreads, the better they can protect themselves. Dr. Gayle wants people everywhere to know that AIDS can be prevented.

Dr. Gayle began her fight against AIDS while she was on the staff of the Centers for Disease Control in Atlanta, Georgia. The centers, known as the CDC, are part of the United States Public Health Service. The main function of the service is to prevent early death among the citizens of the United States. The CDC helps by finding ways to control or prevent diseases like AIDS.

Part of the work of the CDC involves learning how diseases spread. Dr. Gayle kept records of the numbers of people who had AIDS, where they lived, and what their lifestyles were like. Then she studied the data, looking for patterns that explained how the disease was spread and how the spread could be halted.

Gayle has left the CDC but not the fight against AIDS. She currently is chief of the AIDS division of the United States Agency for International Development. The agency has developed a program to improve health care in the developing countries of Africa, Asia, and Latin America, where AIDS is even more of a problem than it is in the United States.

Gayle's job with the agency is to provide health information and medical resources to assist in AIDS prevention. She believes that education is the best way to prevent the spread of AIDS. She wants young people to realize that lifestyle choices they make now may affect them their entire lives.

THINK ABOUT IT

Why is health information a good way to fight disease?

Medical Research

Vaccinations, antiseptics, and antibiotics are just a few of the ways modern medicine can help your body fight disease. They are usually a safe and dependable means of disease prevention and treatment. In this activity, you can learn more about modern medicine.

You will need: reference sources, Science Log

Use resources in your school or community library to find information about new vaccinations, antibiotics, antiseptics, or other ways to fight diseases. Find out about new ways to prevent or treat diseases such as AIDS, chickenpox, and flu. If possible, find specific information about new treatments, such as who developed them and when. How effective are they?

Write a short report in your Science Log. Then share your report with your classmates and discuss the importance of your findings.

QUICK CHECK

LESSON 3 REVIEW

❶ How is receiving a measles vaccination similar to having the disease? How is it different?

❷ Why aren't antibiotics prescribed for colds and flu?

DOUBLE CHECK

SECTION C REVIEW

1. Why are infections caused by viruses more difficult to treat than those caused by bacteria?

2. Why are all disease-causing microorganisms considered to be parasites?

3. Why is Edward Jenner considered a pioneer in medical research?

REFLECT

It's time to think about the ideas you have discovered during your investigations. Think, too, about your many accomplishments.

SUMMARIZE

Answer the following questions in your Science Log.

1. What **I Wonder** questions have you answered in your investigations, and what new questions have you asked?

2. What have you discovered about the structure and function of the human body, and how have your ideas changed?

3. Did any of your discoveries surprise you? Explain.

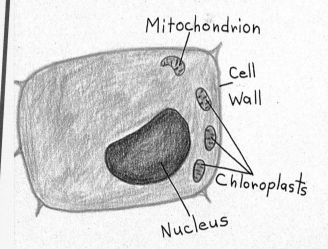

Plant Cell

Mitochondrion

Cell Wall

Chloroplasts

Nucleus

Plant cells have walls, but animal cells do not. Plant cells also have chloroplasts, which are organelles that produce food. Animal cells cannot produce their own food.

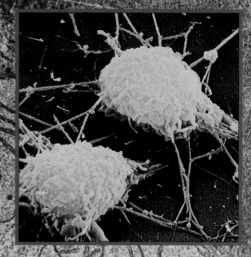

Animal Cell

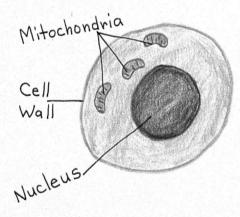

Mitochondria

Cell Wall

Nucleus

CONNECT IDEAS

1. Describe mitosis as a part of the cell theory.

2. Give an example of a structure at each level of organization in humans.

3. Compare the usefulness of antiseptics for preventing infections caused by viruses and bacteria.

4. Describe several ways flu viruses can be passed from one person to another.

5. How does your body protect itself from disease-causing microorganisms carried by insects?

SCIENCE PORTFOLIO

❶ Complete your Science Experiences Record.

❷ Choose several samples of your best work from each section to include in your Science Portfolio.

❸ On A Guide to My Science Portfolio, tell why you chose each sample.

Scientists share their discoveries and ideas and learn from one another. How can you share what you've learned?

Decide

▶ what you want to say.

▶ what the best way is to get your message across.

Share

▶ what you did and why.

▶ what worked and what didn't work.

▶ what conclusions you have drawn.

▶ what else you'd like to find out.

Find Out

▶ what classmates liked about what you shared—and why.

▶ what questions your classmates have.

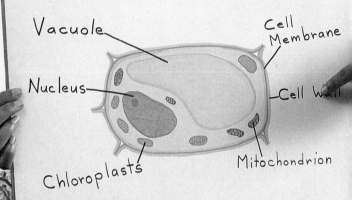

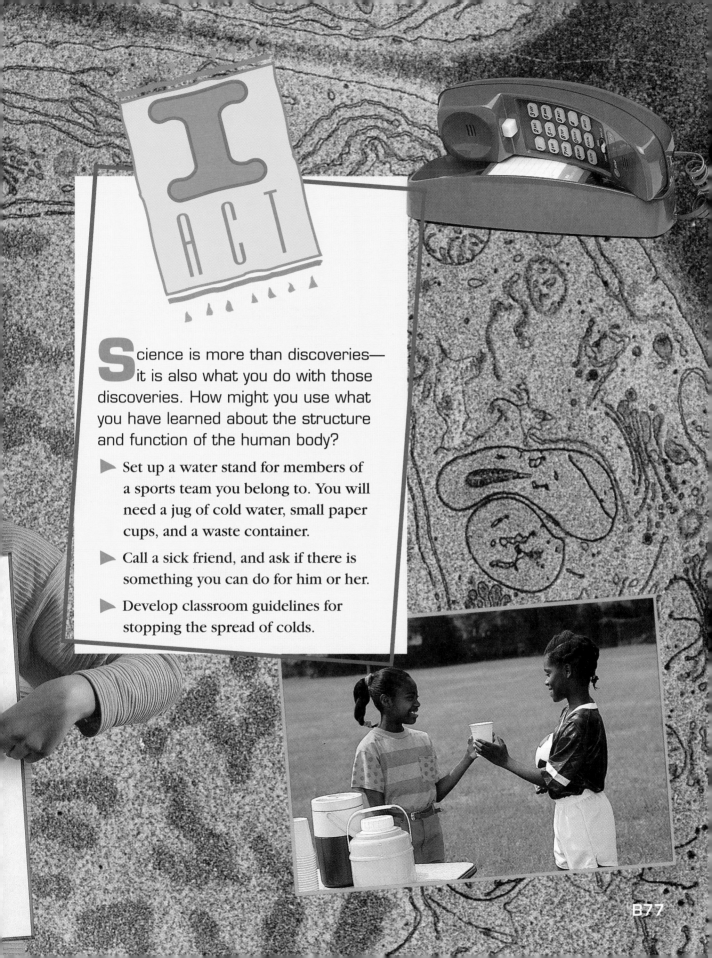

I ACT

Science is more than discoveries— it is also what you do with those discoveries. How might you use what you have learned about the structure and function of the human body?

▶ Set up a water stand for members of a sports team you belong to. You will need a jug of cold water, small paper cups, and a waste container.

▶ Call a sick friend, and ask if there is something you can do for him or her.

▶ Develop classroom guidelines for stopping the spread of colds.

THE LANGUAGE OF SCIENCE

The language of science helps people communicate clearly when they talk about the cells and the human body. Here are some vocabulary words you can use when you talk with friends, family, and others about human structures and functions and things that can affect them.

blood—fluid tissue that moves from place to place. It is made up of *red blood cells,* which carry oxygen to body cells; *plasma,* which is the liquid part of the blood; *white blood cells,* which help protect the body from disease and infection; and *platelets,* which stop the flow of blood at a cut. **(B39)**

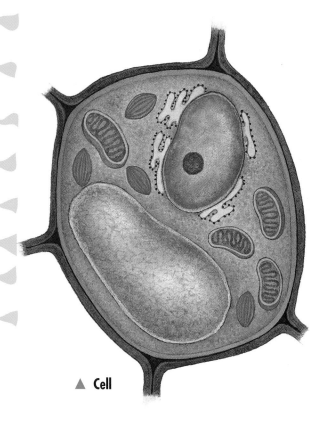

▲ Cell

antibiotics—chemicals that keep bacteria from growing. **(B71)**

antibodies—proteins in your body that destroy or weaken microorganisms. After you receive a measles vaccination, for example, your body produces antibodies that keep you from getting measles. **(B67)**

antiseptics—strong chemicals that kill bacteria. **(B70)**

cell—the basic unit of structure and function in an organism. In many-celled organisms, there are different kinds of cells, each with a different job to do. For example, muscle cells contract to produce movement, while red blood cells transport oxygen. **(B14)**

cell membrane—a protective covering around a cell. It allows certain materials to pass into and out of the cell. **(B16)**

cell theory—one of the major theories of life science. The cell theory has three parts: (1) All living things are made of cells. (2) The cell is the basic unit of structure and function of all living things. (3) All cells come from other cells. **(B15)**

chloroplasts—organelles that make food in plant cells. **(B18)**

chromosomes—structures in the nucleus of a cell that contain the instructions that enable the nucleus to control the activities of the cell. **(B24)**

cytoplasm—the living material between a cell's nucleus and its cell membrane. **(B16)**

dehydration—loss of water. **(B19)**

▲ **Diffusion**

diffusion—the movement of a material into an area that has less of the material. Food coloring spreading throughout a glass of water is an example of diffusion. **(B22)**

mitochondria—organelles that produce the energy a cell needs. **(B17)**

organ—a body structure made of different kinds of tissues that work together to do a specific job. The heart and the stomach are examples of organs. **(B32)**

▶ **Organ—stomach**

organelle—any cell structure that has a specific job to do. **(B17)**

organism—a living thing that carries out all life functions. **(B33)**

osmosis—the diffusion of water through a cell membrane. **(B22)**

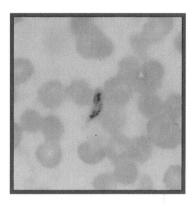

▲ **Parasite that causes malaria**

parasites—organisms that live by feeding on the living tissues of other organisms. The protozoan that causes malaria, for example, is a parasite that can live in mosquitoes and other animals. **(B62)**

system—a group of organs that work together to do a job. The human circulatory system, for example, is responsible for transporting nutrients and oxygen to body cells. **(B33)**

tissues—groups of cells with the same structure and function. The heart, for example, is made of heart-muscle tissue. **(B31)**

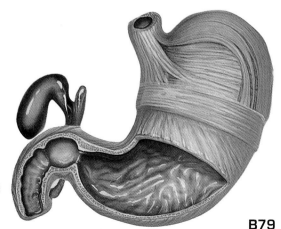

STARBASE EARTH

Unit C

StarBase Earth

The Solar System and Beyond

I WONDER

Wondering about the universe has led to the science of astronomy. What do you wonder about when you look at a starry sky?

Work with a partner to make a list of questions about the universe. Be ready to share your list with the rest of the class.

◀ Spiral Galaxy
▼ Jupiter

I PLAN

You may have asked questions such as these as you wondered about the universe. Scientists also ask questions. Then they plan ways to find answers to their questions. Now you and your classmates can plan how you will investigate the universe.

My Science Log

Why can't we see the stars during the day?

How far away is the sun?

How are the other planets like Earth?

How are the planets alike? How are they different from each other?

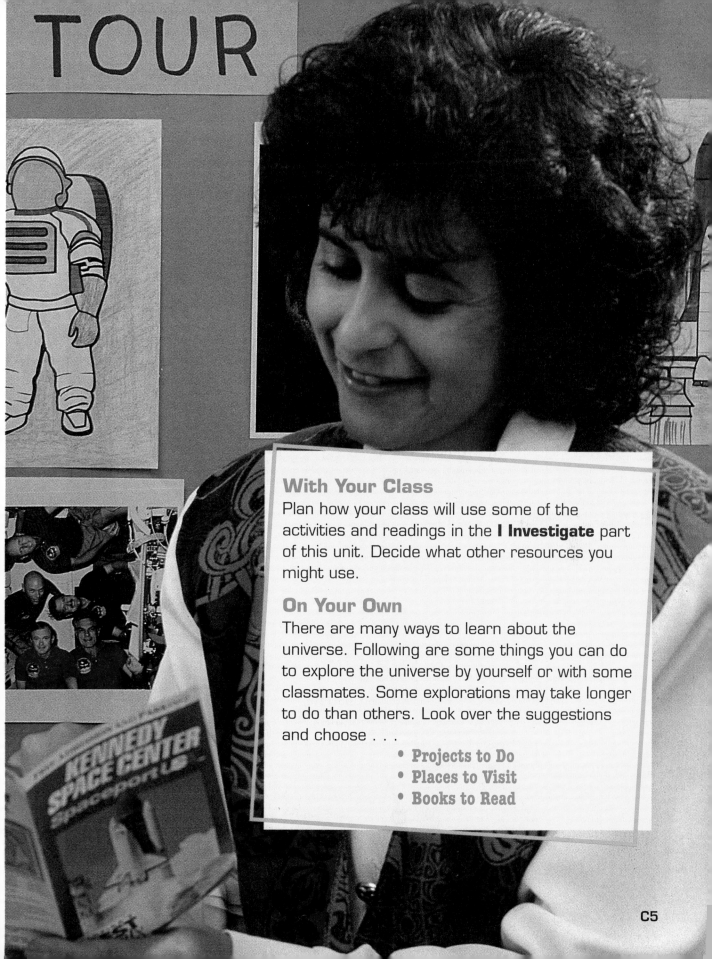

TOUR

With Your Class

Plan how your class will use some of the
activities and readings in the **I Investigate** part
of this unit. Decide what other resources you
might use.

On Your Own

There are many ways to learn about the
universe. Following are some things you can do
to explore the universe by yourself or with some
classmates. Some explorations may take longer
to do than others. Look over the suggestions
and choose . . .

- **Projects to Do**
- **Places to Visit**
- **Books to Read**

PROJECTS TO DO

STARBASE EARTH LOG

Be your own astronomer. Observe the sky on several nights and record your observations in a StarBase Earth Log. You might record the time the moon rises each night for a month. You could draw the moon's phases over that same period. Or you could keep a record of the brightest stars you can see. Set aside several pages in your StarBase Earth Log for each set of observations or drawings.

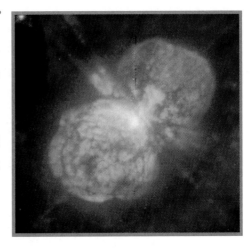

ASTRONOMY UPDATE

Collect information about new discoveries, recent satellite and space shuttle launches, or any other interesting space events. Check newspapers, magazines, radio and TV programs, and up-to-date books. Keep your information in a notebook, and present it in a report titled "Astronomy Update."

SCIENCE FAIR PROJECT

Review the **I Wonder** questions you and your partner asked. One way to find answers to these questions is through a science fair project. Choose one of your questions. Plan a project that would help you answer the question. Discuss your plan with your teacher. With his or her approval, begin work by collecting materials and resources. Then carry out your plan.

PLACES TO VISIT

BRING THE UNIVERSE INDOORS

An observatory or a planetarium is a wonderful place to learn about the universe. Ask your teacher to direct you to an observatory or a planetarium you can visit. Go with your family or with some classmates to see the stars and the exhibits. Present a report to your class about what you learned.

ASTRONOMY CLUB MEETING

Many people who are interested in space science join astronomy clubs. They do so to explore the universe and meet with others who share their interest. Such clubs may meet to observe a meteor shower or an eclipse, to share information on building telescopes, or to take photographs of interesting objects in the sky. Contact a local astronomy club. Ask if you can go to a meeting and an observing session. Tell your class about your visit.

BOOKS TO READ

Wings: The Last Book of the Bromeliad

by Terry Pratchett (Delacorte Press, 1990). Be careful! In this book, you'll read about tiny people called *nomes,* who live everywhere. Their leaders have discovered that nomes originally traveled on a spaceship that is now on the moon. Because life on Earth has become dangerous for them, they want to get their spaceship back so they can escape. Will they achieve their goal?

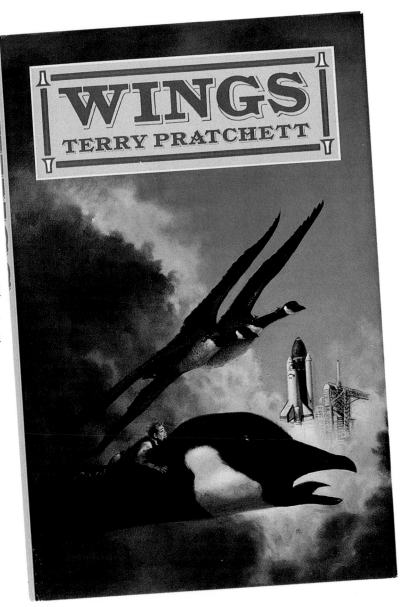

Voyager:
An Adventure to the Edge of the Solar System

by Sally Ride and Tam O'Shaughnessy (Crown, 1992), Outstanding Science Trade Book. Would you like to travel in space for 12 years? You would visit four giant planets that had never been visited before. You would pass through the dangerous asteroid belt. Even astronauts cannot take this trip, but two robot spacecraft did. See the amazing pictures they sent back.

More Books to Read

The Big Dipper and You

by E. C. Krupp (William Morrow, 1989), Outstanding Science Trade Book. For hundreds of years, people all over the world have used the Big Dipper as a guide to the sky. Reading about the Big Dipper in this book will help you learn about the stars in the sky.

Could You Ever Meet an Alien?

by David J. Darling (Dillon Press, 1990). Some scientists hypothesize that if there were intelligent life in outer space, we would have found evidence of it by now. Other scientists hypothesize there could be planets with life on them that we don't even know about. What do you think? This book will help you decide.

Galileo and the Universe

by Steve Parker (HarperCollins, 1992), Outstanding Science Trade Book. Galileo was a mathematician, a physicist, and an astronomer who lived 400 years ago in Italy. In a time when you could be executed for asking questions, he risked his life to carry out scientific experiments and to use mathematics to study the results. Read about this brave scientist and his discoveries.

Raven's Light: A Myth from the People of the Northwest Coast

by Susan Hand Shetterly (Atheneum, 1991). For the ancient people of the Northwest coast of North America, life was hard and uncertain. When they made up stories to explain the world around them, they made Raven, a tricky, clever bird, the creator of the world. Raven made the Earth, but he needed light. How Raven steals the sun from the Kingdom of the Day is told in this book.

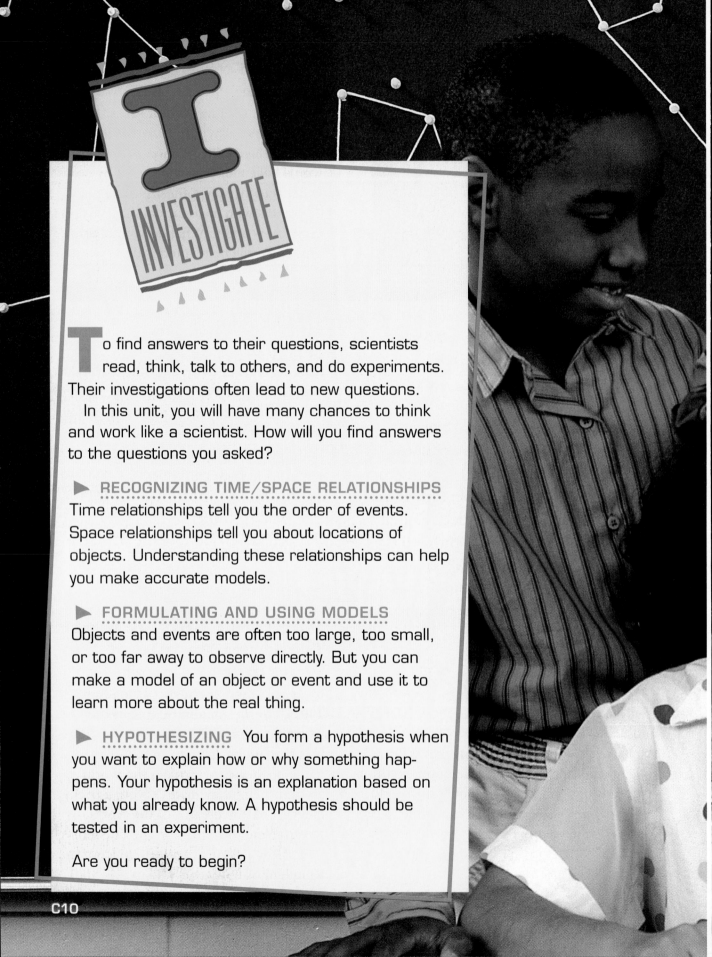

INVESTIGATE

To find answers to their questions, scientists read, think, talk to others, and do experiments. Their investigations often lead to new questions.

In this unit, you will have many chances to think and work like a scientist. How will you find answers to the questions you asked?

▶ **RECOGNIZING TIME/SPACE RELATIONSHIPS**
Time relationships tell you the order of events. Space relationships tell you about locations of objects. Understanding these relationships can help you make accurate models.

▶ **FORMULATING AND USING MODELS**
Objects and events are often too large, too small, or too far away to observe directly. But you can make a model of an object or event and use it to learn more about the real thing.

▶ **HYPOTHESIZING** You form a hypothesis when you want to explain how or why something happens. Your hypothesis is an explanation based on what you already know. A hypothesis should be tested in an experiment.

Are you ready to begin?

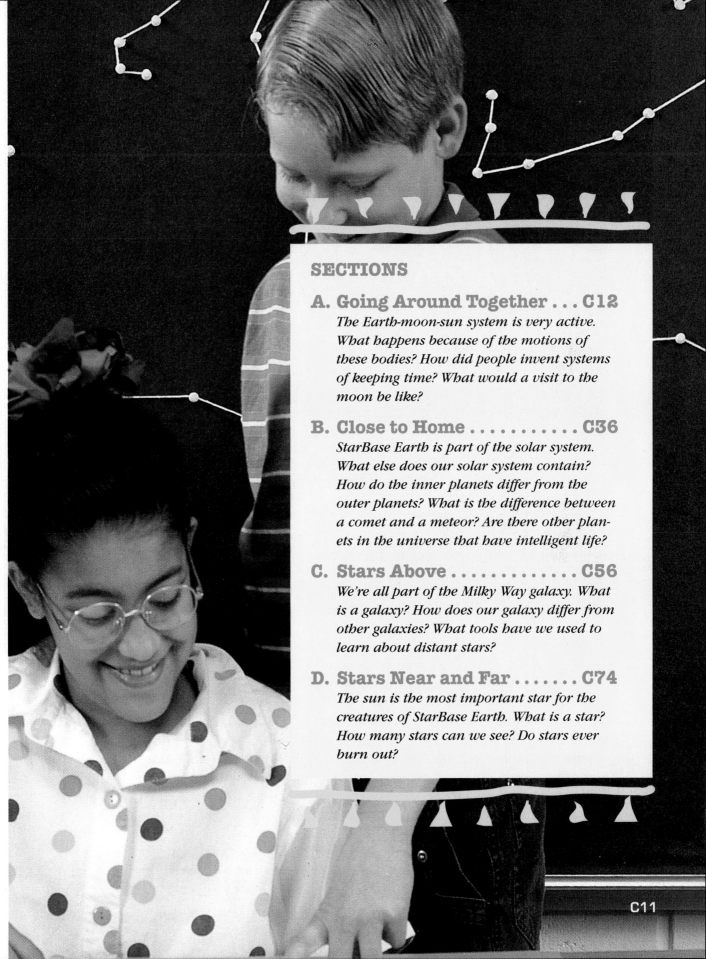

SECTIONS

Going Around Together

▲ The Moon

Have you ever wished you could be an astronaut? Well, in a way, you already are. The Earth itself is like a giant "starbase" traveling around our star, the sun. At the same time, the moon is in orbit around us.

How do the movements of the Earth and the moon in relation to the sun affect you? What do people measure by the movements? In your Science Log, identify three things you find out about StarBase Earth as you work through the investigations that follow.

1 MOVING RIGHT ALONG

People have always wondered about the lights that move across the sky. The two brightest lights are our sun and our moon. In the activities and readings that follow, you will find out about the movements of the Earth-moon-sun system.

ACTIVITY

Out of Sight!

MATERIALS
- small toy ship
- tabletop
- beach ball
- Science Log data sheet

Most ancient people thought Earth was flat. They feared they would sail off the edge. Others thought it was a sphere, like a ball. In this activity, you can test their ideas about the Earth's shape.

DO THIS

1 Squat or kneel beside the table or desk. Push the toy ship away from you across the surface until it falls off the other side.

2 Hold the ball in one hand at eye level. Use your other hand to hold the ship on the surface of the ball. Push the ship away from you across the curve of the ball. Keep holding the ship as it disappears from sight.

THINK AND WRITE

1. What shape do you think the Earth has? Explain how using the two models led you to your conclusion.

2. What happened to the ship as it moved across the ball? Describe its appearance.

So Near, So Far

Like the Earth, the moon and the sun are sphere-shaped. Ancient people noticed that the moon and the sun appeared to be about the same size in the sky. They did not know the actual diameters of the moon and the sun. How could two such different objects appear to be the same size?

MATERIALS

- tennis ball
- smaller ball
- Science Log data sheet

DO THIS

1. Set the tennis ball on a desk.

2. Hold the smaller ball in your outstretched hand in front of you.

3. Slowly back away from the tennis ball. With each step, stop and line up the two balls so that they appear to be next to each other. Observe the apparent sizes of the balls.

THINK AND WRITE

1. What happened to the apparent sizes of the two balls?

2. Why do you think the moon and the sun appear to be the same size?

3. **RECOGNIZING TIME/SPACE RELATIONSHIPS**
   Space relationships can tell you about locations of objects. How did the model you used help you discover the space relationship that affects the apparent sizes of the moon and the sun?

From Myth to Science

To some ancient people, the moon was the hunting goddess Diana. To us, it is the Earth's natural satellite. As you read, think about how ancient people made the leap from telling stories about the universe to scientifically describing how it works.

Early people had no binoculars, telescopes, or computers. They did not even have eyeglasses. However, they were careful observers of the universe. They made very accurate records and predictions based upon its movements. But they did not know what the objects they studied were.

A myth is a story created to explain some-thing in nature. Early people made up myths about the moon, the sun, and the stars. The moon, for example, was said to be good for farmers because its light did not burn the Earth the way the sun's did. So some people created stories about the moon as the goddess of farming. Others saw that there was a connection between the moon and the tides. So they made up stories that featured the moon as the goddess of the sea.

About 2,500 years ago, some Greek astronomers began to seek other ways to explain the universe. They used ways that did not depend upon myths. The Greeks had little technology. They observed, measured, and reasoned to try to understand the universe.

Goddess Diana ▶

Aristarchus (air ihs TAHR kuhs), for example, looked at the Earth's shadow on the moon during an eclipse. He concluded that the sun was much larger than the Earth and that it was much farther away than other people thought. He decided that the sun must be at the center of the universe.

"The Earth and the other planets orbit around the sun," he said. People laughed. Anybody could see that the Earth remained still while everything else moved around it!

Aristarchus also calculated the distance from the Earth to the sun. He used modern methods of measurement and came very close—138,570,000 kilometers (86 million miles). This is only slightly less than the actual distance—150 million kilometers (93 million miles).

Eratosthenes (er uh TAHS thuh neez), another Greek scientist, calculated the Earth's circumference. He did so by measuring the sun's angle at the summer solstice, the time of longest daylight.

Anaximander (uh NAKS uh man duhr) made a timekeeper. First, he stuck a stick into the ground. Then, he watched the stick's shadow change during the day. He made accurate measurements to mark the times of daylight, the times of the seasons, and the length of the year.

THINK ABOUT IT

How is what the Greek scientists did to explain things in the universe different from what the storytellers did?

▼ Earth's movements change the appearance of shadows during the day.

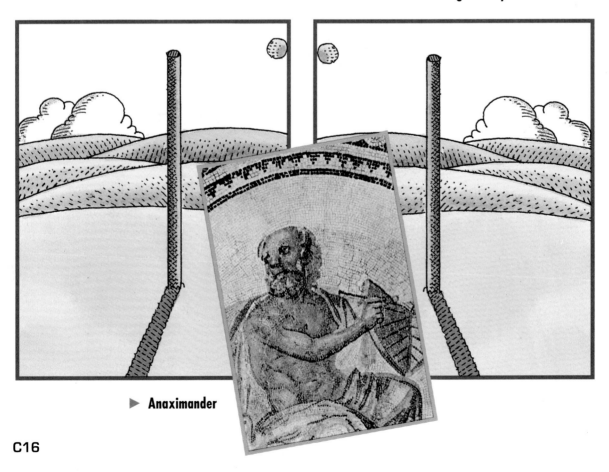

► Anaximander

A C T I V I T Y

That's Stretching It!

As the centuries passed, more and more people began to realize that the Earth and the other planets travel around the sun. It seemed to them that the path the planets took around the sun is a circle. Is it? Complete the activity to find out.

MATERIALS
- 30-cm-square sheet of cardboard
- 2 pushpins
- ruler
- 30-cm piece of string
- pencil
- Science Log data sheet

DO THIS

1 Stick one pushpin into the center of the cardboard. Stick the other one in about 5 cm away in any direction.

2 Loop the string and tie the ends together. Now put the string around the pushpins.

3 Put your pencil inside the loop and stretch out the string with the pencil point. Keep the string tight and move the pencil around the pushpins.

4 Move the pushpins farther apart and draw the path of the pencil. Move them closer together and draw the path of the pencil.

THINK AND WRITE

1. What kind of shape did you draw? How did the shape change when you moved the pushpins farther apart? closer together? The shape of the Earth's orbit is similar to the shape you would draw if you moved the pushpins very close together.

2. **FORMULATING AND USING MODELS**
   In this activity, you made and used a model to understand the shape of the Earth's orbit around the sun. Suppose one thumbtack represents the sun and the pencil's path represents the Earth's orbit. What can you conclude about the Earth's distance from the sun as it orbits the sun?

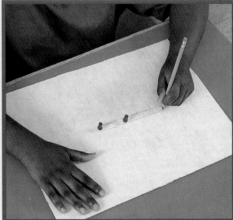

The Face in the Moon

Have you seen the giant "face" in the moon? Each night when the moon is almost full, the same face appears. Why do we see only one side of the moon? Modeling the moon's spin and orbit will help you answer this question.

Place a chair where you can walk around it. Start circling the chair in a counterclockwise direction. When you are halfway around, notice which side of your body is visible from the chair. Is it your left side or your right side? Notice the position of your body again when you are three-fourths of the way around. Also check it when you complete the

circle. Has the right side of your body ever been the side closer to the chair?

What can you infer about the moon's rate of spin in relation to its rate of orbiting the Earth? Now you should know why you always see the same face in the moon.

THINK ABOUT IT

Is the far side of the moon always dark? Explain.

▶ **Can you see the face?**

▼ **This is the moon's far side, photographed by *Luna 3*.**

A C T I V I T Y

Watch Where You're Going!

The Earth, the moon, and the sun have many movements you can observe. As you discovered in a previous activity, the Earth moves around the sun in a not quite circular path. This path is called an *ellipse*. Complete this activity to see how the movements all fit together.

MATERIALS
- beach ball
- volleyball
- tennis ball
- Science Log data sheet

DO THIS

1 Hold the beach ball (the sun). Have a classmate hold the volleyball (Earth) some distance from the sun. Have another classmate hold the tennis ball (the moon) near the Earth.

2 First, the volleyball must spin the way the Earth spins in place. Next, the moon must orbit the Earth in an ellipse. The classmate holding the tennis ball must always keep the same side of the ball toward the Earth. Finally, as these things are going on, the Earth must slowly orbit the sun in an ellipse.

THINK AND WRITE

Which movement takes the least time—the Earth spinning once, the moon orbiting once around the Earth, or the Earth orbiting once around the sun? Which movement takes the most time? Explain.

A Heavy Subject

When you asked your **I Wonder** questions, did you wonder why you don't fall off the Earth? Did you ask why the moon stays in orbit around the Earth? Read about a famous scientist who wondered about these same things.

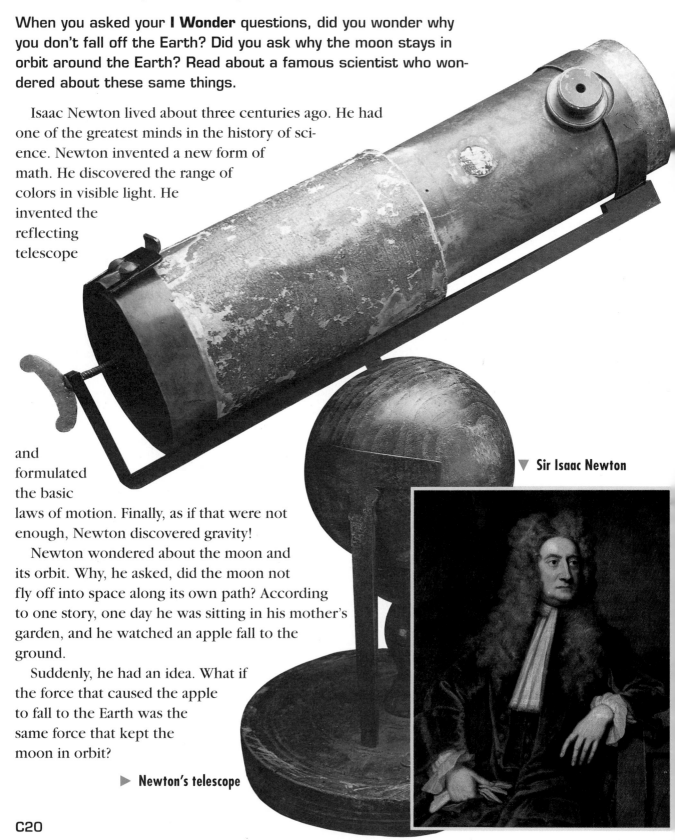

Isaac Newton lived about three centuries ago. He had one of the greatest minds in the history of science. Newton invented a new form of math. He discovered the range of colors in visible light. He invented the reflecting telescope and formulated the basic laws of motion. Finally, as if that were not enough, Newton discovered gravity!

Newton wondered about the moon and its orbit. Why, he asked, did the moon not fly off into space along its own path? According to one story, one day he was sitting in his mother's garden, and he watched an apple fall to the ground.

Suddenly, he had an idea. What if the force that caused the apple to fall to the Earth was the same force that kept the moon in orbit?

▼ **Sir Isaac Newton**

▶ **Newton's telescope**

Newton thought and thought. He was very good at this! He finally came up with the law of universal gravitation. The law says that all bodies in the universe are attracted to all other bodies. This attraction among bodies is **gravity.** The greater the mass—or the amount of matter—of each body, the stronger the attraction. Gravity affects all objects in the universe.

Newton's law explains why the apple falls to Earth. It also explains why the moon is attracted to the Earth and why the Earth is attracted to the sun. Each body acts on the other through the force of gravity. Try the following activity to model the Earth in orbit around the sun.

You will need: safety goggles, a 1-m long string and a key

 CAUTION: Put on safety goggles.

Securely tie a long piece of string to a key. In an open area, away from your classmates, carefully swing the key around your head. What do you feel from the key as you swing it? What path does the key take? What would happen if the string suddenly broke?

THINK ABOUT IT

Why do you think the sun's gravity does not pull the Earth into the sun?

▼ **Orbits of Earth and moon**

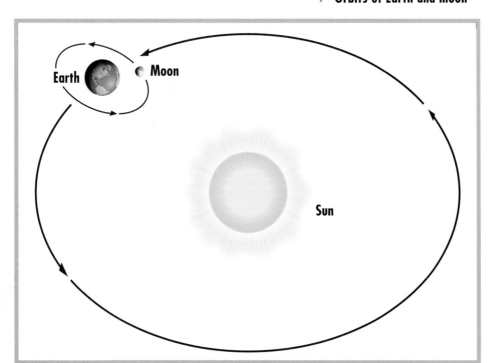

ACTIVITY

Casting Shadows

You might think that with so many objects in the universe orbiting one another, they would cross each other's paths. Well, they do. In the following activity, you will see how the sun and the moon can be darkened, or eclipsed.

MATERIALS

- large flashlight
- basketball
- tennis ball
- Science Log data sheet

DO THIS

❶ Darken the classroom.

❷ Shine the flashlight (the sun) on the wall.

❸ Hold the basketball (Earth) between the sun's light and the wall to show the Earth's shadow.

❹ Move the tennis ball (the moon) between the Earth and the wall. Observe what happens.

❺ Move the tennis ball between the basketball and the light. Observe what happens.

THINK AND WRITE

1. Which action represented an eclipse of the moon?

2. Which action represented an eclipse of the sun?

3. Why does an eclipse of the moon throw the entire moon into shadow? Why does an eclipse of the sun throw only a partial shadow on the Earth?

4. Look at the photograph. Why do you think that the Earth is not completely eclipsing the moon?

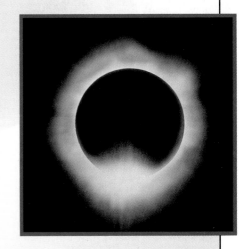

You're Blocking My View!

Ancient astronomers observed and tried to predict eclipses, even if they did not understand them. Read on to see what these people thought was going on in the sky.

The people of many early cultures were frightened by eclipses of the sun and the moon. Some believed that these events were battles between heavenly beings.

The Miwok people of what is now California thought that eclipses were fights between the sun and the moon. The Pomo, also of California, believed that a great bear was walking along the Milky Way and met the sun. The sun would not let the bear pass. So the two fought! The sun was eclipsed when the bear won.

In Viking mythology, wolves tried to eat the sun and the moon and blotted them out. The Chinese believed that the sun's enemy was a dragon. For the Maya, it was a large, fanged snake.

Ancient people would often sing, dance, and make loud noises to scare away these "evil spirits." They thought that this restored the moon and the sun to their rightful place in the heavens.

Why did people's noise and singing always seem to work? What would happen after a period of time?

▲ Solar eclipse   ▼ Lunar eclipse

LESSON 1 REVIEW

❶ Describe the movements of the Earth and the moon in relation to the sun.

❷ What are some beliefs ancient people had about the sun and the moon?

WHAT TIME IS IT?

You've explored the movements of the Earth around the sun and of the moon around the Earth. When viewed from the Earth, these movements occur in regular patterns. Throughout history, people have kept time by these patterns. What patterns can be used to mark the passing of time?

Ancient Astronomers

Astronomy is the oldest science. It began even before written language. People needed to understand the cycle of changes on Earth. Then they could plant and harvest crops, sail safely by sea, and do other important activities. Many ancient people built stone structures and kept calendars as ways to mark the changing skies.

The Babylonians lived in what is present-day Iraq around 3000 B.C. The Babylonians viewed the universe as a disk of land surrounded by water, with Babylon in the center.

About 5,000 years ago, a kind of observatory was built in Britain. It is called *Stonehenge.* Stonehenge is similar to earlier observatories built in Egypt and South America. The builders of Stonehenge arranged huge stones so that

the rays of the rising sun would shine through openings between the stones at certain important times of the year. Thus, Stonehenge may have been a kind of calendar.

El Caracol was a Mayan observatory. Astronomers observed Venus through openings in the top of this structure.

The Anasazi (ahn uh SAH zee) lived in the American Southwest about A.D. 1000. They marked the movements of the moon, the sun, and the stars. Casa Rincañada is an Anasazi kiva, or holy place. It lies in a perfect east-west line.

The Arabs of the Middle East preserved many astronomical records during the Middle Ages. The Arabs also refined the *astrolabe,* an instrument for measuring the altitude of the sun and stars.

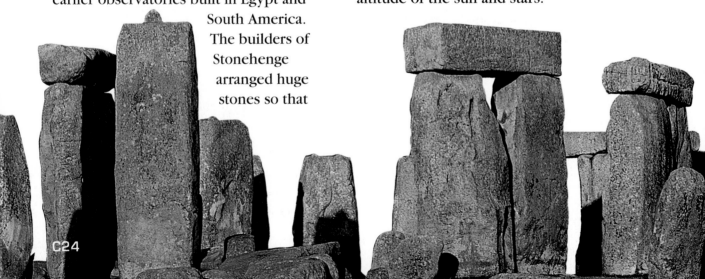

▲ Babylonian view of the world

▲ El Caracol

▼ Stonehenge

▲ Casa Rincañada

▲ Arab astrolabe

THINK ABOUT IT

What kinds of observations would ancient people have had to make over a period of time before they built their observatories and similar structures?

A Long Day's Journey

Once people recognized that the apparent movements of the sun and moon happened over and over, they began to use these cycles to organize their lives. The following activity will help you see why there is always another day.

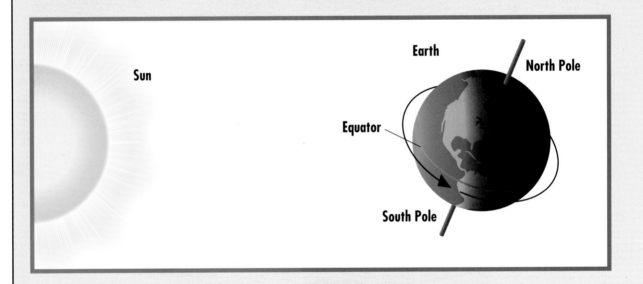

DO THIS

❶ Cut out a strip of paper and write your community's name on it. Tape it to the globe in approximately the correct place.

❷ Darken the room.

❸ Shine the flashlight on the globe.

❹ Rotate the globe in a counter-clockwise direction as seen from above.

THINK AND WRITE

1. What cycle did you just model? Describe it.

2. How does this cycle affect humans, other animals, and plants?

A Seasonal Change

The Earth's rotation causes the cycle of night and day. What kind of cycle does the Earth's revolution, or trip around the sun, cause? Find out in this activity.

MATERIALS
- Earth globe tilted on its axis
- large flashlight
- Science Log data sheet

DO THIS

1 Shine the flashlight (sun) directly on a spot on the globe and then at a slant on the same spot. Record your observations.

2 Hold the globe while someone else shines the light directly on the equator.

3 Rotate the globe slowly while you move around the person with the light. Keep the globe tilted toward the same side of the room. The person with the light should also turn, keeping the light on the equator.

THINK AND WRITE

1. In steps 1 and 2, which was larger—the area in the path of the direct rays or the area with the slanted rays?

2. Which form of the sun's rays—direct or slanted—do you think is brighter and hotter?

3. When the sun's slanted rays hit the Northern Hemisphere, which season does your community have?

4. When the sun's slanted rays hit the Southern Hemisphere, which season do you have?

5. What do we call each of the Earth's revolutions around the sun? How long is it?

The Long and Short of It

You know that there are more hours of daylight in the summer and more hours of darkness in the winter. Why is this so?

The lengths of daylight and darkness in a place depend on two things. They are the time of year and how far from the equator the place is.

Because the Earth is tilted, the amount of sunlight any place receives changes as the Earth moves around the sun. During our summer, the Northern Hemisphere tilts toward the sun. Then we have long days and short nights. As the Earth continues its orbit, the Southern Hemisphere tilts toward the sun. This gives people there long days and short nights, while we have just the opposite. This is our winter.

The day with the most sunlight, June 20 or 21, is called the *summer solstice*. The day with the most darkness, December 21 or 22, is the *winter solstice*. March 20 or 21 and September 22 or 23 are the two days halfway between the solstices. They are called the spring and fall *equinoxes. Equinox* comes from a word that means "equal night."

THINK ABOUT IT

Which parts of the Earth always have days and nights of about equal length? Which parts regularly have very long days or very long nights? Explain.

▼ Earth's tilt and its orbit around the sun cause the seasons.

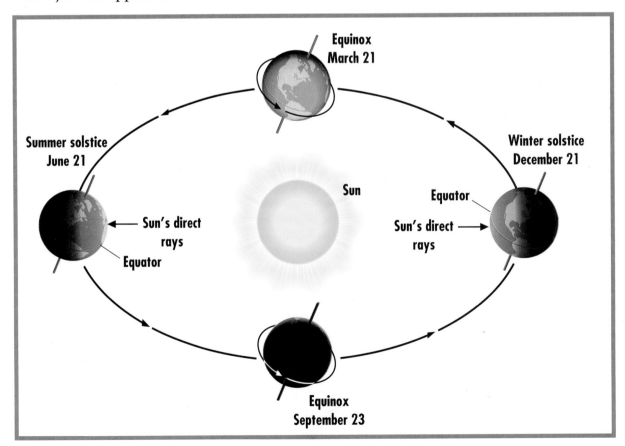

Equinox
March 21

Summer solstice
June 21

Winter solstice
December 21

Sun

Equator

Sun's direct
rays

← Sun's direct
rays →

Equator

Equinox
September 23

Land of the Midnight Sun

The polar areas are the most affected by the Earth's tilt. Each pole receives months of continuous daylight followed by months of continuous darkness. What is life like in these areas?

Norway is a European country that lies above the Arctic Circle. It is called the Land of the Midnight Sun because the sun shines almost all of the time during the summer.

In Norway, children attend school in the dark from mid-November through January because the sun does not shine at all. But in the summer they go to bed while it is light, from mid-May through July.

After months of darkness, children in Norway get a day's vacation from school in late January to greet the returning sun. The continuous darkness in the winter causes some people to feel sad. So Norwegians are always delighted by the appearance of the *northern lights* when the sun doesn't shine.

THINK ABOUT IT

How would periods of daylight and darkness in the Antarctic compare to those periods in the Arctic Circle?

▼ In Norway, the sun still shines after 11:00 P.M. in late June.

▶ The northern lights

ACTIVITY

It's Just a Phase!

Perhaps you have watched the moon go through phases, or changes in its appearance. A new cycle of phases begins about every 29 days. Why do you think this happens? Now try this activity to test your ideas.

DO THIS

1. Darken the room and turn on the lamp.

2. Stand with your back to the lamp.

3. Hold the ball at arm's length above your head so that it is in the light.

4. Rotate counterclockwise, keeping the ball in the same position. Stop each eighth of the way around and draw a picture that shows how much of the ball appears lit.

THINK AND WRITE

1. What did the lamp represent? the ball?

2. Describe how much of the lighted half of the ball you could see and your position at each stopping point in your rotation. What is each similar phase of the moon called?

3. Now what do you think causes the cycle of phases of the moon? Compare your answer with your first idea.

4. What period of time on a calendar is nearly the same as the time it takes the moon to orbit the Earth?

The Moon's Got Pull, Too!

Suppose you visit a beach at the nearest ocean. What effect of the moon's gravitational attraction on the Earth would you see? Read the following and you'll see that the moon's phases are related to another cycle of change.

The Earth's force of gravity keeps the moon in orbit. However, the moon's gravitation has an effect on the Earth, too. It causes the twice-daily cycle of tides in the Earth's oceans.

When the moon's gravity pulls on the Earth's oceans, it causes them to bulge. This causes high tides on the side of the Earth facing the moon, as well as on the opposite side. The areas in between have low tides. As the Earth rotates, different places have high and low tides.

Twice each month, at the new moon and full moon, the sun and moon line up with the Earth. This causes higher and lower tides than usual. These are called *spring tides. Neap tides* occur twice a month also, at the quarter moons, when the sun and the moon form a right angle with the Earth. Neap tides are moderate in height.

Spring tides ▼

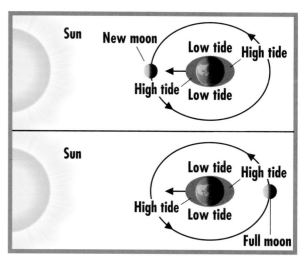

Neap tides ▼

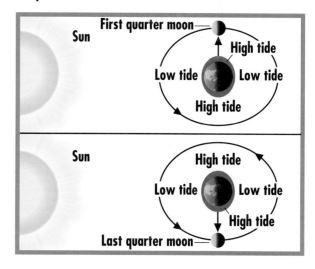

LESSON 2 REVIEW

❶ What effect of the Earth's rotation do we observe?

❷ Suppose the only night you see the moon, it is half lit. How can you tell whether the full moon or the new moon phase is approaching?

3 A TRAVELER'S GUIDE TO THE MOON

Long before the astronauts set foot on the moon, astronomers had mapped it more completely than some parts of Africa had been mapped. We have learned even more from the *Apollo* space missions. On the following pages you will find out what the moon is really like.

Don't Go Out Without a Suit!

Why do astronauts have to wear spacesuits on the moon? Read the following to see what you could and could not do on the moon.

On July 20, 1969, humans stood on the moon for the first time. After landing the lunar module Eagle, astronauts Neil Armstrong and Edwin "Buzz" Aldrin stepped out on the surface. For two and one-half hours they collected rocks and soil. They set up experiments and took pictures. Armstrong took this one of Aldrin.

▶ "That's one small step . . ."

The moon has a very limited atmosphere. There is no oxygen to breathe and not enough atmosphere to even out the temperature. As a result, the moon's surface is very hot during its day and then freezing during its night. The moon's day and night are both about two Earth weeks long. You would be very glad to have a spacesuit there.

▲ The Apollo astronauts were able to leap easily on the moon. They weighed only one-sixth of their Earth weight.

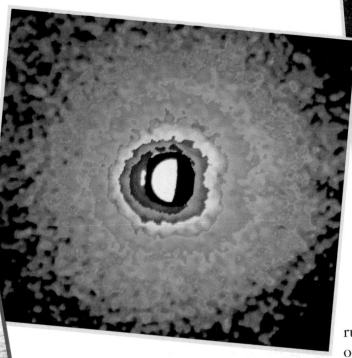

▲ This is the first image of the moon's thin atmosphere.

On the other hand, you would enjoy running and jumping on the moon. It has one-sixth the gravity of Earth, so you would weigh only one-sixth of what you weigh on Earth. Think how easy it would be to slam-dunk a basketball! But remember, you'd have to do it while wearing a spacesuit.

THINK ABOUT IT

Imagine how large a baseball stadium would have to be if you could hit a ball six times farther than on Earth! How would some of your favorite sports change on the moon?

Scope It Out!

People used to think that the surface of the moon was flat and smooth. Read to find out what the moon's surface is really like.

The moon is about the same age as Earth, four and one-half billion years. Some scientists think that when Earth was young, a large body hit it and exploded. The explosion hurled a lot of debris into space. The Earth's gravity captured the debris, which became the moon.

Scientists can find out the relative ages of features on the moon. Large rocks hit the moon long ago, so areas with many craters are the oldest. Volcanoes erupted because the impacts heated up the moon, melting some of the surface, so the smooth areas, called maria, are younger. Craters that sit inside maria are younger than the maria. Also, any crater that partly covers another crater is younger. This is because the rock that produced it had to hit the moon's surface more recently than did the rock that produced the crater underneath it.

▲ The jagged edge of the sun-and-shadow line across the moon proved to observers that its surface has varying heights.

▼ **Surface of the moon**

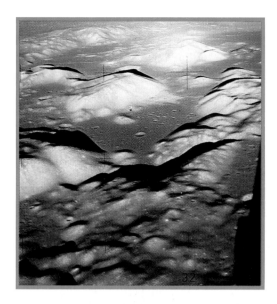

▲ About 85 percent of the moon's surface is light-colored highlands. These were formed by the continuous impact of meteorites. The tallest mountains are only 6,100 meters (20,000 feet) high. They erode very slowly because there is no weather on the moon.

▲ The rest of the moon's surface is *maria,* which means "seas." Early observers thought these areas contained water. They are actually craters that were filled with lava during the moon's volcanic period.

LESSON 3 REVIEW

What area of the moon would you choose to explore? Describe what you would expect to find.

 DOUBLE CHECK

SECTION A REVIEW

1. Why do the sun and the moon appear to be about the same size?

2. What patterns can be used to mark the passing of time? Describe and explain each one.

3. Compare the features of the Earth and the moon.

Close to Home

▲ Planetary space probe

The size of the universe is hard to imagine. Most of us feel more comfortable learning about it by starting with our own solar system. Each member of our solar system was probably formed from the same gas and dust. Yet each member is very different from all the others.

In this section, you will investigate each member of the solar system one by one. Think of three facts you now know about our solar system, and write them in your Science Log. Add to your notes as you work through the investigations of StarBase Earth's neighborhood.

1 OUR NEIGHBORHOOD

Our neighbors in space are the sun, a family of 8 other planets, about 70 known moons, and many comets and asteroids. Together with the Earth, these objects form one vast, continuously moving solar system. Its scale and structure will amaze you.

Wrong-Way Planet

Long ago, astronomers observing the night sky saw that some points of light do not always move in the same direction as the others. One of these points of light, the planet Mars, seems to move backward at times. That is, it appears to move from west to east over several nights, instead of from east to west. Does Mars really move backward? Try this activity and decide for yourself.

▼ **Mars**

You will need: a large open space

Ask a classmate to begin walking slowly in a circle. Then, moments later, begin walking in the same direction in a circle. Make sure your circle has the same center but a slightly smaller radius. Now speed up so that you pass your classmate. How does his or her movement appear to change against the background as you pass by?

Scientists think that the solar system formed about 4.5 billion years ago from a swirling cloud of dust and gas. As this gas cloud condensed to form the sun, it began to spin in one direction. Some of the gas and dust that was thrown off formed the planets. That's why all the planets orbit the sun in the same direction, even though sometimes this doesn't seem to be so.

THINK ABOUT IT

Does Mars really move backward? Explain.

The Big Picture

What do we know about the planets? The pictures on these pages will give you some information about the members of our solar system.

Because the distances in the solar system are so large, astronomers use a measurement called an AU. AU stands for astronomical unit, the distance between the Earth and the sun, or 150 million kilometers (93 million miles).

Saturn

Distance from Sun: 9.5 AU
Length of Year: 29.5 Earth years
Length of Day: 10.25 Earth hours

Neptune

Distance from Sun: 30 AU
Length of Year: 165 Earth years
Length of Day: 16 Earth hours

Uranus

Distance from Sun: 19.2 AU
Length of Year: 84 Earth years
Length of Day: 17.25 Earth hours

Mercury

Distance from Sun:
0.40 AU
Length of Year:
88 Earth days
Length of Day:
59 Earth days

Venus

Distance from Sun:
0.72 AU
Length of Year:
225 Earth days
Length of Day:
243 Earth days

Jupiter

Distance from Sun: 5.2 AU
Length of Year: 11.9 Earth years
Length of Day: 9.8 Earth hours

Earth

Distance from Sun: 1 AU
Length of Year: 365.26 days
Length of Day: 24 hours

Mars

Distance from Sun: 1.5 AU
Length of Year: 1.9 Earth years
Length of Day: 24.5 Earth hours

Pluto

Distance from Sun: 39.5 AU
Length of Year: 248 Earth years
Length of Day: 6.4 Earth days

THINK ABOUT IT

Compare the facts given for the nine planets. What patterns can you find?

ACTIVITY

Let's Scale It Down!

Scientists make scale models to help them understand the real world. Models are especially helpful for studying the solar system because it's so large. In this activity, you can make a model of planet distances from the sun.

MATERIALS
- construction paper
- scissors
- colored pencils
- tape
- long classroom wall
- ruler
- Science Log data sheet

DO THIS

1 Use construction paper, colored pencils, and scissors to draw and cut out a large circular sun. Tape the sun on one end of the wall.

2 Use the scale 10 cm = 1 AU. Draw and cut out a paper Earth, and tape it 10 cm from the edge of the sun.

3 Draw, cut out, position, and tape the other eight planets in place, using the same scale. Refer to pages C38–C39 for the distances of the planets from the sun. Round off the number of astronomical units to make your figuring easier.

THINK AND WRITE

▶ **RECOGNIZING TIME/SPACE RELATIONSHIPS** In this activity, you used a scale to show a space relationship between the real planet distances from the sun and the distances on your model. Why was it important to always measure the distance from the sun instead of from one planet to another?

QUICK CHECK

LESSON 1 REVIEW

1 When seen from Earth, which planets would never appear to move backward in the sky? Explain.

2 How would you describe the way the planets are arranged in the solar system?

2 INNER PLANETS AND ASTEROIDS

The four planets closest to the sun—Mercury, Venus, Earth, and Mars—are called the *inner planets.* You will discover that these planets, along with the asteroids, have something in common.

Mercury and Venus

The United States' *Mariner 10* and *Magellan* space probes showed us the surfaces of Mercury and Venus. See and read what was discovered.

Mercury, the closest planet to the sun, is about the size of Earth's moon. A crust and a deeper rocky layer surround a huge core of iron and nickel. The surface temperature varies from –180°C to 430°C (–292°F to 806°F). The planet is not large enough for its gravity to hold onto a moon or much of an atmosphere.

Venus, about the size of Earth, is made of rock that covers a core of iron. But we're not likely to walk on the surface of Venus, because the atmosphere is dense and hot 465°C, (869°F) and contains carbon dioxide and sulfuric acid! We would be burned, suffocated, cooked, and crushed! Venus has no moon but may have active volcanoes.

The *Magellan* spacecraft used radar imaging to cut through Venus's cloudy atmosphere. The three craters in the picture are large, from 35 to 65 kilometers (22 to 40 miles) wide. The dark areas indicate smooth ground, and the light areas indicate rough ground.

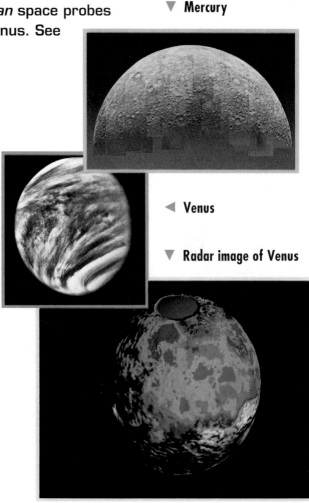

▼ **Mercury**

◄ **Venus**

▼ **Radar image of Venus**

THINK ABOUT IT

What other body in the solar system does Mercury look like? Explain.

Earth

Mercury and Venus are too hot and dry to support life. Find out what makes Earth the right place for life. See how photographs from space show this.

Earth has a solid inner core surrounded by a liquid outer core, a rocky mantle, and a crust. The planet has volcanic eruptions and earthquakes. Sunlight, a nitrogen- and oxygen-rich atmosphere, large oceans, and the greenhouse effect make climates that support life.

A Watery World
Two-thirds of Earth's surface is covered by water. Without water, there could be no life as we know it.

Weather Patterns
Sunlight, the atmosphere, and ocean currents create Earth's weather.

Atmosphere
Earth's atmosphere provides air to breathe. It protects life from harmful solar radiation.

Ozone Holes
A layer of ozone (a form of oxygen) surrounds the Earth. Ozone protects us from harmful ultraviolet rays. Recently, the ozone has thinned out over both poles and in other places.

Polar Ice
Large, growing sheets of ice cover the polar regions. These regions receive the least amount of direct sunlight.

THINK ABOUT IT

Why do you think that Earth is the only inner planet that has life?

Guy Bluford:

Space-Shuttle Astronaut

Satellites provide us with much information about Earth. But human observations and research in space are important also. Guy Bluford knows firsthand about space research. He is a former space-shuttle astronaut.

After graduation from The Pennsylvania State University, Bluford became an Air Force pilot and an aerospace engineer. He became interested in astronaut training when the space shuttle was being developed. The Air Force gave him the opportunity to apply for the space program, and he did so in 1977. He was accepted and immediately began training for his first mission.

Bluford's job on space-shuttle flights was mission-specialist astronaut. Mission specialists run various experiments on board an orbiting space shuttle. In addition to running the experiments, Bluford had to fix the equipment if something broke.

Most space-shuttle experiments can be divided into two categories: materials-processing experiments and life-science experiments. Materials-processing experiments involve making materials, such as computer chips or medicines, in the near-zero gravity of space. Some life-science experiments involve studying plants in orbit, to observe how near-zero gravity affects plant growth.

Mission specialists run many different experiments during a space-shuttle flight. Bluford would sometimes have as many as 75 experiments working at the same time. Learning everything necessary to complete so many experiments successfully is the most challenging part of the job.

In the future, mission specialists will be needed to run experiments on America's orbiting space station. The space station will be a permanent laboratory where scientists will learn even more about Earth.

THINK ABOUT IT

How do mission-specialist astronauts help us learn more about Earth?

Mars and the Asteroids

Of all the planets, Mars and some asteroids are the most likely to be explored and settled by humans. Read to see why this may someday be possible.

Mars is the most Earth-like planet in our solar system. It has a small, solid, iron core. The surface has mountains, deserts, volcanoes, and canyons. A thin atmosphere of carbon dioxide covers the surface. On a Martian day, temperatures may range from a freezing –120°C (–184°F) to a comfortable 25°C (77°F). In 1976 two NASA Viking Landers tested the Martian soil for signs of life and found none.

▲ Mars has the longest canyon in the solar system. Valles Marineris, shown here, is about the width of the United States. The channel-like features suggest that Mars once had running water. There may still be water frozen under the polar areas.

▲ Mars, about half the size of Earth, is large enough to hold onto two moons, Phobos and Deimos. They are oddly shaped objects and may be captured asteroids.

▲ Olympus Mons is the largest volcano in the solar system. It stands three times as high as Mount Everest.

A wide belt of small objects called *asteroids* orbits the sun between Mars and Jupiter. Asteroids are sometimes called *minor planets*. All of them together would not equal the amount of material in our moon. The largest asteroid is Ceres. Asteroids might be the remains of a planet pulled apart by Jupiter's gravity. Or they might be bits and pieces left over from the formation of the solar system.

The asteroids are rich in minerals, and scientists think about mining them. Larger asteroids may be used as research stations someday.

▲ The spacecraft *Galileo* took this close-up of an asteroid in 1993. It is rocky, like everything else in the inner solar system. Notice the tiny impact craters. What do they tell you about the age of this asteroid?

QUICK CHECK

LESSON 2 REVIEW

Make a table to compare the inner planets. Use headings such as *Size, Temperature,* and *Atmosphere.*

3 OUTER PLANETS, COMETS, AND METEORS

From 1977 to 1989, two *Voyager* spacecraft flew by the four large outer planets. The photographs and data collected by the *Voyagers* showed a group of planets and moons with strange features unlike anything seen among the inner planets. Read on to find out how the outer planets differ from the inner planets.

Jupiter

Beyond the orbits of the four inner planets moves Jupiter, the first outer planet. See and read about what makes Jupiter and its moons so strange.

Jupiter is the largest planet. Its atmosphere is cold hydrogen gas. Below that is liquid hydrogen. Examine Jupiter's features shown on the next page.

Like the other giant outer planets, Jupiter has many moons. The four largest, those discovered long ago by Galileo, are called the *Galilean moons* in his honor. They are named Io, Europa, Ganymede, and Callisto. The Voyager spacecraft found 13 additional moons around Jupiter, bringing the known total to 17.

▲ Io is nicknamed "the pizza moon" because of its appearance. Io is one of only two moons in the solar system with active volcanoes.

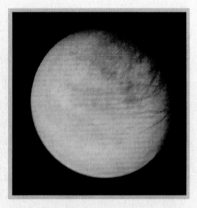

▲ The smooth, icy surface of Europa may hide a huge ocean.

▲ Larger than the planet Mercury, Ganymede has an icy crust with many craters.

North Equatorial Belt
Strong winds blow in opposite directions among cloud belts.

North Temperate Belt
The southern edge is bordered by "red ovals," giant circling movements in the atmosphere.

North Tropical Zone
This bright zone contains high clouds made of ammonia crystals.

Great Red Spot
Jupiter's Great Red Spot is the size of three Earths. Astronomers think it is a giant storm.

▲ Callisto is larger than Earth's moon. It is covered with craters made of ice.

South Polar Region
Within swirling clouds lie "white ovals," gigantic storm systems.

Jupiter's Ring
In January 1979, *Voyager 1* discovered a thin, faint ring made of dark grains of dust.

THINK ABOUT IT

How are Jupiter and its moons different from the inner planets and their moons?

Saturn

Saturn was the farthest of the outer planets known to ancient astronomers. To them, it looked like a pale, yellow light. What is Saturn really like?

Saturn, like Jupiter, is mostly gas, although it is much less dense than Jupiter. In fact, Saturn is so light that it could float on water! Saturn has at least 18 moons, many of them discovered by the two Voyager spacecraft. It also has a large, beautiful system of rings made up of millions of bits of ice.

Encke Division
The innermost moon orbits in the gap between Saturn and its rings.

A Windy Planet
Like Jupiter, Saturn's atmosphere has cloud belts that are blown in opposite directions.

Ring's Edge
The outermost bright ring was discovered in 1979.

Cassini Division
This appeared to be a space between rings. Voyager ships found many faint small rings within the division.

▲ Titan, Saturn's largest moon, is the second largest in the solar system.

THINK ABOUT IT

The appearance of Saturn's rings changes during the planet's orbit. Sometimes we see the topside of the rings. Other times we see their underside. In 1995 and again in 2003, Saturn will appear to be ringless. How will Saturn be facing us during those two years?

Where Is It?

Saturn and all the closer planets can be seen without a telescope. How did astronomers find Uranus, Neptune, and Pluto? Read on to find out.

Uranus was discovered by British astronomer William Herschel in 1781. Herschel also discovered two of the planet's moons and observed that the moons orbit in the same direction that the planet rotates—clockwise.

After Uranus was discovered, astronomers saw that the planet was being pulled off course by the gravity of some unknown body—perhaps another planet. They looked for and found Neptune in 1846.

The odd thing was that Neptune's gravity was not strong enough to affect the orbit of Uranus. So the search went on for Planet X.

American astronomer Percival Lowell began to hunt for Planet X in 1905. He looked at thousands of photographic plates to find an object that moved against the background of stars. But he never found it.

In 1928 American astronomer Clyde Tombaugh continued the search. Like Lowell, Tombaugh compared many images on photographic plates. In 1930 he found a "star" that had moved a long distance over just six days. Clyde Tombaugh thought that he had found Planet X in the area of sky near the constellation Gemini.

▲ Clyde Tombaugh

◀ Refracting telescope

THINK ABOUT IT

What other kinds of objects in the solar system could be found by looking for objects that moved against the background of stars?

ACTIVITY

Searching for Planet X

How do you think you would feel if you discovered a new planet? In this activity, you can re-create the thrill of Clyde Tombaugh's discovery.

DO THIS

1 Look at the top left corner of the two photographic plates.

2 Use one crayon to circle the image that appears on both plates in the same position.

3 Use the same crayon to circle the other images that appear on both plates in the same positions.

4 Do you see an image that is in two different positions? If so, circle the image in both positions with your second crayon. Hurray, you have found a planet!

THINK AND WRITE

1. What is the real name of the planet you circled in different positions on the plates and that Clyde Tombaugh discovered?

2. Why was it possible to see the planet's image change position in just a few nights?

C50

Uranus, Neptune, and Pluto

Circling the cold far reaches of our solar system are the two remaining gas planets—Uranus and Neptune—and a small, rocky planet, Pluto. Each of these planets is mysterious in its own way.

Uranus is blue-green because it has an atmosphere of methane gas. The planet has a set of dark, narrow rings. Astronomers think that its moon Miranda was broken apart by an impact but later fell back together in the strange shape it has now.

Another ringed planet, Neptune, is the bluest planet because of its methane gas atmosphere. The white clouds are methane ice. Neptune's great dark spot is a huge storm. Its moon Triton has volcanoes. Triton's strange surface has caused it to be nicknamed "the cantaloupe moon."

Pluto is the only outer planet without a thick atmosphere. Little is known about Pluto, except that it has one known moon, Charon. Charon is half the size of its planet, so Pluto and Charon are often cosidered a double planet. From Earth, Pluto can be seen only as a small dot, even with the best telescopes.

THINK ABOUT IT

Why are Pluto and Charon sometimes called twin planets?

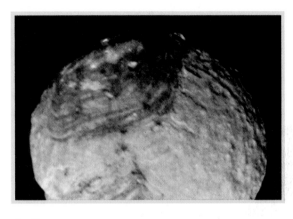

▲ **Uranus**

▼ **Neptune and Triton**

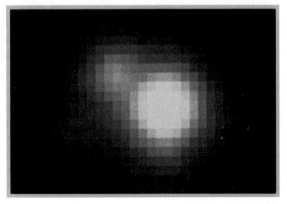

▶ **Pluto and Charon**

Comets Come and Comets Go

People have always marveled at the short visits of ghostly flares spread across the sky. What are these objects? Where do they come from, and where do they go?

Comets are chunks of ice and rock left over from the formation of our solar system. They are often called "dirty snowballs." They move around the sun in long, oval-shaped orbits. Comets may take from about 3 years to many millions of years to complete their orbits. Comets probably come from a large cloud of frozen chunks of material surrounding our solar system.

The strangest feature of a comet is its tail. As a comet approaches the sun, part of the comet melts and vaporizes. This causes a long, visible gas tail to stream behind the comet. Notice how the tail always points away from the sun.

In 1993 astronomers got a real treat. They photographed a comet that had been pulled apart by Jupiter's gravity. The comet's pieces have fallen into Jupiter's atmosphere.

▼ The orbits of some comets.

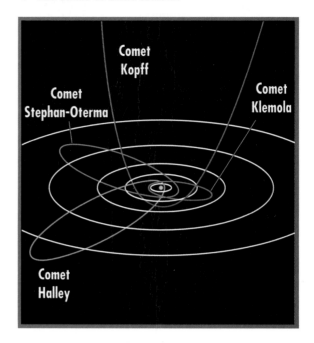

Comet Kopff

Comet Stephan-Oterma

Comet Klemola

Comet Halley

THINK ABOUT IT

Will comets orbiting around the sun last forever? Explain.

▲ A comet's tail always points away from the sun.

Showers of Meteors

Perhaps you've looked up on a star-filled night and seen a light that flashed across the sky and disappeared. You may have heard someone exclaim, "There goes a shooting star!" What are "shooting stars," and when can you see them?

In fact, shooting stars are not stars at all. They are *meteors.* And what are meteors? Let's return to the topic of comets for a moment. Comets leave behind a trail of gas and dust, or *meteoroids,* as they move through the solar system. When the Earth passes through these dust particles, they stream into our atmosphere as meteors. Because most of them are no bigger than a grain of sand, they burn up in a flash of light. Sometimes a meteor is large enough to survive its plunge and hit the surface of the Earth. Then the piece of rock is called a *meteorite.*

▲ **Meteor**

The Earth often passes through the same paths of comet dust each year. This produces yearly showers of meteors. Sometimes you can see several meteors per hour. Other meteor showers may have hundreds of meteors per hour in a spectacular display. The table lists some major yearly meteor showers that you can watch.

METEOR SHOWERS		
Name	**Date**	**Meteors per Hour**
Quadrantids	January 3	50
Lyrids	April 22	10
Delta Aquarids	July 31	25
Perseids	August 12	50
Orionids	October 21	20
Taurids	November 8	10
Leonids	November 17	10
Geminids	December 14	50

LESSON 3 REVIEW

❶ How are most of the outer planets alike? Which one is different? Explain.

❷ During a meteor shower, why are more meteors likely to be seen between midnight and dawn than earlier in the evening?

4 WHAT'S OUT THERE?

Are we alone in the universe? Is Earth the only planet that contains intelligent life? Read this page and do the following activity to see how scientists have looked for other life in the universe.

Message to the Unknown

Some scientists say the conditions that led to life on Earth are rare. Others say there may be millions of planets with intelligent life. Here is one way to find out.

Since 1960 astronomers have been using radio telescopes to detect signs of other intelligent life in the universe. In 1974 American astronomer Frank Drake sent a message from Earth. The message was in code and was beamed into space by the world's biggest radio telescope, at Arecibo, Puerto Rico. The coded message is shown in the diagram. It tells any intelligent observers about Earth. In 1992 a full-scale program called *SETI* (*Search for Extraterrestrial Intelligence*) was begun, using radio channels all over the Earth.

Look at the information in the code. The figure shown in red stands for a human being. The solar system is shown in yellow. Why is one of the objects positioned above the others? Symbols for the numbers 1 to 10, at the top, are in white. The major chemical elements on Earth are in green. The DNA code is in blue.

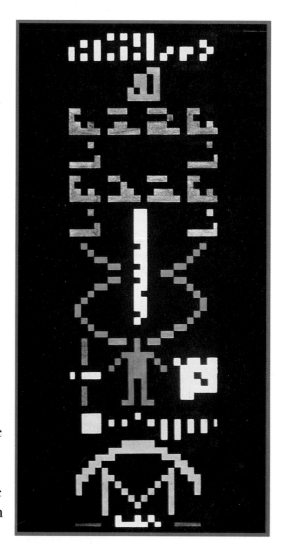

▲ SETI message

THINK ABOUT IT

How would scientists know whether a signal they receive is a message from intelligent life?

ACTIVITY

Contact

Suppose you are going to send a new code into space. The message will tell other life in the universe about our planet. Surprise! You receive an answer. You can communicate with an intelligent being from another planet.

MATERIALS

• colored pencils
• the SETI code
• Science Log data sheet

DO THIS

❶ Make a list of four important things about Earth that you think other intelligent beings should know.

❷ Draw a diagram that shows these things in some way. Use the SETI diagram for ideas.

❸ Color your coded message. At the bottom, show what each symbol in your diagram stands for. Have a classmate try to decode your message.

❹ Draw a picture of what you think the extraterrestrial being would look like.

THINK AND WRITE

Explain why you pictured the extraterrestrial being as you did.

LESSON 4 REVIEW

What are several problems with the SETI approach to the search for other intelligent life in the universe?

✅ DOUBLE CHECK

SECTION B REVIEW

1. Explain how Earth is more like the other inner planets than the outer planets.

2. Explain how astronomers can predict and find previously unknown planets in our solar system.

SECTION C
Stars Above

Have you ever joined others on a clear night for a stargazing party? If not, then try it sometime. It's fun! You can bring a star chart, a pair of binoculars or a telescope, or just your own two eyes and your wondering mind. Whether you enjoy finding patterns of stars or using different kinds of telescopes, this section will help make your stargazing activities a success. You will also explore some possible answers to questions you may have asked about the universe.

What stars appear above the eastern horizon soon after sunset? Do they change? Do some stars seem to be grouped together in a pattern? What star groupings do you recognize? Work through the following investigations. In your Science Log, answer the above questions and describe some of your night-sky observations.

1 THE CELESTIAL SHOW

On any clear night, gaze upward and you can view a sky show. Against a domelike background, patterns of stars march across the sky. You will meet some of the "actors" as they give their stellar performances.

Stars on Stage

Let's set the stage for the nightly parade of stars across the sky. Astronomers use the following model to locate and track stars and planets.

Think of stars as being attached to the inside of a large hollow sphere surrounding the smaller sphere that is the Earth. This imaginary sphere of sky is called the *celestial sphere.* From any point on Earth, you can see only half of the celestial sphere. That half appears as if it meets the Earth at the horizon. In the diagram, you can see the axis, the poles, and the equator of the celestial sphere. They are extensions of the axis, the poles, and the equator of the Earth.

Observe a clear night sky for several hours and you will notice that stars appear to rise above the eastern part of the horizon and set below the western part of the horizon. For convenience, astronomers think of the celestial sphere as rotating. Actually, this is not so. Since the Earth rotates from west to east, the celestial sphere seems to rotate from east to west. One complete rotation takes 23 hours 56 minutes 4.09 seconds—slightly less than a 24-hour day.

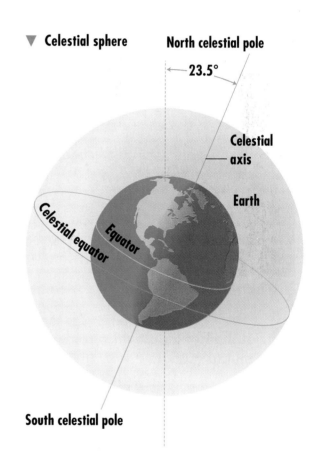

▼ Celestial sphere

North celestial pole

←— 23.5°

Celestial axis

Earth

Celestial equator

Equator

South celestial pole

THINK ABOUT IT

On a certain night at 9:00 P.M., a bright star appears on the horizon. If that star is viewed at 9:00 P.M. on each night during a year, how will its position change?

ACTIVITY

Pictures in the Night Sky

Ancient observers noticed that stars seemed to be arranged in groups, or constellations. These constellations were pictured as figures in the sky. For example, Orion was the great hunter, and Cassiopeia (kas ee oh PEE uh) was the queen on her throne. You can make and project some of these constellations for yourself and others to view.

MATERIALS
- cylindrical oatmeal box (open at one end)
- star charts
- flashlight
- Science Log data sheet

DO THIS

❶ On your paper, draw around the box's bottom.

❷ Choose a constellation, and mark its star pattern heavily in the circle on the paper.

❸ Lay the star pattern face up on top of the sealed end of the box.

❹ Use a pencil to punch a hole in the bottom of the box for each star.

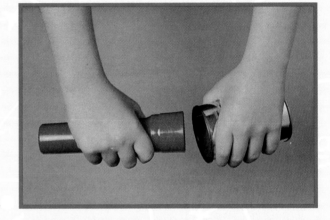

❺ Put the lighted flashlight inside the box, and show your constellation on a wall in a darkened room.

THINK AND WRITE

1. Draw and identify each classmate's constellation. Do research and write a paragraph about the mythology of each constellation.

2. **FORMULATING AND USING MODELS** When making models, you should read through all the steps and gather all the materials you need before you begin. Why do you think you drew the shape of the constellation and placed it on the box before punching holes in the box? What other uses can you think of for your class's constellation projectors?

Finding the North Star

In the last activity, you made a model of a constellation. In this activity, you can use two stars of a well-known constellation to point you to the star closest to the celestial north pole.

MATERIALS
- star chart
- ruler
- Science Log data sheet

DO THIS

1. Find the constellation Ursa Major, which contains the stars known as the Big Dipper, on the star chart.

2. Locate the two stars on the front edge of the Dipper's cup.

3. Line up your ruler along these stars, and then follow the line north until you reach a star.

THINK AND WRITE

1. Which star did you find along the ruler's line?

2. How can you show that this star is indeed the star that is closest to the north celestial pole of the celestial sphere?

Circumpolar stars At the latitude of your location, some stars appear to rise and set just like the sun. Others, called *circumpolar* ("around the pole") *stars*, are always above the horizon. The star you located, Polaris, is the north pole star since it is the star closest to the north celestial pole of the celestial sphere.

The north pole star always appears directly above the Earth's North Pole. Its height above the horizon is the same as the latitude of your location.

ACTIVITY

The Sun's Parade

Did you know that the sun passes through various constellations on the celestial sphere? How could you identify these constellations? In this activity, you will model the Earth's movement around the sun.

MATERIALS
- 12 sheets of poster board
- pencils, crayons
- desk and lamp
- star charts
- Science Log data sheet

DO THIS

1. Draw a constellation pattern on a sheet of poster board for two of the following constellations: Aquarius, Pisces, Aries, Taurus, Gemini, Cancer, Leo, Virgo, Libra, Scorpius, Sagittarius, Capricornus.

2. Clear a large space, and set up the desk with the lighted lamp (sun) on top.

3. Twelve classmates should hold different posters in a circle, facing the sun in the center. They should stand in the order given in step 1, from Aquarius to Capricornus.

4. Other classmates should take turns being the Earth and revolving slowly around the sun, staying between the lamp and the constellations. They should notice both the constellations they face and those behind the sun.

THINK AND WRITE

1. Suppose that while looking away from the sun, you face the constellation Taurus. In which constellation does the sun appear?

2. If you cannot see the sun's position in a constellation because of the sun's light, how can you tell which constellation it is in?

Circle of Animals

In the last activity, you modeled the Earth's revolution around the sun and noted the sun's location in some constellations. Here is how the Earth's revolution is shown on the celestial sphere.

Throughout the year, as the Earth orbits the sun, observers see different constellations in the night sky. Ancient people noted that the sun appeared to move through the same star patterns year after year. They named this path the *ecliptic*. The ecliptic is an imaginary circle on the celestial sphere. It represents the changing position of the sun against the background of stars, as seen from the Earth.

The 12 constellations that lie in the ecliptic's path are called the *zodiac*. This comes from a Greek word that means "circle of animals." Can you see why?

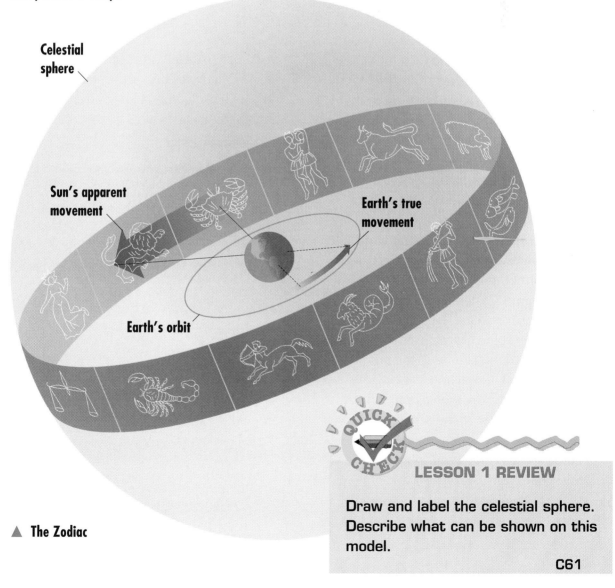

Celestial sphere

Sun's apparent movement

Earth's true movement

Earth's orbit

▲ The Zodiac

LESSON 1 REVIEW

Draw and label the celestial sphere. Describe what can be shown on this model.

2 EYES ON THE SKY

Since the early 1600s, people have had tools to help them view the universe. In this lesson, you can find out about the telescopes that can help you get a better look at the universe.

Starry-Eyed

Read about a group of students who learned firsthand about telescopes.

Seeing Stars

by **Judith E. Rinard**
from ***National Geographic World***

"It was so exciting to see the planets!" says Christina Vitale, 12, a Junior Member from Tucson, Arizona. "My favorite was Saturn. It's just beautiful. We could see its moons and rings. All the rings looked like a rainbow of orange and other colors." Last summer Christina viewed the planets, stars, and galaxies through powerful telescopes when she attended the University of Arizona Alumni Association's Astronomy Camp in Tucson.

The camp session lasted one week. The student astronomers spent the first three days at the university. They toured nearby Flandrau Planetarium and Kitt Peak Observatory. Going behind the scenes, they examined huge telescopes. At the university's mirror lab, they watched as scientists made some of the world's biggest telescope mirrors.

Each evening the campers learned about the night sky and constellations from professional astronomers. They listened to lectures on space, stars, and comets by scientists, experts from NASA, and space artists.

▼ **Telescope domes**

◀ Marian Toro launches her rocket. "I couldn't believe it flew so well."

During the day the campers split up into research teams to do experiments. They investigated planet temperatures, tracked satellites, and built small telescopes and model rockets. Campers came from many different places. One of them, Marian Toro, 17, came from Sells, Arizona. She is a Native American of the Tohono O'odham Nation, once called the Papago. She lives on the reservation, 60 miles west of Tucson.

"I'm really interested in astronomy," says Marian. "Kitt Peak is right on our reservation. It is part of a mountain range that is sacred to us. Our people have always believed that our creator stays in a cave there but dwells throughout the mountains. Long ago, our people looked at the moon and stars to tell if crops would be good. Now people study the stars with telescopes."

The highlight of the week was spending four days and nights using telescopes at the observatory on Mount Lemmon. The telescopes, used by research astronomers, are stationed on the mountaintop, 9,200 feet high.

▲ **Chris Cadle makes a model rocket.**

Through the observatory's open domes, teams used the 40-inch and 60-inch telescopes to observe objects in the night sky. The camp counselors, who were graduate students in astronomy, taught them how to position the huge telescopes to view each object.

"We stayed up until three every morning," says Marian. "I saw Jupiter and its Red Spot. The Ring Nebula, a ring of colored gases, was beautiful."

By the end of the week the campers had great souvenirs—photographs of the night sky they took through special cameras attached to the telescopes. Some of the campers began thinking of careers as astronomers.

"I really enjoyed camp," says Chris Cadle. "It's a neat experience to go to the top of a mountain to see what's out there."

THINK ABOUT IT

Why are many telescopes located on mountaintops?

Catching the Light

Telescopes, like those used by the students at the astronomy camp, gather and focus light. They make distant objects look brighter, clearer, and larger. Read about the invention of two kinds of telescopes used today.

In 1609, Italian scientist Galileo Galilei was the first scientist to use a telescope for astronomy. However, he did not invent it. A Dutch eyeglass maker named Hans Lippershey was looking through different pairs of lenses one day. Suddenly he saw distant objects spring into view as if they were close up. Lippershey had accidentally invented the telescope!

The Lippershey-Galileo telescope is a *refracting* telescope. It uses two glass lenses to refract, or bend, light and focus it to form an image. The objective lens gathers the light. The eyepiece lens magnifies the image. The larger the objective lens, the brighter and clearer the image. Galileo's objective lens was only 26 mil-limeters (1.01 inches) in diameter. Yet it opened up a universe of previously unseen stars to astronomers.

About 60 years later, Isaac Newton invented a *reflecting* telescope. He used mirrors instead of glass lenses to gather and focus light. Newton's objective mirror was only 2.5 centimeters (about 1 inch) in diameter.

THINK ABOUT IT

Why do you think reflecting telescopes with larger and larger objective mirrors are built?

▼ Galileo with his telescope

▲ Sir Isaac Newton

The Refracting Telescope

You can repeat Hans Lippershey's accidental discovery of the refracting telescope. Complete this activity to see for yourself how a refracting telescope works.

MATERIALS
- 2 convex lenses
- Science Log data sheet

DO THIS

① **CAUTION: Never use lenses to look at the sun.** Hold up one lens of the pair, and look through it at a distant object.

② Move the lens back and forth until the image is clear.

③ Keep the first lens in the same position. Then hold the second lens near your eye. Move it back and forth in line with the first lens until you again see a clear image of the object.

THINK AND WRITE

1. When you completed step 2, how did the object appear?

2. When you completed step 3, how did the object appear?

The Reflecting Telescope

Newton reasoned that a certain type of mirror could do the same things as a lens. Complete this activity to discover how a reflecting telescope works.

MATERIALS
- candle in holder
- safety matches
- concave mirror
- table
- magnifying glass
- Science Log data sheet

DO THIS

❶ CAUTION: Be careful near the flame. Your teacher will light the candle and place it at one end of the table.

❷ Place the mirror at the opposite end of the table.

❸ Move the mirror until it reflects the image of the candle onto the wall.

❹ Use the magnifying glass to make the candle image larger.

THINK AND WRITE

1. Describe in your own words how a reflecting telescope works.

2. What advantage does a reflecting telescope with a larger diameter mirror have over one with a smaller mirror?

Skylight!

Most of the telescopes that astronomers use to observe the universe are located on Earth. However, some are located in space. Space-based telescopes allow astronomers to look deeper into the universe. Read about three large telescopes, and find out what makes each one useful.

▲ The Yerkes refractor is often used to track stars and planets.

The largest refracting telescope, with a 1-meter (40-inch) diameter objective lens, is at Yerkes Observatory in Williams Bay, Wisconsin. The telescope was completed in 1897. Since then it has been used to study the planets and to measure star positions and movements. The Yerkes telescope is likely to remain the largest refracting telescope. Glass is heavy and larger lenses would bend, distorting the view.

Reflecting telescopes can be much larger, because mirrors can be made of lightweight material. The Keck I telescope sits at an altitude of 4,203 meters (13,789 feet) on the top of Mauna Kea volcano in Hawaii. It is the largest reflecting telescope in the world. Its main mirror measures 10 meters (33 feet) in diameter. This mirror is made up of 36 smaller hexagonal mirrors. Each smaller mirror's position is controlled by a computer system. As a result, the mirror, as a whole, will focus light properly. Large reflecting telescopes like the Keck I are mostly used to study quasars and faint galaxies.

▼ Keck telescope

Mountaintops offer the best views from Earth. But astronomers have long wanted to put a telescope above the Earth's atmosphere and pollution. In April 1990, the space shuttle *Discovery* placed the Hubble Space Telescope into orbit.

At first, the Hubble Space Telescope did not work as expected. In December 1993, the crew of the space shuttle *Endeavour* made repairs on the telescope. It is now sending back clearer pictures.

Here is what a clear picture means. Think of how a distant car's headlights look as they approach you. At first, the two headlights are a blur, and then, as they get closer, they separate into two distinct lights. The Hubble Space Telescope can separate images of very faint distant stars that are close together better than other telescopes.

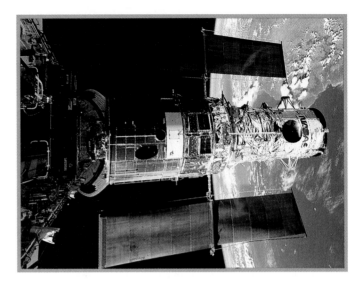

▲ The Hubble Space Telescope is the size of a school bus. Its objective mirror is 2.4 meters (almost 8 feet) in diameter.

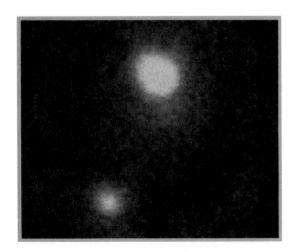

▲ The Hubble Space Telescope's shot of Pluto and its moon Charon (left) is much more distinct than an Earth-based photograph (right).

QUICK CHECK

LESSON 2 REVIEW

Explain in your own words how refracting and reflecting telescopes work. Make a chart to list their similarities and differences.

3 ISLANDS IN THE UNIVERSE

As astronomers on StarBase Earth look deeper into space, they find more and more giant groups of stars rushing away from each other. Where are these star groups going?

The Backbone of Night

A mysterious faint glow in the sky inspired many myths among ancient people. How did the ancients describe this glow?

◄ The star-filled Milky Way Galaxy led to fanciful myths and stories.

Maybe you have seen this softly glowing ribbon of light stretching across the sky. To some ancient Greeks, it looked like a river of milk. So they called it the *Milky Way*.

Ancient people of Botswana, in Africa, saw a different picture. They saw what appeared to be a structure holding up the sky. They called it the *Backbone of Night*.

The ancient Greek thinkers Pythagoras and Democritus hypothesized that the ribbon of light is really a ribbon of stars.

Hundreds of years later, Galileo viewed these stars through his telescope.

Our solar system, the ribbon of stars, and all other stars in the sky form one large group, or *galaxy*. Millions of galaxies spread out like islands in a sea of space. Astronomers still call our galaxy the *Milky Way Galaxy*.

THINK ABOUT IT

How did Pythagoras and Democritus use scientific thinking?

ACTIVITY

It Depends on Your Viewpoint!

The ribbon of stars and the shape of our Milky Way Galaxy suggest the location of our solar system. Based on what you know, where do you think our solar system is located? Now, test your hypothesis.

MATERIALS
- paper to be recycled
- low, flat table
- drawing paper
- Science Log data sheet

DO THIS

1. Make dozens of "stars" by wadding scrap paper into balls.

2. Arrange the paper stars on the table-top in the shape of a spiral, as shown in the diagram. Pile more stars on top of each other in the center, and put fewer along the spiral arms.

3. Look directly across the surface of the table through the paper stars. Draw what you see.

4. Then, look down on the paper stars. Draw what you see.

THINK AND WRITE

1. Compare the pictures you drew in steps 3 and 4 with the diagrams on this page and on page C69. Which drawing is more like this diagram? Which is more like the one on page C69?

2. Where do you now think our solar system is located in our galaxy?

3. **HYPOTHESIZING** A hypothesis is an explanation based on what you already know. In this activity, you formulated and tested a hypothesis. How did your actions test your hypothesis?

▲ Spiral Galaxy

Space in Space

Remember the AU—the unit you used to mark distances in the solar system? Distances beyond the solar system are much greater. Read the following to find out how much greater.

Astronomers do not use kilometers or astronomical units to measure these greater distances. The numbers would be far too large. Instead, they measure distances in *light-years*. A light-year is the distance light travels in a year. With a speed of about 300,000 kilometers (186,000 miles) per second, light travels about 10 trillion kilometers (6 trillion miles) in a year.

Our Milky Way Galaxy contains up to 200 billion stars. The galaxy extends 100,000 light-years from edge to edge. The center is about 10,000 light-years wide. The sun and Earth are about 30,000 light-years from the center of the galaxy, as shown in the diagram.

▼ **Milky Way Galaxy**

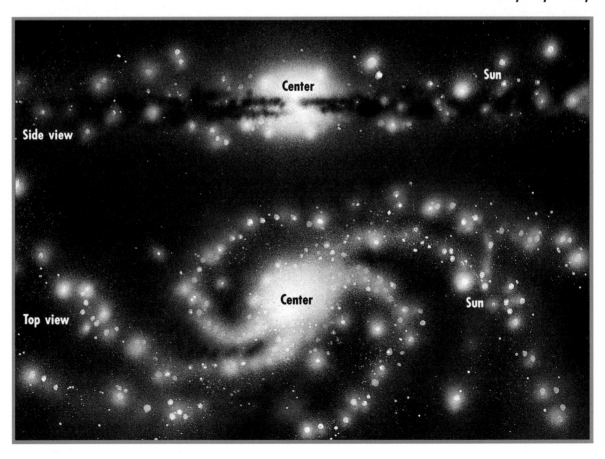

This means that we cannot travel across the galaxy, or even a short way through it. Voyager, traveling much slower than the speed of light, took 12 years to reach Neptune. That distance is only a small fraction of the distance in a light-year.

Telescopes have enabled people on StarBase Earth to locate stars in our own galaxy and to determine its shape. Telescopes can also show astronomers the size and the beauty of other galaxies.

▼ Galaxy M87 has an elliptical shape and contains a thousand billion old red stars.

▼ Galaxy M104 is nicknamed the Sombrero Galaxy because, when seen through a telescope, it looks like a hat. It is 40 million light-years away.

▲ The Andromeda Galaxy is a spiral galaxy like the Milky Way Galaxy. It is one of only three galaxies that can be seen from Earth without a telescope. It is only 2.3 million light-years away.

THINK ABOUT IT

Suppose you could visit a planet like Earth somewhere in each of the galaxies shown. How might the night sky appear from each planet?

Beginnings and Endings

How did the universe begin? Will it ever end? You can act out two theories that astronomers have developed to answer these questions.

▲ Galaxies and clusters of galaxies all speed away from each other as the universe expands.

Many scientists think that about 15 billion years ago, all the matter in the universe was squeezed into a tiny, hot point. Then, in an instant, this matter began to expand outward in all directions, as if a giant explosion had occurred. The matter cooled and clumped together, forming galaxies. Today, the universe is still expanding. The amount of matter and its gravitational attraction will determine whether the expansion continues or stops. Let's act out two possible futures.

On an open field, stand with some of your classmates in a tight circle, facing outward. Other classmates should stand far away from the circle and should observe what happens. You and the others in the circle should begin to walk straight outward until told to stop. Then turn around and look at everyone else's position. Turn to face the center of the

circle and walk inward. When you rejoin the others in a tight circle, stop and face outward again. Now use the theories and your observations to answer the following questions.

What will happen to the galaxies of the universe if the universe continues to expand forever?

What will happen to the galaxies of the universe if gravity stops the expansion and causes them to return to the point where they started?

LESSON 3 REVIEW

❶ How do you know that the sun is located within a spiral arm of our galaxy?

❷ How do some scientists explain how the universe began and what its future might be?

DOUBLE CHECK

SECTION C REVIEW

1. Which stars in the northern hemisphere do not seem to rise and set in the sky? Explain.

2. Why is the Hubble telescope in space able to take better pictures of space objects than the Yerkes telescope in Wisconsin?

Stars Near and Far

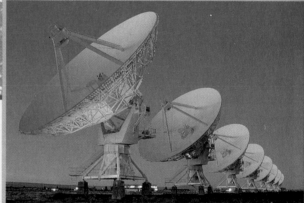

▲ Radio telescopes

Do you ever try to count the stars you see in the night sky? If you do, you will count some bright stars and many more faint stars. Like our star, the sun, the stars you see from StarBase Earth and many billions of fainter stars are all powerful sources of heat and light. This section discusses the kinds of energy that stars produce, why some stars are brighter than others, and how stars are born, age, and burn out.

On a clear night, observe the brighter stars in the sky. What is the color of each bright star? Use a star chart to identify these stars by name. In your Science Log, list each of these and its color. As you work through the following investigations, research the stars in your list. For each one, write three things that you find out.

1 HOME STAR

For about 5 billion years, StarBase Earth has been bathed in the sun's heat and light. An environment has slowly developed in which plants and animals, including humans, can thrive. In this lesson, you will find out what the sun is really like and how it provides the Earth with energy.

Our Sun's Different Looks

StarBase Earth's star, the sun, has been photographed by both Earth-based and orbiting telescopes. Some pictures, taken by regular cameras using visible light, show what we can see with our eyes. Other pictures show a very different kind of sun. See for yourself!

▼ This is a visible-light photograph of sunspots on the sun's surface.

◄ This photograph, taken by *Skylab,* shows a *solar prominence.* It's a huge cloud of burning gas that blasts out from the sun's surface.

◄ This *Skylab* coronagraph was taken by blocking out the sun's surface in order to see the corona, the sun's outer atmosphere.

▲ A radio telescope and a computer made this map of the sun's radio-wave activity. The red spots are clouds of hot gas. They would show up as sunspots in a visible-light photograph.

THINK ABOUT IT

Describe two characteristics of the sun that show it is not a perfectly smooth ball of light.

C75

What's Going On in There?

As you have seen, our sun is much more active than it appears to be. Let's look inside the sun and see how it produces all that energy.

The sun is about 1.4 million kilometers (870,000 miles) in diameter, about 100 times the diameter of the Earth. It is large enough to hold one million Earths. Like all stars, the sun is a large globe of hot gas.

Photosphere
The photosphere, or "sphere of light," is the part of the sun that we see. The sun's energy is given off here, at the surface. The surface temperature is about 5,500 degrees Celsius. At this temperature, the light given off appears to us as yellowish white or orange.

Radiative Layer
This area is warmed by the core and in turn, warms the next layer. The temperature is about 3 million degrees Celsius.

Convective Layer
The energy is moved through this layer the same way it is moved by gas bubbles to the surface of boiling water. The temperature here is about 1.1 million degrees Celsius.

Core
The hydrogen gas at the core of the sun is compressed and heated by the weight of the outer layers. At a temperature of about 14 million degrees Celsius, the hydrogen atoms combine to make helium. The energy produced by this nuclear reaction radiates outward to heat the sun's gaseous outer layers. Only gravity keeps the sun from blowing apart.

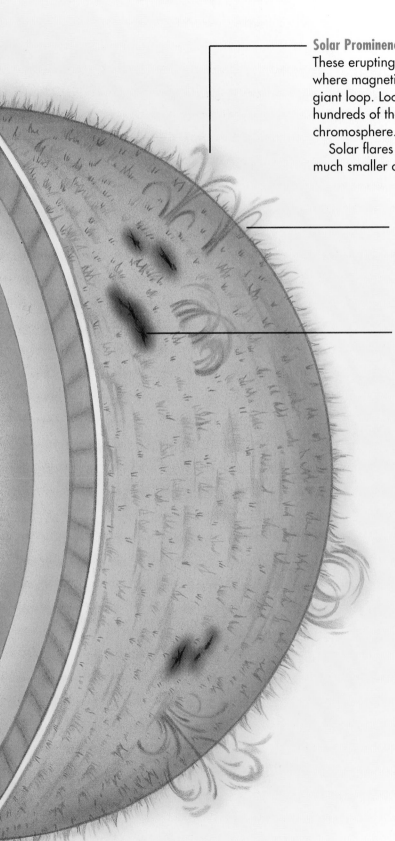

Solar Prominences

These erupting clouds of gas often occur near sunspots where magnetic fields force the rising hot gas into a giant loop. Looped solar prominences can extend hundreds of thousands of kilometers above the chromosphere.

Solar flares are brighter than prominences. They are much smaller and usually disappear after a few minutes.

Corona

The top layer of the sun's atmosphere reaches a temperature of 2 million degrees Celsius! The corona can be seen only during a total solar eclipse.

Sunspots

Sunspots are cooler areas on the sun's surface. Strong magnetic fields can block the flow of heat to the surface.

Chromosphere

The chromosphere, or "circle of color," surrounds the photosphere. Here the temperature reaches 100,000 degrees Celsius.

THINK ABOUT IT

A spacecraft surface that faces the sun becomes very hot. How could you protect a spacecraft from overheating?

ACTIVITY

X Marks the Spot!

You've learned what makes up the sun and its layers. By observing sunspots, you can find out something very important about what the sun does.

DO THIS

① **CAUTION: Never look directly at the sun with your eyes alone or through an eyepiece. You could be permanently blinded!** Point the telescope so that a magnified image of the sun shows through the eyepiece and onto the paper or cardboard.

② If you use binoculars, block one eyepiece with the small piece of cardboard and tape.

MATERIALS
- small telescope, or binoculars with supporting stand
- large sheet of white paper or cardboard
- small piece of cardboard
- tape
- sheet of thin tracing paper
- Science Log data sheet

③ Note the sunspots that appear on the white paper or cardboard.

④ Lay the tracing paper over the cardboard, and trace the outline of the sun. Record the positions of the sunspots over several days.

⑤ About one month later, record the positions of the sunspots again.

THINK AND WRITE

1. What can you conclude about the positions of the sunspots over several days?

2. When observing the sun's surface one month later, did you see any of the sunspots that you had observed before?

3. What can you conclude about the sun's movement, based on your responses to questions 1 and 2? Explain.

The Sun's Bubble

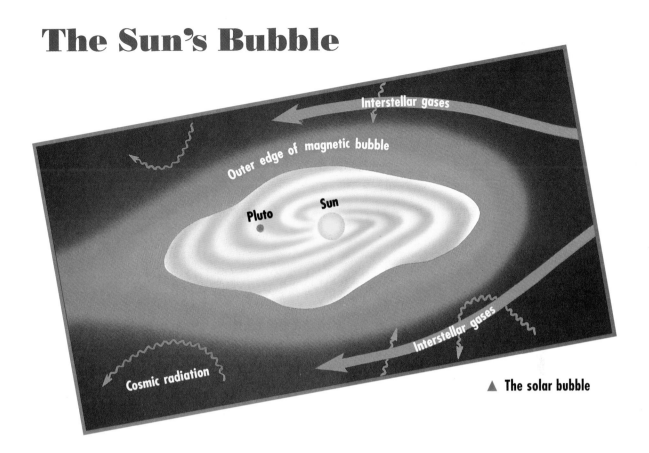

The solar bubble

You probably wouldn't think that it's windy out there in our solar system, but it is. Surprised? Read to find out what the sun blows through the solar system.

It doesn't seem to make sense that there could be a wind in space. After all, space is empty, isn't it? Not really! The sun's corona gives off fast-moving gas that becomes the *solar wind*. The solar wind is a gale of charged atomic particles. These particles race away from the sun at speeds of up to 3 million kilometers (1.9 billion miles) per hour. They generate electric currents and magnetic fields that fill the space in our solar system. The currents flow in a great, thin sheet that ripples as the sun rotates. The magnetic fields form a huge bubble around our solar system. This bubble protects all nine planets from the cosmic radiation that exists in the space between the stars. The cosmic radiation would be harmful to life on Earth. Within the protective bubble are gases that are very hot. However, the gases are spread so thin that people on Earth and astronauts in space do not burn up.

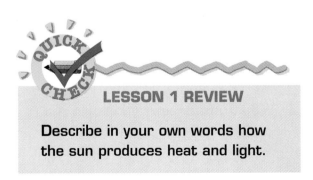

LESSON 1 REVIEW

Describe in your own words how the sun produces heat and light.

2 STAR LIGHT, STAR BRIGHT

Almost all stars give off blindingly bright light, but only our sun appears very bright to us. Some stars appear to be brighter than others. Why is this? How do we rank stars by their brightness? In this lesson, you will explore and answer these questions and others.

ACTIVITY

MATERIALS
- 2 lamps
- bulbs of various wattages: 40, 60
- darkened corridor or room
- Science Log data sheet

Burning Bright!

What causes some stars to look so bright and others to look so dim? This activity will help you test your hypothesis.

DO THIS

1. Place two lighted lamps, one with a 40-watt and the other with a 60-watt bulb, halfway down the corridor. Observe both from the corridor's end.

2. Move the lamp with the 60-watt bulb to the far end of the corridor. Again, observe both from the opposite end of the corridor.

3. Observe bulbs of different wattages at a variety of distances.

THINK AND WRITE

1. In step 1, which lamp was brighter? How did step 2 change the apparent brightness of the two lamps?

2. What other observations did you make with bulbs of different wattages at different distances?

3. Based on your observations, what two factors affect the brightness of stars as they appear to us?

4. **EXPERIMENTING** A hypothesis should be tested by an experiment. How completely did this experiment test your hypothesis?

From Bright to Dim

Today's astronomers use an ancient way of comparing the brightness of stars. You can use this method to find the brightness of any star that you see.

You have probably seen the stars Sirius and Rigel in the night sky. Sirius, called the *Dog Star,* is in the constellation Canis Major, *The Great Dog.* Rigel is in the constellation Orion. Both stars are very bright. In fact, Sirius is the brightest star in the night sky.

▼ **Canis Major (left) and Orion (right)**

Astronomers use the word **magnitude** to refer to a star's brightness. *Apparent magnitude* refers to how bright a star appears to us. Apparent magnitude is based on how much light a star gives off and how far away from Earth the star is.

Over 2,000 years ago, the Greek astronomer Hipparchus (hih PAHR kuhs) classified stars that were visible to the unaided eye into six magnitudes. Magnitude 6 stars were the dimmest. Magnitude 1 stars were the brightest. This scale has been extended to include brighter and fainter stars. Rigel has an apparent magnitude of 0, brighter even than a magnitude 1 star. Sirius has an apparent magnitude of –1.5, even brighter. Today, with very large telescopes, we can see stars as dim as magnitude 25.

The measure of a star's actual brightness is its *absolute magnitude.* Now let's look again at Sirius and Rigel. Which star is really brighter? In terms of absolute magnitude, Rigel is magnitude –6. Sirius has an absolute magnitude of only 1.4. Sirius appears to be brighter because it is much closer to Earth. It is only 9 light-years away (the distance light travels through space in 9 years), while Rigel is 815 light-years away!

▼ This star chart of the midevening winter sky shows some of the brighter stars and their apparent magnitudes. Find Rigel and Sirius. The chart shows that they are among the brightest of stars.

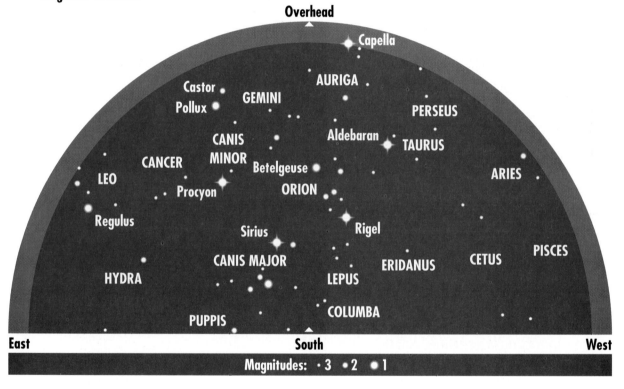

THINK ABOUT IT

Look at the star chart above. What other stars can you find that have very bright apparent magnitudes? Which constellations are these stars in?

Let's Get Warmed Up!

Visible light is just a small part of the energy given off by stars. Another form is infrared radiation, or heat.

We detect light with our eyes. Our bodies detect infrared radiation as heat. An infrared photograph can be used to identify heat sources. White and yellow represent the hottest areas. Blue and green represent the coolest. Astronomers gain useful information about planets, stars, and galaxies from infrared photographs.

Look at the photograph below. Which part shows the most heat? What do you think the man is holding that is so hot? Notice that the man's hand and face—his bare skin—show up warm or hot. Yet the areas around his eyes show up very cool. How do you explain this?

THINK ABOUT IT

How might an infrared photograph of the Earth be useful to scientists?

▼ **Infrared photo**

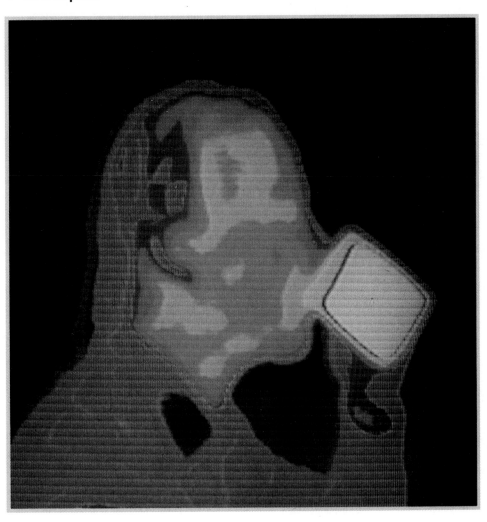

Riding the Waves!

Stars give off a wide range of energy. You have explored two forms of this energy—light and heat. The diagram shows other forms of energy that astronomers measure and record.

▼ Gamma rays are used to preserve foods at less cost than canning or freezing methods.

▼ X-rays are used to take pictures of the inside of the body.

▼ Ultraviolet waves from the sun can burn your skin. Sunscreen lotion protects you from these waves.

▼ Ordinary photographs show the same things that our eyes see in visible light.

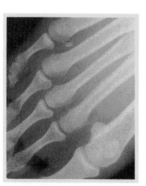

| Gamma rays | X-rays | Ultraviolet waves | Visible-light waves |

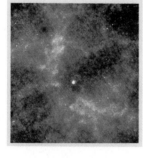

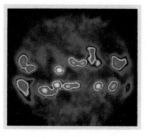

▲ Gamma rays come from very energetic objects in space.

▲ X-rays in space come from areas around stars and from exploding stars.

▲ Ultraviolet waves given off by young stars in a cloud of gas make the gas glow magenta.

▲ A visible-light photograph of a star cluster shows thousands of tightly grouped stars.

Visible light represents only a small part of this energy. Visible light divides into colors when it passes through a prism, a wet atmosphere, or a soap bubble. What are the colors?

All energy travels through space as waves. The waves all travel at the speed of light. But some waves are very long, and some are very short. All these forms of energy can be produced on Earth artificially.

▼ Infrared waves are felt by our bodies as heat.

▼ Microwaves can be used to cook food.

▼ A radar system bounces radio signals off a target and back to the receiver. The radar echo is displayed as an image on a screen.

▼ This radio map shows the intense radio waves coming from the center of our galaxy.

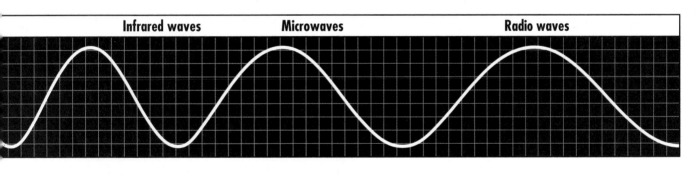

| Infrared waves | Microwaves | Radio waves |

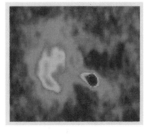

▲ This picture of the center of the Milky Way Galaxy was taken by an infrared camera.

▲ This is a microwave picture of the radiation left over from the beginning of the universe.

LESSON 2 REVIEW

Does a star's apparent magnitude tell everything about how bright the star is? Explain.

3 "LIVES" OF THE STARS

Stars come in many different sizes, temperatures, and colors. As you will see, different stars often lead very different "lives."

You're Not in My Class!

The absolute magnitude of a star is determined by its size, mass, color, and temperature. The diagram below shows you how scientists classify stars according to their properties.

Study the diagram on page C87. Note that temperature readings are along the bottom and absolute magnitude readings are at the left.

The *main sequence* is a group of stars that lie along the curved line running from the top left to the bottom right. Many stars, including the sun, lie on this sequence.

From top to bottom, the stars go from hottest to coolest and from largest to smallest. So, in the main sequence, a large size or mass and a hot temperature mean a high absolute magnitude.

Notice that the diagram also shows stars that lie outside the main sequence. Betelgeuse (BET uhl jooz), in the constellation Orion, is a red star. If it were of an average size and mass, it would not be very bright. But Betelgeuse is a super giant—it's huge! Its size makes up for its low temperature. So Betelgeuse has a very high absolute magnitude. Stars that lie below the main sequence are very small stars. They are usually white or red. Use the diagram to answer these questions.

1. Where is the sun in the diagram? What color is it? What is its temperature? Is it a large, a medium, or a small star?

2. The sun is so close to us that its apparent magnitude is –27! What is its absolute magnitude?

3. Which other star on the diagram is much like the sun?

▼ **Observatory**

C86

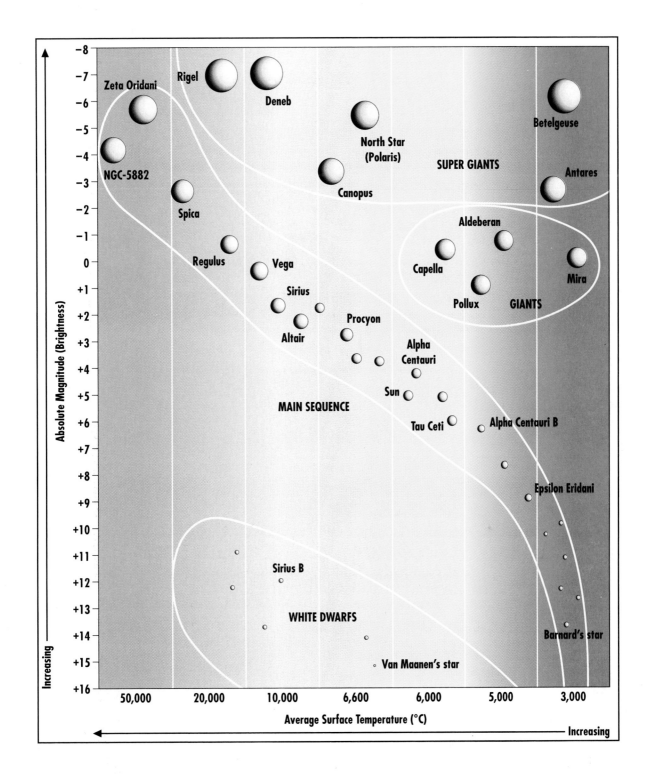

THINK ABOUT IT

What does knowing the absolute magnitude of a star tell you about that star?

Once and Future Stars

Stars have different life spans, just as Earth's creatures do.
Follow the life cycles of the two stars here.

Blue star
A blue star is hotter and brighter
than a yellow star.

Supergiant
The blue star becomes a supergiant
that burns fuel quickly.

Supernova
A supergiant may explode
into a supernova.

Neutron star
After the explosion, the star's
core may shrink and become a
neutron star.

New star forms

New star forms

Yellow star
A yellow star, like our sun, is a relatively small and cool star.

Nebula
All stars probably begin in a *nebula,* a swirling cloud of dust.

Red giant
As a yellow star uses its fuel, it begins to grow larger. It becomes a red giant, and its surface temperature drops.

Black dwarf
When the white dwarf stops giving off light, it becomes a black dwarf, just a black cinder.

White dwarf
When its outer layer blows off, the star shrinks and becomes a white dwarf. It shines with very bright white light.

Black hole

If the core shrinks to a point, it becomes a black hole. Not even light can escape a black hole's gravity.

QUICK CHECK

LESSON 3 REVIEW

Our sun will become a red giant, but it will never become a supernova. Explain.

DOUBLE CHECK

SECTION D REVIEW

Our sun and Capella are both yellow stars. The sun's absolute magnitude is 4.8; Capella's absolute magnitude is 0.4. Compare the sun and Capella. How will their lives differ?

C89

I REFLECT

It's time to think about the ideas you have discovered during your investigations. Think, too, about your many accomplishments.

SUMMARIZE

Answer the following in your Science Log.

1. What **I Wonder** questions have you answered in your investigations, and what new questions have you asked?

2. What have you discovered, and how have your ideas changed?

3. Did any of your discoveries surprise you? Explain.

Jupiter

Uranu

Earth

Mars

Venus

Sun

THE SO

Pluto

Saturn

AR SYSTEM

CONNECT IDEAS

1. How have observations of the movements of the Earth, the moon, and the sun been used for keeping time in days, months, and years?

2. How are stars different from planets?

3. How has technology helped us increase our knowledge of the universe?

4. How do the moon and the sun affect the tides?

5. Compare the inner planets and the outer planets, and explain how the Earth differs from all other planets.

SCIENCE PORTFOLIO

1. Complete your Science Experiences Record.

2. Choose one or two samples of your best work from each section to include in your Science Portfolio.

3. On A Guide to My Science Portfolio, tell why you chose each sample.

I SHARE

Scientists share their discoveries and ideas and learn from one another. How can you share what you've learned?

Decide

▶ what you want to say.

▶ what the best way is to get your message across.

Share

▶ what you did and why.

▶ what worked and what didn't work.

▶ what conclusions you have drawn.

▶ what else you'd like to find out.

Find Out

▶ what classmates liked about what you shared—and why.

▶ what questions they have.

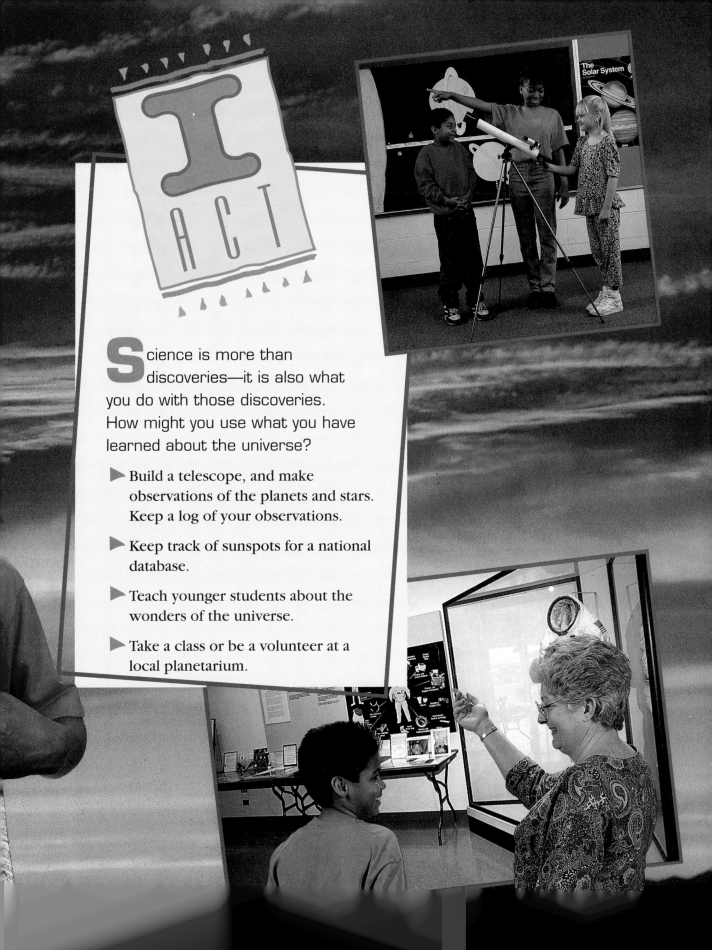

I ACT

Science is more than discoveries—it is also what you do with those discoveries. How might you use what you have learned about the universe?

▶ Build a telescope, and make observations of the planets and stars. Keep a log of your observations.

▶ Keep track of sunspots for a national database.

▶ Teach younger students about the wonders of the universe.

▶ Take a class or be a volunteer at a local planetarium.

THE LANGUAGE OF SCIENCE

The language of science helps people communicate clearly when they talk about the universe. Here are some vocabulary words you can use when you talk about StarBase Earth and the universe with friends, family, and others.

asteroids—small rocky bodies that orbit the sun between the orbits of Mars and Jupiter. **(C45)**

astronomer—a scientist who studies the planets, stars, and other celestial objects in order to understand the universe. **(C15)**

astronomical unit (AU)—the distance between the Earth and the sun, about 150 million kilometers (93 million miles). This unit is used for measuring distances in the solar system. **(C38)**

axis—an imaginary line around which a planet rotates. **(C57)**

▼ **Earth's axis is tilted 23$\frac{1}{2}$°**

Axis

circumpolar—around the poles. Circumpolar stars always appear to circle either the north celestial pole or the south celestial pole. **(C59)**

comets—chunks of ice and rock that travel around the sun in a variety of orbits. Some of the orbits are very long and some are quite short. **(C52)**

▼ **Comet**

Tail

Head

constellation—a group of stars that appear to make a picture of some sort in the night sky. Ursa Major is a constellation. **(C58)**

▼ **Constellation**

core—the central part of any star. In the core, continual nuclear reactions change hydrogen into helium and energy. **(C76)**

corona—the uppermost gaseous layer of the sun's atmosphere. The corona is visible only during an eclipse. **(C77)**

crater—a deep impression left in the surface of a planet or moon by the impact of a meteorite. **(C34)**

▼ **Crater on the moon**

eclipse—a temporary blocking out of the moon (when the Earth passes between the moon and the sun) or of the sun (when the moon passes between the Earth and the sun). **(C22)**

▼ **Eclipse of the sun**

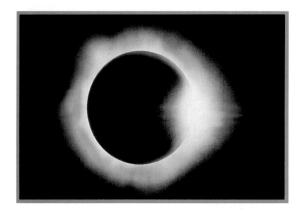

ellipse—a flattened circle, the shape of the orbits of planets and comets. **(C17)**

▼ **Ellipse**

equinox—a day, occurring once in the spring and once in the fall, on which there are equal periods of daylight and night. **(C28)**

galaxy—a vast collection of stars. Our solar system is in the Milky Way galaxy. **(C69)**

gravity/gravitation—the force of attraction between every particle of matter and every other particle of matter. **(C21)**

light-year—the distance light travels in a year, about 10 trillion kilometers (6 trillion miles). **(C71)**

magnitude—the degree of brightness of a star. *Apparent magnitude* is how bright a star appears to observers on Earth. This magnitude is determined by the star's distance from Earth and its actual brightness. *Absolute magnitude* is how bright a star really is. This magnitude is determined by the star's size, color, and mass. **(C81)**

meteor—a meteoroid that enters Earth's atmosphere. When meteors enter Earth's atmosphere, they burn, causing bright flashes of light. **(C53)**

meteorite—a meteor that plunges to Earth in one piece. **(C53)**

▼ **Meteorite impact crater in Arizona**

meteoroid—dust, gas particles, and rocks thrown off by comets. **(C53)**

moon—the Earth's natural satellite. Other planets also have moons. **(C14)**

orbit—the path one object takes around another, such as the path of the Earth around the sun or of the moon around the Earth. **(C16)**

phase—one of the apparent shapes of the moon. The full moon is one phase. **(C30)**

▼ **Phases of the moon**

planet—one of the nine large, solid, nearly spherical objects revolving around the sun. The planets are Mercury, Venus, Earth, Mars, Jupiter, Saturn, Uranus, Neptune, and Pluto. **(C37)**

revolution—the movement of one object around another. One complete revolution of the Earth around the sun takes one Earth year. **(C27)**

rotation—the spinning of a body about its axis. One period of rotation of the Earth takes one Earth day. **(C26)**

satellite—a natural or artificial body that orbits another body. The moon is a natural satellite. **(C43)**

solar system—the sun, its family of planets (including Earth), and all the asteroids, comets, and meteors. **(C37)**

solstice—a day that has the most hours of daylight (summer solstice) or the fewest hours of daylight (winter solstice). **(C28)**

star—a large globe of hot gas, shining by its own light. Different stars go through different stages in their lives. The sun will someday become a *red giant* and then a *white dwarf*. Massive stars may explode into incredibly bright objects called *supernovas*. Then, collapsing in on themselves, they may become *black holes,* from which no light escapes. Some massive stars explode and become very small and dense *neutron stars*. **(C76)**

sun—the star in our solar system. **(C75)**

▼ **Sun's layers**

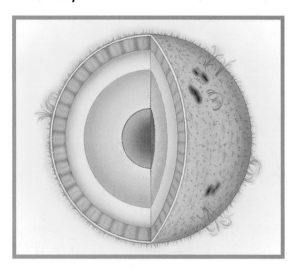

telescope—a device that makes distant objects appear larger, brighter, and more detailed. A *refracting telescope* uses glass lenses to gather light and focus the image. A *reflecting telescope* uses mirrors for the same results. **(C64)**

universe—everything there is—all the planets, solar systems, galaxies, gas, dust, and matter everywhere. **(C72)**

COOKING WITH SCIENCE

Phase Changes

Andre filled a tall glass with ice cubes and added lemonade. A few minutes later, water was dripping from the outside of the glass. Andre wondered why.

In the ice-cube experiment, you observed *phase changes*. The three states, or *phases*, of matter are solid, liquid, and gas. When the ice cubes melted, they changed from one phase (solid) to another (liquid). When the water evaporated, it changed from a liquid to a gas.

Phase changes are caused by heating or cooling a material. Water, for example, is a liquid at room temperature. When its temperature is lowered to its freezing point of 0 degrees Celsius (32 degrees Fahrenheit), it changes to a solid: ice. You can see this happen by placing an ice-cube tray full of water in the freezer. When you allowed the ice to sit in a cup at room temperature, it changed to its liquid phase. If enough heat is applied to make water boil, it changes from a liquid to a gas. This

▲ **Condensation is an example of a phase change.**

occurs at its boiling point of 100 degrees Celsius (212 degrees Fahrenheit). Other materials have different freezing and boiling points.

Other phase changes include *condensation* and *evaporation*. You observe condensation when water droplets collect on a glass containing a cold drink. That's what Andre saw on his glass of lemonade. The water vapor (gas) in the air is cooled when it touches the cold glass, so the water changes back to its liquid phase. You saw evaporation in your ice-cube experiment. The water gradually disappeared as it changed from a liquid to a gas.

THINK ABOUT IT

Name some examples from nature in which phase changes take place.

Going Through a Phase

In the last activity, you observed an example of a phase change in water. Here are other examples of phase changes.

▲ Although you do not normally see liquids evaporate into water vapor, you can see evidence that it is happening.

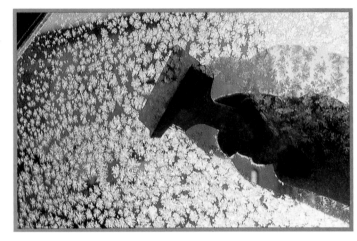

▲ The frost you see on a car window is water vapor that froze as it touched the window.

▲ To go from a liquid to a solid, the gelatin had to be refrigerated.

▲ Water in the air becomes liquid as it cools on the side of the glass.

THINK ABOUT IT

What would you have to do to make juice bars out of juice? Explain why.

It's Natural

In the poem "January," poet and novelist John Updike describes some everyday phase changes.

January

by **John Updike**

The days are short,
The sun a spark
Hung thin between
The dark and dark.

Fat snowy footsteps
Track the floor.
Milk bottles burst
Outside the door.

The river is
A frozen place
Held still beneath
The trees of lace.

The sky is low.
The wind is gray.
The radiator
Purrs all day.

LESSON 3 REVIEW

❶ What determines which phase the water you find will be in?

❷ Think of something you eat that goes through phase changes when it is cooked, and describe whether the phases are solid, liquid, or gas.

DOUBLE CHECK

SECTION A REVIEW

1. Identify three physical properties of a food item of your choice and tell which property best identifies it.

2. How does SI help scientists?

Changes in Matter

Students in Mr. Washington's
class had begun to bring in the ingredients
for their recipes. They found that many of their recipes used the same
basic ingredients—flour, salt, sugar, vegetable oil. Yet the foods would
taste very different after different amounts of the ingredients had been
combined in various ways.

Like the ingredients in recipes, matter combines in various ways to
make all the substances in the world. How do recipe ingredients combine? Common processes used in cooking include mixing, stirring, and
heating. Do similar processes produce the various substances in our
world? Keep careful notes in your Science Log as you work through
the following investigations.

1 ATOMS AND ELEMENTS

The ingredients Mr. Washington's students are using are all made up of matter. But what is matter made up of? You'll find the answer to this question in these investigations.

Small, Smaller, Smallest

When you're served peas, do you ever eat them one at a time? How about grains of rice or grains of salt? In this investigation, you'll find out how difficult it is to see and handle very small objects.

Pour out a small amount of sand. Using your fingers, try to separate just one grain of sand from the rest. It isn't easy, is it?

Jaime is planning to make the dish *arroz con pollo* (ah ROHZ kahn PAW yaw). He needs to mix a number of different ingredients together to make it. If you separated *arroz con pollo* into its smallest parts, you would have containers of rice, chicken, vegetables, water, and spices. Each of these ingredients, however, is made of much smaller particles.

The basic building block of matter is the *atom*. A single grain of salt or a grain of rice is made up of millions of atoms. Atoms are too small to be seen, except with very powerful microscopes.

THINK ABOUT IT

▲ Ingredients for *arroz con pollo*

How would you explain to a person that all matter is made of particles too small to see?

Mystery Object

Scientists use indirect ways to learn about atoms. They can do things to a material, such as add chemicals, and then observe what happens. The way the material reacts gives them information about the atoms in it. Here's an activity that will help you discover properties of an unseen object.

MATERIALS
- mystery object
- 40-cm x 60-cm piece of cardboard
- 1 marble
- Science Log data sheet

DO THIS

1 Work with two or three classmates. One of you should get the "mystery object" from your teacher.

2 Without showing the object to your partners, place the object on the table and hold the cardboard over the object.

3 Other students should take turns gently rolling the marble under the cardboard to hit the object. Keep a record of the angle at which the marble approaches the object and the angle at which it bounces off. Observe the sound made when the marble strikes the object.

4 The partners should decide what they think the object is and give reasons for their decision.

THINK AND WRITE

1. What senses did you use to make your observations? What properties did you identify? What properties were you unable to describe?

2. **FORMULATING AND USING MODELS** Models can be used to represent methods or structures. What did you model in this activity? How does the model help you understand how scientists have learned about atoms?

Is There Iron in Your Cereal?

You may not be able to see atoms, but you can sometimes observe very small amounts of some kinds of materials. Sometimes materials that are mixed together can be easily separated. For example, your cereal may be made up of several different food ingredients. In this activity, you can discover one of them. You might be surprised at what you can find in your breakfast cereal.

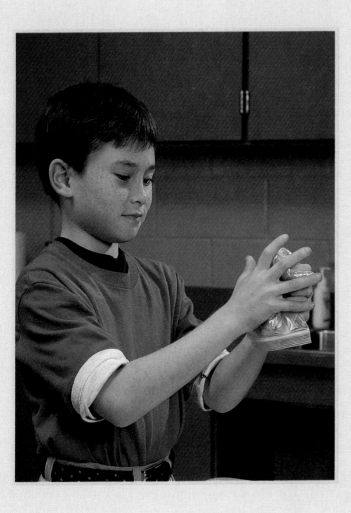

DO THIS

1 Put the cereal and some water in the small bag. Seal the bag.

2 Put this bag and the bar magnet in the larger bag.

3 Knead the cereal to break it into small bits. Position the magnet near a corner of the smaller bag. Record your observations.

THINK AND WRITE

1. What was the substance you observed near the magnet?

2. Why is this substance in cereal?

It's Elementary

All matter is made up of atoms. Some substances have only one kind of atom. Others have more than one. Read to find out what these substances are.

The iron you observed in the cereal is an element. An **element** is made up of only one kind of atom. Iron atoms are all the same, and they all behave in the same way. Scientists have identified 109 elements, which means that there are 109 different kinds of atoms that we know of. Some other elements besides iron are oxygen, hydrogen, copper, uranium, carbon, and sodium.

Of course there are more than 109 kinds of matter. As you look around your classroom, you can probably see quite a few. This is because atoms combine in thousands and thousands of different ways. For example, water is not an element. It consists of a combination of the elements hydrogen and oxygen.

Few of the things you see around you are pure elements. For example, you may be sitting at a desk that has some parts made of wood or plastic and others made of steel. Wood, plastic, and steel are made of molecules that consist of many different atoms. A substance made of two or more elements chemically combined is called a **compound.** There are thousands of natural and artificially-made compounds.

When two or more atoms combine they form a **molecule.** A water molecule consists of one atom of oxygen and two atoms of hydrogen. Any other combination of oxygen and hydrogen would not have the properties of water.

Water molecule ▶

▲ Lady Falls, British Columbia, Canada

QUICK CHECK

LESSON 1 REVIEW

❶ Can you tell by looking at something whether it is an element? Explain.

❷ How does iron differ from wood?

2 MIXTURES

Because many of his students had been trying out recipes, Mr. Washington decided to talk about something they'd been doing a lot of—mixing. You can do some of the same activities his class did to learn about different kinds of mixtures.

ACTIVITY

Separating Mixtures

Sometimes we have to separate the ingredients in a mixture. For example, some kinds of beans need to be soaked in water, which is then discarded before the beans are cooked. How can the bean-and-water mixture be separated into the parts that make it up?

MATERIALS
- 2 clear plastic cups
- dried pinto beans
- water
- Science Log data sheet

DO THIS

❶ Fill one cup $\frac{1}{4}$ full of beans.

❷ Pour in water up to the halfway point on the cup.

❸ Find a way to separate the mixture so that the beans end up in one cup and the water in the other.

THINK AND WRITE

Were you able to remove all the water from the beans? Why not? What utensils would have helped you do a better job?

Mixed Together

Most of the recipes the students in Mr. Washington's class are preparing call for mixing different ingredients. Are all the mixtures alike? Read to find out.

In the activity, you probably separated the two substances by pouring the water into the second cup, leaving the beans in the first cup. This method of separating a mixture is called *decanting.* Another method is using a filter or a strainer. Think of times in the kitchen when a filter or a strainer is used to separate the solid parts of a mixture from the liquid parts.

▲ **Utensils for straining and filtering**

In a **mixture,** the parts keep their own properties, even though the parts are mixed together. Because of this, they can be separated by physical means. Some mixtures, like fruit juice, have the same composition throughout. You can't see the separate ingredients. You might not even be able to tell they are mixtures when you look at them. Other mixtures, like vegetable soup, are not the same throughout. The different substances in them can be seen as separate.

▼ **Common food mixtures**

THINK ABOUT IT

All of the substances pictured above are mixtures. Which ones have the same composition throughout? In which can you see the separate ingredients?

Pasta and More

Dominic is preparing a pasta dish for the food festival. He found a poem about pasta that he liked, and he decided to include it on his pasta poster. Here it is.

Ready For Spaghetti
by Peggy Guthart

Pasta ribbons, pasta bows,
Pasta spirals, pasta O's,
Some is white and some is green,
Some comes with spinach in between.

It's shaped like tubes and wheels and strings
And named all sorts of funny things:
Ravioli, tortellini,
Macaroni and linguini.

In my book it is supreme;
I like it best with peas and cream.
Pasta — there's no way to beat it.
The only thing to do is eat it!

THINK ABOUT IT

What mixture is mentioned in the poem? Could it be easily separated into its various ingredients?

Solutions

Terry made a pitcher of lemonade. She added water and sugar to lemon juice and then stirred. As she put the pitcher in the refrigerator, she thought to herself that it certainly wouldn't be easy to separate this mixture. What do you think?

Terry's lemonade is a solution. **Solutions** are mixtures in which the composition is the same throughout. Solutions are made of two parts—the *solvent* and the *solute.* Most of a solution is the solvent, or the material in which the solute is dissolved. The solute is the material that dissolves in the solvent. When you make a fruit-flavored drink, water is the solvent and the flavored powder and sugar you add are the solutes.

Do you know the favorite solution of people in Japan, China, and England? It's tea, of course! Many drinks are solutions. Coffee is another popular solution, as are soft drinks. What is the solvent in all these drinks?

THINK ABOUT IT

List four solutions you are familiar with. In each, what is the solvent and what is the solute?

▶ Solutions are a kind of mixture.

Suspensions

Heather's project is an example of another kind of mixture. Read and find out why.

Heather is planning to bring her aunt Ronnie's famous green salad to the festival. As she watches her aunt prepare the salad dressing, she notices that the spices settle to the bottom, while the oil and vinegar separate into two layers at the top. "Oh, no!" Heather wails. "I can't take the dressing to school like that! If everyone has to shake it up, it's sure to end up all over the walls!"

"Don't worry," says her aunt calmly, as she puts the dressing in her blender and turns the blender on for a minute. "Just blend the dressing well, and the ingredients will stay mixed for a while."

Heather's aunt has made a *suspension,* a mixture in which one of the parts is a liquid. Unlike in a solution, the particles settle out of a suspension, because they do not dissolve in the liquid.

Suspensions are very common in everyday life. For example, many of the liquid medicines you are familiar with are probably suspensions. Have you noticed that paint stores have special machines that shake paint cans to mix the ingredients before you take the paint home? That's because many paints are also suspensions.

THINK ABOUT IT

Suppose your doctor prescribes a medicine that is labeled "Shake well before using." What do you know about the medicine? Why is it important to follow this direction?

▶ Blenders help mix suspensions.

Colloids

Janine and her father are making another kind of mixture.
Read how it is different from a suspension.

Janine and her father are making a gelatin dessert mold. The gelatin in the dessert is a mixture called a **colloid.** In a colloid, the particles do not dissolve, but they are so small that they do not settle out. They remain suspended because they are constantly moving.

There are several kinds of colloids. Some of Mr. Washington's students are using colloids in their recipes. You can probably find examples of all of them in your home. *Gels,* such as jelly, have liquid particles suspended in a solid. The gelatin Janine and her father are making is a gel. Another familiar gel is stick deodorant. With an adult, look in your family's medicine cabinet for other examples of gels.

Mayonnaise and milk are emulsions. *Emulsions* are made of two liquids. In milk, the two liquids are cream and skimmed milk, which is largely water. Unprocessed milk, if left to sit, will separate into two layers, with the cream at the top. In milk processing plants, the cream and skimmed milk are emulsified, or mixed evenly throughout, so that the two liquids do not separate.

Before pouring the gelatin into the mold, Janine's father sprayed the mold with a nonstick cooking spray so that the gelatin could be easily removed

from the mold. The cooking spray is an aerosol. *Aerosols* are colloids in which solid or liquid particles are suspended in a gas. You may have aerosols at home, such as nonstick cooking spray, air fresheners, and cleaning products. Fog and smoke are also examples of aerosols. What is suspended in the gas in each case?

THINK ABOUT IT

Why are colloids important to the food industry?

A C T I V I T Y

Make Your Own Colloid

Janine and her father made a gelatin dessert. In this activity, you'll make a gelatin dessert, too. Once it has set, you can enjoy eating the colloid.

MATERIALS
- package of presweet-ened gelatin dessert powder
- water
- measuring cup
- mixing bowl
- spoon
- refrigerator
- banana
- plastic knife
- paper cups
- plastic spoons
- Science Log data sheet

DO THIS

1 **CAUTION: Stir the gelatin and water carefully so that you do not splash boiling water on yourself.** Read and follow the directions on the package of gelatin. Your teacher will boil the water and pour it into your mixing bowl.

2 Place the gelatin mix in the refrigerator, allowing it to partially set.

3 Remove the gelatin from the refrigerator, and slice the peeled banana into the gelatin. Stir the mixture and return it to the refrigerator. After the gelatin sets completely, enjoy it with your classmates.

THINK AND WRITE

Is your gelatin dessert a suspension as well as a colloid? Explain.

A C T I V I T Y

Solution or Colloid?

Colloids and solutions look the same throughout. How can anyone tell them apart? Find out in this activity.

MATERIALS

- 4 clear plastic cups
- tea
- flashlight
- milk of magnesia
- 2 mystery liquids
- Science Log data sheet

DO THIS

1 Pour the tea into a clear cup. Shine the flashlight through the tea. Notice how the beam of light looks. Tea is a solution. The beam of light passes through in a straight line.

2 Pour the milk of magnesia into another cup. Shine the flashlight through it. How does the light look? This is a colloid, and the suspended particles scatter the light.

3 Repeat the procedure with the mystery liquids provided by your teacher. Try to determine whether each is a solution or a colloid.

THINK AND WRITE

What characteristics of solutions and colloids did you notice?

QUICK CHECK

LESSON 2 REVIEW

Copy and complete the following table.

Types and Characteristics of Colloids			
Gel		suspended in	solid
Emulsion	liquid	suspended in	
Aerosol		suspended in	

D48

3 COMPOUNDS

You've discovered properties of different kinds of mixtures.
Compounds are different from mixtures. What are compounds?
You will find the answers to this and other questions as you
complete this lesson.

A C T I V I T Y

How Is a Compound Formed?

In this activity, you'll form a common compound.
See if you can predict what the compound will be.

MATERIALS

- pencil
- steel wool
- 2 test tubes
- beaker
- water
- masking tape
- ruler
- Science Log data sheet

DO THIS

1 Using the pointed end of the pencil, push a small wet ball of steel wool to the bottom of one test tube.

2 Fill the beaker halfway with water.

3 Place the test tube with the steel wool and an empty one upside down in the beaker. Tape them to the side so that they will stand up.

4 Measure and record the height of the water in each test tube once a day for 4 days.

5 How did the steel wool change? What compound formed?

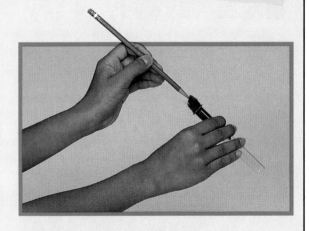

THINK AND WRITE

1. What would prevent the compound from forming?

2. MEASURING Making careful measurements can help you make comparisons. How would your conclusions be affected if you did not make careful measurements? Explain.

Rising to the Occasion

Arthur is making a German coffeecake for the festival. On his first attempt, the dough didn't rise enough. For dough to rise properly, conditions must allow one of the ingredients to react to form gas bubbles in the dough. Do you know what that ingredient is? As you do this activity, think about what might have gone wrong with Arthur's coffeecake.

DO THIS

1. Pour 1 cup of warm water into one bag and 1 cup of cold water into the other.

2. Sprinkle 2 tablespoons of yeast in each bag of water. Seal the bags, removing as much air as possible.

3. Predict in which bag the yeast will produce the gas that would make a cake rise. Record your prediction.

4. Mix the yeast and water by kneading each bag. Record what you observe.

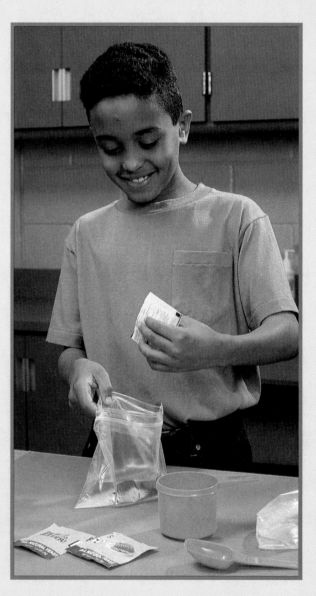

THINK AND WRITE

What might be one reason that the dough for Arthur's coffeecake did not rise enough?

Compound It

The common compound water is made up of two atoms of hydrogen and one atom of oxygen. Hydrogen and oxygen are gases, but when they combine as H_2O, they form the clear liquid water. Read to find out more about compounds.

In the first activity in this lesson, you observed the formation of rust, a compound. Recall that compounds such as rust are formed when two or more elements combine chemically. When elements combine to form a compound, a chemical change occurs. You end up with something you didn't have before. For example, the rust in the activity resulted from the combining of atoms of the element oxygen in water with atoms of the element iron in the steel wool.

Think of elements as being like the letters of the alphabet and compounds as being like the words formed by combining letters. From just 26 letters we can spell all the words in our language. From the 109 elements, millions of compounds can be formed.

Another compound you know is salt. It is made up of the elements sodium and chlorine. As an element, sodium is a solid that is dangerous to handle because it can burst into flames. Chlorine is a poisonous gas. But when sodium and chlorine are

▲ **Rust is a compound.**

combined chemically in the ratio of one atom of sodium to one atom of chlorine, they form salt (NaCl), a white crystal that is safe to handle and eat.

THINK ABOUT IT

Tell how a compound is different from an element.

▼ **Components of salt**

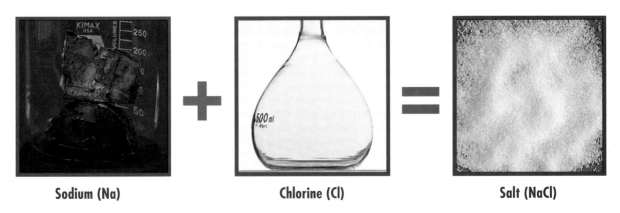

| Sodium (Na) | Chlorine (Cl) | Salt (NaCl) |

ACTIVITY

Testing for Sugar and Starch

Have you ever wondered what is in the snacks you eat? In this activity, you will test for the presence of two compounds, glucose (sugar) and starch.

MATERIALS

• 4 test tubes
• test-tube rack
• wax pencil
• water
• 50-mL graduate
• egg white
• green onion (scallion)
• saltine cracker
• stirring stick
• 4 glucose test strips
• iodine solution
• droppers
• Science Log data sheet

DO THIS (CAUTION)

1. Using the wax pencil, label the test tubes 1–4. Put 5 mL of water in each. Place a small amount of egg white in test tube 1, some green onion bits in test tube 2, and a piece of cracker in test tube 3, and stir. Leave only water in test tube 4.

2. Test for sugar. Dip a different glucose test strip into each test tube. Note any color change in the strip. A purple color indicates that glucose is present—the darker the color, the more glucose. Record the color of each strip.

3. **CAUTION: Iodine is poisonous and can also damage your skin. Do not inhale its vapors. Do not allow it to contact your skin.** Test for starch by dripping a few drops of iodine solution into each test tube. Look for a color change in the test tubes. If starch is present, the color will turn to bluish black. Record the color changes.

THINK AND WRITE

1. Which test tubes contained glucose? Which contained starch?

2. Sugar can provide quick energy. If you needed quick energy, which of the foods tested should you eat?

Feed Me!

Mr. Washington's class is preparing a variety of foods for the festival. Read to find out why these foods are not only delicious but also important to your health.

Your body needs certain kinds of nutrients, or fuels, to stay alive and grow. These are called *essential nutrients*. Many of the foods the students are preparing for the festival, such as bread, pasta, and rice, supply *carbohydrates*. These foods make up a large portion of the diet in many cultures. Carbohydrates are an important source of fuel for the body's cells. They are compounds made of carbon, hydrogen, and oxygen.

Examples of carbohydrates are sugars, starches, and cellulose. One type of sugar is glucose, which you tested for in the last activity. Your body's cells use glucose as fuel. Other kinds of sugars are fructose and sucrose, or table sugar. All of these sugars are sources of quick energy.

Starch is a molecule that your body must break down into smaller molecules before

it can be used. Pastas and the crackers you tested in the activity contain starches. Besides carbohydrates, your body also gets energy from *fats*. Foods such as margarine, mayonnaise, cheese, whole milk, and vegetable oils are high in fats. Fats are nutrients that produce a great many calories when used by your body. When the energy from food is not used, it is stored in the form of body fat.

Eggs, cheese, and whole milk also contain *vitamins*. Vitamins help cause specific reactions that keep your body working properly. Vitamins are found in vegetables and many of the other healthful foods that you eat.

Another necessary nutrient is *protein*. When you drink a tall glass of milk, you are providing your body with proteins it needs. Cheese, eggs, meat, cereal grains, beans, and peas are other foods that provide proteins.

THINK ABOUT IT

Prepare a menu for a meal that would be part of a healthful diet.

◀ **A healthful choice of foods**

Yummy!

It's doubtful that the students in Mr. Washington's class will be serving caterpillars or slugs at their festival, but who knows what mysterious delicacies might be hidden in a salad or stew? As you read, think about the kinds of nutrients each dish might provide. You might even decide to try some!

Incredible Edibles: Unusual Foods from Around the World

by Elizabeth Keyishian from *3•2•1 CONTACT*

LITERATURE   Some foods that are a favorite taste treat in one country wouldn't be touched, never mind *eaten,* by people in other countries. That's because what you think is yummy depends on what you're used to eating. If you had been snacking on slug soup or stewed caterpillars all your life, you probably wouldn't think they were icky.

In fact, caterpillars are full of protein. That doesn't mean it's safe for you to snack on your backyard caterpillars. (They might have just walked through poisonous insecticide.)

But it is safe to read all about them—and other unusual foods—from around the world.

Caterpillars

In Africa, the "mopane worm"—or caterpillar—is stewed, canned, fried, and eaten fresh...right off the tree. Some people say caterpillars have a nutty flavor. Others say that caterpillars taste like dried beef. Crunchy or chewy, a meal of 20 caterpillars is packed with vitamins.

▲ **Exotic foods**

Moths

In Australia, moths are a taste treat for some people. Sitting around a campfire at night, people eat handfuls of toasted moths. The moths are thrown in the fire and then eaten off a stick—just like toasted marshmallows.

Dandelion Flowers

The bright yellow dandelion flower grows all over the United States—in gardens, pastures, lawns, and along the side of the road.

Dandelion-eaters say the flowers taste good boiled or in a fried sandwich.

▲ **Dandelion flowers**

▲ **Sushi**

Sushi

Sushi is raw fish that is a national dish of Japan. Today, it is very popular in the U.S. It's important that the fish is very clean and fresh.

Sushi chefs are very skilled at cutting and shaping the fish. The small pieces of fish are placed on mounds of rice and flavored with ginger and horseradish.

Frog Legs and Snails

Frog legs and snails are mostly eaten in France. But they are gaining popularity in the U.S. Believe it or not, frog legs taste just like chicken. Snails are chewy and taste a little like clams.

Snails are taken out of the shells to be cooked. When they are served, they are placed in pretty serving shells. We promise: Your friends won't think you're—um—"shell-fish" if you decide to share the treat.

▶ **Escargot, or snails**

▼ **Caviar**

Caviar ·······················

You might have heard people talk about how much they'd like to dine on champagne and caviar—at least in the movies.

Caviar is most popular in the former Soviet Union. It is also eaten all over Europe and in the U.S.

Caviar is actually tiny eggs from the sturgeon—a kind of fish. The eggs taste very salty and very fishy. That's why most people have to develop a taste for them. Remember that black stuff that Tom Hanks tried in the movie *Big*? That was caviar.

Rattlesnake ·······················

Rattlesnake meat is very popular in Texas even though hunting rattlesnake is dangerous.

You can buy rattlesnake meat in many parts of the U.S. But most people outside of Texas eat it so that they can tell everyone that they ate a rattlesnake!

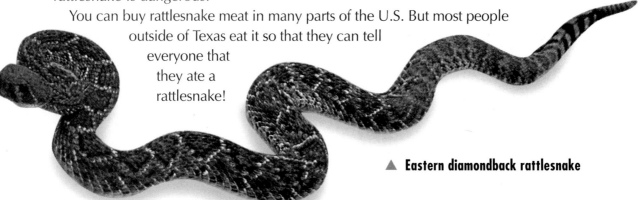

▲ **Eastern diamondback rattlesnake**

Bird Nests ·······················

In China, there are many delicacies that might sound strange to people from other countries. Here's a sampling: bear paws, shark fins, monkey brains, and bird nests.

Bird nests are not eaten right off the tree. The nest is made into a soup. The nests taste crunchy. What else would you expect?

THINK ABOUT IT

Do you think that people from other cultures might think some of the foods you eat are unusual? Explain.

Check the Label

You grab a box of cereal and pour yourself a big bowl. What's in the cereal you are about to eat? You can find out by reading labels.

You will need: 3 boxes that contained different kinds of breakfast cereal, Science Log

Work in groups. Identify the percentages of vitamins and minerals in each of the cereals. Record the amount of salt in each cereal.

Look at each list of ingredients. The ingredients are listed in order from the one that is used most to the one that is used least. Look for different names for types of sugar—for example, *glucose, sucrose, molasses, fructose,* or *corn syrup.* Which cereal seems to have a lot of sugar? Is there cholesterol in the cereal? How much?

Check the recommended serving size. Do you think the size is smaller than the serving most people usually eat? Explain why.

If you're trying to eat less salt, which cereals should you eat? Too much sugar is not good for you either. Which cereal should you eat to get the least sugar? If you want to get the most vitamins and minerals possible, which cereal should you eat?

◀ Labels provide nutritional information.

A Little Extra

Did you see niacin on the list of ingredients in the cereals? Niacin and other ingredients are often added to foods. Read to find out why.

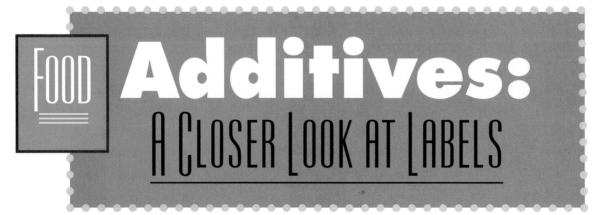

FOOD Additives: A Closer Look at Labels

from **Current Health**

 Chocolate pudding was Joe's favorite dessert. He liked to help make it. His recipe used milk, sugar, cornstarch, vanilla, and unsweetened chocolate.

Sometimes Joe's family used prepared mixes for making other foods. They also bought ready-made meals to eat at home. Why, Joe often wondered, did labels on store-bought products list so many ingredients? His homemade recipes called for fewer items.

One day Joe asked a neighbor about it. Mr. Sanchez worked as a chemist at a food company.

What Do Additives Do?

"Many of those extra ingredients on labels are called additives," Mr. Sanchez told Joe. "Their names may be hard to say or pronounce, but their uses are easy to understand.

CHOLESTEROL, mg		0
SODIUM, mg	220	0*
POTASSIUM, mg	160	280
		360

PERCENTAGE OF U.S. RECOMMENDED DAILY ALLOWANCES (U.S. RDA)

PROTEIN	6	
VITAMIN A	15	15
VITAMIN C	**	20
THIAMIN	25	2
RIBOFLAVIN	25	30
NIACIN	25	35
CALCIUM	**	25
IRON	100	15
VITAMIN D	10	100
VITAMIN B₆	25	25
FOLIC ACID	25	25
VITAMIN B₁₂	25	35
PHOSPHORUS	15	25
MAGNESIUM	15	20
ZINC	25	30
COPPER	10	10

*2% MILK SUPPLIES AN ADDITIONAL 20 CALORIES, 2 g FAT, AND 10 mg CHOLESTEROL.
**CONTAINS LESS THAN 2% OF THE U.S. RDA OF THIS NUTRIENT.

▲ **Typical ingredient label**

"Some additives make food more nutritious," he went on. "Extra vitamin D in milk helps prevent rickets, a disease in which bones become soft or twisted. Adding niacin to the bread and cereal we buy has helped keep us healthier, too. Iodine, now present in some packages of table salt, is also a help. And we almost never hear of *scurvy, pellagra,* or *goiter.* Many people got sick with diseases like these before some of today's additives came into use.

"Ascorbic acid (vitamin C) is another term you may often see listed on boxes. This helps keep cooked fruits from turning brown. It also helps them last longer," said Mr. Sanchez.

"*Sodium nitrates* aid in keeping meats, fish, chicken, and turkey from giving us food poisoning. They help meats stay fresher, too.

"Peanut butter and salad dressing would separate into oily and dry layers if chemicals called *emulsifiers* were not used. Emulsifiers mix together ingredients like oil and water, which otherwise would normally separate. *Stabilizers* keep them from separating later on.

"Breads and cakes would be flat without baking powder or yeast. *Humectants* keep shredded coconut moist. Take away the *glycerine* used in making marshmallows and they might not be as soft and fluffy at all.

"Sugar and salt make some foods seem to taste better. They're additives, too. So are mustard and pepper.

"Margarine would look white instead of yellow without extra color. Even strawberry ice cream owes some of its rosy color to an extra helping of pink tint."

Mr. Sanchez continued, "There are about 2,800 additives in use today. They keep our packaged foods safer, and help them last longer as well as look and taste better. They also give us nourishment we might not get otherwise."

Natural and Synthetic Chemicals

"Often we hear that additives are really chemicals," said Mr. Sanchez. "Is that bad? Not when you know that everything is made up of chemicals, even air."

Mr. Sanchez liked talking about this. "Some of the chemicals we add to food come from plants. Others are manufactured. Though there are people who feel that 'natural' is better than *synthetic,* others believe there is little difference to the body. Your body, they say, digests natural and synthetic chemicals the same way.

"Some food scientists believe that synthetic additives are better because they are more *consistent,*" Mr. Sanchez added. "This means that the color will be the same in every package of pudding mix or ice cream of the same brand that we buy. The flavor will be consistent from box to box, too.

"The treats you make at home need fewer additives because they're made from fresh ingredients. Once cooked, they're not stored very long, either."

In the Old Days...

"Long ago families grew and cooked only their own foods," said Mr. Sanchez. "They ate only what was right there. Most of the time it was fresh, in season. Sometimes it was pickled (to preserve using a vinegar solution) or dried. Later, food was canned and refrigerated to help it stay fresh longer.

"As more people moved to cities, they had to find new ways to get food. They wanted it to be easier to cook and to take less time. It still had to taste good and to be high quality. It also had to travel further to reach them, so it had to keep its freshness. To help food stay fresh and be safe to eat, companies like the one where I work began using additives.

"The government tests all additives for safety before they can be used. The labels on food packages must list all ingredients. That way, shoppers can make choices for themselves as to what they want to eat—or not eat.

▲ **There were few food additives in the old days.**

"During this century, eating has become much safer. In the old days, food spoiled quickly. A few companies used unsafe colors to make food look better. Sometimes they used unhealthful ingredients, too.

"Other companies were not always honest about what they were selling. They might put coloring and flavors in a jar and call it jam without using any fruits at all."

Nowadays...

"New laws were passed to make food safer and much more nutritious," explained Mr. Sanchez. "The U.S. Food and Drug Administration (FDA) was started around the same time. One of its jobs is to check up on the safety of the foods we eat.

"Today, people buy just about everything their family eats. Often the food comes from far away, even from other countries. Along with the extra additives in their foods, they are buying consistency, good taste, and nourishment. Their foods are safe, and they are saving a great deal of time in cooking.

"Well, I guess I said a mouthful about food," laughed Mr. Sanchez. "Do you have any more questions about food labels or ingredients, Joe?"

"Only one question, Mr. Sanchez," said Joe. "All this talk about food has made me hungry. Where can I get a safe, nutritious, good-tasting snack?"

▲ **The use of food additives helps keep foods fresh.**

QUICK CHECK

LESSON 3 REVIEW

❶ How have food additives improved some of the foods we eat?

❷ Which of the following are necessary nutrients: carbohydrates, emulsifiers, protein, elements? Explain.

4 CHEMICAL OR PHYSICAL?

Cooking involves change. Cold foods are made hot, powders dissolve in liquids, foods become soft or hard or change color. In this lesson, you will identify some of these changes.

Clues to Change

Mr. Washington's students wondered about the difference between physical and chemical changes. If a chemical change produces a new chemical, how do we know when this has happened?

After much discussion, Mr. Washington's class decided the following: There are two types of changes. In a **chemical change,** a new chemical is formed. Burning is one kind of chemical change. In a **physical change,** no new chemical is formed. Boiling, dissolving, evaporating, and freezing are physical changes.

They noted some clues that a chemical change had occurred:

- A new substance forms.
- The color changes.
- Heat or light is given off.
- Bubbles form.
- The change is not easily reversible.

▶ Chemical change

THINK ABOUT IT

Think of the changes that occur when breakfast is cooked. Which do you think are chemical changes? Explain your answers.

▲ Physical change

A C T I V I T Y

What Kind of Change?

When you cook at home, you can see changes taking place. This activity will give you a chance to observe a number of changes. You can decide whether they are physical or chemical.

DO THIS

CAUTION: Iodine is poisonous and can also damage your skin. Do not inhale its vapors or allow it to contact your skin.

Do the following tests. Record your results in a table.

1. Take a drinking straw and blow *slowly* into a test tube one-quarter full of limewater.

2. Add a drop or two of iodine solution to a slice of raw potato.

3. Add a few drops of water to baking powder.

4. Add 3 dropperfuls of vinegar to 25 mL of milk.

5. Add a dropperful of vinegar to a piece of eggshell.

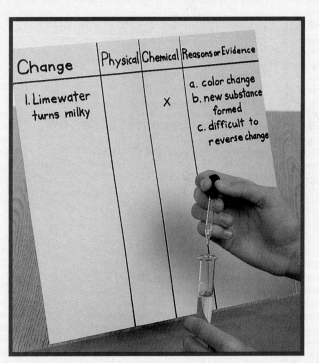

THINK AND WRITE

What conclusions did you reach? Explain your reasoning.

ACTIVITY

Watch the Bubbles!

Mr. Washington's class listed "bubbles form" as one clue to a chemical change. But does the formation of bubbles always mean that a chemical change is occurring? Decide for yourself as you do this activity.

MATERIALS
- hot plate
- beaker
- water
- carbonated soft drink
- seltzer tablet
- measuring cup
- 10 mL molasses
- packet of yeast
- vinegar
- baking soda
- Science Log data sheet

DO THIS

1 **CAUTION: Never use a heat source without adult supervision.** Heat water in a beaker until it boils.

2 Examine a recently opened carbonated drink.

3 Drop one-quarter of a seltzer tablet into water. Is this a chemical change?

4 Let a cold glass of water reach room temperature.

5 To 50 mL of water, add 10 mL of molasses. Make a yeast mixture by stirring half a packet of yeast into 25 mL of warm water. Add this to your molasses solution. Place the solution in a warm spot, and record all changes over the next few days. Does a chemical change occur?

6 Add a few drops of vinegar to baking soda. How are these bubbles like those you observed above?

THINK AND WRITE

Make a list of all the clues you can use to recognize a chemical change. Why is there always a clue to a chemical change?

Doctor U, Chemical Change Detective

Mr. Washington read the following story to his students and asked them to find all the physical and chemical changes mentioned in it. You can do the same. Write your own story and ask a classmate to find the physical and chemical changes.

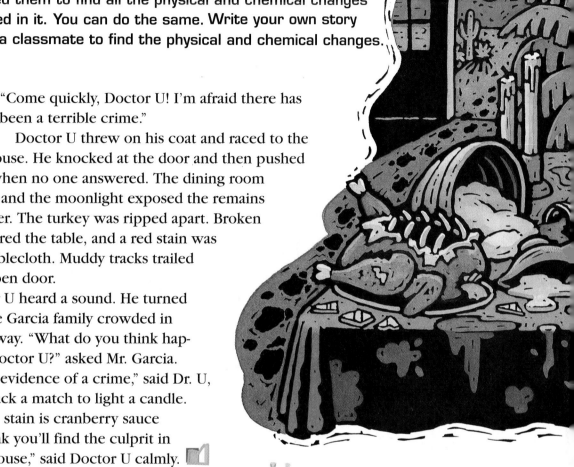

"Come quickly, Doctor U! I'm afraid there has been a terrible crime."

Doctor U threw on his coat and raced to the Garcia house. He knocked at the door and then pushed it open when no one answered. The dining room was dark and the moonlight exposed the remains of a dinner. The turkey was ripped apart. Broken glass littered the table, and a red stain was on the tablecloth. Muddy tracks trailed out an open door.

Doctor U heard a sound. He turned to see the Garcia family crowded in the doorway. "What do you think happened, Doctor U?" asked Mr. Garcia. "I see no evidence of a crime," said Dr. U, as he struck a match to light a candle. "That red stain is cranberry sauce and I think you'll find the culprit in the doghouse," said Doctor U calmly.

QUICK CHECK

LESSON 4 REVIEW

Give one example each of a physical change and a chemical change from the story. Tell how you knew the difference.

DOUBLE CHECK

SECTION B REVIEW

1. Use drawings or models to explain atoms, molecules, and elements and the relationships among them.

2. Think of three or four everyday mixtures. Tell what kind of mixture each is, and explain how you decided what it is.

SECTION C
Heat

Are you comfortable right now? Thanks to modern heating and cooling systems, you can adjust a room's temperature. Too hot? Turn on a fan or an air conditioner. Too cold? Turn up the heat.

What is heat? How do we measure it? Consider these and other questions as you explore the ideas in this section. Remember to keep careful notes in your Science Log as you work through some of the following investigations.

1 MOVING MOLECULES

With the International Festival only a few days away, Mr. Washington's room was teeming with activity. Students were hard at work on their costumes and recipes. Read and discover how some of them used heat in their projects.

Popping Up

Barbara was preparing a Native American treat, popcorn.

Recipe for Popcorn

popcorn
popcorn popper or pot with lid
cooking oil
hot plate or stove

Count out 100 kernels of popcorn, and place them in the popcorn popper or pot. Add a small amount of cooking oil. Place the pot on a hot plate and turn the heat to high. Shake the popper as the corn pops. After the corn has popped, remove it from the popper or pot.

As Barbara passed around samples of popcorn, Mr. Washington asked, "What makes popcorn pop?" Students compared the unpopped and popped kernels. They noticed that the hard outer shell of the popcorn had burst open in popping. They wondered what could have caused these "mini-explosions" and why the popped kernels were so much larger than the unpopped kernels.

THINK ABOUT IT

How would you explain what happened to the popcorn?

ACTIVITY

Pop! Goes the Popcorn

Prepare popcorn according to Barbara's recipe.
As you observe the changes in the popcorn, think
about the questions: "What makes popcorn pop?"

MATERIALS
- balance
- popcorn
- vegetable oil
- pot with lid
- heat source
- potholders
- Science Log data sheet

DO THIS

1. Find the mass of the unpopped kernels.

2. **CAUTION: Never use a heat source without adult supervision.** Make popcorn, using Barbara's recipe.

3. Find the mass of the popped and unpopped kernels after popping.

4. Determine the percentage of kernels that did not pop by counting the unpopped kernels and by dividing by 100.

THINK AND WRITE

1. Did the popcorn's mass change after popping? Explain why you think this happened.

2. What do you think caused the popcorn to "explode"?

What Is Heat?

You had to heat the popcorn to make it pop. But what is heat? How do objects gain and lose heat? Find out for yourself.

MATERIALS
- 3 plastic–foam cups
- 50-mL graduate
- cold and hot water
- spoon
- thermometer
- Science Log data sheet

Changing Temperatures					
Cold Water		Hot Water		Mixture	
Amount	Temperature	Amount	Temperature	Predicted	Actual
20 mL		20 mL			
20 mL		40 mL			
40 mL		20 mL			

DO THIS

❶ Copy the table provided, and use it to record your observations.

❷ Label the cups *1, 2,* and *3.*

❸ Pour 20 mL of cold water into cup 1 and 20 mL of hot water into cup 2. Record the temperature of the water in each cup.

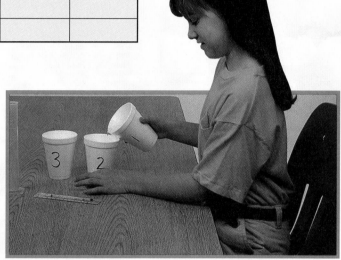

❹ Predict what the temperature will be if you mix the water in cups 1 and 2.

❺ Pour the water from each cup into cup 3. Stir. Record the temperature of the mixture.

❻ Repeat steps 3 through 5, using 20 mL of cold water and 40 mL of hot water. Repeat again, using 40 mL of cold water and 20 mL of hot water.

THINK AND WRITE

1. In which mixture did you record the highest temperature? Why was this the highest?

2. Think of several situations in which a cold substance comes in contact with a warmer substance. What is the result in each?

In the Heat

Scientists now know that heat is a form of energy. As an object becomes hotter, its atoms and molecules move faster. As an object loses heat, its atoms and molecules move more slowly. What do you think happened to the water molecules in the activity you just did?

You can determine how hot something is by taking its temperature. *Temperature* is the measure of the average energy of the moving atoms and molecules in a substance or an object. We measure temperature with a thermometer.

THINK ABOUT IT

How have you used thermometers?

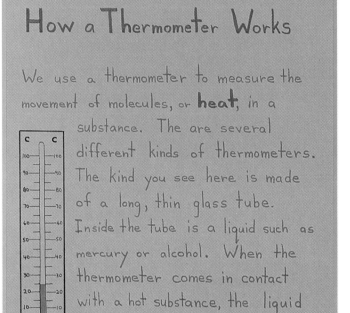

How a Thermometer Works

We use a thermometer to measure the movement of molecules, or **heat**, in a substance. The are several different kinds of thermometers. The kind you see here is made of a long, thin glass tube. Inside the tube is a liquid such as mercury or alcohol. When the thermometer comes in contact with a hot substance, the liquid expands. It rises in the tube. When the thermometer touches a cold substance, the liquid contracts and goes down in the tube.

▲ Thermometers are useful in projects.

Moving Matter

You have discovered how heat is measured. Now, read and find out how heat moves.

We know that all matter is made of tiny particles called *atoms* and *molecules*. These particles are in constant motion. Molecules are too small for us to see. Scientists use a model based on properties they can observe to explain movement of molecules and heat.

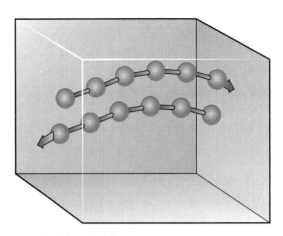

▲ **Liquid molecules**

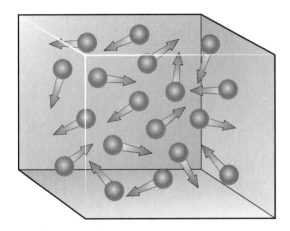

▲ **Gas molecules**

The model shows that molecules of gases are not attached to each other. They move quickly, bumping into one another and against the container's walls. This is why a gas fills its container and does not have a particular shape. Gas molecules are like beads moving about freely in a box.

In liquids, molecules are attached to each other in stringlike formations. They move much more slowly than individual gas molecules. The volume of these molecules remains the same because each formation can move on its own, causing the liquid to take the shape of its container. You could picture liquid molecules as behaving like hundreds of short strings of beads.

In solids, the molecules are very close together and seldom move apart. Generally, they just bend and stretch. This is why a solid keeps its shape. You might think of molecules in a solid as being like beads in a box that is so full, the beads have very little room to move around.

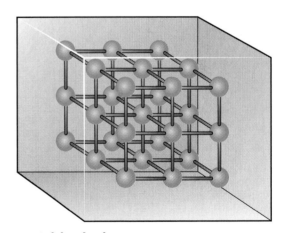

▲ **Solid molecules**

THINK ABOUT IT

Think of other things that can be used to demonstrate the movement of molecules of matter.

Expanding with Heat

Carrie and her dad were going to spend the day at a hot-air balloon rally. Before they left for the rally, Carrie filled two cups to the rim with water for some tea. She placed one cup in the microwave while her dad watched. When she went to take the cup of hot water out of the microwave, she found that the water had spilled over the cup rim. She wondered why.

As Carrie was cleaning up the spilled water in the microwave, her dad said, "I see you filled the cup too full of water."

"What do you mean, Dad?" she asked.

Carrie's dad explained that as a substance is heated, its molecules begin to move faster. They spread out and take up more room. Since Carrie had filled the cup completely, the water spilled out as it expanded.

Dad told Carrie that whenever she heats a liquid, she should not completely fill the container. That way the liquid is less likely to spill out after it begins expanding.

Carrie was curious about what happens to solids and gases when they are heated. "Do they expand, too?" she asked.

▷ Hot air expands and rises.

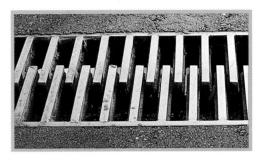

"Remember how hot it was last summer? It was so hot that sections of the road buckled. This happened because the molecules of cement began moving farther apart. Before long, the molecules had no room to expand, so the road buckled, or bulged out and cracked. That's why most roads and bridges are built with expansion joints. The joints are flexible. They allow the pavement to expand so that the roadway won't crack."

"I think I understand, Dad," Carrie replied. "The same thing must happen to gases, right? Today, at the rally, the balloonists will turn on their heat jets. That will warm the air in the balloons. Then the warm air will expand and the balloons will rise."

"That's exactly what will happen. Well, I've finished my tea. Let's wash the dishes, and go to the rally!"

▲ Cracked road surface.

THINK ABOUT IT

What do you think can happen if gases in an enclosed container are heated? Explain.

How People Got Fire for Cooking

Emilio's family came to the United States from Tonga, a Polynesian island chain in the Pacific Ocean. He decided to prepare a Polynesian dish for the festival. As his grandmother helped him, she told him the Polynesian myth of how people first got fire for cooking.

▼ Polynesia

Long ago, people did not have fire. Everything they ate was uncooked. They ate raw meat and fish and uncooked plants. Maui, like other people, did not know what cooked food tasted like.

Then Maui's mother came to visit him. She lived with the gods, who had fire for cooking and warmth. She brought with her cooked food. Maui ate it and marveled at how delicious it was.

He asked why it tasted so much better than the food he was used to. His mother explained that the gods had fire and that they used it to cook food. She also said that the gods would never share fire with people.

Soon, Maui's mother had to return to the land of the gods. Maui followed her and heard the words that would allow him to enter the land of the gods.

He decided to visit and bring back fire. Once there, he met a relative who warned him of the danger of trying to outwit the guardian of the fire. "He is a huge giant and a master fighter, and he will never give up fire," the relative explained. But Maui insisted that he needed fire for the people and would get it at any cost.

The relative helped Maui pass through a deep canyon so that he could get to the place where the fire guardian lived. As

▲ Maui had questions.

D74

soon as Maui arrived there, the fire guardian came out and asked where he was from. Maui told him that he was from the land of the people and that he had come to get fire for them.

The fire guardian thought that he could fool Maui. To get rid of him, the giant gave Maui some glowing embers. When Maui put these in water, they went out. He knew that he had not been given the secret of fire. The guardian continued to try to trick Maui, but he did not succeed. Finally, Maui challenged him to a tossing fight.

The giant went first and tossed Maui high into the air. But Maui did not fall. Instead, he paddled his arms as if they were the oars of boats and glided gently to the ground.

The giant was sure Maui could not toss him into the air. But Maui grabbed the giant and tossed him high into the air. The giant went higher and higher. Maui began to sing an enchanted song that kept the giant in the air.

The giant begged Maui to stop singing. Maui told the giant that if he stopped singing the giant would fall to Earth and be injured or killed. The giant told Maui to leave him in the air if that was the case. But Maui said the giant would starve to death if left in the air. Then the giant pleaded with Maui to catch him as he fell. Maui promised to catch the giant if he would give Maui the secret of fire.

▶ **Maui and the giant**

The giant agreed, and Maui caught him before he hit the ground. The guardian of the fire kept his word. He went into his hut and brought out two fire sticks—one was long and thin, and one was flat like a stone. He showed Maui how to twirl the long stick in his hands against the flat stick to produce fire. He also gave Maui a torch to light his way home to the land of the people. The giant told Maui that he could pass through the canyon without harm because he had defeated the great guardian of the fire.

Carrying the fire sticks and torch, Maui returned to the land of the people. He showed the people how to use the fire sticks. They learned how to cook their food over the fire, and the food tasted better. They warmed themselves by the fire. They also were protected by the fire because dangerous animals would not come near it. The people were happy, and every time they lit a fire, they sang the song that Maui had sung to keep the guardian of the fire in the air.

QUICK CHECK

LESSON 1 REVIEW

Explain each of the following in terms of the moving-molecules model.

- **An inflated balloon that is left in a hot car bursts.**

- **On a cold day, automobile tires look a bit flat.**

- **Julie can't slip her ring on her finger on an especially hot day.**

▼ **The people could cook!**

2 ON THE MOVE

Much of cooking involves transferring heat energy from one material to another. As you complete the investigations in this lesson, think about ways heat is transferred.

ACTIVITY

Too Hot to Handle

How does heat move from one substance to another? This activity will give you a chance to explore that question.

MATERIALS
- pan
- water
- egg
- heat source
- stopwatch
- potholders
- Science Log data sheet

DO THIS

1. Carefully place the egg in the pan. Fill the pan with enough water to cover the egg.

2. **CAUTION: Never use a heat source without adult supervision.** After putting the pan on the heat source, turn on the heat. Allow the water to boil for 7 minutes. Use the stopwatch.

3. Turn off the heat. Using the potholders, remove the pan from the heat source. Pour out the hot water, keeping the egg in the pan. Refill the pan with very cold water.

4. Take the egg out of the water after 20 seconds and hold it.

THINK AND WRITE

In which direction did heat travel as you held the egg?

Heat Transfer by Conduction

Ana was washing the dishes she used to prepare an onion dip. She filled the sink with warm water and detergent. The warm, soapy water felt good on her hands. Do you think heat was being transferred? How do you know? Explain your reasoning.

When Ana put her hands in the warm water, heat from the water transferred to her hands and warmed them. You experienced the same thing as you held the egg. Heat was transferred from the egg to your hands. Did the egg become too hot to handle? In the activity, you experienced an example of conduction, one way in which heat energy moves. **Conduction** is the movement of heat that occurs when atoms or molecules bump into one another.

In conduction, the fast-moving molecules in a hot substance (such as the egg) hit the slower-moving molecules in a cooler substance (such as your hand). The slower-moving molecules speed up, and the faster-moving molecules slow down. Remember, the faster the molecules are moving, the more heat the substance has. Solids, liquids, and gases can all be heated by conduction because they are all made up of molecules. In the activity, what do you think happened to the contents of the egg as your hand heated up?

THINK ABOUT IT

Name two other examples of heat being transferred by conduction.

▼ Food in a Wok (below) and a hard-boiled egg (left) are cooked by conduction of heat.

D78

ACTIVITY

Currents of Heat

In the last activity, heat was transferred from the hot plate to the pan. From the pan, the heat traveled to the water. From the water, the heat traveled to the egg. Then the heat went from the egg to your hand. In the following activity, you will explore another way heat moves.

DO THIS 🔆CAUTION

❶ Fill the beaker $\frac{2}{3}$ full of water, and drop in the piece of candy. Set the beaker on the hot plate. DO NOT TURN ON THE HEAT YET. Leave the beaker undisturbed for 5 minutes.

❷ **CAUTION: Never use a heat source without adult supervision.** Turn on the heat, being careful not to disturb the water.

❸ Record what you observe, and then turn off the heat.

THINK AND WRITE

1. In what way was the heat you observed moving?

2. What do you think this may have to do with the transfer of heat?

3. **FORMULATING AND USING MODELS** Using models is a way to show how something works. In this activity, you constructed a model to demonstrate convection currents. Explain how this models the heating system in your classroom.

Heat Transfer by Convection

Enrico placed a pan of water on the stove and turned the burner on. When the water started to boil, he added noodles. He watched as the noodles were tossed up and down in the water, and he wondered what caused this to happen. Read to find out.

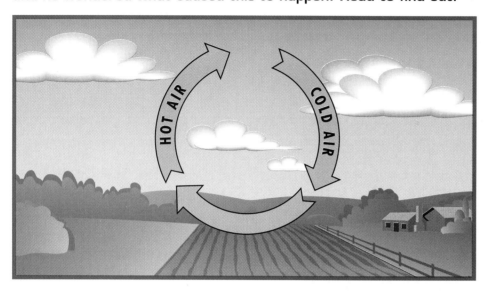

◄ Convection currents

When a liquid or a gas is heated, its molecules speed up and begin to move in currents. Enrico's noodles were being moved within the currents of water.

When you heated the candy in the water, you observed convection. **Convection** is the transfer of heat by currents of molecules in liquids and gases. As the water near the heat source becomes hotter, its molecules begin moving faster and spreading out. The warmer water is less dense than the cooler water, so the warmer water is pushed up by the cooler, more dense water. This produces currents of warm water that carry heat.

Have you ever noticed that roads seem to shimmer on a hot afternoon? This shimmer is caused by convection currents in air. Convection currents in air help produce weather. Warm air near the Earth's surface is moving faster and is less dense than the cooler air in the atmosphere. The warm air rises, and the cooler air rushes in to replace it. Winds that ripple a flag or bend trees are produced by these convection currents of air.

THINK ABOUT IT

In the last activity, was the beaker heated by convection or by conduction? Explain.

Solar Heating

Think how it feels when the sun shines on your skin. Does the feel of the sun differ depending on whether you are in bright sunshine or in shade? In this activity, you will measure the effect of this kind of heating.

MATERIALS

- 2 cardboard boxes, same size
- scissors
- clear plastic wrap
- tape
- 2 thermometers
- Science Log data sheet

DO THIS

1 Cut a large hole, or "window," in one side of each box. Make sure the holes are the same size.

2 Cover the holes with the plastic wrap. Tape the plastic wrap tightly to the cardboard, leaving no gaps.

3 Put a thermometer inside each box.

4 Place each box in direct sunlight. Place one box with its window facing the sun and the other box with its window away from the sun. Wait 20 minutes.

5 Read and record the temperature on each thermometer.

THINK AND WRITE

1. Was there a difference between the temperatures you recorded? Why or why not?

2. **EXPERIMENTING** Scientists experiment to test hypotheses. How could you further test solar heating?

Heat Transfer by Radiation

How does heat from the sun get all the way to the Earth? Do molecules bump into each other, one after the other, for 150 million kilometers (93 million miles) through space, until they reach Earth? How long would such a process take? It seems that this kind of heat transfer must work differently from the others. How is the sun's heat transferred?

In conduction and convection, the movement of molecules transfers heat. The sun's heat does not require the movement of molecules. Instead, the heat is transferred by **radiation,** or by infrared rays. Infrared rays are like light rays, but they cannot be seen. These rays travel in straight lines as fast as light. The sun's rays travel through space to Earth and produce radiant heat.

You can feel radiant heat when you're out in the sun. Radiant heat is what your hand feels next to a light bulb. Another example of radiant heat is the warmth you feel from a fireplace.

▲ Radiant heat

THINK ABOUT IT

Write a paragraph in which you describe someone's experience with all three forms of heat transfer.

Cooking for a Living:
A Tasteful Experience

Many students in Mr. Washington's class enjoyed cooking foods for the International Festival. They wondered what it would be like to be a chef. What would they have to learn, and what would they do every day as chefs? Read and learn about the career of one chef.

So You Wanna Be a *Chef?*

Be Prepared to Train Like an Athlete

by **Joanne Koch** from *Career World*

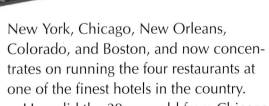

▲ Restaurant dining

 How would you like to make dinner for Michael Jordan? What about cooking for ballet star and gourmet Mikhail Baryshnikov? Or perhaps you'd like to prepare lunch for America's best-known chef, Julia Child.

Michael Kornick, executive chef of the Four Seasons Hotel in Boston, has taken up all of these challenges with gusto. Kornick has cooked for celebrities in New York, Chicago, New Orleans, Colorado, and Boston, and now concentrates on running the four restaurants at one of the finest hotels in the country.

How did the 29-year-old from Chicago, Illinois, reach these heights so fast? Hard work, careful preparation, training under other excellent chefs, and an expanding marketplace for people in the food service—all have contributed.

Working His Way Up the Food Ladder

▲ School for chefs

Kornick has worked the whole gamut of jobs, from the lowliest helper chopping onions for $5 an hour to his current position as a highly paid executive chef.

His first paying job in the food industry was at age 16 when he bused tables at a neighborhood restaurant. Wanting to get involved in the actual preparation of food, he moved on to a restaurant in downtown Chicago, where he was a line cook, preparing food for their large buffet.

Kornick began to realize that becoming a chef would require more education and training. He decided to apply to the Culinary Institute of America in Hyde Park, New York.

At the institute, the chef is regarded as an important figure who demands respect. "Every student has to wear the proper uniform of starched white double-breasted jacket and apron, high chef's hat (toque), perfectly pressed pants, white socks, and black shoes," says Kornick. "Classes are taught by the greatest chefs in the world. The entire U.S. Culinary 'Olympic' Team was teaching there when I attended." (The Culinary Olympics, in which 180 countries compete, takes place every four years in Frankfurt, Germany.)

The competition at the institute is intense. Kornick compares the rigors of the program to military training. There's a definite chain of command and the kitchen troops have to learn to take orders and to respond immediately.

"It's also like athletic training," says Kornick. "People are competitive but they must also work as a team, able to move as a unit quickly and expertly under pressure."

▲ **Gourmet meal**

The first few years of low pay and extraordinary hard work were vital to Kornick. He served an apprenticeship with a European-trained chef, Andrew Stahl, at the Windsor Court Hotel in New Orleans.

"You have to cut hundreds of chickens and prepare a thousand sauces before you feel mastery. Repetitive production is the key in this industry." Having proven that he could assist in producing quality food time and again, Kornick moved up from line cook to *chef de partie*—a specialist position. He served as *saucier,* in charge of preparing sauces and later as *poissonnier,* in charge of preparing the fish dishes.

Much of the terminology of cooking is French. Kornick says it helps to know French, but in terms of dealing with staff, it's important to know Spanish as well, since many people in the American food industry are Spanish speaking.

By age 24, Kornick was offered the *sous chef* (under the chef) job with his mentor, Andrew Stahl, in New Orleans. This time he got a chance to show his leadership skills. This position varies, but in a large restaurant or hotel, the sous chef supervises the staff and reports directly to the chef.

Kornick's big break came when he was hired as chef at Gordon restaurant in Chicago. At Gordon, he had the thrill of cooking for basketball champion Michael Jordan and for ballet star Mikhail Baryshnikov, as well as for many superstars of food preparation.

▼ **New Orleans**

Becoming a Culinary Master

▲ **Four Seasons Hotel**

When Kornick was asked to come and show his cooking ability to the head of the Four Seasons Hotel in Boston, he was only 28. But he already had 12 years of experience, counting part-time work in high school and his two years of formal training at the Culinary Institute of America. He impressed the management of the hotel with his skill.

It was only when he began to work at the hotel and felt the full impact of being in charge of an $11.5 million food operation, with four restaurants and 450 hungry, demanding guests that he felt a little shaky.

"One of the hardest things is breakfast. Some hotel guests may eat their other meals out, but everyone eats breakfast at the hotel. That makes it the most difficult and thankless part of my job. People don't think to call and praise, but they certainly will complain."

▼ **Breakfast**

Almost a year into the job, Kornick still arrives every day at 7 a.m. to make sure that breakfast is up to par. He plans menus, supervises his staff of 45, and creates dishes and recipes. Kornick spends some of his 12- to 15-hour day interviewing prospective employees. What does he look for? "Enthusiasm, energy, and the love of food. I also look for a well-coordinated person. I'm very happy if they have had some experience with a sports team. People who have played in bands also do well.

"I'm looking for someone who will mix well with the group, but feel confident enough to take on responsibility. If the position is for a specialist chef, I look for leadership, the ability to tell people what to do, such as someone who might have been the captain of a sports team or the leader of a band.

"Here at the Four Seasons Hotel we require at least three years of experience, plus some serious training, such as a certificate from a culinary institute or training under a good chef.

"This is a physically draining job. The hours are long and there is less time off than in other fields. But if you've got that love of food, that love of the action—there's no place on earth like it."

THINK ABOUT IT

What science skills would a chef use in planning and cooking meals?

▲ **Cooking staff**

Festival Day

▼ Festival projects

The day of the festival had finally arrived. The students had invited their families to the festival. Mr. Washington's classroom was buzzing with activity. The students were wearing colorful clothes from Kenya, Mexico, Russia, and many other countries. Foods from around the world had been prepared. Posters, masks, statues, and other items students had made were on display. Soon the students' families would arrive to watch the international pageant, to view the exhibits, and to taste the ethnic foods.

Before the guests arrived, Mr. Washington asked the students to think about what they had learned about science when preparing their festival projects. Barbara explained that she had learned that heat is a form of energy. She also said that as she prepared popcorn, she learned that moving particles produced heat. She explained that the popcorn popped because the molecules of moisture in the kernel began moving so rapidly and expanding so much that the kernel could no longer hold them.

Luis said that he had learned about different kinds of mixtures. He pointed out that Terry's lemonade is a solution, Heather's salad dressing is a suspension, and Janine's gelatin mold is a colloid.

Kathryn explained that she had learned the importance of precise measurements as she cut the pattern for her Bolivian skirt and as she prepared the Bolivian corn-filled pies known as *humitas*.

◀ **Festival food**

Dominic said that learning about the phases of matter interested him the most. He said he was surprised to learn that water is the only matter on Earth that exists naturally in all three phases—gas, solid, and liquid.

You can have the same kind of learning experience the students in Mr. Washington's class have had. Plan your own International Festival. When you have your own festival, remember most of all that you can have fun with science—anytime and anywhere— even in the kitchen!

LESSON 2 REVIEW

Here are three examples of heat transfer that are used in cooking. Decide which is conduction, which is convection, and which is radiation.

- baking bread in an oven
- boiling potatoes
- broiling fish

✓ **DOUBLE CHECK**

SECTION C REVIEW

1. Describe the relationship between atoms, molecules, and elements.

2. Here is a recipe for making bread. Use the following terms to identify the ingredients and processes: mixture, solution, suspension, colloid, emulsion, element, compound, physical change, chemical change, conduction, convection, radiation.

- Dissolve 1 package yeast in 4 cups warm water. Combine with 2 cups heated milk, 2 tablespoons sugar, 2 teaspoons salt, and 1 tablespoon melted margarine. Cool until lukewarm.

- Add 2 cups flour. Knead until smooth. Place in a bowl and let rise in a warm place until it doubles in size. Punch down.

- Divide into 2 equal portions. Put each in a loaf pan and let rise until it doubles in size. Bake at 400°F about 35 minutes.

I REFLECT

It's time to think about the ideas you have discovered during your investigations. Think, too, about your many accomplishments.

SUMMARIZE

Answer the following in your Science Log.

1. What **I Wonder** questions have you answered in your investigations, and what new questions have you asked?

2. What have you discovered about matter and its physical and chemical changes? How have your ideas changed?

3. Did any of your discoveries surprise you? Explain.

MIXTURES

These are different kinds of mixtures a mixture in which you can se substances. Lemonade is a mixtu you cannot see the separate ingre

1. Describe five properties of matter, and tell how you measure them.

2. Watch someone prepare a meal in your home. List the physical and chemical changes that are involved.

3. Tell whether the heating system in your home uses conduction, convection, or radiant heat.

4. Draw models of water, salt, and oxygen molecules and label their atoms.

5. Look around your home. List examples of a mixture, a solution, an emulsion, a colloid, a gel, and an aerosol, and describe what life-would be like without them.

Ready For Spaghetti
by Peggy Guthart

Pasta ribbons, pasta bows,
Pasta spirals, pasta O's,
Some is white and some is green,
Some comes with spinach in between.

It's shaped like tubes and wheels and strings
And named all sorts of funny things:
Ravioli, tortellini,
Macaroni and linguini.

In my book it is supreme;
I like it best with peas and cream.
Pasta — there's no way to beat it.
The only thing to do is eat it!

SCIENCE PORTFOLIO

❶ Complete your Science Experiences Record.

❷ Choose one or two samples of your best work from each section to include in your Science Portfolio.

❸ On A Guide to My Science Portfolio, tell why you chose each sample.

I SHARE

Scientists share their discoveries and ideas and learn from one another. How can you share what you've learned?

Decide

▶ what you want to say.

▶ what the best way is to get your message across.

Share

▶ what you did and why.

▶ what worked and what didn't work.

▶ what conclusions you have drawn.

▶ what else you'd like to find out.

Find Out

▶ what classmates liked about what you shared—and why.

▶ what questions your classmates have.

I ACT

Science is more than discoveries—
it is also what you do with those
discoveries. How might you use
what you have learned about the
characteristics of matter?

▶ List several ways you could use the
radiant heat from the sun (solar
energy). You could look in books
to see how to make a simple solar
collector. Discuss your plans with
your family.

▶ Use what you know about mixtures,
heat, and physical and chemical
changes to create or improve a recipe.

▶ Apply what you have learned about
heat and temperature
by finding out which
areas of your home
are most efficiently
heated and why.

THE LANGUAGE OF SCIENCE

The language of science helps people communicate clearly when they talk about nature. Here are some vocabulary words you can use when you talk about the properties of matter with friends, family, and others.

atom—the basic building blocks of matter. **(D37)**

chemical change—a change in which a new chemical forms from another type of matter. Burning charcoal is an example of a chemical change. **(D62)**

▲ **Chemical change**

colloid—a mixture in which the very small particles do not separate but remain suspended. Homogenized milk is a colloid. **(D46)**

compound—two or more elements that have combined chemically and can be separated only by chemical changes. Water is a compound of hydrogen and oxygen. **(D40)**

element—matter made up of only one kind of atom. Iron is an element. **(D40)**

heat—a form of energy that is produced by the movement of molecules in a substance. Heat moves through *conduction,* as particles hit one another; through *convection,* as currents of molecules flow; and through *radiation,* as electromagnetic waves travel. **(D70)**

International System of Units (SI)—the standard system of measurement used by scientists. **(D26)**

mass—the amount of matter in a substance. **(D28)**

matter—anything that has volume and mass. Gases, liquids, and solids are all made up of matter. **(D13)**

▲ **The gas inside the balloon, the river's water, and the tree are all made up of matter.**

mixture—matter containing two or more substances that are not chemically combined. Lemonade is a mixture of lemon juice, water, and sweetener. A mixture such as lemonade has the same composition throughout. A mixture such as salad is not the same throughout. **(D42)**

▲ **Mixture with same composition** ▲ **Mixture with different composition**

molecule—the smallest particle of an element or a compound that can exist with the properties of that element or compound. **(D40)**

physical change—a change in matter that does not form a new chemical. Boiling, dissolving, evaporating, and freezing are examples of physical changes. **(D62)**

▲ **Physical change**

properties—the characteristics used to identify a substance. Color, taste, and smell are examples of properties. **(D13)**

solution—a mixture that includes a solvent and a solute, the substance that is dissolved in the solvent. In salt water, the water is the solvent and the salt is the solute. **(D44)**

suspension—a mixture in which solid particles can separate slowly from a gas or a liquid. Salad dressing with spices in it is an example of a suspension. **(D45)**

▲ **Suspensions slowly separate.**

temperature—the measure of the motion of the molecules in a substance or an object. **(D70)**

volume—the amount of space an object takes up. **(D27)**

weight—the measure of the pull of gravity on an object. **(D28)**

PRAIRIE DOG TALES

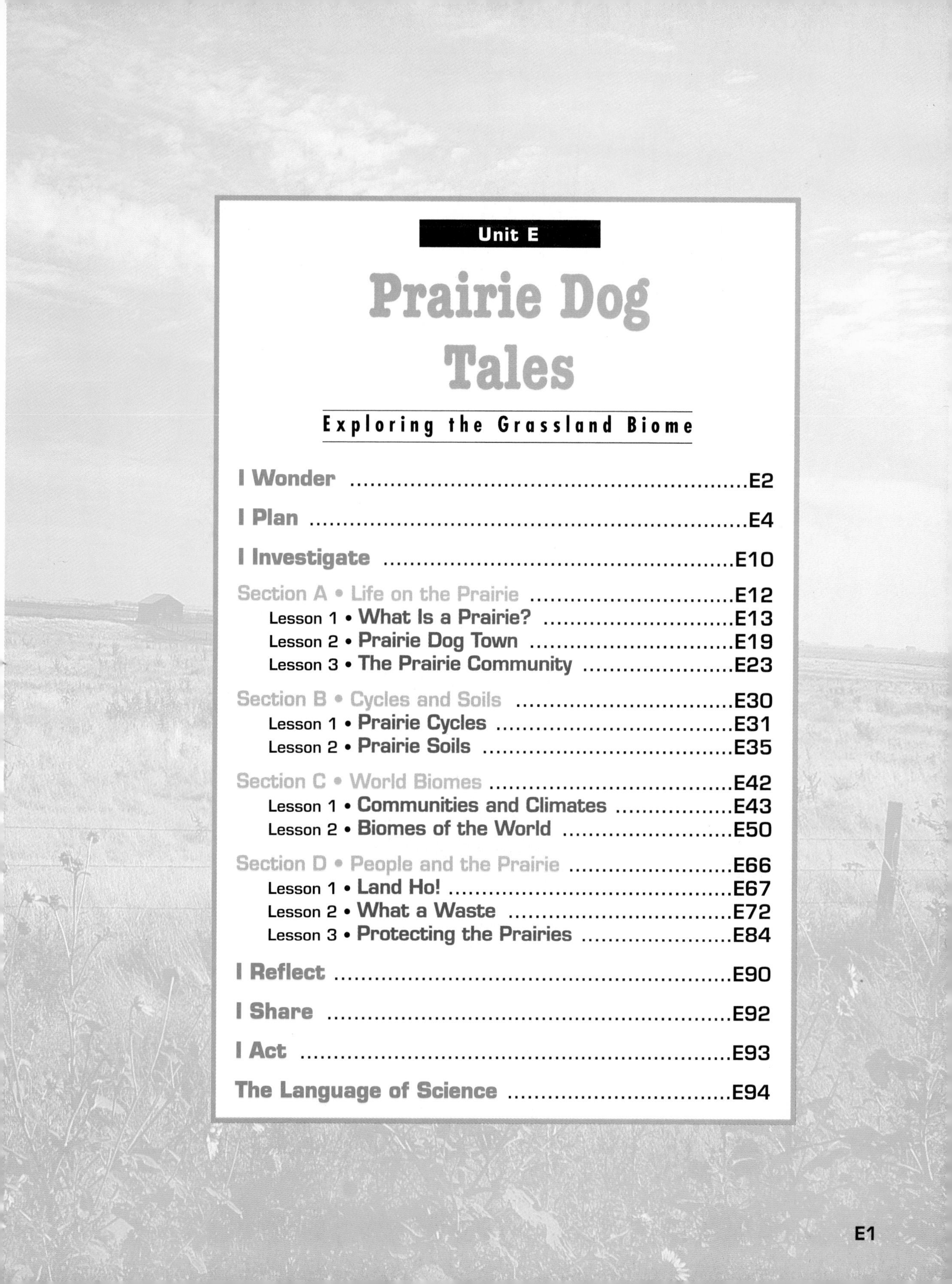

Prairie Dog Tales

Exploring the Grassland Biome

I WONDER

Science begins with wondering. What do you wonder about when you look at these photographs of a prairie and a prairie flower?

Work with a partner to make a list of questions you may have about prairies. Be ready to share your list with the rest of the class.

Prairie
Sunflower

I PLAN

You may have asked questions such as these as you wondered about prairies. Scientists also ask questions. Then they plan ways to help them find answers to their questions. Now you and your classmates can plan how you will investigate prairies.

My Science Log

What kinds of plants grow on a prairie?

What kinds of animals live on a prairie?

What kind of climate does a prairie have that makes it different from other areas?

How have people changed prairies and other natural areas?

With Your Class

Plan how you will use the activities and readings from the **I Investigate** part of this unit. Decide what other resources you might use.

On Your Own

There are many ways to learn about prairies and other natural areas. Following are some things you can do to explore prairies by yourself or with some classmates. Some explorations may take longer to do than others. Look over the suggestions and choose...

- **Projects to Do**
- **People to Contact**
- **Books to Read**

PROJECTS TO DO

LOCAL HISTORY

Use library resources to find out about prairies or other natural areas that have been developed for houses, stores, offices, and factories. Find out what these areas were like before building began and after the buildings went up. Make a map or a chart that shows the amount of undeveloped land in your area 50 years ago and the amount remaining today.

COMMUNITY PROJECT

Find out whether your city or town has a group that tries to save prairies, forests, wetlands, or other natural areas. Talk with people in the group about projects they are working on. Then think of a project that you and a group of friends or classmates could do. Share the idea with your classmates and your teacher. Plan the project, find the materials you need, and begin. You may want to work with the group you contacted.

ENVIRONMENTAL FORECAST

Collect information from magazines, local newspapers, and radio and TV broadcasts about natural areas near your home. Look for information about areas that are being saved or lost. Use your information to present a report explaining what you think will happen to any remaining natural areas and why.

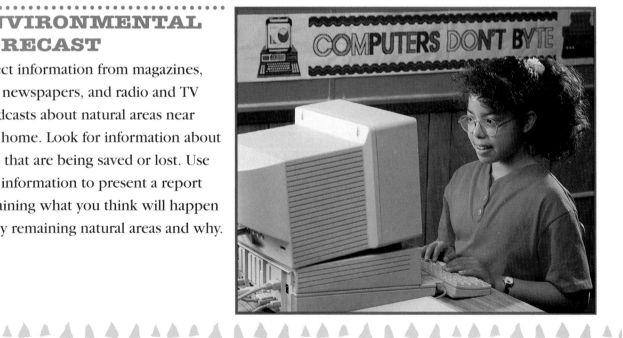

PEOPLE TO CONTACT

IN PERSON

To learn about natural areas near you, talk to people who have lived in your area for a long time. Find out if there are still any prairies or other natural areas near you, and if not, what happened to them.

Some people are interested in saving native plants and in planting gardens of wildflowers. Talk to someone who does this. Find out what plants the person has chosen and why.

- National Audubon Society
- Nature Conservancy
- Sierra Club
- Student Conservation Association
- Grassland Heritage Foundation
- National Wildlife Federation

BY TELEPHONE

In some places, people have saved prairies or other natural areas and turned them into nature preserves. Sometimes these people belong to national organizations, and sometimes they are members of a community group that tries to preserve and restore a local natural area.

There are many groups you can call to find people who are concerned with nature and wildlife. Here are some agencies and groups you might contact.

BY COMPUTER

If you have the use of a computer with a modem, you can connect to networks that carry information about natural areas. Different networks offer nature "magazines," conversations with people interested in protecting natural areas, and free or inexpensive software.

If your school is connected to Internet, an international computer network, you can talk with students in other parts of the world and share information on prairies and other natural areas.

BOOKS TO READ

The Place of Lions

by Eric Campbell (Harcourt Brace, 1991). Imagine leaving everyday life to live in Africa! Chris was doing just that. But the plane carrying him and his father crashes, and the pilot is killed. Chris's journey begins as he goes to find help for his injured father. An old lion, too, is on a journey. He is returning home to die. Read this book to find out what happens when their paths cross and how their journeys become a legend.

American Bison

by Ruth Berman (Carolrhoda, 1992), Outstanding Science Trade Book. The Native Americans of the plains and the pioneers depended on the bison for food and shelter. Millions of bison lived on the plains before people started hunting them, but by 1900 there were only 500 left! People tried to save them from extinction. Read this book to find out whether the bison will survive in their shrinking habitat and harsh living conditions.

More Books to Read

The Elephant Family Book

by Oria Douglas-Hamilton (Picture Book Studio, 1990). In Africa there is a man who studies elephant families. The pictures in this book will show you how elephant families live. Many elephants are dying because humans are destroying their habitat and because poachers kill them. We need to learn about elephants in order to save them.

Heartland

by Diane Siebert (Crowell, 1989). Read this book to learn about the heartland of America, where the land stretches wide and flat. People with machines farm the land for wheat and other crops, but here Earth and sky rule. The winters are harsh, and in summer the sun beats down.

Giraffes, the Sentinels of the Savannas

by Helen Roney Sattler (Lothrop, Lee & Shepard, 1989), Outstanding Science Trade Book. A giraffe is a watchtower on the African plains. It can see danger a kilometer away. All the animals run away when a giraffe is frightened, because they know danger is approaching. This book is full of information about this interesting animal whose ancestors were here 20 million years ago.

The Wild Horse Family Book

by Sybille Kalas (Picture Book Studio, 1989). The ponies that live on the grasslands of Iceland are very much like the ancestors of horses. They arrived on the island more than 1,100 years ago on Viking ships. In this book, you will read about a herd and of the land they live on.

I INVESTIGATE

To find answers to their questions, scientists read, think, talk to others, and do experiments. Their investigations often lead to new questions.

In this unit, you will have many chances to think and work like a scientist. How will you find answers to questions you asked?

▶ **COMMUNICATING** When you communicate, you give information. In science, you communicate by showing results from an activity in an organized way—for example, in a chart. Then you and other people can interpret the results.

▶ **OBSERVING** You use your senses of sight, hearing, smell, and touch to observe the world around you. Sometimes you use instruments to extend your senses.

▶ **CLASSIFYING/ORDERING** When you classify objects, you put them into groups according to how they are alike. Ordering is putting things in an order. For example, you might order things from first to last, smallest to largest, or lightest to heaviest.

Are you ready to begin?

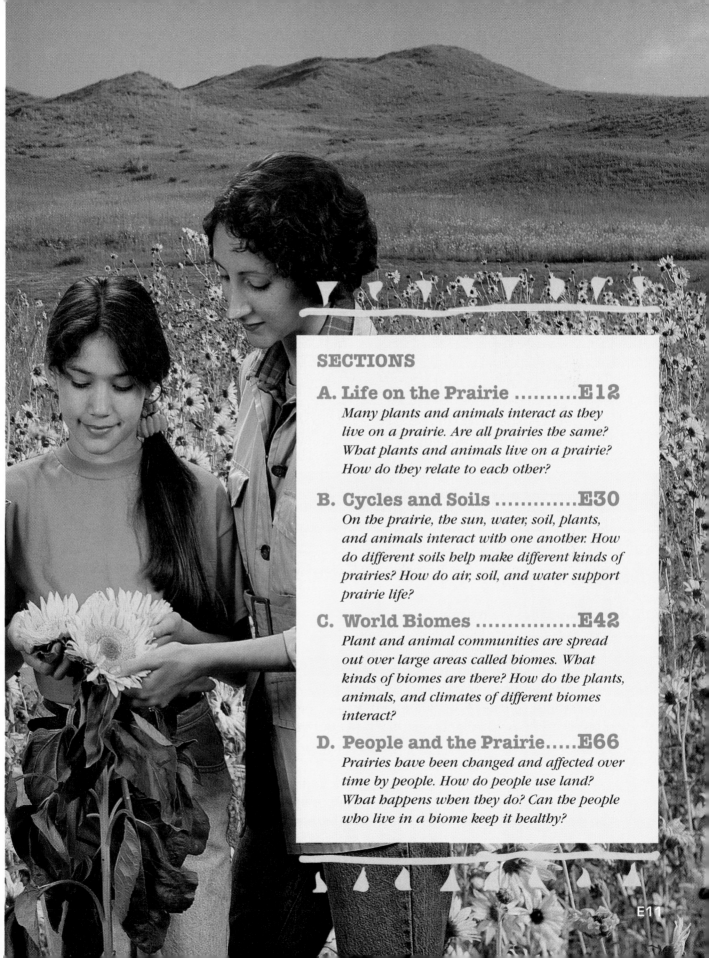

SECTIONS

Life on the Prairie

Do you live in an area where most of the land is grassy and either flat or gently rolling? If you do, you probably live on a prairie. Perhaps much of the land around you is now used for farms or for grazing sheep or cattle. But you can still see natural prairies if you know where to look. Roadsides and unused land are often like wild prairie. This section is about prairies' open, grassy lands. If you've ever seen a prairie, you're about to learn some interesting things.

Are all prairies the same? What plants and animals live on a prairie? How do they relate to one another? Keep careful notes in your Science Log as you work on some of the investigations in this section.

1 ▶ WHAT IS A PRAIRIE?

Some people may think that every prairie is the same. But there are many kinds of prairies, and each kind presents a different picture of plant and animal life. There are many things you can discover about prairies when you look carefully.

Prairie Seasons

On a prairie, just as in other places, the seasons bring changes in plant and animal life. This activity will help you understand how living things on the prairie are affected by the changing seasons.

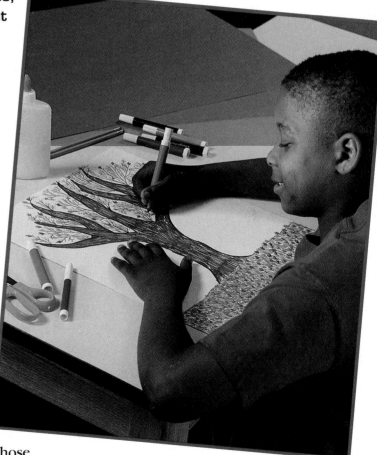

You will need: poster board; crayons, paints, or markers; reference books

Close your eyes and listen while your teacher reads aloud the first two paragraphs from *Seasons of the Tallgrass Prairie.*

Think about what you have just heard. This is the prairie in the summer. Picture the prairie in one of the other three seasons.

Make a poster about the season you chose. You may use information from what your teacher read and also from reference books to help you. In class, explain why you chose to show that season the way you did.

Then discuss how the seasons where you live are like or different from the seasons described in the book. List what happens in each season where you live. Compare your area's seasons with the prairie's seasons.

A Little Piece of Grassland

As you saw in the last activity, prairie life can change as the seasons change. There are many kinds of plants and animals found in a prairie. In many ways, a lawn or a patch of wild grass is like a part of a prairie. In this activity, you will see a variety of things found in a small, grassy spot.

MATERIALS
- meter stick
- string
- scissors
- sharpened pencils
- hand lens
- paper
- Science Log data sheet

DO THIS

1 Cut a length of string about 4.2m long. Then choose a grassy spot. Use the meter stick and the string to mark out spaces 1 meter square. Push a pencil into the ground at each corner of the square.

2 Look for both living and nonliving things within the square. Use the hand lens. On your paper, draw the living things you find. Make lists of plants, animals, and nonliving things.

3 In class, report on what you found in your square. Compare your findings with those of your classmates.

THINK AND WRITE

1. Did your classmates find exactly the same things in their squares? What was the same? What was different?

2. **OBSERVING** Sometimes you use instruments to extend your senses. In this activity, you used a hand lens to observe living and nonliving things. How did this tool help you make more accurate observations?

A Grassy Ocean

You can learn about prairies by visiting one or by studying living things in other grassy places. You can also learn more about prairies by reading about them. On these pages, you will find some information about prairies. As you read the following story, written by a student who lives near Chicago, think about how prairies are like the open, grassy places you have seen.

A few years ago, I had never seen a prairie. But now, just north of our town near Chicago, people are making a small prairie where an old farm used to be.

A nature group bought the land, which was no longer being used by people. Experts on prairies collected all kinds of seeds from places where prairie plants still grow--by roadsides, near old railroad tracks, and even on certain parts of golf courses. Some people from our town volunteered to help plant the seeds. But first, the plants already growing on the land had to be burned! Someone from the nature group came to speak to the volunteers. She explained that controlled burning of the land would do two things. It would get rid of plants that weren't prairie plants, and it would do what natural fires do on a wild prairie—make it possible for new plants to grow.

Our new/old prairie is a tallgrass prairie. It's the kind of prairie that has more rain than other prairies. Most of the grass is higher than my head. From far off, it looks like a grassy ocean, with waves of blue, yellow, and green. But up close, seen from the trails we follow to explore it, it looks like a forest of grass—big bluestem grass, and wild rye, and in the low, damp places, cordgrass.

▲ Unused farmland

▲ **Prairie wildflowers in bloom**

Even the flowers are tall. They have to be to reach the sunlight. Gray-headed coneflowers, looking like big yellow daisies with woolly gray centers, nod in the wind. Rattlesnake masters wave their heavy white flower heads from tall stems. Sunflowers raise their huge blossoms above the grasses, turning toward the light. In some places you can find wild asters and purple prairie clover.

When you first look at our prairie, most of the living things seem to be plants. But when you take a closer look, you can see that lots of animals live there, too. Many kinds of insects live in the growth of prairie grass and flowers. Grasshoppers eat the plants, and butterflies feed on the nectar of wildflowers.

Where there are seeds and insects, you will find meadowlarks, vesper sparrows, and other prairie birds-but you have to know where to look. These birds nest on the ground among the tall grasses. At one edge of the prairie, where there is a pond, water birds come to nest and raise their young.

Where there are so many plants and seeds to eat, rabbits and mice move in. Of course, the animals that hunt them move in, too! Snakes burrow in and around the roots of prairie plants, and they hunt mice and other small animals. Hawks circle overhead and dive to catch the same prey.

▲ **Hawk**

At the information center there's a piece of sod someone cut and saved from the prairie that was here many years ago. It's more than a foot thick-and it's all roots! The guide told us that on some prairies, the roots of plants grow 3.5 meters (over 11 feet) down.

▼ **Hiking in the prairies**

▲ **Shortgrass prairie**

My aunt Molly writes that in Kansas, where she lives, the prairie is different. The climate is drier and windier, and other kinds of plants are mixed with the taller grasses. She says that on the mixed-grass prairie, shorter grasses also grow: little bluestem, green needlegrass, Junegrass, and many others. The grass isn't so much like a sea there-in some places, it grows in clumps, like little islands. There are lots of ground squirrels there, and even some prairie dogs. Aunt Molly says that when prairie dogs aren't disturbed by people, they dig so many burrows that they help loosen and mix the soil.

Farther west, Aunt Molly writes, you find shortgrass prairie. There isn't much rain there, because the Rocky Mountains block some of the rainfall from storms that come from the west. There are still some grasses, like blue gamma and buffalo

▲ **Mixed-grass prairie**

grass. But, as my aunt tells me, you begin to see sagebrush and even cactus mixed with the grasses.

Next year my great-aunt and great-uncle in Oklahoma are having a family reunion. We're going, and I'll get to see all the prairie I want!

THINK ABOUT IT

What makes some prairies different from others?

E17

Grass Roots

In the story of any prairie, one of the most important parts takes place underground. This activity will help you see how prairie growth depends on "grass roots" support.

DO THIS

1. **CAUTION: Make sure you have permission to dig in the spot you choose.** Work with a partner. Dig out a small plug of grass, about the size of your palm. Be sure to include the roots.

2. Lay the grass on a clean sheet of paper and look at it through the hand lens. Notice how the roots are shaped.

3. Carefully pull apart the roots.

4. Choose three blades of grass. Measure the lengths of each root and blade. Write down your measurements.

5. Draw each grass sample. Label the root and the blade on each one. With your partner, display your drawings and explain what you found.

THINK AND WRITE

Look up the term *grass roots* in the dictionary. Based on this activity, why you think people use the word in the way the dictionary shows.

QUICK CHECK

LESSON 1 REVIEW

1. What kinds of plants are you most likely to see on a prairie?

2. What are some things that cause prairies to change?

PRAIRIE DOG TOWN

To really understand how many kinds of animals there are on a prairie and the kinds of roles they have in prairie life, you have to know where to look. Some creatures are easy to see on the open land or in the sky. To find others, you need to look closely at the earth, the flowers, and the grasses. In this lesson, you will explore how one animal, the prairie dog, makes its home on the prairie.

A Prairie Dog Watcher

Have you ever observed a group of animals for a short period of time? Maybe you watched ants make crisscross patterns in front of you as they searched for food. Read to find out about the animals one boy watched.

I SPY ON PRAIRIE DOGS

by **Mark Hoogland**
as told to **Gary Turbak**
from ***Ranger Rick***

LITERATURE

"Buffalo! Watch out," I called down to my dad from our lookout tower. The shaggy creature was charging straight for him. Dad sprinted for the nearest tree and scrambled right up—just in time.

That wasn't the first time he'd been chased by a charging buffalo. (It's the same animal some people call a *bison*.) When you study prairie dogs, as we do, you learn pretty fast to keep an eye out for buffaloes.

▶ **Bison**

▲ **Seeing the world as a prairie dog sees it.**

I've been helping my dad with prairie dogs since I was two years old. I don't think I was really much help then, but he says I'm a big help now.

My dad is a biologist who works at Wind Cave National Park in South Dakota. He's been studying a town, or colony, of about 150 black-tailed prairie dogs there for 15 years. Prairie dogs hadn't been studied much when he first started watching. Now he's found out some surprising things about them, and I've helped him.

Prairie dogs are in the ground squirrel family. Like other ground squirrels, they live underground in deep burrows. An adult weighs about two pounds (1 kg) and is about a foot (30 cm) long, not counting its tail. They're just a little bigger and heavier than the gray squirrels you often see in parks and backyards.

Prairie dogs pop out of their burrows every morning to eat grass and other plants. And every day from February to June, my dad and I watch them from a

tower. Since my mom and dad are my only teachers, I usually bring my assignments along to work on while I watch. In spring the male prairie dogs fight a lot. When I see a fuzzball rolling around in the dirt, I know it's two males at it again. They fight to get control of burrows and to win the right to mate with females. Each winning male becomes head of a family group of three or four females and their young.

▼ **Prairie dog family**

Catching and Painting Prairie Dogs

Studying prairie dogs is fun, But the part I like best is catching babies in "live traps" so we can mark them. The trap is a little cage with a trick door. When a prairie dog walks into the trap, the door closes behind it.

We sometimes put 15 traps around one burrow opening. After all the traps are in place, we climb up the tower. When the babies come out, they have no place to go but into a trap. As soon as we see that several babies have been caught, we climb down and collect them.

First I put on gloves. Then I carefully open a trap and take out a prairie dog. I hold the baby while my dad uses black dye to put a special mark on its fur. He might paint a stripe along one prairie dog's side and give another one a black head. The dye doesn't hurt the prairie dogs, and it lets us identify each one from the tower. We also put a numbered tag in each dog's ear before we let it go.

Usually it runs right right down into a burrow. But one day a baby started to follow me. Wherever I went, it went too. I think the baby thought I was its mother! I finally had to pick it up and nudge it down the burrow. Then I ran away before it came back out.

A Strange Discovery

A few years ago, my dad and I discovered something weird. He thought some of the females might be killing—and eating—the babies of other females. But he didn't have proof that they were.

One day we caught a female that had been in another female's burrow. I noticed something strange stuck in her fur. It turned out to be the leg of a newborn prairie dog. We realized then that she had killed and eaten the other mother's babies!

◀ **Trapping prairie dogs for identification**

E21

Now we know this happens often when a mother leaves her babies to find something to eat. In fact, over half of the babies born are killed by other prairie dogs.

Why do they do it? The main reason seems to be that eating meat is a quick way for a mother to make enough milk to feed her own babies.

This may be important news for ranchers who live near prairie dog towns. Some of the ranchers worry that the towns could quickly spread over land that is used by their cattle. But because prairie dogs often eat their babies, the towns don't usually grow very fast. For example, our prairie dog town hasn't grown a bit in all the years my dad and I have been working there.

Watching for More Than Prairie Dogs

Besides prairie dogs, my dad and I sometimes get to see their enemies, such as coyotes, bobcats, or falcons. And once, a prairie dog just barely escaped from an eagle right in front of our tower.

When the prairie dogs see an enemy, they bark a warning and run to their burrow mounds. They watch the enemy until it leaves and dive into their burrows only if the enemy comes too close. Prairie dogs are really good at warning each other and escaping. Some years we haven't seen even one get killed.

There are also a lot of buffaloes living in our park. Some days a hundred or more will wander past our tower. Other days they wallow in the dirt or just lie around. But they don't always pick a good place to rest. When a buffalo lies down on one of our traps, the trap gets squashed flat!

Usually the buffaloes are peaceful, but we can't trust them—my dad has been chased more than 50 times! So while the prairie dogs have to watch for enemies and warn each other, we have to keep an eye out for trouble too. But that's what makes studying animals outdoors so interesting. You never know what will happen next!

LESSON 2 REVIEW

What could you find out by studying the same population of prairie dogs for many years?

▼ Prairie dog in its habitat

3 THE PRAIRIE COMMUNITY

A prairie is a community. It has populations of grasshoppers and prairie dogs and clover, just as a city community has a population of people. And members of a prairie community depend on one another in many ways. These activities will show you how they need each other to survive.

ACTIVITY

Where's the Food?

What is the food supply of a prairie animal? What happens if there are too many hunters or if the food runs out? This activity will help you see how food is obtained in a prairie community.

MATERIALS
- colored game markers, 25 each of 3 colors
- name tags
- small plastic bags
- Science Log data sheets

DO THIS

❶ Put on a tag that identifies you as a grasshopper, a snake, or a hawk.

❷ Play the game in 30-second turns. On the first turn, grasshoppers collect markers, and place them in their bags. On the next turn, snakes feed on grasshoppers by tagging them and taking their bags. Grasshoppers continue to feed. On the third turn, hawks can feed on snakes. Grass-hoppers and snakes can continue to feed.

❸ Sort and count the markers.

THINK AND WRITE

Which animals had the most food when the game ended? Write a paragraph explaining why you think this happened.

Go With the Flow

Each kind of plant and animal in the prairie community has a place. Each plays an important part in "passing along" the energy the community needs to live. As you read, notice the many kinds of living things that move energy from one living thing to another.

▲ **Deer mouse (herbivore)**

▼ **Peregrine falcon (carnivore)**

Think about the "menu" a single prairie plant can offer: leaves for grazing buffalo or pronghorn, flower nectar and stem juices for insects, and seeds for birds.

Plants are **producers.** They get energy from the sun and use it to make food from nutrients in the soil and air.

Animals are **consumers.** They can't use energy from the sun directly to make food, so they must get energy from other living things—either plants or other animals.

On a tallgrass prairie, bison or pronghorn graze. On a shortgrass prairie, prairie dogs nibble grasses and woody stems. Everywhere, mice, rabbits, and ground squirrels nibble greens, roots, and seeds. These animals are **herbivores**—plant eaters. They get their energy directly from plants.

Eventually, the herbivores become food for other animals. Owls and snakes feed on mice, rabbits, and other small plant eaters. Badgers, coyotes, and even hawks and eagles carry off prairie dogs. These animals are **carnivores**—meat eaters. When they make a meal of a herbivore, the energy gets passed along to them.

Some animals, such as bears and raccoons, are **omnivores**— they eat anything! They use energy from both plants and animals.

It seems as if the use of energy in a chain would end with the last animal to have a good meal, but it doesn't. When an animal dies, other animals may feed on it and begin the process of breaking it down. Animals that eat dead animals are **scavengers.**

Finally, insects, fungi, and bacteria, which are **decomposers**, break the animal into small parts that become part of the soil. Even an eagle that ate a prairie dog that nibbled the grass will someday become part of the soil that helps the grass grow. Energy from the sun flows from herbivores to carnivores and omnivores to scavengers and finally to decomposers. We call this the **food chain**.

◀ Prairie rattlesnake (carnivore)

▶ Turkey vulture (scavenger)

▼ Bear (omnivore)

▲ Fungi (decomposer)

THINK ABOUT IT

What would happen if decomposers were destroyed on a large scale?

Please Pass the Energy

On different kinds of prairies, the roles in a food chain may be taken by different plants and animals. In this activity, you will investigate how energy is passed along a food chain.

MATERIALS
- index cards
- crayons or markers
- pushpins
- yarn
- bulletin board
- Science Log data sheet

DO THIS

1. Divide into six groups—producers, herbivores, omnivores, carnivores, scavengers, and decomposers.

2. Work with your group to discuss what your role is.

3. Have each person draw on an index card a plant or an animal that plays that role in a prairie community.

4. Form teams that are made up of one member from each group. Arrange your team's pictures to make a food chain.

5. Pin your pictures to the bulletin board. Use yarn to connect the parts.

6. Explain how energy passes through the food chain.

THINK AND WRITE

1. Think what would happen if one member of your food chain were eliminated. Write down your ideas.

2. CLASSIFYING/ORDERING When you arranged your team's pictures to make a food chain, you placed your pictures in a specific order. Look at your groups pictures again. Could you rearrange them in order? Why or why not?

Community Circle

Besides food, what do the plants and animals in a community need? What happens if one of those things is missing? This activity will help you find out.

You will need: Science Log

Do this activity with the whole class. Count off by fours to form four groups. Each group will take a part:

Group 1—food
Group 2—water
Group 3—shelter
Group 4—space

Make a circle in 1-2-3-4 order. Face the center and stand shoulder to shoulder. Then face right, and take one step inward toward the center. Put your hands on the waist of the person in front of you.

Keep hold of the person's waist. When your teacher signals, sit on the knees of the person in back of you while the person ahead of you sits on yours.

Did it work? If not, decide what to change and try it again.

What did your class have to do to make the community circle work? Would it work as well if you stood farther apart? What would happen if one of the groups left the circle? Explain. How does this relate to plant and animal communities?

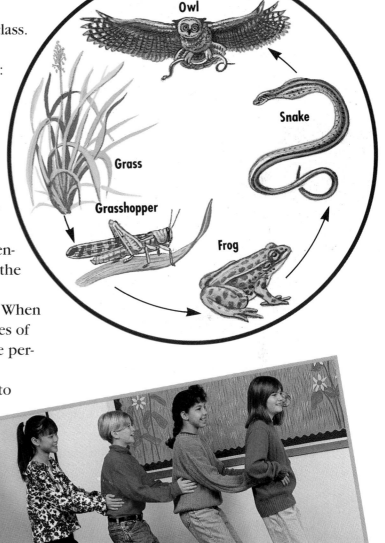

E27

Counting Leaves and Noses

Many kinds of plants and animals make up a prairie *community*. As you saw in the last activity, they depend upon food, water, shelter, and space to survive. What happens to a prairie community if one of its populations changes? Read to find out.

▲ **Horned owl**

In an oak forest near the prairie's edge, horned owls live. At night they fly silently over the prairie and the prairie farms, hunting mice. But one day the forest is cut down, and because their homes are destroyed, the owls are gone. What happens now?

The mice are no longer in danger from owls, so their population grows. Soon there are too many mice for the available food. Some of them don't survive.

On a shortgrass prairie, coyotes eat many things—insects, rabbits, mice, and prairie dogs. But sometimes they also hunt goats or sheep from the farms and ranches. Then farmers begin to hunt or poison coyotes.

Many of the small animals the coyotes hunted live longer now, so their numbers begin to grow. They damage crops and land. Finally, as food becomes scarce, some of them starve.

A prairie community, like other environments, is composed of all the plant and animal *populations* that live in it. Changing one population may make the other populations change, too.

Animals depend on plants in the community for food, but plants depend on animals, too. Prairie clover and some other prairie flowers depend on bees to pollinate them. If the bees die or move away, fewer flowers are pollinated.

When this happens, the plant populations of the prairie begin to change. As they change, the animal populations change, too. The animal populations that grow are the ones that don't need those flowers to survive.

▶ Bee pollinating prairie flower

Of course, conditions on the prairie are always changing. Seasonal changes in bring changes in the water supply, the number of plants, and the food and shelter that animals get from them.

But sometimes there are permanent changes. Taking land for buildings or farms, using up the water, and building roads can change populations of plants and animals until the prairie community is almost entirely different.

▼ Coyotes on the prairie

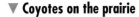

LESSON 3 REVIEW

❶ How does energy pass from plants to animals?

❷ What would happen to the food chain if suddenly there were a large increase in the population of one animal?

❸ Describe a situation in which the same animal can be both predator and prey.

DOUBLE CHECK

SECTION A REVIEW

1. Are the same kinds of plants and animals found on every prairie? Why or why not?

2. Draw an example of a food chain. Use at least 3 plants or animals to create your food chain.

SECTION B
Cycles and Soils

I n a prairie community, just as in any natural community, the plants and animals interact with the physical environment — the
water, the air, and the soil. For example,
the rainfall a prairie receives and the quality
of the soil found there determine what kinds of plants can grow. The
kinds of plants that grow on a prairie determine the kinds of herbivores
that live there – and, in turn, the kinds of carnivores that live there.

How do air, soil, and water interact to support prairie life? Keep
careful notes in your Science Log as you work through the following
investigations on cycles and soils.

1 PRAIRIE CYCLES

In the last section, you investigated prairie food chains and the flow of energy through the prairie community. But what about the matter that makes up the community? How does water, for example, move through a community? In this lesson, you will investigate movement of matter in a community.

ACTIVITY

Water, Water Everywhere

As in any community, water is vital to the prairie. The rains fall, the plants take what they need, and the rest runs off the land or soaks into the ground. But how does water get into the air to produce rain? In the following activity, you can model this process.

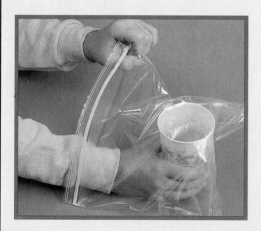

MATERIALS
- small plastic cup
- water
- plastic bag that seals
- Science Log data sheet

DO THIS

1. Working with a partner, half fill the cup with water.

2. Open the plastic bag. Place the cup inside the bag. Hold the cup steady while your partner seals the bag.

3. Carefully set the bag in a sunny place. Make sure you set the bag down without spilling any water.

4. Leave the bag in the same place for 3 or 4 days. Draw a picture of how the bag and cup look each day.

THINK AND WRITE

1. What happened to the water in the cup? Why do you think this happened?

2. Where did the water in the bag come from?

A Prairie-Go-Round

The process you observed in the last activity is the same one that occurs in nature. As you read the following journal entries of Molly Tallchief, a woman who has spent many years observing the shortgrass prairies of western Kansas, think about how water moves through the prairie community.

JULY 13TH

Only two hours after sunrise, and it's already hot. The dew on the little bluestem has dried, and the water in the pond is a little lower than it was yesterday. I watch a fox trot silently homeward through the dry grass, panting as it runs.

Out to the west, as far as I can see, the horizon is rimmed with purple clouds, and the wind is rising. Maybe there'll be rain today.

JULY 14TH

It rained last night; a real gully washer. In fact, there are still a few showers around this morning. Rain is always welcome on the prairie — plants and animals need it just to survive. As the showers continue, I sit on my porch and think about where the water goes after a storm.

It often rains hard in western Kansas, the water pounding the dry earth. A lot of it runs off into the Arkansas River, then southeast to the Gulf of Mexico. If it rains long enough, some of the rain soaks into the ground, down to the roots of the grasses.

▼ **Kansas rainstorm**

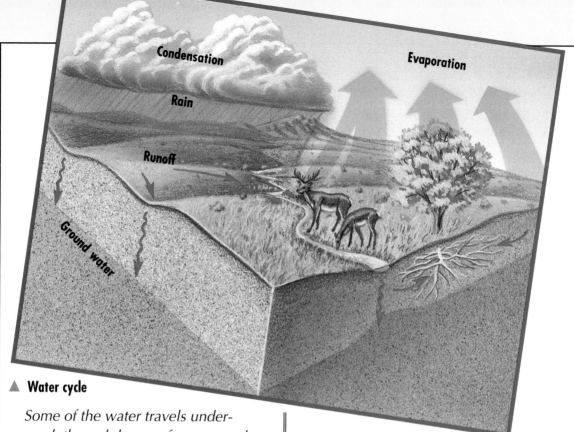

▲ **Water cycle**

Some of the water travels underground, through layers of porous rock. Eventually it finds its way into a pond or the river.

Looks as if the rain has stopped. Drops of water glisten on sunflowers along the pasture fence. The sun slowly begins to peek out from behind a dark cloud.

When the sun is shining brightly, I can see what happens to some of the rain that falls. From the fields and ponds, water evaporates into the air. This is part of the water cycle.

If water in the air remained as vapor, sooner or later the prairie plants and animals would run out of the water they need to live. However, as the air cools, water vapor condenses, forming clouds. The droplets grow larger and fall as rain or, in the winter, snow.

I learned long ago to be careful with the water I use. We constantly reuse the same water, and we need to be mindful of what we put into it since all the prairie plants and animals, and people too, depend on this water to survive.

Bison, prairie dogs, deer, foxes, and other animals drink from my pond. They also give off water. Their bodies lose water when they breathe, perspire, pant, or leave their wastes.

▼ **Bison drinking at a pond**

JULY 20TH

It's rained a lot this week, so I've had time to think about other cycles on the prairie. All matter cycles through a community. Matter moves constantly from water, air, and soil to living things and back again. It's part of a "trade agreement" between plants and animals and the nonliving environment.

For example, some of the herbivores I see daily-insects, bison, prairie dogs-need nitrogen, carbon, and oxygen to live. They take oxygen from the air and nitrogen and carbon from the plants they eat, and their bodies turn it into materials and energy they need to live and grow. These animals give off a gas called carbon dioxide and wastes containing nitrogen.

Prairie producers, such as little bluestem and rattlesnake master, use the carbon dioxide and the nitrogen the animals give off to make food. In addition to producing food, plants release oxygen into the air. The herbivores use the food and the oxygen, and the cycle continues.

Other animals, such as hawks, snakes, and coyotes, are carnivores. They take in carbon and nitrogen when they eat animals that have eaten plants.

The wastes of these animals are broken down by decomposers, and when they die, more carbon dioxide and nitrogen are released and go into the cycle to be used by plants and animals once again.

These cycles are repeated over and over on the prairie. Without the matter cycles, plants and animals couldn't survive.

QUICK CHECK

LESSON 1 REVIEW

❶ Describe the water cycle in words or pictures.

❷ How do herbivores use nitrogen, carbon, and oxygen to live?

▼ Oxygen-carbon cycle

Oxygen

Carbon Dioxide

Carbon Dioxide

Oxygen

2 PRAIRIE SOILS

To some people, soil is just "dirt," but the life of a prairie depends on soil. The growth of plants can be affected by the quality of the soil in which they grow. The following activities will help you find out what soil is and how it forms. You will also see how plants grow in different types of soil.

ACTIVITY

Sifting Through Soil

You know that plants need good soil to grow. But what is good soil? Doesn't all soil contain the same materials? In this activity, you will examine soil to find answers to these questions.

MATERIALS
- soil sample
- balance
- 3 different-sized sieves
- newspaper
- hand lens
- Science Log data sheet

DO THIS

1 Use the balance to measure out 100 g of your soil sample. Place the soil in the large sieve, and shake it over the newspaper for 1 minute. Use the hand lens to observe the material in the sieve.

2 Determine and record the mass of the remaining soil, and put it in the medium sieve. Shake it over a clean sheet of newspaper for 1 minute. Use the hand lens to observe the material in the sieve.

3 Determine and record the mass of the remaining soil, and put it in the small sieve. Shake the sieve over another clean sheet of newspaper for 1 minute. Use the hand lens to observe what is in the sieve.

THINK AND WRITE

Compare and contrast the materials left in the sieves.

ACTIVITY

Blue-Ribbon Soil

In the last activity, you separated soil into various materials. Some of the materials were organic — the remains of once living organisms. The rest of the materials were inorganic — not from living organisms. Which materials and in what combinations make the best soil? In this activity, you will make and test different soil mixtures.

DO THIS

1 With a pencil, carefully punch several drainage holes in the bottom of each cup. Label the cups *A*, *B*, *C*, and *D*.

2 Fill cup *A* with equal amounts of peat moss and clay, cup *B* with equal amounts of peat moss and sand, and the cup *C* with equal amounts of clay and sand. Fill the cup *D* with a mixture of equal amounts of all three materials.

3 Plant three seeds in each cup and water them thoroughly. Place the cups in an area that gets plenty of sunlight. Water them every other day, and wait for the seeds to sprout.

4 When the sprouts are a week old, measure the length of the tallest sprout in each cup, and record the data. Repeat this procedure one week later.

5 Make a bar graph that shows the size differences between the plants in the four cups at the end of each week.

THINK AND WRITE

1. Which soil mixture is best for growing bean plants? Explain.

2. **COMMUNICATING** Drawing bar graphs is one way of communicating information visually. Why do you think bar graphs are easier to interpret than data tables?

The Good Earth

In the last activity, you saw the importance of good soil for growing healthy plants. Without good soil, life as we know it would not be possible. We often take soil for granted, yet it takes from 100 to 1,000 years for 1 centimeter of soil to form. As you read, think about the soil you made and how soil forms in nature.

The next time you're walking along a path, stop and look at the soil. Under your feet is a story of animals, plants, and minerals — a story thousands of years old.

Soil is formed from *parent material*, or rock, that is on or near the Earth's surface. Wind, water, and other forces break down the parent material into small pieces. This process is called *weathering*. That's how the story of soil begins.

▼ **Rock is weathered by wind and water.**

▲ **Pioneer plants**

Hardy plants, called *pioneers*, begin growing in the rock pieces. A few small animals, mostly insects, move in. As the plants and animals die, they break down and become part of the soil. In warm, moist climates, the soil changes quickly. Plants grow and decay faster, enriching the soil.

Over many years, layers of soil, or horizons, build up. The newest horizon is the A horizon. This is sometimes called topsoil. The bottom layer, mostly pieces of rock, is the C horizon. Where soil forms slowly, there may be only two horizons. Where soil forms rapidly, new topsoil forms over the old. Then the old topsoil becomes a B horizon.

▲ **Mt. Lassen, California**

In cold or dry climates, soil forms slowly, because water is in short supply. In all climates, water is the most important factor in forming soil. It seeps into cracks in parent material. In some climates, cycles of freezing and thawing split the rock into pieces. Water dissolves minerals in the parent material and washes them into the soil. Water helps plants grow and it speeds up decay.

What the soil under your feet is like depends on where you are. On a tallgrass prairie, you may be standing on topsoil a meter or more deep. On a steep hill, you may have only a few centimeters of soil under you. What is the soil like near your school?

THINK ABOUT IT

Why is the soil of the tallgrass prairie deep and rich?

A C T I V I T Y

Disappearing Soil

Although the soil of the tallgrass prairie is deep and rich, some farmers are concerned, because the soil in their fields is disappearing. This activity will help you find out how this happens and how it can be stopped.

MATERIALS

- 2 baking pans
- potting soil
- sod
- watering can
- goggles
- fan
- 2 bricks, same size
- dishpan
- 2-L bottle of water
- Science Log data sheet

DO THIS

1. Working with a partner, fill two baking pans with potting soil.

2. Cover the soil in one pan with a piece of sod. Water the sod every day for a week, but keep the pan of bare soil dry.

3. **Caution: Put on safety goggles before turning on the fan. Stand behind the fan.** At the end of the week, put the fan in front of the pan of bare soil and turn it on for 5 seconds. Note what happens to the soil in the pan. Do the same thing to the pan that has the sod covering the soil.

4. Now put a brick under one end of each pan. Place a dishpan under the lower edge of the pans.

5. Slowly pour half the water in the bottle into the top of the pan with bare soil. Slowly pour the rest of the water into the top of the pan with sod.

THINK AND WRITE

What effect did the covering of sod have on the soil in the presence of wind and running water?

Stop That Soil!

In some parts of the United States, soil wears away faster than it forms. Good soil is one of the Earth's most important resources, but soil that took thousands of years to form can disappear in an afternoon thunderstorm. In the last activity, you saw how plants help stop soil from disappearing. As you continue reading, you will find out about other ways to protect valuable soil.

Wind can pick up uncovered soil and blow it far away. Runoff, water from rainstorms and melting snow, can carry soil into streams and rivers.

There are many ways to prevent soil from disappearing. Plants that cover soil, for example, allow water to soak into the ground, while the roots of the plants help keep the soil in place.

Plant cover helps keep the wind from blowing soil away, too. Because of this, farmers often plant a *cover crop* in the fall, when the regular crop-growing season is over. In spring, the cover crop is plowed into the soil, and the field is ready for planting the regular crop once again.

▲ Wind erosion

▲ Water erosion

Farmers can also plant rows of crops across hills rather than up and down the hills. This is called *contour farming*, since it follows the natural contours of the land. The small mounds of soil across the hills keep the runoff of heavy storms from washing the soil down the hills.

LESSON 2 REVIEW

1. How does weathering help form soil?

2. How would a row of trees planted along the side of a field keep the soil from disappearing?

DOUBLE CHECK

SECTION B REVIEW

1. Draw and label a diagram showing the layers of prairie soil.

2. How are the water and nitrogen-oxygen-carbon cycles important to the plants and animals on the prairie? What would happen if one of these cycles no longer existed?

SECTION C
World Biomes

▶ **Parrots**

Prairie communities may have various grasses and wildflowers, but they don't have large trees or shade-loving ferns. Forest communities develop in areas with conditions that are different from those of prairies because forest plants and animals need certain conditions to live and grow. In different parts of the world, similar conditions exist.

How many kinds of communities are there in the world? Are the interactions in different communities similar to those in prairie communities? As you work through the investigations in this unit, use your Science Log to keep notes about the similarities and differences in various communities.

1 COMMUNITIES AND CLIMATES

If you compare two prairie communities, you will find some minor differences. But in important ways, they are alike. Their plants, for example, are similar, since only certain kinds of plants can survive the prairie climate. In the following activities, you will find out what the climate of a prairie is like, and what kinds of communities develop in areas with different climates.

ACTIVITY

Weather Watchers

What is the weather like on a prairie? How does it change from day to day? In this activity, you will be able to see how weather patterns develop and move across a prairie.

MATERIALS
- weather maps
- scissors
- 10 sheets of white paper
- tape or glue
- stapler
- Science Log data sheet

DO THIS

1 Cut out and save the national weather map from a newspaper for ten consecutive days.

2 Tape or glue one map in the lower right corner of each of the sheets of paper.

3 Put the pages in order, with the oldest map on the bottom and the most recent map on top. Staple the sheets together to make a book.

4 Flip the pages from back to front to observe how weather systems move across the prairies.

THINK AND WRITE

In which direction did the weather systems move? Write a paragraph summarizing the prairie weather for the ten days.

Grasslands in Other Countries

Prairie-like communities are found in many parts of the world. Some have different plants and animals and support different uses, but the climate is basically the same as that in North American prairies. Here are two reports, written by different students, describing grassland communities in their countries. As you read the reports, think about how these grasslands are similar to and different from North American prairies.

▼ Cattle on the pampas

A FARM ON THE PAMPAS

Most of my aunts and uncles and cousins are *porteños* people who live in the port city of Buenos Aires. But my family lives on a farm in the country.

It's a small farm, but it's big enough to feed our family. The soil is very rich, and there is enough rain to raise wheat. The grass is good, too. We raise some cattle — not as many as the big farms, but there are always some to sell.

Sometimes I go to the city with my father, and sometimes I go with him to look at cattle or horses. When we travel, we see a lot of the *pampas*. On some big ranches, the open grasslands stretch for many kilometers, and you still see *gauchos* on horseback herding cattle.

They keep the cattle moving from place to place, wherever the grass is good. Although the pampas are full of farms and

ranches, wild animals still live there. We often see *armadillos* — they usually feed at night. And if we're quiet, we sometimes see flocks of *rheas* near a pond or a river. They look something like ostriches, and like ostriches, they can't fly. They live near water, where they take baths and even swim.

My father says that the pampas were once wild, and that gauchos made their living catching wild cattle and horses that roamed the land. I would like to have seen what the land was like then. When my father and I drive through land that is part of a very large ranch, we sometimes travel through places where you can't see any houses or roads — except the one we're on. Then I almost feel as if I've gone back in time to when the pampas were endless grassy plains.

ARGENTINA — Pampas

▼ Farm in Argentina on pampas

◄ Flock of rheas

E45

The steppes of
ASIA

If you travel east or west from where I live, you will see many kilometers of land like this—open plains, with hardly any trees. And every hectare of it is farms! That's because this part of the *steppes*—the grasslands that stretch across parts of Russia, Mongolia, and China—has some of the richest soil in the world. It's dark brown in some places, and in other places it's almost black. It will grow just about anything.

The farms here are big. Many people, including my family, work on them. My father manages the farm my family works on.

On this part of the steppes, the weather is warm in summer, but not hot. The winters are cold and long, and the growing season is very short. Part of my father's job is finding crops that will grow quickly.

We don't get a lot of rain, but we get enough to raise grain. Our farm raises mostly oats and wheat, but part of our land

is left in grass to feed livestock. We also raise a little corn to feed cattle and hogs.

On these farms, you have to look carefully if you want to see any wildlife. Of course, there are birds and squirrels, just as there are in cities. Wild hamsters used to live everywhere, but they don't stay where land has been farmed.

At night, if I stand and watch very quietly, I sometimes see *jerboas*. They're like tiny jumping mice with enormous back legs and tails. They can walk on their hind legs, and when they jump, they seem to fly!

There are wolves, too, but they don't like the open fields. I hardly ever see them,

▼ **Hamster**

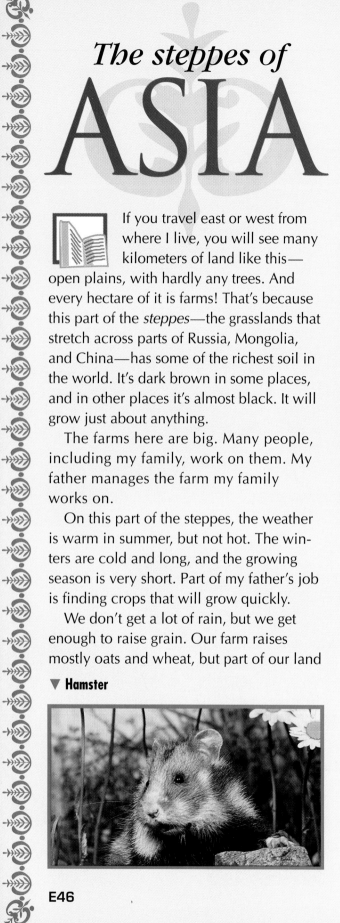

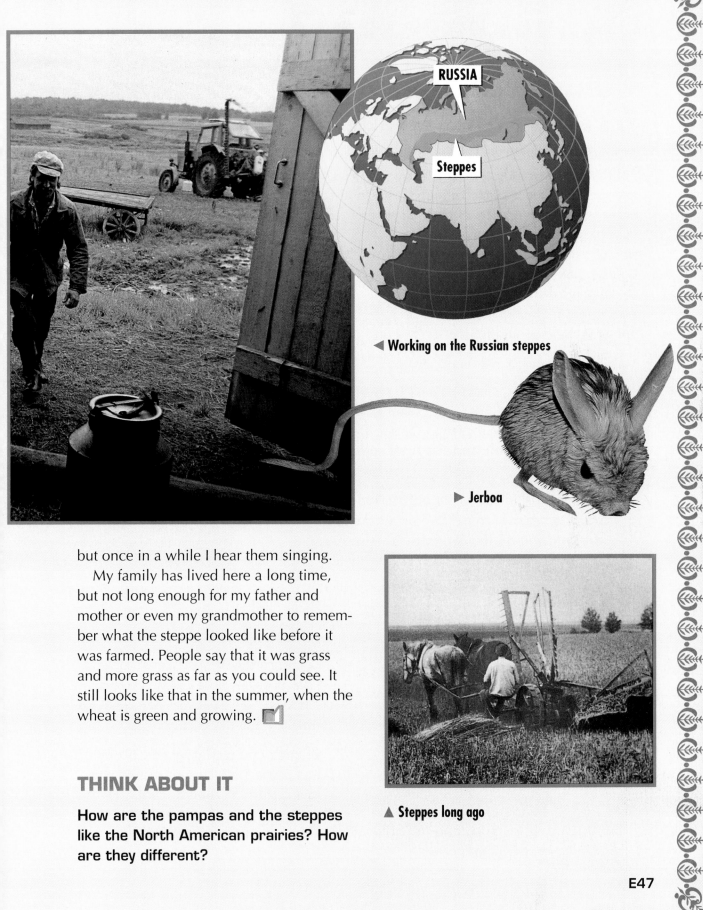

RUSSIA

Steppes

◀ **Working on the Russian steppes**

▶ **Jerboa**

but once in a while I hear them singing.

My family has lived here a long time, but not long enough for my father and mother or even my grandmother to remember what the steppe looked like before it was farmed. People say that it was grass and more grass as far as you could see. It still looks like that in the summer, when the wheat is green and growing. 📖

THINK ABOUT IT

How are the pampas and the steppes like the North American prairies? How are they different?

▲ **Steppes long ago**

Comparing Grassland Climates

Although the plants and animals are different, the pampas and steppes are very similar to grasslands everywhere. One way to compare grassland communities is to make graphs of their climates, particularly temperature and precipitation. This activity will show you how to make and compare these graphs, which are called *climatograms*, for three different grassland communities.

Grassland

North American Prairies

Asian Steppes

South American Pampas

MATERIALS
- graph paper
- ruler
- table on page E49
- Science Log data sheet

DO THIS

1. Work with a partner. Use graph paper to make three climatograms. Label the left side *Precipitation* and the right side *Temperature*.

2. Use the data in the table on E49 for each area. Remember to put the numbers for precipitation on the left and the numbers for temperature on the right.

THINK AND WRITE

1. Compare the finished climatograms. How are they alike? How are they different? What is very different about the pampas region?

2. Choose one climatogram. Study the patterns of temperature and precipitation. Then describe what you think the weather would be like in summer and in winter.

PRECIPITATION AND TEMPERATURE IN THREE GRASSLAND COMMUNITIES

		Month										
	Jan.	Feb.	Mar.	Apr.	May	Jun.	July	Aug.	Sep.	Oct.	Nov.	Dec.
Precipitation (CM)	7	5	5	10	8	5	5	5	7	2	3	5
Temperature (°C)	–7	–9	–5	2	7	16	24	26	22	6	4	–1
Precipitation (CM)	5	4	2	2	1	0	0	0	1	1	4	5
Temperature (°C)	–18	–20	–15	4	12	18	20	22	20	16	5	2
Precipitation (CM)	12	13	10	5	3	3	3	2	2	5	11	11
Temperature (°C)	23	28	19	14	12	8	8	10	12	15	18	20

BIOMES A **biome** is a large community of plants and animals. Biomes are determined by climate and the kinds of plants that are found in the area. There are six major land biomes in the world — tropical rain forests, deciduous forests, boreal forests, arctic tundra, grasslands, and deserts. In the next section, you will read about each of these biomes.

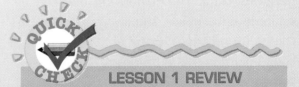

LESSON 1 REVIEW

Describe the climate where you live. How does the climate affect the types of plants and animals that live there?

2 BIOMES OF THE WORLD

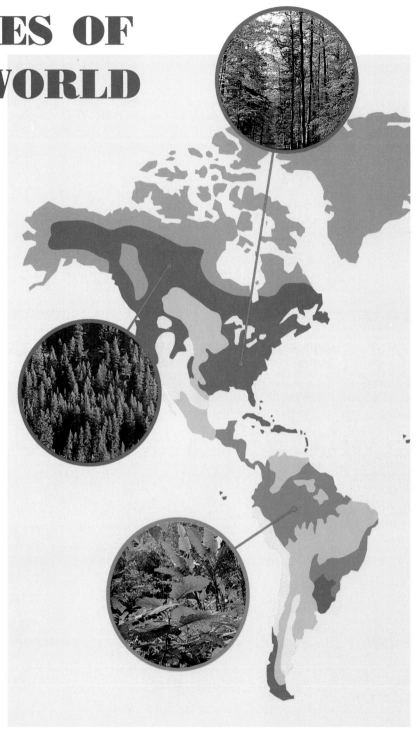

Grasslands are one of the six major land communities, or biomes, of the world. What kinds of climates do the major biomes have? What are the dominant plants and animals of each biome? The following activities will help you explore biomes and determine how climate affects the plants and animals that live in each.

Biomes and Climate

Climate is weather over a long period of time. The climate of a biome determines the living things found there. Each of these biomes has a different temperature range and amount of precipitation.

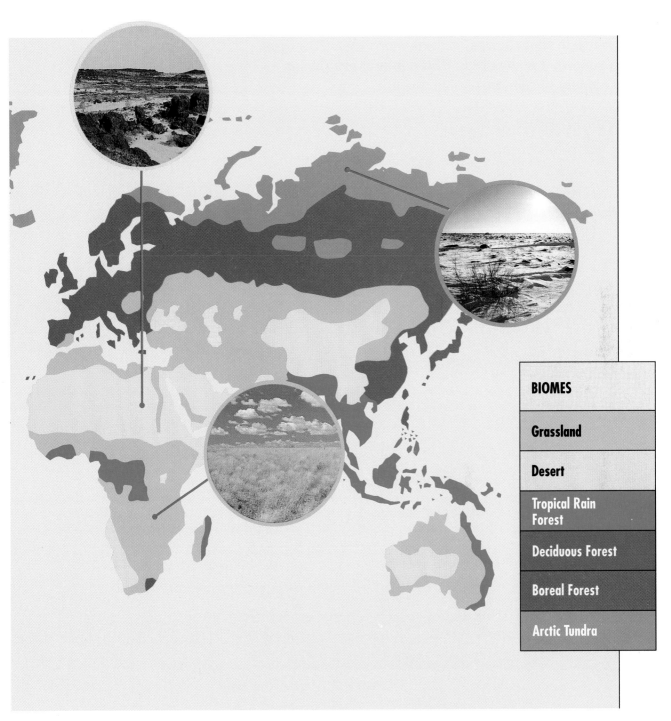

BIOMES
Grassland
Desert
Tropical Rain Forest
Deciduous Forest
Boreal Forest
Arctic Tundra

THINK ABOUT IT

Locate on the map the biome where you live. What is the climate like in your biome?

Tropical Rain Forests

Tropical rain forests grow where the climate is warm and rainy. In those areas, it rains more than 200 days each year, and as much as 660 centimeters (about 260 inches) of rain may fall in a year.

from *Journey Through a Tropical Jungle*

by Adrian Forsyth

The jungle was the greenest place I'd ever seen. There were more shades of green in this forest than anyone could ever name. One reason it seemed so green was that every tree seemed to support its own little world of other plants. On the tree trunks and branches, mosses, orchids, and even other small trees were growing.

In such warm, wet climates, trees grow rapidly. The tallest trees may tower 60 meters (about 200 feet) above the forest floor. In the heavy shade of the tall trees, plants that don't get any sun die. Vines survive because they climb toward the light. Other plants, such as orchids, grow on tree branches that get some sun.

Much of the animal life of a tropical rain forest is found right in the trees. Many kinds of birds, bats, insects, monkeys, and even frogs, spend their entire lives in treetops. They find food, shelter, and everything else they need there. The ground supports other animals, including deer, snakes, and large predators. Some animals move from trees to the ground.

Rain forests are important because they produce oxygen that supports life. But as they are cut down for timber and cleared for farms, they are destroyed faster than they can regrow. Today tropical rain forests are in danger of disappearing.

THINK ABOUT IT

What do you think would happen if all the rain forests were destroyed?

▲ Rainforest snake

Deciduous Forests

If you traveled through a broadleaf forest at different times of the year, you could probably infer what the climate was like. Deciduous forests have warm or hot summers and cold winters. There is enough rain and snow—more than 75 centimeters (about 30 inches)—to keep the forest moist throughout the year.

from *The Roadside*

by David Bellamy

Farther on, where the old track goes through the woods, ferns and mosses nestle in the damp coolness beneath the trees. A toad sits motionless on a stone… The fallen trunk of a silver birch is full of holes made by woodpeckers searching for insects, and clusters of bracket fungi are growing on the dead wood… Just beyond the woods the foxes have their den under a hedgerow of sweet chestnut and dog-rose bushes.

Deciduous trees lose their leaves every fall and then grow new ones in the spring. Deciduous trees grow large, but not as large as trees in a rain forest. Through their spreading branches, plenty of light reaches the forest floor. So between the trees, other plants fill in. Berry bushes and small fruit trees grow in the more open places. In different seasons, violets, May apples, and other low plants blanket the forest floor.

For animals the deciduous forest is a well-stocked pantry. Squirrels and seed-eating birds find plenty of food. Snakes, foxes, owls, and other small predators find good hunting. Deer browse on grass and shrubs.

Many deciduous forests have been logged or cleared for farming. But in some areas, they regrow. On abandoned farms, shrubs and small trees take over the fields. Later, hardwood trees take root, and the land becomes forest again.

▲ Gray squirrel

THINK ABOUT IT

Describe how climate in a deciduous forest supports the plant and animal life.

▲ Cardinal

Boreal Forests

Boreal forests grow where most deciduous trees can't survive — in places with very cold, snowy winters and short growing seasons. Precipitation in the boreal forest is only about 50 centimeters (about 20 inches) yearly.

from **Lumberjack**

by **Stephen W. Meader**

They opened the bars at the entrance to an old wood-road, and stepped into the cool shadow of the pines. It was quiet in the woods, and dark, except where filtered patches of sun came through to sprinkle the brown needle carpet with flecks of gold. A soft sound, like the *hush-sh-sh . . . hush-sh-sh* of waves on a beach, descended from the far green roof of the forest.

Boreal forests contain mostly conifers — trees that produce cones — such as pines. Conifers are **evergreens.** This means that they shed their old leaves and grow new ones throughout the year, so their branches are never completely bare. The soil of a boreal forest is usually not rich, but there is enough light and space for shrubs and small plants to grow. Layers of mosses or lichens often cover the forest floor.

In a boreal forest, seeds and insects provide plenty of food for jays, creepers, and other birds. Snowshoe hares and beavers find plants for browsing. The forest also supports deer, moose, and predators such as bears and wolves.

Boreal forests are sometimes destroyed by forest fires. Where this happens, the forest may regrow with a mixture of conifers and deciduous trees, such as aspen or birch.

THINK ABOUT IT

How is a boreal forest different from a deciduous forest?

Black bear ▶

Arctic Tundra

On the Arctic tundra, the air is dry. Less than 25 centimeters (about 10 inches) of precipitation falls each year. Winters are long and very cold, and summers are short and cool.

from *Life on Ice*

by **Seymour Simon**

Along the protected sides of small valleys grow low-creeping shrubs such as bearberry, crowberry, and cranberry. Here and there in a protected spot you may find a small willow tree or a dwarf birch. But if you continue moving north, even these few trees disappear. The land stretches to the horizon in a rolling, treeless plain called the Arctic tundra.

Most of the year, the tundra lies frozen under a thin layer of snow. In the short summer, only the surface of the ground thaws. Underneath is *permafrost*, soil that stays frozen all year. Because the ground stays frozen, water has no place to drain when the snow melts. This makes tundra soil wet and swampy. Some tundra plants are trees, but you wouldn't recognize them! They are the size of small bushes. Other plants are flowers that grow and bloom quickly in the short summer.

Animals on the tundra are adapted for cold weather. They are also adapted to blend in with the snow-covered landscape. The Arctic hare, willow ptarmigan (TAHR muh guhn), and snowy owl grow white fur or feathers in the winter. Caribou and musk oxen move constantly, following the food supply. Many birds are "summer guests" on the tundra and they migrate south in winter.

Some tundra lands are rich in minerals and oil. But with its short growing season and cold climate the tundra is very fragile. Too much mining or building could destroy its plant and animal life.

THINK ABOUT IT

How are animals on the tundra adapted for the cold weather?

▶ Willow ptarmigan

Grasslands

Grasslands, also known as prairies, are areas that don't receive enough precipitation during the year to allow for the growth of large trees and other plants. Winters are cold and snowy, and summers are hot and dry. Precipitation is usually about 50 centimeters (about 20 inches) each year, but much of it falls as winter snow, when the plants are not growing.

from *Seasons of the Tallgrass Prairie*

by **Carol Lerner**

The only sound on the vast grassland is the murmur of plant against plant as the wind ruffles the thick, low growth. Only a few dark shapes stand without moving on the sea of swaying grasses—here and there the sturdy forms of bur oak trees and far off a line of willow trees marking the place where a shallow stream bed cracks the smooth plains. The same green sea stretches in all directions as far as the skyline—flat, unbroken, monotonous.

Although they are drier than forests, grasslands do receive enough summer rain to support the grasses and wildflowers that cover them. These plants have extensive networks of roots that hold the soil and help keep moisture in. When the plants die and decay, they build up the soil.

Many small animals, such as ground squirrels, prairie dogs, birds, and insects, are found in grassland biomes.

Antelope and bison were once common on North American grasslands, but today most of the large grazing animals have been replaced by domestic cattle and sheep.

Because of the richness of the soils, many grasslands have been turned into farmland. Most of the world's grains—wheat, corn, and soybeans—come from areas that were once covered with big bluestem, rattlesnake master, and cornflowers.

THINK ABOUT IT

Why do you think that antelope and bison are no longer very common on the North American grasslands?

Deserts

Most deserts receive very little rainfall, less than 25 centimeters (about 10 inches) a year, although some deserts do have a very short rainy season. During that time, flowering plants sprout, bloom, and die in only a few weeks. But for most or all of the year, a desert has almost no rainfall at all.

from *The Hidden Life of the Desert*

by Thomas Wiewandt

Every spring, the Sonoran Desert is a wonderland of flowering trees, shrubs, and cactuses. These tough plants can endure long periods of heat and dryness. Most can bloom every year because they store much food and water in their stems and roots. In the morning sun, big, beautiful blossoms open on the fat, juicy stems of prickly pears. And paloverde trees wear a veil of tiny golden flowers. The paloverde has very long roots that reach deep into the ground for water.

The plants in a desert are widely separated so that they don't compete for the small amount of moisture in the ground. This wide spacing of plants leaves the ground open, and the soil is likely to blow away in the wind. In a desert, where the plant covering is thin, the soil doesn't form a rich layer. Plants and animals live in a landscape of gravel, sand, dry earth, or rock.

The plant community of the North American desert supports many small animals, such as pocket mice and shovel-nosed snakes, as well as coyotes and other larger predators. In drier deserts of the world, such as the Sahara of Africa, some plants and animals survive in *oases*, places in the desert where springs supply enough water for plant and animal life.

Although many people think of deserts as wasted land, deserts often contain deposits of valuable minerals and metals, such as gold and silver. Many desert communities have been damaged or destroyed by mining or by people unaware of the fragile nature of the deserts.

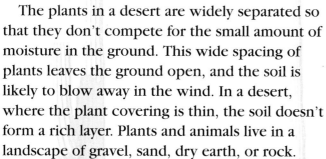

◀ Fennec fox

THINK ABOUT IT

What do all deserts have in common? How are they different from one another?

Biome Bound

Within any biome, there is a relationship between climate and the dominant kinds of plants. The animals of a biome are also adapted to the conditions of the biome. There are many other relationships among the members of a biome community. Use some of the following activities to learn more about biomes around the world.

A Community Creation

Working in groups or as a class, use sand, rocks, clay, and any other materials you can think of to create a model or diorama of a biome. Include both plants and animals. As part of your display, make a key that will help viewers know what features you have included.

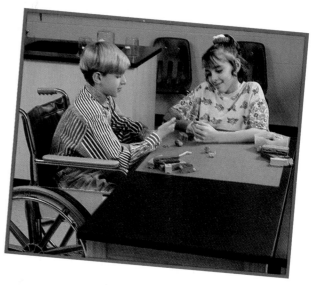

Worth a Thousand Words

Work in groups. With your group, choose a biome anywhere in the world. Look through travel books, photography books, nature magazines, and magazines about different parts of the world, such as *Natural History* or *National Geographic,* for pictures and information about the biome you choose. Find out about plant life, animal life, rivers, and other natural features. Make a booklet on all the information your group finds.

Tours and Travel

Work in groups. Your group is a travel agency! Write a brochure, based on your display, that will make tourists want to take a nature tour of your biome.

LESSON 2 REVIEW

❶ Choose one of the six land biomes and write a paragraph describing the climate and some of the plant and animal life found there.

❷ Think about the biome you live in. Describe what it might have been like 100 years ago.

 DOUBLE CHECK

SECTION C REVIEW

1. How is the climate of an area related to the kind of biome that develops there?

2. What kinds of things can cause a biome to change?

People and the Prairie

Most of the land you see on the prairie is land that has been modified by people for some specific use, such as building houses. Anytime land is used by humans, the natural biome changes. If the land is not used carefully, the plant and animal communities, the water, the soil, and even the air over the community may be destroyed.

▲ Tilling

How do people use land wisely? What happens when they don't? Can people live in harmony with a natural biome? As you work through the investigations in this section, write your ideas about these questions in your Science Log.

LAND HO!

When humans change part of a biome, the changes can affect even the parts of the biome that are left untouched. As you work through the following readings and activities, look for ways in which minor changes can affect an entire biome.

ACTIVITY

Home on the Range

There are limits to how big a community can get — both a human community and a natural community. This activity will help you find out what these limits are, and what produces them.

DO THIS

1 You are going to find out how many foxes a prairie will support. Your teacher will give you a grid that is 6 squares long and 6 squares wide. This represents your prairie. Counting chips will represent foxes.

2 Your teacher will read certain "fox facts" for each year. You will calculate how many foxes to add to or take from your prairie. Only one "fox" can go in each square of your grid.

THINK AND WRITE

1. How many years did it take for the foxes to completely fill your prairie? Compare your results with those of your classmates.

2. List some things that limited the fox population. Tell what would have happened without these limiting factors.

Putting Land to Work

Growing populations need more space, so they often spread out into nearby areas. But what happens to a natural area when people change it to meet their needs? As you read the article Molly Tallchief wrote for a newspaper in Iowa, note the way people change the land they use.

The CHANGING LAND

▲ Iowa cornfield

by **Molly Tallchief**

 A plow slices deep into the Iowa prairie, tearing through the native grasses. A year later, corn stands where the tall grasses were. This is a typical scene on the prairies of North America.

People need certain things to live. They need food, homes, and jobs. They also need products to make their lives easier and more productive.

All these needs require land. But land covers less than 30 percent of the Earth's surface. The rest is water. And only about 13 percent of the land can be used for farming.

On good farmland, crops are planted year after year. Crops take nutrients from the soil. After a while, the nutrients are used up and must be replaced. In much of the world, chemical fertilizers are added to the soil, and the farms produce good crops every year. In some places, natural fertilizers are used. Manure (animal wastes), bone meal, or even dead fish have nutrients that plants can use. But in a

▲ **Clearing land**

few areas, farmers simply move on, clearing more land when the old land becomes unproductive.

It's hard for people to raise the food they need and take care of the land, too. Using chemical fertilizers year after year leaves harmful substances in the soil and water. Using natural fertilizers requires a lot of human labor and limits the amount of food that can be produced. Moving and clearing new land destroys valuable resources, such as rain forests.

Some land is not good enough for growing crops, but it can be used for grazing animals. Cattle, sheep, and goats can live on pasture grasses and produce meat, wool, and milk.

Although animals can be grazed on land too poor for farming, if too many animals graze, or if they graze too often on the same pasture, plants are killed. This leaves the land open to erosion by wind and runoff.

Forested lands are generally not good for either cropland or grazing land, but they are valuable in their own way for producing wood and related products. In the United States, most of our timber is used for lumber or for paper. In some countries, wood is used for fuel.

Timberlands can be replanted after cutting or allowed to sit idle until new trees grow. But in areas where people need wood for heating and cooking, trees are cut so often that the forests don't grow back.

Because humans are increasing in numbers, more land is needed every year. Learning to use land wisely, without using up what the land provides, is one problem people need to solve.

▼ **Sheep grazing**

THINK ABOUT IT

What is one problem connected with humans using land? What could be done to solve the problem?

Land Use Around the World

In different parts of the world, people use the land in different ways. This activity will help you compare ways land is used on five continents.

You will need: Science Log

Look at the circle graphs, and compare the ways fertile land is used on each continent. Determine which continent has the highest area of land in farming, in grazing, and in timber. Write a paragraph comparing and contrasting the way fertile land is used on each continent.

These figures will probably change in the future. Make a list of some things that could cause them to change.

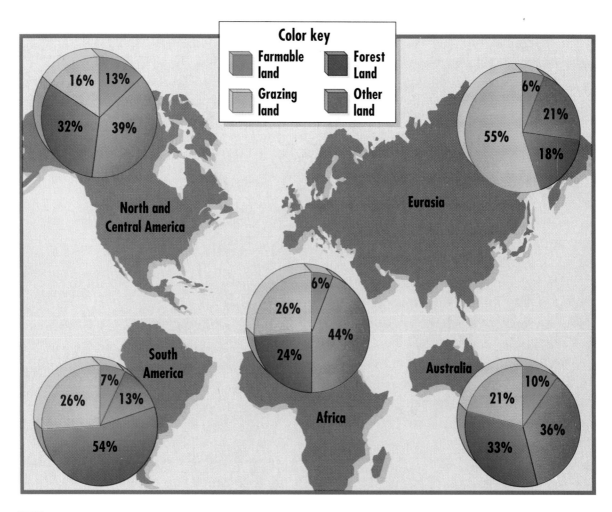

Color key
- Farmable land
- Grazing land
- Forest Land
- Other land

North and Central America: 13%, 16%, 32%, 39%

Eurasia: 6%, 21%, 18%, 55%

South America: 7%, 13%, 26%, 54%

Africa: 6%, 26%, 24%, 44%

Australia: 10%, 21%, 33%, 36%

Wascally Wabbits

Land provides for human communities the same things it provides for natural communities: food, water, and living space. But what happens when people and nature try to share the same land? You can find out as you read about the problems in Buffalo Plains.

Buffalo Plains is a small farm town surrounded by some of the Midwest's finest farmland. It is located between two large cities that are growing and using more and more land as their suburbs spread out.

As new homes are built, natural areas have disappeared. This has caused a problem for the farmers of Buffalo Plains: there has been uncontrolled growth of the rabbit population.

A long time ago, when farmers first settled in the area, they killed off the natural predators of the rabbits — foxes. The fox was seen as a troublemaker since it killed chickens as well as rabbits. With few predators, the rabbit population grew quickly. But it wasn't much of a problem then, since there was plenty of open prairie for rabbits to feed on.

Now, the open prairie, the rabbits' natural habitat, is being turned into subdivisions, and the rabbits have started feeding on the farmers' crops. The town of Buffalo Plains is considering several ways to solve the rabbit problem. The following solutions have been suggested:

- Provide free hunting licenses to encourage rabbit hunting
- Pay farmers for the damage rabbits do to their crops
- Use poisons to get rid of the rabbits
- Reintroduce natural predators into the area

Of course, everyone in town has opinions about the proposals. What would your opinion be if you were a developer? a homeowner? a farmer? a hunter? a conservationist?

LESSON 1 REVIEW

❶ What are three important ways land is used? How is most of the land used in your area?

❷ The building of towns and cities uses land. List some ways in which rapidly growing towns or cities can change the ways they use the land.

2 WHAT A WASTE

People use materials from plants, animals, and the Earth itself to make the things they need. As they make these things, they produce wastes. Wastes may be as harmless as sawdust from a lumber mill, or they may be chemicals that destroy the air, the water, or the soil. As you work through the activities that follow, notice how the land is affected by wastes.

ACTIVITY

Polluter's Pond

As you read earlier in Molly Tallchief's article, chemical fertilizers sometimes end up in water, such as farm ponds. In this activity, you can observe what happens to pond water when fertilizer gets into it.

DO THIS

❶ Working in small groups, fill the jars with pond water. With the marker, label the jars *1*, *2*, and *3*.

❷ In the small bottle, mix 30 drops of liquid plant food with 30 drops of water to make a weak solution of fertilizer.

❸ Put 10 drops of fertilizer in jar *1*. Put 50 drops of fertilizer in jar *2*. Don't put any fertilizer in jar *3*. Close the jars, and place them in the sun. Check them every day for two weeks.

MATERIALS
- pond water
- 3 jars
- marker
- small bottle with cap
- dropper
- liquid plant food
- water
- Science Log data sheet

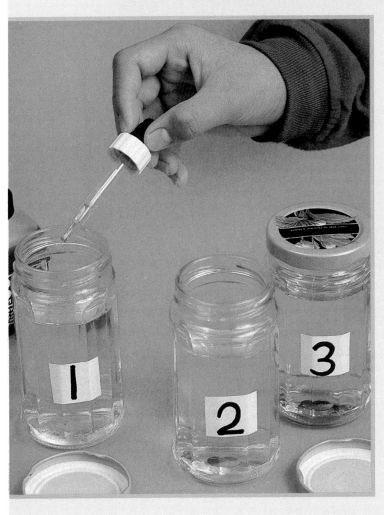

THINK AND WRITE

1. Which jar has the most growth? Which has the least?

2. How can runoff from fertilized fields change the plant life in a pond or river?

3. OBSERVING Making observations is an important part of the scientific process. What do you observe about the use of different strengths of fertilizer?

Where's the Poison?

In addition to using chemical fertilizers, farmers and gardeners spray plants with *pesticides* — chemicals that kill plant pests but that can also harm other animals. What happens when animals eat food containing pesticides? The following game will help you find out.

You will need: colored markers, animal game tags, and the "food" bags from the Where's the Food? activity in Section A.

Play the game again, following the directions on page E23. Grasshoppers feed on the first turn, snakes and grasshoppers on the second turn, and hawks, snakes, and grasshoppers on the third turn. After each turn, the animals that were "eaten" (tagged) or didn't find enough food sit down.

When the last turn ends, go back to the classroom. Markers of one color represent food contaminated with pesticides. Your teacher will tell you which color.

Count how many grasshoppers, snakes, and hawks have contaminated food. Then count the total markers for each group and find the three highest totals for players. Which group has the highest total? Which players have the highest totals? What group are they in?

Give a Hoot . . .

Pesticides and chemical fertilizers aren't the only kinds of wastes. People create wastes when they use things and when they make things they need. As you read the following, think about ways you produce wastes.

Did you use a paper napkin today? How about a hair dryer? Did you take the bus to school, or did someone give you a ride? None of these are bad things to do, but all of them affect the environment.

All of these things used only *natural resources*, or materials from the Earth. Many of them produced some form of waste as well. The paper mill used trees to make the paper and chemicals to bleach it. The chemicals may have ended up in a river somewhere. The electric energy plant burned coal and produced smoke, which may have gone into the air. And the car or bus burned fuel made from oil and produced exhaust that fouled the air.

Unwanted or harmful wastes in the air, water, or soil are called *pollution*. Some kinds of pollution are very visible, and so are the problems they cause.

Suppose you throw that paper napkin you used into the trash. Your trash, along with the trash of thousands of other people, probably goes to a landfill. Landfills use land that could be used for raising food or building houses. When the landfill gets full, the trash must go somewhere else, so another landfill is made.

Some kinds of pollution are not so visible. At an electric energy plant, a fuel such as coal is burned. Chemicals from the burning coal go up the smokestack and into the air. When some of those chemicals mix with water vapor in the air, they form an acid. The acid droplets that form over a prairie smokestack may be carried by the wind to fall as acid rain on a forest hundreds of miles away! What do you think acid rain does to plants? You can find out in the next activity.

▲ **Trees damaged by acid rain**

◄ **Landfill**

▲ **Industrial pollution**

THINK ABOUT IT

List five things you did today, and explain how each may have caused pollution.

E77

The Acid Test

What does rainwater containing chemicals from the air do to plants? In this activity, you will find out how acid rain affects plants.

MATERIALS
- 4 potted bean seedlings
- marker
- 4 spray bottles
- water
- vinegar
- ruler
- Science Log data sheet

DO THIS

❶ Work in small groups. With your group, choose 4 potted seedlings of about the same size. Mark the pots *A*, *B*, *C*, and *D* with the marker.

❷ Fill one spray bottle with water. With the marker, label it *A*. Fill the second spray bottle with a solution of $\frac{3}{4}$ water and $\frac{1}{4}$ vinegar, and label it *B*. Fill the third spray bottle with a solution of $\frac{1}{2}$ water and $\frac{1}{2}$ vinegar, and label it *C*. Fill the fourth spray bottle with a solution of $\frac{1}{4}$ water and $\frac{3}{4}$ vinegar, and label it *D*.

❸ Once a day for ten days, spray seedling *A* with the bottle marked *A*. Spray seedling B with the bottle marked *B*. Spray seedling C with the bottle marked *C*. Spray seedling *D* with the bottle marked *D*.

❹ On days 1, 5, and 10, measure the seedlings, and record the measurements and any other observations on your data sheet. When the experiment ends, make a graph showing the growth pattern of each of the seedlings in your group. Then compare your graph with the graphs made by other groups.

▲ Acid rain damage

THINK AND WRITE

1. How did the plants change from day 1 to day 10?

2. Did the amount of acid in the "rain" make a difference? Use your data to explain your answer.

3. **COMMUNICATING** In this activity, you made a graph of the growth of the seedlings. Graphing is a good way to communicate the results of an experiment. How did graphing make it easier for you to compare your data with the data obtained by other groups?

... Don't Pollute

As human populations grow, will pollution continue to get worse, or can it be controlled? No one knows for sure, but people are finding ways to control some kinds of pollution. Continue reading to find out what you can do to help.

Of course, people must farm in order to raise food. They also need to mine for minerals, drill for oil, cut trees, and manufacture things. People need transportation, too, in order to get to work and to school and to move materials and products. All of these activities can cause pollution, and they all use natural resources and energy.

One way to control pollution is to reuse things as much as possible. This is called *recycling*. Aluminum cans, for example, can be made into new cans. This saves both aluminum—-a natural resource — and energy. Recycling reduces the amount of waste that goes into landfills, too, saving land.

► Ladybug

Reducing the amount of waste is also a way to cut down on air pollution. Manufacturing plants and energy stations can use equipment that prevents harmful chemicals from getting into the air. Some of these chemicals can even be reused.

Farmers can use fewer chemical fertilizers and pesticides. They can bring in natural predators to get rid of insects and other pests that harm their crops.

Another way to cut down on pollution is to use materials that can be broken down by organisms in the soil and water. Bacteria and other decomposers can get rid of these wastes, turning chemicals into harmless materials that can even make the soil richer.

We may never completely stop pollution, but we can sometimes reverse its effects. The next activity will show you how polluted water can be cleaned up.

THINK ABOUT IT

How does recycling save natural resources and eliminate some pollution?

◄ Pitch in!

Waterworks

Acid rain, poisoned runoff from farms, and even soil can get into a water supply. This activity will let you try out some ways of cleaning up water.

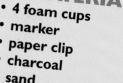

MATERIALS
- 4 foam cups
- marker
- paper clip
- charcoal
- sand
- gravel
- muddy water
- measuring cup
- Science Log data sheet

DO THIS

1 Work with a partner. With the marker, label the cups A, B, C, and D. With a paper clip, carefully punch 10 holes in the bottom of cup A, B, and C.

2 Put a layer of charcoal and a layer of gravel in cup A. Put a layer of sand and a layer of gravel in cup B. Put a layer of sand and a layer of charcoal in cup C.

3 Pour about 150 mL of muddy water into cup A. Catch the runoff in cup D. Observe the runoff and record your observations. Repeat step 3 with cups B and C.

THINK AND WRITE

Which combination of materials seemed to clean the water best? How might this method be used on a large scale to clean polluted water? Write down some ideas.

David Powless:
Conservationist

Earlier in this unit, you read about Molly Tallchief, a Native American woman who lived on and studies the shortgrass prairie of western Kansas. In the following interview, you will meet someone who works to protect the prairie environment. David Powless is a conservationist. In the interview, he answers questions about his training and about the kind of work he does. After reading the interview, maybe you, too, will become interested in conservation.

Q. What is a conservationist?

A. A conservationist is a person who is concerned with protecting the environment. He or she works to conserve natural resources and to prevent unnecessary loss and waste.

Q. What kinds of things do you do?

A. I'm involved in environmental testing. I do complete chemical tests on soil, air, and water. In addition, I test waste water, ground water, and drinking water for pollution. I also test hazardous wastes and toxic substances, and I do some checking of air quality.

Q. In your job, do you work with other people?

A. Yes, I work with twenty-three people who are technicians. These technicians have a variety of degrees in chemistry, biology, geology, and biochemistry.

Twelve of these people are Native Americans. You see, the company I work for is owned by the Oneida Tribe of Indians of Wisconsin, of which I am a member. Our tribe believes that people are responsible for taking care of the Earth and for doing something about environmental problems.

Q. Are computers and other instruments important in your work?

A. Yes, computers are used to record and store test information. Computers are also used to prepare reports. Other instruments are used to measure hazardous and toxic substances down to parts per billion.

With these instruments, I'm able to determine all the pollutants in the materials that have been tested.

Q. **What kind of career opportunities are there in this field?**

A. There are many career opportunities in conservation, especially in chemistry. Environmental groups are setting very strict guidelines about the levels of pollution to be allowed in manufacturing

processes. Trained technicians are needed to operate the new machines to measure these levels. In addition, more technicians are needed to work in the laboratory to prepare the samples of test materials.

Q. **For this type of work, what subjects should students study?**

A. I would suggest that students study biology, chemistry, geology, and zoology. For the higher levels of science, mathematics is an absolute requirement. Computer skills will also be important.

Q. **What is your educational background?**

A. I studied petroleum engineering at the University of Oklahoma and then got a degree in marketing and economics at the University of Illinois. First I worked in the steel industry; then I received a National Science Foundation grant, the first given to a Native American. I used this grant to develop a process to recycle hazardous waste in steel mills.

Q. **Do you think people will be able to stop pollution and clean up the Earth's problems?**

A. Yes, I do. We are coming to a point of choice. The earth will always be here, but will we be able to keep living on it? The choice is up to us. I believe that we can do it.

LESSON 3 REVIEW

1 Predators, such as hawks and owls, can be affected by pollution. Explain how this can happen.

2 How can pollution change a biome? Give several examples.

3 PROTECTING THE PRAIRIES

Nature may change a prairie over hundreds or thousands of years, but people can change it in just a few years. It would be impossible to undo all the changes that have happened to the North American prairies since people first settled there. But how do biomes change, and what can people do to make sure that future changes will protect natural communities? The following readings and activity can give you some

ACTIVITY

Pond Today, Prairie Tomorrow

In any environment, some changes occur naturally. This activity will help you understand what happens to a pond over time, and why.

DO THIS

1 Put the soil into the aquarium or bowl. Bank the soil high around the edges, leaving a low spot in the center.

2 Plant several water plants in the center. Slowly pour in water until about half the soil is covered.

3 Sprinkle some seeds anywhere in the container.

4 Every other day, sprinkle some more seeds in the container. Make observations about the water level, the number of seeds that have sprouted, and whether the water plants are growing. Do not add water.

5 Draw a picture showing how your "pond" looks at the end of one week. Compare your observations with those of others.

Succession The process that changed your "pond" into a "meadow" is called *succession*. In nature, succession is usually a slow process, occurring in stages. The first, or *pioneer*, stage includes plants and animals that can survive unfavorable conditions. These organisms are gradually replaced by plants and animals that are more like those found throughout the natural biome. For example, the final, or *climax*, community of a prairie might include grasses, wildflowers, and prairie dogs. Next, you can read about an experiment to artificially restore a tall-grass prairie in Illinois.

THINK AND WRITE

How do you think a natural pond turns into a meadow? Use the results of your activity to describe the process.

▲ Pond succession

Return with Us Now

The damage humans do to natural communities can't always be undone. But sometimes a small area can be returned to its natural condition. The following describes the work of John Csoka, an 11-year-old who helped restore part of a natural community near his home.

Preserving the Prairie *A Return to Tallgrass*

from *Current Health*

"The first settlers to travel west came out of the woods into a huge sea of grass. That's part of our heritage. That's why it's important to restore the few acres that remain." So says John Csoka, who, at the age of 11, decided to do something about preserving the prairie for the future.

John has always been interested in ecology and "plants, animals, birds, anything that's alive, basically." He is an active member of the Prairie Woods chapter of the Audubon Society in his hometown of Palatine, Illinois. He decided to help the group rebuild a natural prairie.

"We were delighted that someone as young as John was so ready to give us a lot of his free time," says Nancy Wedow, who is a past president of the chapter. "His example got even more kids interested. And he's really stuck with it."

John started spending his weekends and afternoons helping to clear the land for planting. "Even though the park district owns it, the place was just allowed to grow wild," he says. And he learned that "wild" is not necessarily the same thing as "natural."

▶ Prairie wildflowers

▲ **Illinois cornfield**

The dandelions and daisies that are everywhere today in the Midwest were unknown on the original tallgrass prairies that swept from the edge of eastern U.S. woods across the middle of the country to the Missouri River. You can still see short-grass prairies ripple in the sun throughout the Great Plains west of the river. But the rich and colorful tallgrass acres have almost disappeared.

Pioneers' Plants

That's because when the settlers came, they began to change the landscape. They plowed under prairie and discovered some of the richest farmland in the world. Native prairie plants have deep and tangled root systems that keep the plants alive underground in winter. The roots store nitrogen and other minerals and carry them down into the soil. Important crops like corn and wheat grew quickly once the ground was cleared of prairie grass and flowers.

▶ **Burning of prairie tallgrass**

The pioneers also brought along things to remind them of home. Plants, shrubs, even trees were loaded onto wagons and replanted in the Midwest. Some of them came all the way from Europe. In the fertile soil, they soon overgrew the native plants and killed them with too much shade or strangled their roots. Forests began to overshadow what had once been open prairie.

"The trees might not have taken over so completely if the settlers had paid attention to what the Indians already knew," John says. "Every year or so the top growth on the prairie needs to burn off, so new little plants near the soil can get enough sunlight to grow."

Prairie Fires

Prairie fires usually started in the fall, when the sun was still hot and the leaves were drying out. Lightning, the heat of the sun, or the Indians themselves could spark the flames. Indians often used prairie fires to make buffalo herds stampede toward waiting hunters who killed them for food and to use their tough, warm hides for shelter and clothing.

▲ **Working on prairie restoration**

"A burned prairie looks black and dead, but it's not," says John. "A lot of the seed heads manage to stay above the flames and don't drop until the fire is out. By then, the ashes from the plants have released minerals back into the dirt, and the seeds have a fertile place to grow when spring comes." Young tree saplings that might otherwise grow up and kill the prairie with shade usually don't survive the fire.

Three years after he began working on the prairie patch, John is the official steward in charge of the project. He gets help from volunteers and his friends in the ecology club at Palatine High School, where he is a sophomore.

You can tell their hard work has made a difference. Acres of flowering grasses have replaced woods and shrubs. Teachers bring their students to see what Palatine looked like before settlers arrived.

Create a Prairie in Your Backyard

Seven and a half acres is a lot of ground to work on. But you can help create a prairie right in your own backyard, and that's just what the kids at the Elizabeth Blackwell Elementary School in Schaumburg, Illinois, have done. With the help of PTA mom Penny Kurz, Tracy Kurz and her fifth-grade classmates began clearing a small patch of land behind the school in 1990.

Today the spot is alive with birds, butter-flies, and flowering grasses of all kinds.

"I firmly believe that the survival of our native plants and animals is going to depend on our backyards," says Ms. Kurz, who is the school's environmental adviser. "If you have a 2-foot patch of prairie grasses that helps butterflies get from one spot to another, that's an important step."

She also hopes that showing students the way a prairie looks and grows will help them appreciate it more. "It's very different from the formal lawns and gardens we're used to in the suburbs," she says. "At first it looks a little wild and raggedy. And it's cer-tainly taller!" Some prairie grasses are more than 6 feet tall in midsummer.

But, she explained, there's a lot more life in a prairie than in a traditional yard. "We bring classes outside on the lawn and have them close their eyes. Then they describe what they see, hear, feel, and smell. On plain old grass, there's not much," she says.

"But once we go into the prairie and try the same thing, kids are amazed. There's texture, sounds, songs, and wonderful sweet scents."

Another advantage of prairie gardens is that once they're established, they pretty much take care of themselves. Except for occasional weeding to keep out non-native species, and for a controlled burn every year or two, prairies grow just fine on their own.

If you live in a state that used to be cov-ered with tallgrass prairie and want to try growing your own prairie garden at home or at school, first do your homework, John advises. Read everything you can find about the native plants that once grew there. Talk to your local park district. Organizations such as the Audubon Society, the Sierra Club, and the Nature Conservancy all have prairie restoration projects under way. You may be able to volunteer some time to help them out.

Rebuilding the natural landscape takes time, patience, and commitment to the project. But John and Tracy agree, "It's worth it!"

LESSON 3 REVIEW

What kinds of harmful changes to an environment can be undone? Explain how this can happen.

DOUBLE CHECK

SECTION D REVIEW

1. **What could you do at home or at school to eliminate some kinds of pollution?**

2. **Describe several ways in which a biome might change naturally.**

3. **Why isn't it practical to restore all communities to their natural condition?**

I REFLECT

It's time to think about the ideas you have discovered during your investigations. It's time to think, too, about your many accomplishments.

SUMMARIZE

Answer the following in your Science Log.

1. What **I Wonder** questions have you answered in your investigations, and what new questions have you asked?

2. What have you discovered about prairies, and how have your ideas changed?

3. Did any of your discoveries surprise you? Explain.

Hawks and Sna
feed on small
rodents

wer Seeds and Pollen
d insects and birds

90

Grass and Grass Seeds
feed mammals and birds

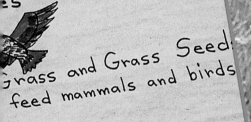

CONNECT IDEAS

1. Name two biomes and compare the plants and animals in them.

2. What characteristics make prairies part of the grassland biome?

3. What makes a grassland different from other biomes?

4. How does energy flow through the plants and animals in a grassland biome?

5. Why are there different kinds of soil in different biomes?

6. Describe several different ways that people have changed the prairie.

SCIENCE PORTFOLIO

1 Complete your Science Experiences Record.

2 Choose several samples of your best work from each section to include in your Science Portfolio.

3 On A Guide to My Science Portfolio, tell why you choose each sample.

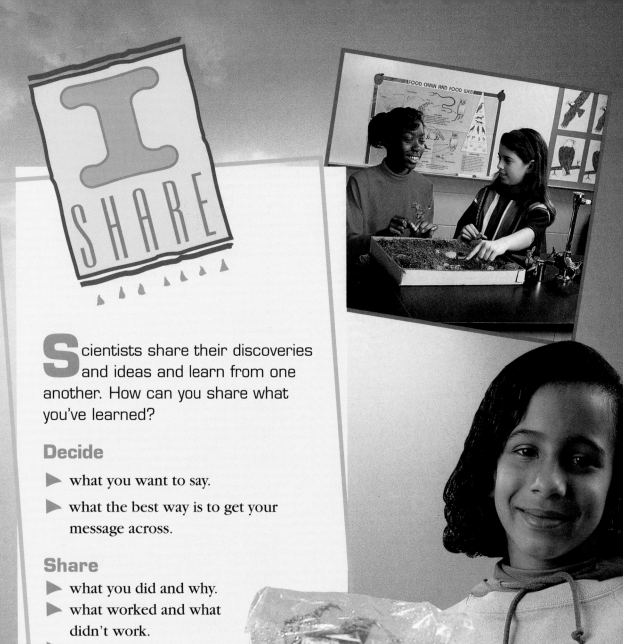

I SHARE

Scientists share their discoveries and ideas and learn from one another. How can you share what you've learned?

Decide

▶ what you want to say.

▶ what the best way is to get your message across.

Share

▶ what you did and why.

▶ what worked and what didn't work.

▶ what conclusions you have drawn.

▶ what else you'd like to find out.

Find Out

▶ what classmates liked about what you shared—and why.

▶ what questions your classmates have.

I ACT

Science is more than discoveries—it is also what you do with those discoveries. How might you use what you have learned about prairies and biomes?

▶ Get involved in creating a nature area. Talk with nature groups to find out what you and your friends can do.

▶ Join a group that works to protect plants and animals, or help count birds or other animals for a nature group.

▶ Take part in a clean-up day, or set up a recycling center.

THE LANGUAGE OF SCIENCE

The language of science helps people communcate clearly when they talk about nature. Here are some vocabulary words you can use when you talk about prairies and biomes with friends, family, and others.

consumer—an organism that gets energy by eating other living things. Animals are consumers. **(E 24)**

decomposer—any living organism that breaks down dead plants and animals into nutrients that can be used by other living organisms. Most bacteria and many different kinds of fungi are the main decomposers. **(E 25)**

▲ **Birch tree rot fungus**

food chain—the path of producers and consumers along which energy passes through a community. A food chain ends when there is no energy left to pass along. **(E 25)**

biome—a type of large-scale environment with a similar climate and similar plants and animals throughout. The major biomes include tropical rain forests, deciduous forests, boreal forests, Arctic tundra, grasslands, and deserts. The North American prairies are part of the grassland biome. **(E 49)**

carnivore—a meat-eating animal. **(E 24)**

community—groups of plants and animals that live in the same environment. Grasses, wildflowers, bison, and prairie dogs might be part of a prairie community. **(E 28)**

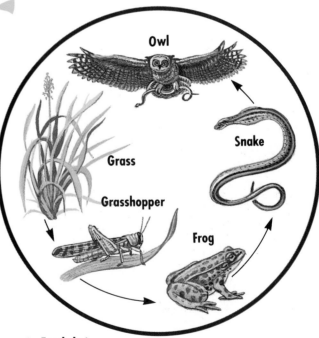

Owl

Snake

Grass

Grasshopper

Frog

▲ **Food chain**

herbivore—a plant-eating animal. **(E 24)**

omnivore—an animal that eats plants and animals. **(E 24)**

population—all the plants or animals of one kind that live in an area, such as all the prairie dogs living on a Kansas prairie. **(E 28)**

producer—an organism that makes its own food. Grasses are the main producers on the prairies. **(E 24)**

▲ **Population of prairie dogs**

▼ **World biomes**

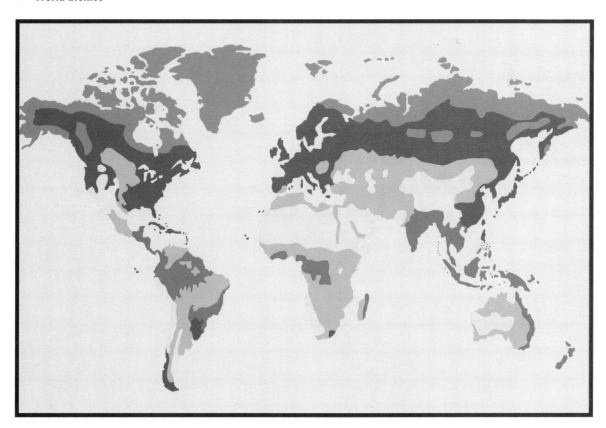

AMUSEMENT PARK

Amusement Park

Experiencing Forces and Motion

I WONDER

Have you ever been to an amusement park? Is there a park you would really like to visit? What do you wonder about all the movements and forces at work in amusement park shows and rides?

With a partner, make a list of questions that you may have about the different motions and machines at an amusement park. Be ready to share your list with the rest of the class.

State Fair of Texas

Thrill ride

F3

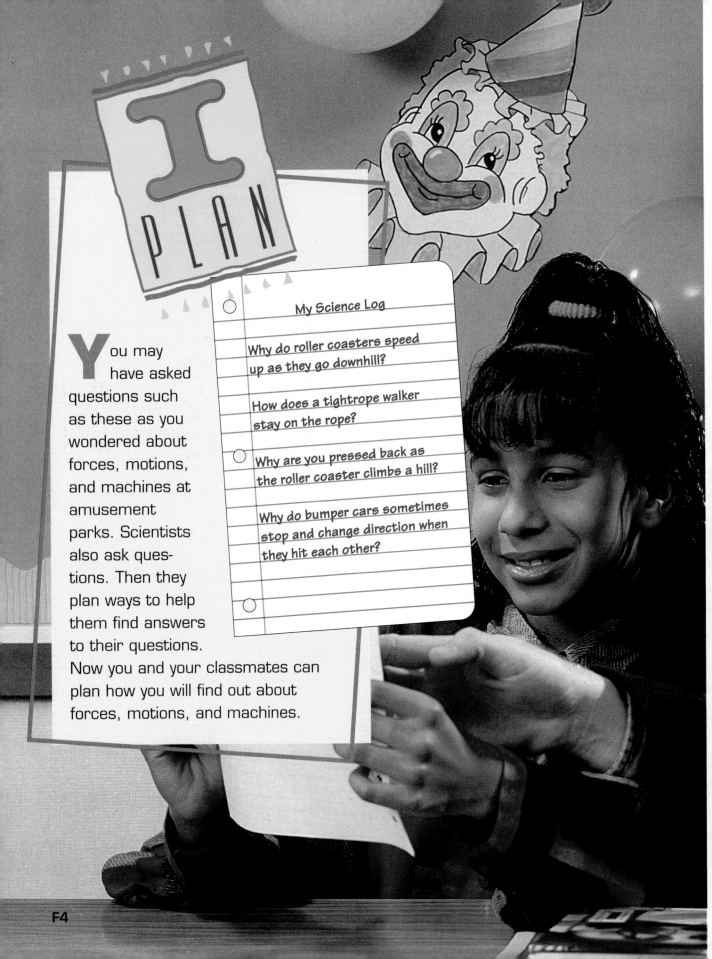

I PLAN

Y ou may have asked questions such as these as you wondered about forces, motions, and machines at amusement parks. Scientists also ask questions. Then they plan ways to help them find answers to their questions. Now you and your classmates can plan how you will find out about forces, motions, and machines.

My Science Log

Why do roller coasters speed up as they go downhill?

How does a tightrope walker stay on the rope?

Why are you pressed back as the roller coaster climbs a hill?

Why do bumper cars sometimes stop and change direction when they hit each other?

With Your Class

Plan how your class will use the activities and readings from the **I Investigate** part of this unit. Decide what other resources you may need.

On Your Own

There are many ways to learn about forces, motions, and machines. Following are some things you can do to explore forces, motions, and machines by yourself or with some classmates. Some explorations may take longer to do than others. Look over the suggestions and choose . . .

- **Projects To Do**
- **Places To Visit**
- **Books To Read**

PROJECTS TO DO

MODEL CARNIVAL

Have you ever had fun playing the games and riding the rides at an amusement park or a carnival? Why not extend that fun at home by making carnival games and constructing model rides? Be creative in your use of materials. Think about the forces that will affect how well your games and rides work.

SHOW TIME

On with the show! Get together with some friends, and prepare a show similar to one you might see at an amusement park. Be sure to include juggling, balancing acts, and clown routines. As you and your friends prepare your show, discuss the forces that affect each type of performance. After rehearsing, find an audience and present your show.

SCIENCE FAIR PROJECT

Review the **I Wonder** questions you and your partner asked. One way to find answers to these questions is through a science fair project. Choose one of your questions. Plan a project that would help you answer questions about forces, motions, and machines. Discuss your plan with your teacher. With his or her approval, begin work by collecting materials and resources. Then carry out your plan.

PLACES TO VISIT

AMUSEMENT PARK

Organize a trip to a nearby amusement park or game room. As you enjoy the rides or games, think about what makes them work. Report to your class about the rides or games you enjoyed most and how you think they worked.

DESIGN STUDIO

Today, computers are used to design cars, appliances, and even roller coasters. Arrange to visit a studio that specializes in designing mechanical objects. Before the visit, jot down questions that you have about the kinds of forces the designers must consider in making their designs.

PLAYGROUND

Your local playground is an excellent place to see how forces interact and to see some simple machines such as swings, slides, and seesaws. Before visiting the playground, ask your teacher to talk about the forces and machines involved in playground equipment. Then have some fun playing on the equipment, just as you did when you were younger.

BOOKS TO READ

Burton's Zoom Zoom Va-Rooom Machine

by Dorothy Haas (Bradbury Press, 1990). Meet Burton the inventor. As he sees it, kids cannot move fast enough, and he wants to invent something that will solve the problem. An out-of-the-ordinary skateboard is his solution. He needs to learn about speed and motion and what makes things fly. Professor Savvy promises easy answers, but can he be trusted? Read to find out what happens, if you can take the excitement!

Burton's latest invention *really* takes off!

Dorothy Haas

Eureka! It's an Automobile!

by Jeanne Bendick (Millbrook Press, 1992).
First, you need a wheel. Luckily someone has already invented that. Then, you need something to make the wheel turn. Someone has already invented that, too. From there, it's not too big a step to add a platform. How can it be powered? This book tells the story of the automobile.

More Books to Read

Wheels at Work

by Bernie Zubrowski (William Morrow, 1986), Outstanding Science Trade Book.
Look around you. How many wheels do you see? Don't look only for those on bicycles and cars. You could not spend a day without using something that has a wheel. In this book, you will learn how the wheel works to help us, and you can make many different projects to demonstrate the value of the wheel.

The Science Book of Motion

by Neil Ardley (Harcourt Brace, 1992).
You move many times during the day and night. Things are always moving. From air around us to machines on the street, it takes force to make something move. This book will show you what makes things move and how it is done. There are fun projects and experiments to help you understand motion.

Zekmet the Stone Carver: A Tale of Ancient Egypt

by Mary Stolz (Harcourt Brace, 1988).
In ancient Egypt, the all-powerful Pharaoh commanded his servant to build a monument to last forever. This book is the story of a humble stone carver who, using simple tools, shows the servant a beautiful idea for a statue—half man, half lion. Many slaves labored for years to build it in the desert.

Bathtubs, Slides, Roller Coaster Rails

by Christopher Lampton (Millbrook Press, 1991). The inclined plane is a wonderful idea. You use one when you go down the slide at the playground. A screw that holds things together is another type of inclined plane. You see inclined planes all around. This book will show you how they help us

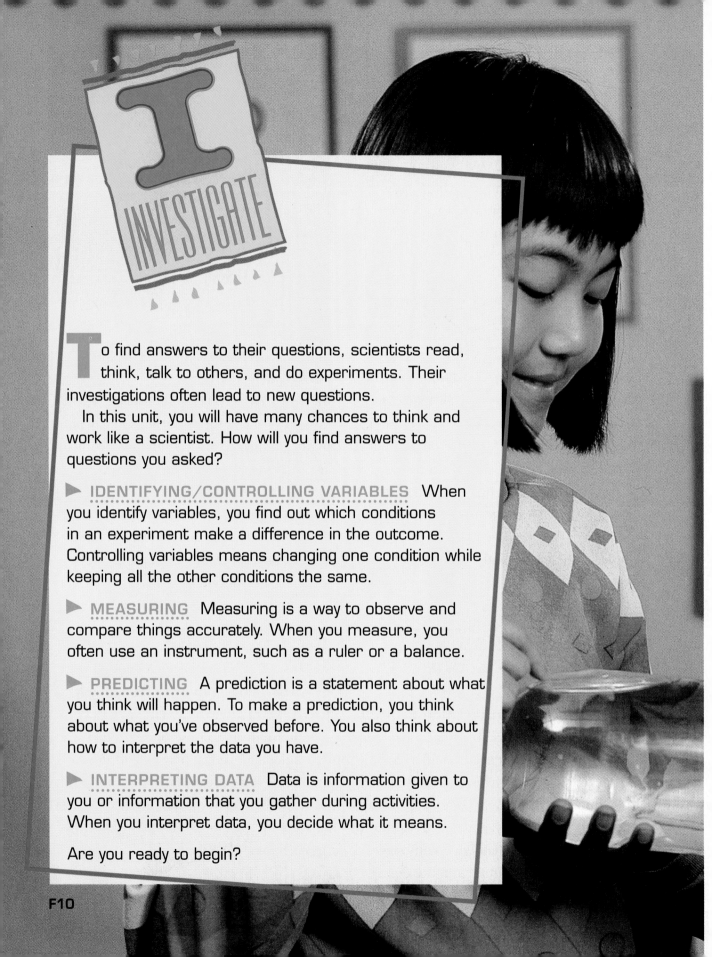

INVESTIGATE

To find answers to their questions, scientists read, think, talk to others, and do experiments. Their investigations often lead to new questions.

In this unit, you will have many chances to think and work like a scientist. How will you find answers to questions you asked?

▶ **IDENTIFYING/CONTROLLING VARIABLES** When you identify variables, you find out which conditions in an experiment make a difference in the outcome. Controlling variables means changing one condition while keeping all the other conditions the same.

▶ **MEASURING** Measuring is a way to observe and compare things accurately. When you measure, you often use an instrument, such as a ruler or a balance.

▶ **PREDICTING** A prediction is a statement about what you think will happen. To make a prediction, you think about what you've observed before. You also think about how to interpret the data you have.

▶ **INTERPRETING DATA** Data is information given to you or information that you gather during activities. When you interpret data, you decide what it means.

Are you ready to begin?

SECTIONS

SECTION A
How Does It Move?

You and some friends are going with your family to an amusement park. You can't wait to ride the roller coaster and to get aboard the water rides. The amusement park is a great place to be. It offers live entertainment, thrilling rides, and all kinds of food. The day will be filled with motion. In this section, you'll find out how scientists describe some of the motion at amusement parks.

Are there some rides you enjoy more than others? Maybe you like the whirling rides, or maybe you prefer rides that combine up-and-down motion with dizzying speeds. Did you ever stop to consider exactly how an amusement park ride moves? In your Science Log, describe some rides found at amusement parks and tell how they move. Add to your descriptions as you work through the investigations that follow.

1 HEY—IT'S MOVING!

When you describe movement, do you think about where you are and how you're moving? In this lesson, you will look at some everyday images of motion. Then you will relate these images to understand the motion of things around you.

A Moving Experience

Have you ever thought about how you can tell when something is moving and when it is not? If you are sitting in a moving car, does it always feel as if you are moving? As you read, think about how you describe movement.

You and your family are leaving for a vacation at a major amusement park. Excited, you hop into the car. A few minutes later, you turn to say something to your sister. You notice out of the corner of your eye that the trees by the side of the road seem to be moving. But you know they're not. The car is moving, and you're moving with it.

▼ Is the car moving, or are those trees moving?

You arrive at the airport and soon you are high in the sky in an airplane. As you look out, it seems as if the plane isn't moving. You know that the airplane is moving at a very rapid speed.

Once on the ground, you and your family set out in a taxicab. The cab is taking you to a hotel near the amusement park. As you head toward the park, you can see in the distance many different rides rising into the sky.

It looks to you as though none of the rides are moving. However, as you get nearer to the park, you see movement. One ride seems to move faster than another. One appears to be moving in your direction. Or perhaps it's moving away from you. From where you are, you can't tell for sure.

All the movements are described relative to your frame of reference. Each time you describe something that is moving, you are comparing it with some object or background that you assume is *not* moving. This background or object is your **frame of reference**. When you change your frame of reference, your perception of motion changes, too. Your sister was not moving in relation to the car. With the car as your frame of reference, you saw your sister as sitting still. The trees were what seemed to be moving.

THINK ABOUT IT

Describe a time when a shift in your frame of reference changed the way you saw something.

An Early Frame of Reference

What is the most basic frame of reference that people on Earth share? Is it moving or not? Hold on tight as you find out about our shared frame of reference.

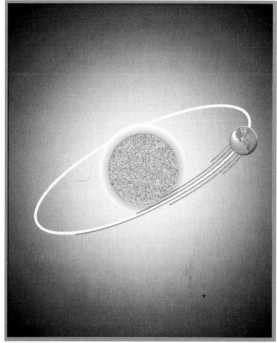

The most basic movement is the movement of the Earth around the sun. We don't feel as if we're moving, but we know that we are. The Earth is revolving around the sun, and it makes one complete rotation on its axis every day. Early people observed the Earth's relationship to the sun and the stars. South of Phoenix, Arizona, the ruins of Casa Grande sit in the hot, dry desert. *Casa Grande* means "big house" in Spanish. It was built in the early fourteenth century by Native Americans called the Hohokam. Casa Grande is a four-story building topped by a watchtower with several openings. Scientists have found that the openings in the watchtower line up with the positions of the rising and setting sun on the first day of each season. This guided the Hohokam in their planting and other activities at different times of the year. Just as the Hohokam did many years ago, we use the Earth as our frame of reference today.

▶ **Casa Grande National Monument, Arizona**

QUICK CHECK

LESSON 1 REVIEW

What is our frame of reference for telling time by the sun?

2 UP TO SPEED

Some rides at amusement parks are fast, and others are slow. Some twirl you around, and others take you up and down in circles. An amusement park provides an ideal setting for observing many types of motion. In this lesson, you will discover how motion is measured.

What a Ride!

What is it like to ride a speeding roller coaster up and down hills and around in circles? Read to find out about the experience of two friends on one roller coaster.

The MONSTER KUMBA

▼ Kumba

 Shortly after my friend Ira and I entered Busch Gardens in Tampa, Florida, we could see the roller coaster of our dreams up ahead. We had read about it. We had seen pictures of it. A couple of people we know had actually ridden it—and survived.

The roller coaster's name is Kumba. As we waited in line to board, we heard non-stop screams from the people riding before us. The giant Kumba looked like a fierce, twisting snake. Part of me couldn't wait to get on, and part of me wanted to run in the other direction!

I might have backed out but Ira said, "What's the big deal?" I wasn't going to let him know that I was scared.

At last, it was our turn to board. We climbed in, and we were on our way!

The coaster climbed the first big hill slowly. Then it started sliding downhill. It felt as though we were falling. My heart stopped while my stomach seemed to fly in some other direction. I couldn't believe that any ride would ever move so fast. Another hill—this time we slanted to the left, and I felt whipped to the side. Could I fall out? Ira screamed. He was the one who had asked, "What's the big deal?" Then we turned to the right, then to the left, and then we took a great big loop upside down. We did go upside down, didn't we? It was so fast. Then we took another small hill and another fast turn and another loop. Or was it two? Whoa!

Then the monster slowed down and stopped. I wanted to sit for a while, just to get used to being still. But we had to get up. I stumbled out of the car. Ira almost fell over. I asked him if he wanted to get back in line right away. He replied that he'd rather wait a while. I thought it was the best idea he'd had all day! 📖

THINK ABOUT IT

What words in the article were used to describe rates of motion and directions of motion?

ACTIVITY

Round Races

After riding a roller coaster, you may have wondered how fast you were traveling. In this activity, you will use measurements to determine an object's speed.

MATERIALS
- 2 meter sticks
- masking tape
- marble
- stopwatch
- calculator (optional)
- Science Log data sheet

DO THIS

1 Tape two meter sticks to the floor, about 2 cm apart.

2 The racer places a marble at one end of the pathway between the two meter sticks. On a signal from the starter, the racer rolls the marble toward the other end of the sticks. At the same time, the timer starts the stopwatch.

3 The flagger calls out "Stop" at the moment the marble crosses the end of the sticks. At the same time, the timer stops the stopwatch.

4 The recorder records the race number, the distance traveled, and the time the race took.

5 Repeat the activity five times. Calculate the marble's average speed. Use this formula: Speed equals distance divided by time (S = D/T or S = D ÷ T). First, find the total distance traveled in all five races and the total time taken for all races. Then, divide the total distance by the total time. Record the average speed.

THINK AND WRITE

1. How would you define the term *speed*?

2. **MEASURING** When you measure, you often use instruments. What measurement instruments did you use in this activity? What measurements could you make without instruments? How can you determine the average speed of a roller coaster ride?

Give Me Direction!

Many of us are thrilled by the speeds of the rides at an amusement park. Speed does not tell us everything about a ride's motion. Read to find out how to describe motion more completely.

A ride at the amusement park may run at a constant speed, but its velocity is constantly changing. **Velocity** is the speed of an object in a certain direction. When direction changes, velocity changes. As you examine the pictures, think about how velocity and speed are different.

▲ A roller coaster climbs a hill at a speed of 5 kilometers (3 miles) per hour. Its velocity is 5 kilometers per hour *upward.*

▲ As the roller coaster comes down the hill at a speed of 40 kilometers (24 miles) per hour, its velocity changes to 40 kilometers per hour *downward.*

▲ On this length of flat, straight track, the roller coaster's speed is 25 kilometers (15 miles) per hour and its velocity is 25 kilometers per hour *straight ahead.*

▲ While the roller coaster makes a sharp turn, even if its speed remains the same, its velocity changes as its direction changes.

LESSON 2 REVIEW

❶ When might it be useful to record average speed?

❷ When a roller coaster travels on a flat, straight path, does it have velocity? Explain.

HURRY—THIS WAY!

At times, you may want to describe how your velocity changes. This lesson shows how to observe changes in velocity.

A C T I V I T Y

Accelerometer

In this activity, you will build an accelerometer. You can use it to show changes in velocity.

DO THIS

❶ Fill the bottle with water, leaving enough space for a small air bubble. Add a tiny piece of bar soap so that the bubble will not get "stuck" on the side of the bottle.

❷ Cap the bottle, and set it on its side on a tabletop. The bubble should move to the center of the side that is up.

❸ Predict what will happen to the bubble if you slide the bottle in different directions.

❹ To test your predictions, quickly push the bottle straight ahead. What happens to the bubble? Quickly pull the bottle back. Where does the bubble go now?

❺ Carry your bottle as you walk in a straight path and then turn to your left and walk in a straight path. Observe the bubble as you are walking.

MATERIALS
- clear plastic bottle with cap
- water
- small piece of bar soap
- Science Log data sheet

▲ Accelerometer

THINK AND WRITE

1. What types of movement made the bubble move?

2. **PREDICTING** In science, you make predictions based on previous observations and experiences. On what did you base your predictions in this activity? How did you test your predictions? How can you explain any differences between your predictions and your actual results?

It's Accelerating

As you look around the amusement park, you see one ride, called the Phantom, that is moving very slowly. Suddenly it speeds up and twirls around. The riders are pushed back against their cages as the entire ride seems to spin through the air. How do we determine the change in the velocity of a ride like this?

In the last activity, you made a bottle accelerometer. With it you can observe a change in velocity. The rate of change in velocity is known as **acceleration**. Whether an object is speeding up, slowing down, or changing direction, it is accelerating. Most amusement park rides involve acceleration.

On a downhill slope or a sharp curve, a ride will probably increase in velocity or accelerate. While moving uphill or in a straight line, it may decrease in velocity, or *decelerate.*

Other than on amusement park rides, when can you experience acceleration? What is your favorite sport? In all sports, many accelerations take place.

Look at the photographs of athletes. Tell whether each person is accelerating.

▲ Is this skater accelerating? If so, how?

▲ Are these runners accelerating? If so, how?

Think about the acceleration changes you go through while playing your favorite sport. Write about these changes in acceleration. Remember, you are accelerating when you speed up, slow down, or change direction.

◄ Is this player accelerating? If so, how?

LESSON 3 REVIEW

A car is waiting at a traffic light. The light turns green. The car speeds up to cruise on a straight road at a constant speed. Then the car rounds a gradual curve while maintaining the same speed. Finally, the car slows and stops in a parking lot. Tell when the car is accelerating. Explain how it is accelerating.

F23

4 IT'S MECHANICAL

The sights, sounds, and motions of the amusement park bring out your own feelings of energy. You want to move, move, move. What is energy? What kinds of energy are related to motion? This lesson will help you answer these questions.

▼ Greatest potential energy

Mechanical Energy

The roller coaster stops for a moment at the top of a hill before it begins to descend. Does the roller coaster have energyas it pauses at the top of the hill? How about when the roller coaster races down the hill? Read to find out.

The roller coaster crawls up hills, speeds down them, zooms through loops, and turns through curves. Scientists look at the motion of the roller coaster as a form of mechanical energy. **Energy** is the ability to cause change, and *mechanical energy* is the energy that moves objects. There's no doubt that a moving roller coaster has mechanical energy.

When it's stopped at the top of a hill, a roller coaster also has potential energy. *Potential energy* is the energy stored in an object because of its position. At any moment, the roller coaster cars could be speeding down the hill. As a result, the roller coaster has the potential for motion when it is stopped at the top of a hill.

As the roller coaster descends, its potential energy is converted to kinetic energy. *Kinetic energy* is the mechanical energy of a moving object. Anything that has mass and movement has kinetic energy.

◄ Least potential energy

THINK ABOUT IT

Using something other than a roller coaster, describe an example of potential energy being converted into kinetic energy that is then converted back into potential energy.

A C T I V I T Y

On the Carousel

You're looking at a beautifully decorated carousel. All the horses are brightly painted. They bob up and down, to the delight of the young children riding them. In this activity, you will discover how a model carousel uses energy.

MATERIALS
- tall, plastic dish-detergent bottle
- long, thin rubber band
- toothpick
- tape
- wire
- bead
- 2 long, thin wooden dowels
- 4 paper cups
- string
- scissors
- Science Log data sheet

DO THIS

1 Your teacher will make a hole in the bottom of the bottle and pop off the cap's nozzle.

2 Loop one end of the rubber band over a toothpick, and, from the outside, feed the other end into the hole in the bottle. Tape the toothpick to the bottom of the bottle.

3 Make a small hook with the wire, and catch the free end of the rubber band inside the bottle. Pull the rubber band through the top. Thread the wire through the bottle cap. Slip the bead over the free end of the wire. Tighten the cap on the bottle.

4 Cross the wooden dowels, and tape them together. Attach the cross to the bottle by winding the free end of the wire around the cross.

5 Tape strings to the paper cups, and tie the strings to the ends of the dowels. Wind up your carousel, and then let go.

THINK AND WRITE

1. When does your carousel have the greatest potential energy? What gives the carousel potential energy?

2. When is the potential energy converted to kinetic energy?

The Whirl-a-Gig

Your model carousel used the energy stored in a stretched, twisted rubber band to operate. What kind of potential energy is this? Read to find out.

The Whirl-a-Gig catches your eye, so you try it out. On this ride, a suspended car takes you to a certain point, nearly stops, and then turns you in another direction. It feels as if the whole thing is run by rubber bands that are stretched and released.

You know that the energy stored in an object because of its position is potential energy. If you stretch a rubber band, it stores *elastic potential energy.* That energy is released as the rubber band returns to its natural shape. Elastic potential energy can be stored in anything that stretches, compresses, or bends and then returns to its original shape. Stretched springs, soft rubber balls, and a bent vaulter's pole have elastic potential energy.

The Whirl-a-Gig no doubt contained springs that whipped you around. Springs are frequently involved in our daily uses of elastic potential energy.

Most of us overlook our daily use of elastic potential energy. The spring that slows down a closing door uses this energy. If you think about your daily uses of this type of energy, you could probably make a very long list.

THINK ABOUT IT

How do a diving board, a trampoline, and a bow and arrow use elastic potential energy?

A C T I V I T Y

The Surprise Roller

Using what you know about mechanical energy, see whether you can explain the unusual behavior of the Surprise Roller.

MATERIALS
- oatmeal box
- scissors
- string
- heavy metal nut
- rubber band
- 2 toothpicks
- tape
- Science Log data sheet

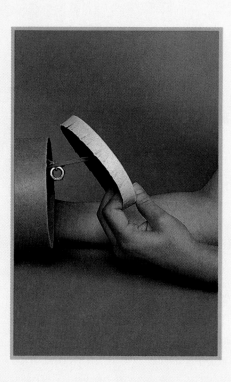

DO THIS

❶ **CAUTION: Be careful when using the scissors to make holes in the box.** Make a small hole in the center of the box bottom and lid.

❷ Use the string to tie the nut onto the middle of the rubber band. Cut off the excess string

❸ Put the rubber band in the box, and push one end through the hole in the bottom. Put a toothpick through the loop of the rubber band to hold it in place. Tape the ends of the toothpick to the box bottom to secure it.

❹ Pull the other end of the rubber band through the hole in the box lid, and secure it with a toothpick. Tape the toothpick down. Put the lid back on the box.

❺ Gently roll your box away from you, and observe what happens. Push the box harder, and observe what happens.

THINK AND WRITE

1. What do you think happened to the rubber band as the box rolled away from you?

2. When do you think the rubber band had the greatest elastic potential energy?

3. What happened as the released elastic potential energy was converted to kinetic energy?

More Potential

Your Surprise Roller stored elastic potential energy. Are there other types of potential energy? You may find some answers as you continue your tour through the amusement park.

You hear young children laughing. You look to see what is happening. The children have just watched a clown on ice skates trip and spill a basket of plastic fruit. Just before the fruit spilled out, it had *gravitational potential energy* because it had the ability to fall.

At a Mexican exhibit, you notice piñatas hanging from the ceiling. Piñatas are clay or papier-mâché figures filled with surprises. A piñata may be shaped like a bird, a donkey, or other figures.

On special occasions, a piñata is hung from the ceiling or a tree. Blindfolded children take turns swinging at the piñata with a stick, trying to break it open. When they succeed, the toys and candy inside come showering down. The toys and candy stored in the piñata have gravitational potential energy.

THINK ABOUT IT

To play a video game at the arcade, you put a coin into a slot. The coin drops into a container, and the game begins. When does your coin have maximum gravitational potential energy?

ACTIVITY

It's a Splash

Have you ever seen a film of high divers? Some divers seem to produce bigger splashes than others. This activity can help you understand why.

MATERIALS
- old newspapers
- round baking dish
- sand
- measuring tape
- masking tape
- 2 small marbles
- 2 large marbles
- Science log data sheet

DO THIS

1 Spread newspaper on the floor next to a wall. Put the baking dish on the paper.

2 Fill the dish with sand to a depth of at least 3 cm. Tape the measuring tape vertically to the wall. Place the 0-cm mark even with the top of the baking dish.

3 Drop one small marble from the 20-cm level into the pan. Observe the marble's effect on the sand.

4 Turn the dish. Drop the second small marble from the 50-cm level. Observe its effect on the sand.

5 Turn the dish and repeat steps 3 and 4 using the larger marbles.

THINK AND WRITE

1. Which marbles—small or large—had the greater gravitational potential energy and the greater kinetic energy? Explain.

2. **IDENTIFYING/CONTROLLING VARIABLES** Controlling variables means changing one variable while keeping all other conditions the same. Explain how you changed one condition at a time while keeping all the other conditions the same. How did each of the variables you controlled affect the results?

A C T I V I T Y

Collision Course

Is it more difficult to stop a roller coaster when it's going fast or when it's going slow? In this activity, you can find the answer.

MATERIALS
- meter stick
- masking tape
- 2 dynamic carts
- removable labels
- long rubber band
- 2 heavy weights
- Science Log data sheet

DO THIS

1 Make a table to record your observations. Tape the meter stick to a table. Label the carts as *1* and *2*. Attach the rubber band to the two carts.

2 Place the carts facing each other on the table, next to the 50-cm mark of the meter stick. Pull the carts apart until both of their front ends line up with the ends of the meter stick.

3 Release the carts at the same time. Note where along the meter stick they collide. Determine the distance each travels before and after the collision. Also note the direction each cart travels before and after the collision—forward or backward. Record your findings.

4 Tape a weight to one cart, and repeat steps 2 and 3. Add a second weight to the same cart, and repeat steps 2 and 3 again.

THINK AND WRITE

1. Did adding mass to one cart affect its velocity? Explain.

2. How did the added mass in the one cart affect the distance and direction the cart traveled after the collision?

Momentum A bowling ball and a basketball roll along at the same speed. Which ball would be easier to stop with one hand? Why? The basketball is easier to stop because it has less momentum. An object's *momentum* is its mass multiplied by its velocity. If its mass or velocity is large, an object will have a large momentum. The more momentum an object has, the harder it is to stop the object or to change the object's direction.

LESSON 4 REVIEW

❶ What kind of energy does a rotating carousel have? How can that energy change form?

❷ Why is it more difficult to stop your bike when you are going fast than when you are going slow? Explain.

❸ When would it be easier to stop a roller coaster—when it is full or when it is empty? Explain.

DOUBLE CHECK

SECTION A REVIEW

1. Using the terms *mechanical energy, potential energy, velocity, acceleration,* and *momentum,* describe a ride on a roller coaster.

2. Compare the terms *speed, velocity,* and *momentum.*

Pushes and Pulls

The amusement park is crowded today. Parents push babies in strollers. A bumper car rams another one and sends it crashing into a third bumper car. Someone throws a baseball at a pyramid of milk bottles, trying to knock them over. A ride operator pulls a lever and a ride starts spinning. All of these actions have something in common. What is it? This section discusses the actions of pushing and pulling and shows how to determine the size of a push or a pull.

On an ordinary day, what do you do that involves a push or a pull? How do your actions vary in strength? On each of the next few days, record in your Science Log two of your actions that are a push or a pull. Describe the strength of each action.

1 FORCE IT!

Forces are all around you—at the amusement park and everywhere else. What are forces? The readings and activities in this lesson will help you find out about the characteristics of any force.

A Piece of the Action

As you read about action at an amusement park, you will find many examples of forces. Use these examples to define *force*.

"Let's head for the game arcade," you suggest to your friend. "I want to win a prize." As you enter the arcade, you see a model crane in a booth full of toys. You decide to try it. You push a coin into the slot. The model crane swings back and forth as you push and pull on a joystick. Then, the claws open and drop right on top of the prize you want. You press a button and the claws grasp the prize. But as the crane and claws tug on the prize, it slips out of the claws. "Oh, well," you sigh. "Let's go play the basketball free-throw game."

► **List all of the pushes and pulls you use when operating the prize crane.**

"We're sure to have more luck tossing basketballs," you say. You have 12 tries to make 8 baskets. You grab a ball and take careful aim. You throw the ball toward the basket, and it swishes through. You miss a few times, but you still have a chance to win a prize. You need to make only one more basket. You wish you could slam-dunk it, but you have to stay behind the line. You eagerly pull the basketball toward you, raise it to eye level, and pitch it forward. It hits the rim, bounces up, and goes through the hoop. You win! The attendant pulls the prize you want off a shelf and pushes it toward you. As you grab your prize, your friend moves on to the next booth—the balloon-pump game.

Here, your friend has one minute to pump enough air into the balloon to make it burst. She presses down on the pump handle and tugs it up over and over again. The balloon gets bigger and bigger. But it doesn't break. She tries again, pumping harder, and this time, she wins!

THINK ABOUT IT

The game players were applying forces to objects as they paid for and played the games in the arcade. Think about the words used to describe the forces. Use them to make up a definition of *force*.

Give It Direction

Now that you have an idea of what a force is, you can check your definition of *force.* You can also find out more about forces.

You probably concluded that a **force** is either a push or a pull. A force can start an object moving, change the direction and rate of its motion, or change the shape of the object.

Any force acts in a specific direction with a specific size, or strength. When scientists diagram forces, they often use an arrow to indicate direction and size of a force. The head of the arrow shows the direction of the force. The tail end of the arrow identifies the point where the force is exerted. The length or the thickness of the arrow represents the size, or strength, of the force. Now see if you can identify some forces.

You will need: Science Log

For each picture below, sketch the scene. Decide which person, animal, or object is applying force and which is receiving force. Then draw arrows indicating the direction of each force and the point where each force is being applied.

THINK ABOUT IT

Using the pictures shown, list the forces in order from strongest to weakest.

ACTIVITY

Give Force a Hand

What happens when people applying forces combine their efforts? How can the outcome of an action change? Try this activity to find out.

DO THIS

1 Use masking tape to mark a starting line about 3 m from a wall.

2 Place the cardboard box behind the starting line, and then fill it with books.

3 Push the box to the wall. Then pull the box back to the starting line. Did you have to push hard on the box, or did you push lightly?

4 Ask another group member to help you push the box to the wall. Then one of you should push as the other pulls the box back to the starting line. Was it easier to move the box alone or with help? Explain.

5 Now have one group member try to pull the box in one direction as you try to pull it in the opposite direction. What happens?

THINK AND WRITE

Sketch your actions in steps 3, 4, and 5. Draw force arrows, and describe what happened in each step.

QUICK CHECK

LESSON 1 REVIEW

1 What do force arrows drawn on a diagram indicate? Explain.

2 If you needed help moving a desk, what combination of forces would be most helpful? Explain.

2 GRAVITY HELPS

A basketball falls through the hoop at the free-throw game, and someone else wins a prize. In this lesson, you will discover how activities involve forces, including the force of gravity.

ACTIVITY

At the Drop of a . . .

MATERIALS
- 6 balls of different masses
- table
- ruler
- Science Log data sheet

Suppose three balls of different masses are fired from three different launchers at the same time. Which ball will land first? Do this activity to test your prediction.

DO THIS

1 With a partner, choose any three of the balls. Predict the order in which the balls will hit the floor when they are rolled off the edge of the tabletop at the same time.

2 Line up the three balls near an edge of the table-top. Use the ruler to push all three balls off the table at the same time. Observe the paths of the balls, and note the order in which they hit the floor.

3 Repeat steps 1 and 2, using different combinations of balls. Record your observations.

THINK AND WRITE

1. What did you observe about the order in which the balls hit the floor?

2. **PREDICTING** To predict, you sometimes think about how to interpret data. How did the data you gathered in this activity affect your prediction?

The Pull of the Earth

In the last activity, you found that objects having different masses, falling together, will land at the same time. Read on to find out why this is so.

Gravity is the force that pulls all objects in the universe toward one another. Earth is surrounded by a gravitational field. Scientists describe the strength of this gravitational field by an object's acceleration toward Earth's center. The stength of Earth's gravitational field decreases as the distance from Earth increases.

Think of the forces of gravity between Earth and a nearby smaller object as acting like the magnetic forces between a large magnet and a small magnet. Which magnet exerts the greater force? Why? Based on this model, what do you think determines the size of the force of gravity between any two objects?

The size of the force of gravity between any two objects is determined by the distance between the objects and their mass. Mass is the amount of matter in an object.

The balls in the activity fell from the same height at the same time, but had different masses. Since the force of gravity was stronger on the more massive ball, why did all three balls hit the floor at the same time?

If one ball has twice the mass of another ball, it requires twice the force to start it moving. Since the force of gravity on the more massive ball is twice as strong, the balls hit the floor at the same time.

THINK ABOUT IT

Suppose you roll a ball off a table that's on top of a high mountain and the ball falls several feet to the ground. Do you think the acceleration of the ball would be the same as the acceleration of the balls in the activity? Why or why not?

▼ The Earth is surrounded by a gravitational field.

A C T I V I T Y

What Goes Up . . .

An old saying about the force of gravity states that "what goes up must come down." Is it possible that what goes up sometimes stays up? Try this activity to help you decide.

MATERIALS
- table-tennis ball
- large, straight plastic straw
- Science Log data sheet

DO THIS

1 Hold the ball above your head.

2 Put one end of the straw in your mouth. Center the straw on the bottom of the ball. Blow through the straw against the bottom of the ball, and release the ball.

3 Repeat steps 1 and 2 as necessary until you are able to balance the ball in the air, above your head.

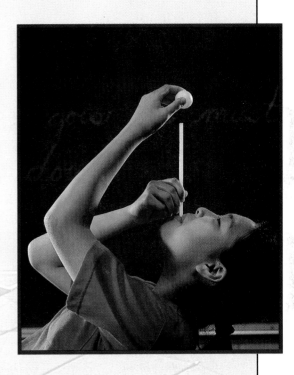

THINK AND WRITE

1. What force kept the ball in the air? How did the direction of this force oppose the force of gravity trying to accelerate the ball?

2. What other ways can you think of to oppose the force of gravity?

Balancing Act

In one of the shows at the park, an acrobat walks across a tightrope stretched high in the air. How does the tightrope walker keep from falling? This activity will help you investigate this question.

MATERIALS
- balancing figure pattern
- scissors
- pencil or marker
- poster board
- 2-m string
- masking tape
- stiff wire
- clay
- Science Log data sheet

DO THIS

1 Cut out the balancing figure. Then trace the figure onto poster board, and cut it out.

2 Stretch the string tightly between two desks. Use masking tape to hold the string in place.

3 Try to balance the figure on the string. If you cannot balance the figure, tape a piece of wire to the back. Add clay to each end of the figure until it balances on the string.

THINK AND WRITE

What did you have to change to make your tightrope sitter balance? Explain.

Center of Gravity Every object, including your tightrope sitter, has a center of mass. The *center of mass*, or *center of gravity*, is the point at which gravity seems to act. For example, the center of mass of a sphere is the center of the sphere. If you place a sheet of paper on your desk and its center of mass is not on the desk, the paper falls. If you shift the paper so that its center of mass is on the desk, it will not fall.

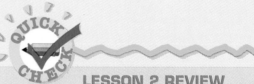

LESSON 2 REVIEW

Suppose you dropped two blocks of the same size from the same height. One block is wood; the other is iron. Which block would hit the ground first? Explain.

3 TAKE ITS MEASURE

You watch people testing their strength at one game booth. When you try, the lead ball rises only halfway up the scale. Why couldn't you apply enough force to ring the bell? How much force is enough? In this lesson, you will measure forces and test your strength.

Feel the Pull

A clown strains and sweats as he tries unsuccessfully to lift one of two huge, identical-looking barbells. In walks another clown. She glances at her struggling partner and then easily picks up the other huge barbell. She laughs and carries it offstage. You wonder how she did that.

Although the barbells are the same size, one is hollow and made of plastic. The other is made of solid iron. Do you think the barbells weigh the same? **Weight** is the force of gravity pulling an object toward the center of another object. So on Earth, the weight of an object is simply the force of gravity acting on that object. Although the barbells look identical, the plastic barbell weighs less than the other one. Why?

Were you able to keep the table-tennis ball in the air by blowing on it in an earlier activity? Do you think you could do the same with a baseball? A baseball has more mass than the table-tennis ball, so it weighs more. You would need to apply more force to resist the pull of gravity on the baseball.

Suppose you could take a trip to the moon. Would you weigh the same on the moon as you weigh on Earth? The moon has less mass than the Earth and so attracts with less force. Although your amount of matter, or mass, would not change, you would weigh less on the moon.

THINK ABOUT IT

On Earth, sea level is closer to Earth's center of gravity than a mountaintop is. Would your weight be different on a mountaintop than at sea level? Explain.

ACTIVITY

Measure the Pull

There are many forces at the amusement park. You can't see a force, but you can measure the size of its effect. In this activity, you will build a force meter to measure the gravitational force on some objects.

MATERIALS

- suction or adhesive hook
- large rubber band
- masking tape
- adding machine tape
- scissors
- marker
- ruler
- 3 100-g masses
- objects of unknown weight
- string
- Science Log data sheet

DO THIS

1 Make a table like the one shown, to record your results.

WEIGHT OF SOME OBJECTS	
Object	Weight (N)

2 Attach the hook to a wall at about eye level, and hang the rubber band from it.

3 Tape a strip of adding machine tape to the wall, next to the hook. Place the top end of the adding machine tape level with the top of the rubber band. Tape the bottom end to the wall, near the floor.

4 Use the ruler and marker to draw a line on the tape, next to the bottom of the rubber band. Mark the line *0 N*.

5 Hang a 100-g mass on the rubber band. Draw a line on the tape, at the bottom of the rubber band. Mark the line *1 N*.

6 Hook a second mass to the bottom of the first one. Draw a line at the bottom of the rubber band. Mark this line *2 N*. Then add the third mass, draw a line, and label it *3 N*.

7 You now have a force meter that you can use to weigh small objects in your classroom. Do this by tying an object to the bottom of the rubber band. Record the name and weight of each object. If a measure lies between two of your marks, estimate the weight. For example, if the bottom of the stretched rubber band is about halfway between the *1-N* and *2-N* marks, record its weight as *1.5 N*.

THINK AND WRITE

1. If an object has a mass of 1,000 g, or 1 kg, what is its weight in N?

2. A bag of sugar has a mass of 2,300 g. What is the force of gravity on the bag?

3. If the force of gravity on an object is 2.5 N, what is its mass in grams?

4. **INTERPRETING DATA** In the activity, you recorded data about the weight of objects you use in the classroom. Based on your data, state how grams and N are related.

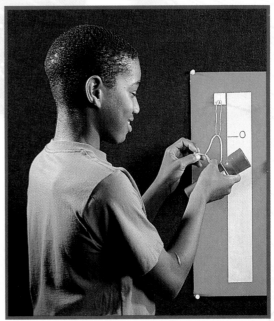

ACTIVITY

Test Your Strength!

At the amusement park, you tested your strength by trying to ring the bell. In this activity, you can test your strength by using bungee cords.

MATERIALS
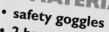
- safety goggles
- 2 bungee cords with a hook on each end
- 2 wooden dowels, each about 30 cm long
- meter stick
- masking tape
- spring scale
- Science Log data sheet

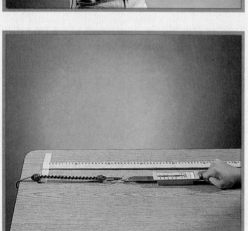

DO THIS

❶ Attach the hooks of one bungee cord to the two dowels.

❷ **CAUTION: Put on safety goggles.** Pull the dowels to stretch the bungee cord as far as you can. Have a partner measure the length of the stretched cord in centimeters. Record the measure.

❸ Repeat steps 1 and 2 using two bungee cords as shown.

❹ Reverse roles with your partner and repeat steps 1, 2, and 3.

❺ Hook one bungee cord to the edge of a table. Tape the meter stick to the table-top so that its zero end is even with one end of the cord. Pull the cord with a spring scale until the cord's length matches the length that you stretched it to in step 2. Read the force meter and record the measure in N.

❻ Repeat step 5 using two bungee cords. Again record the measure in N.

THINK AND WRITE

Compare the amounts of force you and your partner used with those of other pairs. Who is the strongest in your class? Explain.

Measuring Force In the activity on pages F42–F43 and in this activity you measured forces. You recorded your measurements in "N." Just what is N?

N stands for *newton*, the unit used to measure force. One newton is equal to the force of gravity exerted by the Earth on a 100-g mass. So, on Earth, a newton is approximately equal to the weight of a 100-g mass. Newtons can also be used to measure the amount of force you need to move something a certain distance—as when you stretch a bungee cord.

DOUBLE CHECK

SECTION B REVIEW

1. Does standing up require force? Explain.

2. Suppose two balls are dropped from shoulder height at the same time. The balls fall the same distance but do *not* hit the ground at the same time. Explain how this could be.

3. Are mass and weight the same thing? Explain.

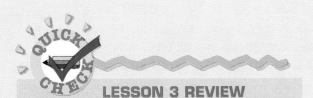

LESSON 3 REVIEW

❶ What are you measuring when you weigh an object?

❷ How could you use wooden dowels and bungee cords to test the strength of other muscles in your body?

The Forces Are with You

Here it is! Here it is! You wave your friends over to get into the line for the water-chute ride. You slowly climb the ramp, and finally you're next in line. You climb into your seat, stretch the seat belt over your lap, and clamp it closed. For a minute nothing happens, but then . . . The motor starts, and your car slides down a water chute, splashes hard into a pool of water, and glides across the water until it reaches another chute. Down the car plunges, slamming hard into the water below. You're soaking wet but smiling.

Think about the forces involved in this scene. Did the forces affect how you and the car moved? Did some forces produce greater speed than others? In this section, you will look at forces and how they affect motion. In your Science Log, tell how forces would affect you on the water-chute ride. Add to your ideas as you investigate forces and motion in this section.

1 WHEN MOTION CHANGES

"Look at the way the human cannonball arcs through the air!" "The Centrifuge ride makes me dizzy as it swings me around and around!" "Watch the green bumper car ram the red car into the guardrail!" These statements describe some of the effects of forces that you will investigate in this lesson.

Forcing Changes

In each picture below, a force applied to an object makes it move. A second force will act on the moving object. For each picture, describe the object's beginning motion. Identify the second force that will act on the moving object. Then describe the effect of the second force.

▲ What do you think pulls on the ball as it heads for the batter?

▲ What keeps these riders from flying away?

▲ What forces act on these bumper cars?

THINK ABOUT IT

What do you think would happen if the second force acting on the baseball, on the airplane, or on the puck were not there?

F47

Falls, Twirls, and Crashes

MATERIALS
- safety goggles
- 3 table-tennis balls
- plastic tube (20 cm long)
- rubber ball
- S-shaped hook
- nylon string (50 cm long)
- large plastic bowl
- lead sinker
- Science Log data sheet

On the preceding page, you described how certain forces would affect the motions of objects. You recognized the effect that gravity would have on the flight of a ball, the effect that holding a control wire would have on the swings, and the effect of a push on a bumper car. In this activity, you will further explore the effects of gravity, circular motion, and collisions.

DO THIS

PART A: GRAVITY AND MOTION

❶ Think of as many ways as you can to demonstrate how the force of gravity alone can change the motion of an object. These ways can involve starting motion, changing the speed of motion, or changing the direction of motion.

❷ Use a table-tennis ball to test your ideas. For each demonstration, sketch a diagram that shows how motion changed. Draw arrows to show the beginning direction of motion, if any, and to show the direction of the force of gravity. Some of your diagrams may be similar to each other. An example is given for a ball that rolls off a table.

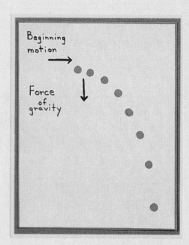

PART B: FORCE AND CIRCULAR MOTION

❶ **CAUTION: Put on safety goggles for this part of the activity.** Assemble a circular-motion device as shown.

❷ Hold the tube in a vertical position. Move the top end of the tube gently in a small circle. As the ball begins to swing in a circle, speed it up until the string points straight out from the tube. Does speeding up the ball make the string pull on it harder? How can you tell?

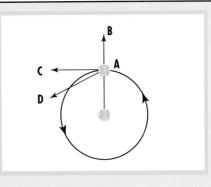

3 Predict how the motion of the ball would change if the string broke while the ball was moving in a circle.

4 Test your prediction by placing the bowl upside down on your desk or table with a table-tennis ball inside it. Move the bowl in circles to get the ball rolling in a circular path. Then lift one edge of the bowl to let the ball escape. In which direction does it go—toward B, C, or D in the diagram or in some other direction?

PART C: COLLISIONS

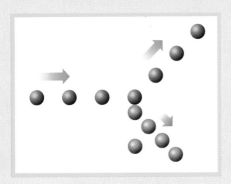

1 Think of as many ways as you can to demonstrate how collisions involving balls can change motion. The collisions might start motion, stop motion, change the speed of motion, or change the direction of motion.

2 Use the table-tennis balls to test your ideas. For each demonstration, sketch a diagram that shows how the motion of balls was changed. Draw arrows to show the directions of the forces. An example is given for a collision between two identical balls.

THINK AND WRITE

1. In an arcade ball-toss game, you get three tries to hit a circular target. For each try after the first, the target is moved farther away from you. On the first try, you throw the ball directly at the target and miss. How should you change the direction and strength of your toss on each of the two remaining tries? Explain.

2. When you rolled the ball inside the bowl, what supplied the force that kept the ball moving in a circle?

LESSON 1 REVIEW

1 Describe the two main ways in which an applied force can change the motion of an object.

2 How does the change in motion caused by gravity on a ball in flight differ from the change in motion of a ball involved in a collision?

2 IN BALANCE OR NOT

Earlier in this unit, you examined what happened when forces combined. Some combinations resulted in movement, and some did not. How did the forces combine, and why did the combinations have different effects? This lesson will help you find out.

In Balance

Can forces be exerted on an object without causing the object to move? Think about this question as you draw some diagrams.

You will need: drawing paper, pencil

Suppose that you and a friend have a rope with a flag attached to the middle. The rope lies on the ground in a straight line. You mark a spot on the ground underneath the flag. Then the two of you pick up opposite ends of the rope and tug with the same amount of force.

What do you think would happen? On a sheet of paper, sketch the scene. Add force arrows to show the size and direction of the force each of you applies to the rope. Explain the outcome.

Now suppose that you and your friend are on opposite sides of a swinging door. The two of you push against the door with equal force. Draw arrows to show the directions and sizes of the forces acting on the door. Describe what happens to the door.

Two forces that are equal in size but opposite in direction are *balanced forces*. Balanced forces produce no change in the position of an object.

THINK ABOUT IT

Do your sketches of the two scenes show balanced forces? Explain.

Out of Balance

You've seen that balanced forces result in no change in motion. How, then, are an object's motion and its velocity changed? This activity can help you answer the question.

- water
- tissue paper
- empty squeezable detergent bottle
- small paper cup
- Science Log data sheet

DO THIS

1 Moisten the tissue paper, and shape it into a plug for the bottle. Use it to plug the opening of the bottle.

2 Place the cup upside down over the top of the bottle.

3 Squeeze the bottle as hard as you can. Observe what happens to the cup.

THINK AND WRITE

1. What two forces were acting to cause what you observed?

2. How did these two forces compare? Describe their directions and relative sizes.

3. Could balanced forces have caused what you observed? Why or why not?

Starting and Changing Motion

Balanced forces never cause a change in motion. What kind of forces do you need in order to move an object or to change its motion? Studying Speed Chutes will give you a clue.

Chute for the (Sports) **STARS**

from *National Geographic World*

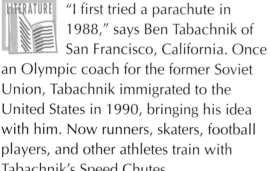

LITERATURE "I first tried a parachute in 1988," says Ben Tabachnik of San Francisco, California. Once an Olympic coach for the former Soviet Union, Tabachnik immigrated to the United States in 1990, bringing his idea with him. Now runners, skaters, football players, and other athletes train with Tabachnik's Speed Chutes.

The chutes attach to a special belt. As an athlete starts to pick up speed, the chutes open. Air pushing against the open chutes creates resistance and running against resistance helps improve both speed and endurance. An athlete can wear

additional chutes in front and run or skate backward.

Professionals and amateurs say the chutes improve performance. "My start is more powerful," says a fullback for the Denver Broncos. "What's more," adds Tabachnik, "the chutes' bright colors make athletes feel good."

Suppose you decide to use a Speed Chute during your running workouts. You begin by standing still, facing into the wind with the chute open behind you. Are the forces applied by the wind and your legs balanced? Why or why not?

You're ready to start your run against the wind. As you begin to step, you increase the force applied by your legs against the ground and you accelerate to a comfortable, steady running speed. How would you describe the directions of the wind force and leg force? How do the sizes of the forces compare?

Now you're ready to pick up the pace. What must you do to increase your velocity? How will the directions of the forces compare? How will the relative sizes of the forces change?

"Good workout!" you exclaim as you end your run and remove the Speed Chute. What kinds of forces made your workout so tough? When your legs applied force against the ground equal in size and opposite in direction to the force of the wind against the Speed Chute, you did not move. These forces were balanced.

As you began running, the forces were still opposite in direction, but they were no longer equal in size. You changed your velocity by applying even greater force with your legs. Starting and changing motion require *unbalanced forces*. Unbalanced forces are opposite and unequal.

THINK ABOUT IT

Suppose two forces are exerted on an object, and the object does not move. Are the forces balanced or unbalanced? Explain.

LESSON 2 REVIEW

❶ When a car is moving at a constant velocity, are the forces exerted on it balanced or unbalanced? Explain.

❷ If a car is turning a corner, are the forces balanced or unbalanced? Explain.

3 FOCUS ON FRICTION

Suppose you go to the "Test Your Strength" game. Here you must hit a platform with a sledge hammer to make a bell ring. But the sledge hammer is lying on the ground several feet away from the platform. Would it be easier to drag the sledge hammer or to carry it? This activity will help you decide.

ACTIVITY

A Rocky Test

Suppose you're riding a bicycle and the front and rear brakes lock so that the wheels cannot spin. Would it be easier to drag your bicycle or to carry it? This activity will help you decide.

MATERIALS
- scissors
- empty shoe box with lid
- long, thick rubber band
- pencil
- 5 rocks
- masking tape
- tabletop
- measuring tape
- piece of carpet
- Science Log data sheet

DO THIS

1 **CAUTION: Be careful when using the scissors.** Work with a partner. Use the scissors to punch a small hole in one end of the shoe box. Thread one end of the rubber band through the hole, and secure the rubber band with the pencil as shown.

2 Put the rocks in the box. Put on the lid and tape it shut. Then lift the box by carefully pulling the free end of the rubber band. Observe what happens.

3 Measure in millimeters how far the rubber band stretches at the point when the box begins rising. Record the measurement.

4 Try to drag the box across the tabletop by pulling the free end of the rubber band. Measure in millimeters how far the rubber band stretches just before the box moves. Record the measurement. Then, measure how far the rubber band stretches while you drag the box. Record the measurement.

5 Repeat step 4. Only this time, drag the box across a piece of carpet.

THINK AND WRITE

1. What is the relationship between the amounts of force needed to slide an object on a smooth surface and on a rough surface?

2. What is the relationship between the weight of an object and the amount of force needed to slide the object? Would you drag or carry the sledge hammer? Explain.

Friction The rubber band stretched because the surface of the table and the bottom surface of the box "grabbed" at each other. **Friction** is the force that resists motion between the surfaces of two touching objects. When you pulled the rubber band hard enough to overcome friction, the box began sliding across the table. When objects slide over one another, the friction that results is called *sliding friction*.

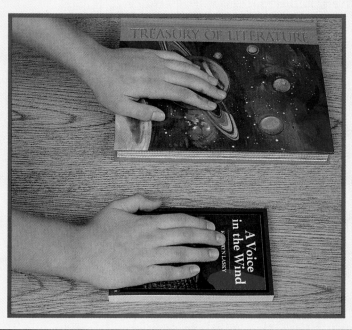

One cause of the friction between two touching objects is the roughness of their surfaces. All surfaces are rough, even those that look smooth, like a tabletop. The weight of objects also affects the amount of friction between them. Why do you think a heavier book would create more friction than a lighter book as it is pushed across a table?

Reducing Sliding Friction

In the last activity, you had to overcome sliding friction to move the box of rocks. Is there a way you could have reduced the sliding friction? Try this activity to find out.

MATERIALS

- 8 round pencils
- smooth floor
- shoe box and rocks from the preceding activity
- measuring tape
- Science Log data sheet

DO THIS

1. Work with a partner. Place the pencils on the floor. On top of them, put the shoe box holding the rocks, as shown.

2. Pull the rubber band to move the box

3. Measure how far the rubber band stretches just before the box moves. Record the measurement.

4. Measure how far the rubber band stretches as the box moves on the pencils.

THINK AND WRITE

Compare the measurements of the stretched rubber band from steps 3 and 4 of this activity with the measurements from step 4 in the previous activity. Did the rubber band stretch more or less in this activity? Why?

Slide or Roll

We often take the force of friction for granted. What would happen to some of our favorite activities if their uses of friction were changed? You can figure out for yourself just how important the right kind of friction can be.

Suppose activities that are made possible by wheels were to be performed without wheels, and suppose sliding activities were performed with wheels. Would friction affect the results? Look at each picture at the right, and answer the accompanying question.

The friction produced by round objects such as wheels and balls is called *rolling friction.* Friction is reduced when the opposing surfaces are separated by something round.

▲ **What would a roller coaster ride be like without wheels on the cars? Describe such a ride.**

▲ **Do you think you could figure-skate on ice while wearing roller blades? Based on what you know about friction, describe an effort to roller-blade on ice.**

THINK ABOUT IT

Why do you think the force needed to move an object against rolling friction is less than the force needed to move an object against sliding friction?

ACTIVITY

In the Air

Can the wind cause friction? This activity will help you answer the question.

MATERIALS
- single-hole paper punch
- 3 squares of sturdy fabric (one with 30-cm sides, one with 40-cm sides, and one with 50-cm sides)
- 12 pieces of string of the same length
- stapler
- 3 cone-shaped coffee filters
- 6 lumps of clay (10 g each)
- stopwatch
- Science Log data sheet

DO THIS

1 Use the paper punch to make a hole in the four corners of each fabric square.

2 Tie one end of a string through each hole in the fabric squares. Staple the free ends of the four strings on each square to the sides of a coffee filter to make a parachute.

3 Press a lump of clay into the bottom of each filter.

4 Drop the parachutes from the same height one at a time, and record how long each takes to hit the floor. Observe what happens to each parachute.

5 Choose one of the parachutes. Experiment with different amounts of clay in the filter. Record the amounts of clay and your time measurements.

THINK AND WRITE

1. What forces acted on the parachutes? Explain.

2. How did added weight affect the length of time a parachute was in the air? Explain why you think the weight had this effect.

3. **IDENTIFYING/CONTROLLING VARIABLES** In any experiment, you control variables by changing one condition while keeping all the others the same. What variable did you change in step 5? What variables did you keep the same in step 5?

Going Against the Flow

You have seen how the velocity of a falling object can be changed by using the friction from a parachute. See if you can find out how this type of friction works.

Fluid friction is the force exerted by a fluid on an object moving through the fluid. The fluid can be a liquid or a gas. The direction of the force is the opposite of the direction in which the object is moving. Air is a gas, so *air resistance* is an example of fluid friction. In the activity, air resistance acted on the parachutes. Water is also a liquid, so it exerts fluid friction.

Look at each pair of pictures, and decide which object encounters less fluid friction.

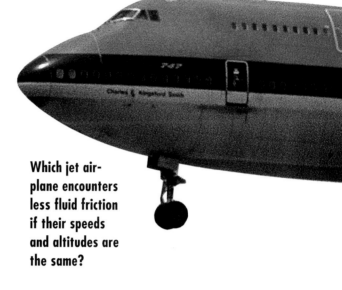

Which jet airplane encounters less fluid friction if their speeds and altitudes are the same?

Which of these identical boats encounters less fluid friction?

THINK ABOUT IT

What two factors do you think determine the size of the force of fluid friction in air or water? Is fluid friction greater in water or in air? Why?

ACTIVITY

Reducing Friction

You have discovered that fluids can cause resistance as objects move through them. This activity will help you find out how fluids affect sliding friction between two objects.

MATERIALS
- stack of old books
- large, smooth metal baking sheet
- flat rubber eraser
- stopwatch
- vegetable oil
- paper towel
- Science Log data sheet

DO THIS

1 Use the stack of books and the baking sheet to make a ramp.

2 Put the eraser at the top of the baking sheet and push it. Use the stopwatch to time how long it takes for the eraser to slide to the bottom of the ramp. You may have to push the eraser again if it stops on its way down the ramp. Record the time.

3 Pour a small amount of vegetable oil on the baking sheet, and use a paper towel to spread it evenly over the surface.

4 Repeat step 2.

THINK AND WRITE

1. What effect did the oil have on the time for the eraser to slide down the ramp?

2. How did the fluid friction compare with the sliding friction on the eraser?

3. Why do you think people use oil to lubricate the moving parts of machines?

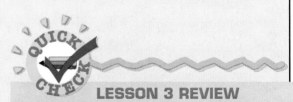

LESSON 3 REVIEW

1 How does sliding friction help you walk?

2 If you accidentally walked through a small oil puddle, would it be easier or more difficult for you to walk after that? Explain.

3 Think of three tasks you perform every day. Describe how friction affects each task.

4 IT'S THE LAW

Sir Isaac Newton was one of the most influential scientists of the seventeenth century. He proposed the law of gravitational force. He also developed three laws of motion. In this lesson, you will investigate Newton's three laws of motion.

A C T I V I T Y

A Lawful Trick

MATERIALS
• small glass
• playing card
• dime, nickel, quarter
• Science Log data sheet

Have you ever seen a show in which the performer pulled a tablecloth out from under a dinner setting without disturbing the dishes or utensils? In some ways, this trick demonstrates Newton's first law of motion. You can try something similar in this activity.

DO THIS

❶ Place the glass on a table, right side up.

❷ Put the card on top of the glass, and place the dime in the center of the card.

❸ Hit the card sideways very quickly with your finger. Where does the coin fall?

❹ Repeat steps 2 and 3 using the nickel and the quarter.

THINK AND WRITE

Describe the position of the coin each time before and after you hit the card.

ACTIVITY

Buckle Up!

Why do you think it's important to use the safety bar when you ride a roller coaster or to wear a seat belt when you ride in a car? Do this activity to find out. You will also discover more about Newton's first law of motion.

MATERIALS

- 5 thick books
- board
- modeling clay
- rolling cart
- meter stick
- thread
- Science Log data sheet

DO THIS

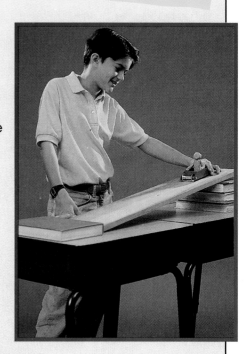

1. Make a ramp with the books and the board. Lay one book against the bottom of the ramp, as shown, to form a barrier.

2. Use some of the modeling clay to make a simple human figurine that will easily fit in the cart.

3. Set the figurine in the cart. Set the cart near the top of the ramp and release it. Let the cart crash into the barrier at the bottom of the ramp. Observe what happens to the cart and to the clay passenger.

4. Where does the clay passenger come to a stop? Measure in centimeters the distance from the barrier to the passenger.

5. Use more clay to make a larger human figurine. Repeat steps 3 and 4.

6. Use thread to tie the clay passenger to its seat. Try another crash test. What happens?

THINK AND WRITE

1. The cart and its clay passenger were in motion together on the ramp. Did this motion together change? If so, how?

2. How did the mass of the clay passenger affect its motion?

3. Why does wearing a seat belt while riding in a car make you safer than not wearing one? Explain in terms of motion and force.

Don't Change This Motion!

The results of the coin trick and of the crash tests demonstrate Newton's first law of motion. Read to find out how.

During the coin trick, the coin on top of the card started out at rest. You applied an unbalanced force to the card by flicking it. But you applied no unbalanced force against the coin. So, for a brief moment, the coin remained at rest in the same position. Then, when the support of the card was taken away, gravity pulled the coin to the bottom of the glass. This trick demonstrated that an object at rest will remain at rest unless acted upon by an unbalanced force. You often assume that objects will remain where you place them. Why is your assumption usually true?

The crash tests demonstrate another part of the first law of motion. Compare the crash tests with your own experience. Suppose your books are on the back seat of a moving car. The car stops suddenly. What happens to your books? How is this similar to what happened to the clay passenger in the cart?

Newton's *first law of motion* states that objects at rest tend to stay at rest, and objects that are moving tend to continue moving. This tendency of objects to resist changes in motion is called **inertia.** The greater the mass, the greater the inertia. The greater the mass, the greater the force that is needed to overcome the object's inertia.

THINK ABOUT IT

Describe what happened to the different coins in the coin trick and the different figurines in the crash tests in terms of inertia.

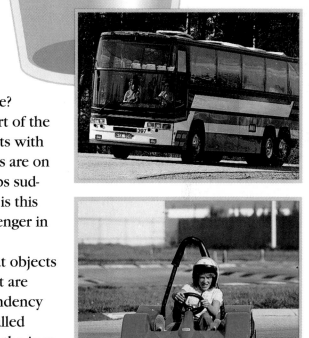

▲ Which vehicle is easier to stop? Use the concept of inertia to explain.

Newton Racers

Which would produce a greater change in the motion of an object—a small force or a large one? How does an unbalanced force acting on two objects of different masses affect their motions? Before trying to answer questions like these, stage a race and gather some information in this activity.

DO THIS

PART A: FORCE AND ACCELERATION

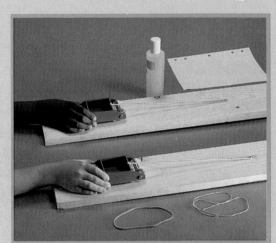

1 Work with a partner. Screw a hook into the middle of one of the boards, 50 cm from one end. Your partner should do the same to the other board. Place the boards side by side so that the hooks line up even with each other.

2 Each of you should attach one rubber band to a skate and to a hook on a board. Pull the skates to the same fixed point, stretching the rubber bands, and hold them in place as shown.

3 Release your skates at the same instant. What happens? Do the skates reach the finish line, or the end of the board, at about the same time?

4 Try a second race. Repeat steps 2 and 3. Only this time, one of you should attach two rubber bands to the skate and the hook. The other racer should use only one rubber band as before. What happens? Repeat this race with the other racer using two rubber bands. Does one skate reach the finish line much sooner than the other? If so, which skate?

PART B: MASS AND ACCELERATION

1 Try a third kind of race. Use one rubber band on each skate. Increase the mass of one skate by filling the bottle with water, fastening the cap tightly, and using string to tie the bottle to the skate as shown.

2 Each of you should pull your own skate to the same fixed point, stretching the rubber band. Release both skates at the same instant. What happens? Repeat this race—only this time, the other racer should use the water bottle. Does one skate reach the finish line much sooner than the other? If so, which skate?

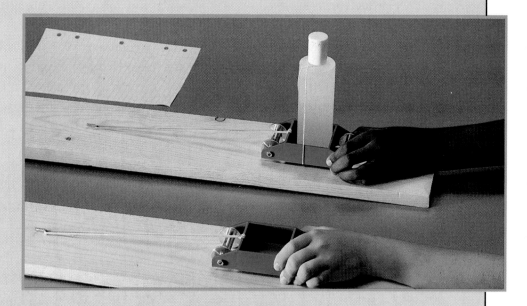

THINK AND WRITE

1. In the first race, how did the forces applied to the skates compare?

2. In the second race and the repeat of it, which skate had the greater change in velocity? Explain.

3. Indicate how the results of the races in Part B support the following statement: If identical unbalanced forces act at the same time on objects having different masses, the smaller mass undergoes a greater change in velocity.

Clowning Around with the Laws

The clown show is about to begin. Take a seat, and read how acceleration, inertia, and friction can all be stars in the clown act. Keep in mind the results of the races in the preceding activity.

A big clown pulling an empty wagon runs across the stage and exits. Seconds later, the clown returns, but this time there's another clown riding in the wagon. Over and over again, the clown enters and exits the stage, each time pulling one more rider in the wagon. Each time the clown returns, he is pulling the wagon more slowly. His pace becomes slower and slower until he finally stops and falls down, exhausted. Why does the wagon become harder to pull? What forces are acting on it?

The clown pulling the wagon shows how Newton's *second law of motion* works. According to this law, when an unbalanced force is applied to an object, the object accelerates. The law goes on to say that the amount of acceleration depends on the mass of the object and the amount of force applied to it. A greater force applied to an object results in greater acceleration. Increases in mass result in less acceleration.

With each additional clown, mass was added to the wagon. The pull of gravity on the wagon, or its weight, became greater, as did its inertia. Friction between the wheels and the floor also increased with the added mass. The pulling force of the clown decreased as the clown's fatigue increased.

THINK ABOUT IT

According to Newton's second law of motion, would a sports car or a locomotive be able to accelerate more easily? Why?

ACTIVITY

You've Got Pull

MATERIALS
- 2 spring scales
- Science Log data sheet

While roller-skating at the amusement park skating rink, you nearly run into a wall. Standing inches away from the wall, you push against it. You roll away from the wall. How can you explain this? In this activity, you will test how forces act on two different objects at once.

DO THIS

❶ Connect the two spring scales by hooking them together.

❷ Have a partner hold one scale in a fixed position. Predict how the readings on the scales will compare when you pull on the other scale. Record your predictions and then test them. Record the readings on the scales.

❸ What do you think will happen if you pull harder? Record and test your prediction. Record the readings on both scales.

THINK AND WRITE

1. Did the scales show the same or different readings? What do the readings indicate about the sizes of the forces involved?

2. How would you describe the forces acting on the two spring scales at the same time?

3. Where did the forces come from to make you roll backward as you pushed forward against the wall? What does this tell you about these forces?

ACTIVITY

Observing Action and Reaction

MATERIALS

- empty soft-drink can with pull-tab attached
- string
- water
- deep sink
- Science Log data sheet

In the previous activity, one spring was affected by the force placed on another spring. A pair of forces acted on different objects. How else can pairs of forces affect objects? Do this activity to find out.

DO THIS

1. Your teacher will use a hammer and nail to punch evenly spaced holes around the can, near the bottom.

2. Pull the can's tab straight up, and tie the string to it.

3. Holding the free end of the string and the can, fill the can with water under a faucet in a deep sink. Using the free end of the string, lift the can away from the tap and see what happens.

THINK AND WRITE

1. What happened to the water? to the can?

2. Do you think one action resulted in the other? Explain.

Equal and Opposite

In one activity, one spring scale reacted to the pull on the other scale. In another activity, the can's spinning also was a reaction to an action. What was the action? How is what happened related to the third law of motion? Read to find out.

When you jump on a trampoline, its springs are pushed down. Then they recoil, and you are bounced back up. Over and over again, the springs stretch and recoil and you bounce up and down. It's a lot of fun, and it is also an example of Newton's third law of motion.

Newton's *third law of motion* states that for every force, there is an equal and opposite force. These forces are called *action forces* and *reaction forces*. In the spinning-can activity, the force of the water streaming out of the can caused the can to spin. The water pouring out was the result of the action force. The can spinning was the result of the reaction force.

Examples of the third law of motion can be found at the amusement park everywhere you look. Describe actions and reactions you might see there.

QUICK CHECK

LESSON 4 REVIEW

❶ Describe Newton's three laws of motion and give an example of each.

❷ Use action-reaction force pairs to explain the readings on the two spring scales in Pull on It.

✔ DOUBLE CHECK

SECTION C REVIEW

1. Which has greater inertia—a refrigerator on wheels or one without wheels? Explain.

2. Why do unbalanced forces accelerate an object?

3. How do Newton's laws of motion apply to motion affected by gravity, to circular motion, and to collisions?

Work and Machines

Y ou might think of the amusement park as just a place of fun and excitement. But there's a lot of work that goes on at an amusement park—work that even involves you. When you throw a baseball at a milk bottle in the arcade, you're doing work. You don't have to work when you ride the roller coaster or other rides, however. The rides do the work for you. This section discusses work and the machines that do work.

Just what is work? What are machines, and what do they do? In your Science Log, jot down some of your ideas about work and machines. Add to or revise your notes as you do the investigations in this section.

1 WORK AND POWER

How can the fun you have at an amusement park be work?
In this lesson, you will examine work and power.

Work Out

You won! It took three tries, but you finally won a huge stuffed animal at the ringtoss game. Is carrying your prize doing work? Let's find out.

Carrying the animal seems to be hard work. By holding the animal still and pushing it forward as you walk, you are doing work on the animal. You are also pulling up on the animal so that the animal does not leave your hands. This is work, too. The animal moves when you move and

stops when you stop. The amount of work done on the animal in one direction completely cancels the work done in the opposite direction.

When you picked up your prize from the ground, you were doing work. In science, **work** is using a force to make something move in the same direction as the force.

How much work did you have to do? You can find out by using the following equation:

Work = force × distance.

In the equation, force is measured in newtons. Distance is measured in meters. A unit of work is 1 newton-meter, which is equal to 1 joule (JOOL). A joule is the unit of measure of work. Suppose your stuffed animal weighs 22 newtons. If you had lifted it 1 meter off the ground in the game booth, you would have done 1 × 22, or 22, joules of work.

THINK ABOUT IT

Suppose you push a model race car 5 meters with a force of 50 newtons and then let go. How much work are you doing?

ACTIVITY

So Much Work

You've seen how you had to work when you lifted your prize. How do you think lifting the animal could have been made easier? This activity can help you find out.

DO THIS

❶ Make a table like the one shown.

❷ Stack the books. Measure and record the height of the stack in meters.

❸ Attach the bag of marbles to the spring scale. Use the scale to lift the bag to the top of the book stack. Record the force you used in newtons.

❹ Calculate the work done. Record this information in the table.

❺ Make a ramp by propping the cardboard against the books. Measure and record the length of the ramp in meters. Tie one end of the string to the bag of marbles and the other end to the spring scale. Use the spring scale to pull the bag up the ramp. Record the force you used.

❻ Compute the work done. Record this information in the table.

MATERIALS
- 5 books
- meter stick
- bag of marbles
- spring scale
- calculator (optional)
- heavy cardboard (15 cm x 40 cm)
- long piece of string
- Science Log data sheet

FORCE AND WORK			
	Force	Height	Work (force x height)
Lifting Marbles			
Pulling Marbles			

F72

THINK AND WRITE

1. Did you have to use more force to lift the bag of marbles or to pull it? Explain.

2. **INTERPRETING DATA** When you interpret data, you decide what it means. Based on your data, how was the amount of work affected by the ramp?

Power You know that scientists define *work* as the use of a force to move something in the same direction as the force. Notice that their definition of work doesn't say anything about the time it takes to do the work. Scientists use the term *power* to describe the amount of work done in a certain period of time. Then they use this equation to determine power:
Power = work divided by time. Work is given in joules. Time is measured in seconds. So power is the number of joules per second.

Suppose it took you 5 seconds to move the bag of marbles up the ramp. You know from the activity how much work you did. Now use the equation to determine how much work you did.

▼ **Inclined plane**

LESSON 1 REVIEW

❶ How much work does an amusement park weight lifter do when lifting a 1000-newton barbell 2 meters? Show your work.

❷ If it takes the weight lifter 2 seconds to lift the 600-newton weight 2 meters, how much power does the weight lifter use? Show your work.

2 MACHINES AT WORK

At the amusement park, machines are all around you. Some of them are easy to identify. The roller coaster and the Ferris wheel are machines that you recognize easily. But some of the machines at the park may not look at all like machines to you. In this lesson, you will discover what machines are and how they help you.

Amusement Parks Without Machines

Suppose there were no machines. What would the amusement park be like? Read to find out what machines are and what they do.

Without machines, the roller coaster ride would be quite different. You couldn't walk up the ramp to the roller coaster platform. You would have to pull yourself up the wall. That would take a lot of effort on your part. As you climbed into the roller coaster car, you would notice that it didn't have wheels. Finally, several ride operators would get behind your car and begin to push it uphill.

A machine doesn't have to be complicated and have a lot of moving parts. It can be as simple as the ramp you climb to get to the roller coaster. The ramp, the wheels on the roller coaster car, and the equipment

that makes the roller coaster move are all machines. A **machine** is any device that makes a task easier or faster.

THINK ABOUT IT

How have machines made a task easier or faster?

Making It Easier

By doing the activity and reading the explanations that follow, you can see how machines make your work easier.

 You will need: safety goggles, board with a nail pounded halfway into it, hammer

CAUTION: Be careful when using the hammer. First, try to remove the nail with your fingers. Then, hook the nail with the claw of the hammer. Pull down toward you on the grip of the hammer. What does the hammer do for you? Why is a hammer considered a machine?

The use of machines involves two types of work. Work goes into a machine, and work comes out of the machine. The work that goes into the machine is called *work input.* This is the effort you supply, like pulling down on the hammer. The work done by the machine is the *work output.* The claw of the hammer does the work of pulling the nail up and out.

A machine does not increase the amount of work that is done. Whether you use your fingers to pull a nail out of a piece of wood or remove it with the claw of a hammer, the same amount of work is done. But what a difference the hammer makes!

Machines make work easier by changing the size or the direction of the force needed to do the work. A machine may decrease the amount of force, called the *effort force,* you need to use. It does so by increasing the distance over which you have to apply the force to overcome the resistance force. *Resistance force* is the force that works against the effort force.

THINK ABOUT IT

A wooden crate is nailed shut. Which would make opening it easier, a small hammer with a claw or a long crowbar? Explain.

▼ A crowbar changes the direction of a force. When you push down on one end, the other end moves up and lifts the board. How does the crowbar decrease the effort required?

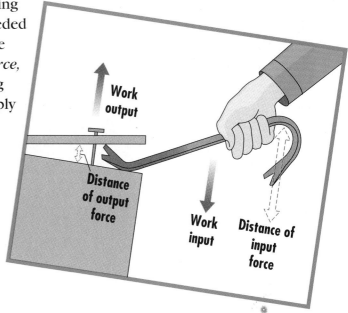

Work output

Distance of output force

Work input

Distance of input force

Helping Machines

The ramp made reaching the platform easier. The hammer made pulling out the nail easier. But just how helpful are machines? You can find out by determining how well they work and how much they reduce the input work needed.

The work output of a machine is never greater than the work input. In fact, often the work output is less than the work input. Friction acts on all machines. Some of the work the machine must do is to overcome the force of friction.

Scientists compare a machine's work output to the work input. The result of this comparison is the *efficiency*. No machine is completely efficient, because all machines must overcome friction. Some of the effort that you used to pull the nail out of the board was used to overcome the friction between the nail and the board.

QUICK CHECK

LESSON 2 REVIEW

❶ How does a machine make work easier?

❷ Can the output work of a machine ever be more than the input work? Explain.

3 SIMPLE MACHINES

Anything that makes work easier is a machine. Simple machines have only one or two parts. In this lesson, you will investigate six simple machines.

ACTIVITY

Use the Lever

When you pulled the nail out of the board with the hammer claw, you were using a machine. In this activity, you can see how this simple machine works.

MATERIALS
- chalkboard eraser
- rigid meter stick
- book
- Science Log data sheet

DO THIS

❶ Place the eraser under the 50-cm mark of the meter stick, and put the book on the 100-cm mark so that the book is half on and half off the meter stick.

❷ Measure the distances on the meter stick from the eraser to the end with the book and from the eraser to the free end.

❸ Press down on the free end of the meter stick. Notice how hard you have to push to lift the book. Notice how far the book rises.

❹ Move the eraser farther away from and closer to the book. Each time you move the eraser, repeat steps 2 and 3.

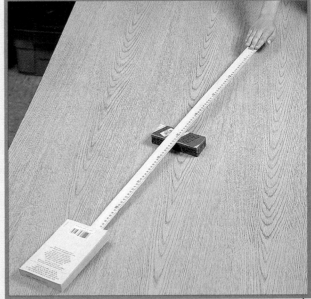

THINK AND WRITE

1. How did the amount of force you used to lift the book depend on the placement of the eraser?

2. How did the distance you pushed down and the distance the book rose depend on the placement of the eraser?

F77

The Lever

In the activity, you used the meter stick as a lever. You have probably played on a lever, too—a playground seesaw. Read to find out how your meter stick, the seesaw, and other levers work.

The seesaw on the playground has two arms of equal length. If you and a friend of equal weight sit on opposite ends of the seesaw, you will balance it. But if you shift your weight slightly back and your friend shifts forward, your friend will go up and you will come down. All **levers,** including the seesaw, are bars that move about fixed points.

In the activity, you used the eraser as the fixed point. The fixed point is known as the *fulcrum.* The side of the lever that you push down is the *effort arm.* The other side of the lever is the *resistance arm,* which comes up as you push down.

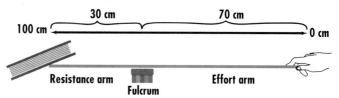

When you moved the eraser, or fulcrum, you changed the effect of the effort arm. When you pressed down on the meter stick, the simple machine either reduced or multiplied your effort. Also, a shorter effort arm required a greater effort to move the resistance a greater distance. A longer effort arm required less effort to move the resistance a shorter distance.

THINK ABOUT IT

Is a lever more useful when the effort arm is longer or when it is shorter? Explain.

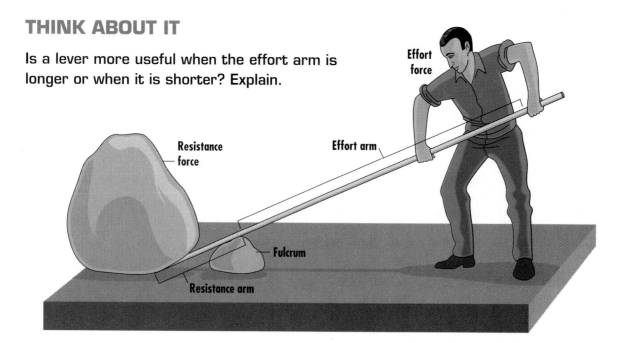

So Many Levers

Do all levers work in the same way as your meter-stick lever? Study the pictures and diagrams to help you answer that question.

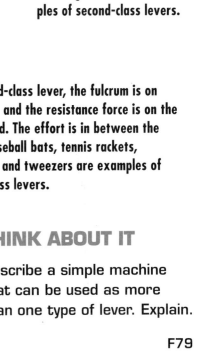

▼ In a first-class lever, the fulcrum is between the resistance force and the effort force. Pliers, hammers, and seesaws are all first-class levers.

Effort
Resistance
Fulcrum

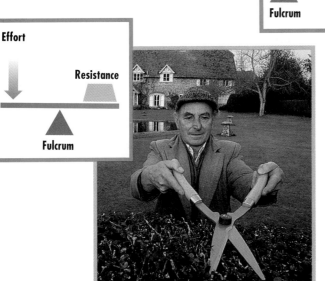

Effort
Resistance
Fulcrum

▲ In a second-class lever, the fulcrum is at one end of the lever, and the effort force is at the other end. The resistance force is in between. Nutcrackers, wheelbarrows, and hinged doors are examples of second-class levers.

Effort
Resistance
Fulcrum

◄ In a third-class lever, the fulcrum is on one end, and the resistance force is on the other end. The effort is in between the two. Baseball bats, tennis rackets, shovels, and tweezers are examples of third-class levers.

THINK ABOUT IT

Describe a simple machine that can be used as more than one type of lever. Explain.

Ramps

We use ramps a great deal. You can see them everywhere at the amusement park. You use them to get on and off rides, and workers use them to load and unload equipment. What kind of simple machines are ramps?

Ramps are inclined planes. An **inclined plane** is a simple machine with a flat, slanted surface. Inclined planes do not have any moving parts. They decrease the effort force needed to move you or an object from one height to another. They do this by increasing the distance over which you or the object must move.

▲ **Movers can load the truck more easily by using a ramp.**

THINK ABOUT IT

Explain how ramps make lifting something to a platform easier.

A C T I V I T Y

How Does Your Wedge Work?

MATERIALS
- 4 wooden blocks
- glue
- safety goggles
- nail
- small hammer
- Science Log data sheet

Simple machines can be used in many ways to make them into other kinds of machines. For example, in this activity you will discover another use for the inclined plane. Try the activity and find out which item is the inclined plane.

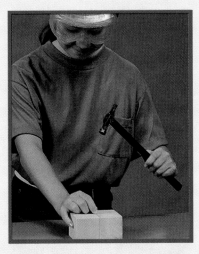

DO THIS

❶ Glue the wooden blocks together to form two larger blocks. Allow the glue to dry.

❷ Try to pull one of the larger wooden blocks apart.

❸ **CAUTION: Put on safety goggles.** Be careful when hammering the nail. Insert the nail between the two smaller blocks of the other large block. Use the hammer to pound gently on the nail.

THINK AND WRITE

How did the nail help you do work? How did it change the direction of your effort force?

Wedge The pointed end of a nail is a wedge. A **wedge** is an inclined plane that is moved to do work. Most wedges are made up of two inclined planes that are back to back. A long, thin wedge requires less effort force to overcome the resistance force. That's why sharp blades on knives and axes cut better than dull blades. The sharpening of these common wedges makes them thinner.

▲ The blades on a plow are a series of wedges. So, too, are the teeth of the zipper in your jacket.

Screws

A *screw* is an inclined plane that is wound around a cylinder. In fact, an inclined plane is related to a screw in the same way in which an ordinary staircase is related to a spiral one.

Screws make use of friction to hold things tightly together. Without friction, screws would easily twist back out. The furniture in your home would certainly fall apart. The inclined plane, the screw, and the wedge are all members of the same family of simple machines.

◀ **Ordinary staircase**

▼ **Spiral staircase**

◀ **Screw**

▼ **Inclined plane**

Wheel and Axle

At the amusement park, you climb aboard a spinning ride. On this ride, you control the spinning. You and your friend grasp the steering wheel and begin turning it. Soon you're spinning in circles. This ride uses another kind of simple machine. What do you think this machine is, and how does it do work? The next activity will help you discover the identity of this simple machine.

MATERIALS

- manual pencil sharpener
- long shoelace
- 2-kg weight
- Science Log data sheet

DO THIS

1 Remove the cover from the pencil sharpener.

2 Tie one end of the shoelace to the shaft of the sharpener, and tie the other end to the weight.

3 Lower the weight off the table, letting the string hang straight down. Then turn the handle of the sharpener and observe what happens.

THINK AND WRITE

1. What happened to the weight? Why?

2. Which turned faster—the handle of the sharpener or the shaft?

On Wheels and Axles

On the spinning ride at the amusement park, you turned a steering wheel that then turned an axle to start you spinning. It didn't take much time or effort to get you spinning quickly. Read to find out why.

The ride had wheels and axles. A **wheel and axle** make up a simple machine consisting of one large circular object and one small one. The wheel is the large circular object, and the axle is the small one. Every time a small force is applied to the wheel, the axle multiplies the small force to result in a larger force.

In the activity, you turned the handle of the pencil sharpener that, in turn, rotated the shaft. Which was the wheel, and which was the axle?

If you ride the bumper cars at the amusement park, you use only a small amount of force to turn the steering wheel. The axle multiplies the force you apply. Before you know it, your bumper car is facing in the opposite direction.

THINK ABOUT IT

Name two examples of a wheel and axle that you use.

▼ The driver applies a small force to the wheel of a steering wheel. This force is multiplied by the shaft to turn the front tires of a car.

▼ You can stop a faucet from running by turning the handle. The handle turns the shaft, which presses down on a washer. The washer stops the flow of water.

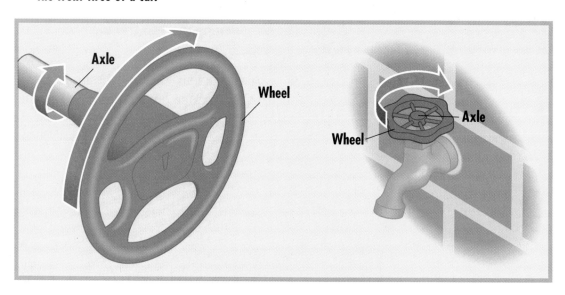

Connie Ensing:

CART Race Official

The pit crew doesn't have a second to waste. They need to get the race car back onto the track. They quickly change its tires and refuel it. Making sure they do it right are Connie Ensing and her team of volunteers. Ensing is a technical official for CART, Championship Auto Racing Teams, Inc.

Ensing's job takes her to racetracks throughout the United States. There, she trains volunteers to help her. Before the race, Ensing's team inspects each race car. They need to make sure that all cars meet safety and design standards. They even measure the width of the car's wheels. Ensing lets a car's pit crew know if the car has to be fixed before it will be allowed to race.

During the race, Ensing's team is kept very busy. They watch for oil leaks and mechanical problems with the cars. They make sure the pit crews follow safety rules as they fuel and maintain the car. Safety is a major concern for technical officials. Ensing gives warnings if she finds out that a crew did not follow the rules.

After the races, Ensing's teams may recheck some cars. They want to make sure that the cars have not been changed during the race. Ensing can have cars disqualified if they have been altered. This could change the outcome of the race.

Connie Ensing enjoys being a technical official for CART. If you like car racing, math, and science, you might enjoy this kind of work, too.

THINK ABOUT IT

Use what you know about forces and motion to explain why safety is an important concern of **CART** officials.

Lift It Easier

You've seen how the wheel and axle lifted the weight in the preceding activity. Another simple machine is designed specifically to lift and lower weights. In this activity, you will make two kinds of these machines.

MATERIALS
- insulated wire, 10 cm
- empty thread spool
- heavy string
- weight
- Science Log data sheet

PART A: FIXED PULLEY
DO THIS

1 Thread the wire through the hole in the spool, and tie the ends together.

2 Hang the tied ends from a hook or have a partner hold them.

3 Tie one end of the string to the weight, and loop the other end over the spool.

4 Pull down on the free end of the string. Observe what happens to the weight.

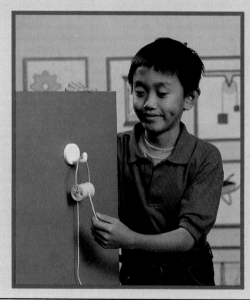

PART B: MOVABLE PULLEY
DO THIS

1 Remove the machine made in Part A from the hook, and tie the weight to the tied ends of the wire.

2 Tie one end of the string to the hook, or have a partner hold it.

3 Loop the other end of the string around the machine, and pull up on it. Observe what happens.

THINK AND WRITE

1. How did the simple machine from Part A help you do work? How did it change the direction of the force you used to lift the weight?

2. How is the second machine you made more helpful than the first machine?

Pulleys The simple machines you just made are pulleys. A **pulley** is a wheel that turns on an axle. Ropes are attached to the pulley to lift and move objects. The first pulley you made was a *fixed pulley,* or a pulley that stays in the same place. With a fixed pulley, you change the direction of the force, but not the amount of force needed.

The second pulley you made was a *movable pulley.* With a movable pulley, the amount of force that is needed is reduced.

Sometimes sets of pulleys, or multiple pulleys, are used to lift heavy objects. Very heavy weights, such as pianos, car engines, heavy freight, or even animals like horses, are lifted with multiple pulleys.

Compound Machines

You've seen simple machines working on their own. Did you know they can be combined to form compound machines? See if you can identify the combinations of simple machines in each picture.

Where can you find simple machines at the amusement park? Take a look at the rides, concession stands, and games all around you. They are made up of combinations of simple machines. With a little time, you could name dozens—or maybe even hundreds. But you'll probably notice that most of them are found in larger, more complicated machines.

The exciting rides and most of the equipment in the park are examples of compound machines. **Compound machines** are machines that are made up of two or more simple machines.

▲ Levers are used to turn on the power for rides, to release passengers "locked" into their seats, and to flip over a container full of fresh popcorn.

◀ How is an ax both a wedge and a lever?

▲ Screws hold the wooden and steel parts of the rides together. Huge screws inside shafts lift riders into the air and twirl them around.

▲ Pulleys and levers are used to stretch and tighten the cable used in a circus high-wire act.

▲ Wheels and axles turn gears inside a carousel to move the riders in a circle.

As your day at the amusement park ends, you think about the great time you had. But take a moment to remember all the forces you saw at work and the machines that made the day such a fun-filled one. Without these forces and machines, your day at the park would not have been as exciting.

LESSON 3 REVIEW

❶ What kind of lever is formed by your elbow, forearm, and hand? Explain.

❷ Identify at least two simple machines in a bicycle.

DOUBLE CHECK

SECTION D REVIEW

1. List in a table the six simple machines, with an everyday example of each.

2. Is an ax a compound machine? Explain.

I REFLECT

It's time to think about the ideas you have discovered during your investigations. Think, too, about your many accomplishments.

SUMMARIZE

Answer the following in your Science Log.

1. What **I Wonder** questions have you answered in your investigations, and what new questions have you asked?

2. What have you discovered about forces, motions, and machines, and how have your ideas changed?

3. Did any of your discoveries surprise you? Explain.

First-Class Lever

Effort

Resistance

Fulcrum

Fulcrum

Resistance

Second-C

Resist

Resistance

Fulcrum

Resistance

Effort

In this unit, I learned about different k...
to learn that my tennis racket becomes...

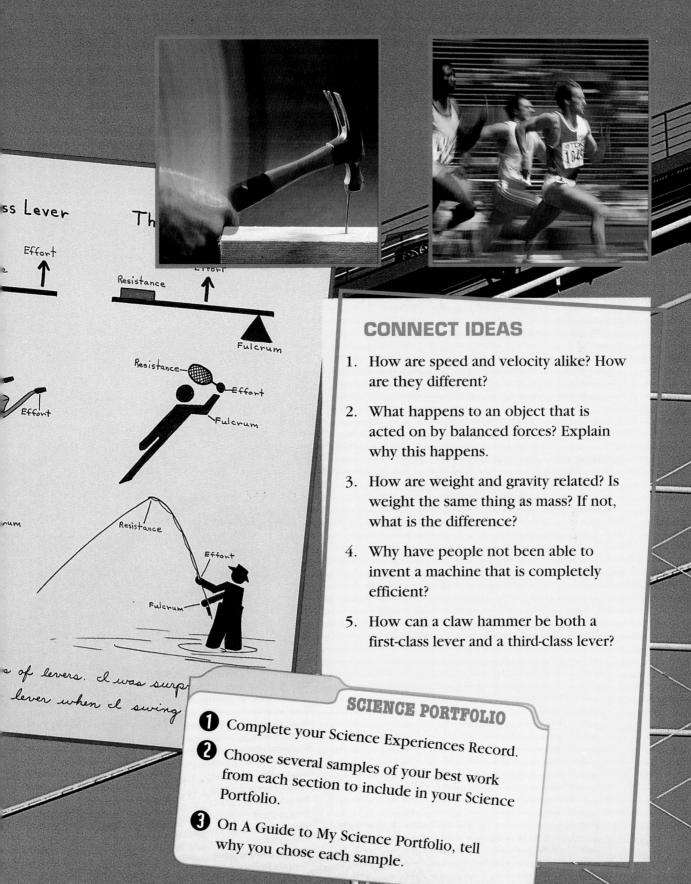

CONNECT IDEAS

1. How are speed and velocity alike? How are they different?

2. What happens to an object that is acted on by balanced forces? Explain why this happens.

3. How are weight and gravity related? Is weight the same thing as mass? If not, what is the difference?

4. Why have people not been able to invent a machine that is completely efficient?

5. How can a claw hammer be both a first-class lever and a third-class lever?

SCIENCE PORTFOLIO

❶ Complete your Science Experiences Record.

❷ Choose several samples of your best work from each section to include in your Science Portfolio.

❸ On A Guide to My Science Portfolio, tell why you chose each sample.

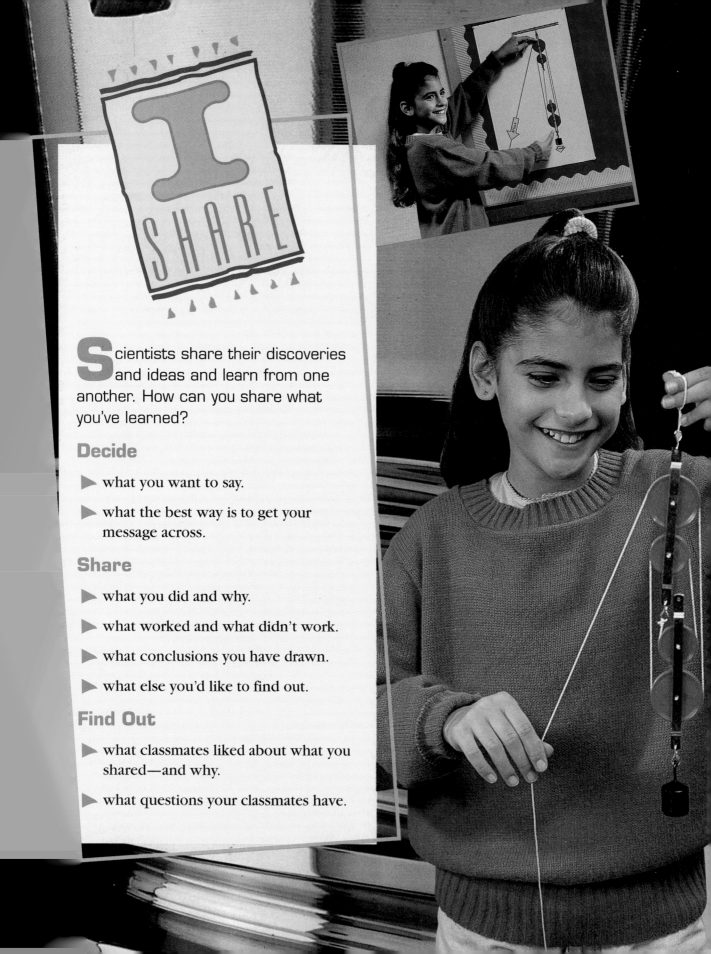

I SHARE

Scientists share their discoveries and ideas and learn from one another. How can you share what you've learned?

Decide

▶ what you want to say.

▶ what the best way is to get your message across.

Share

▶ what you did and why.

▶ what worked and what didn't work.

▶ what conclusions you have drawn.

▶ what else you'd like to find out.

Find Out

▶ what classmates liked about what you shared—and why.

▶ what questions your classmates have.

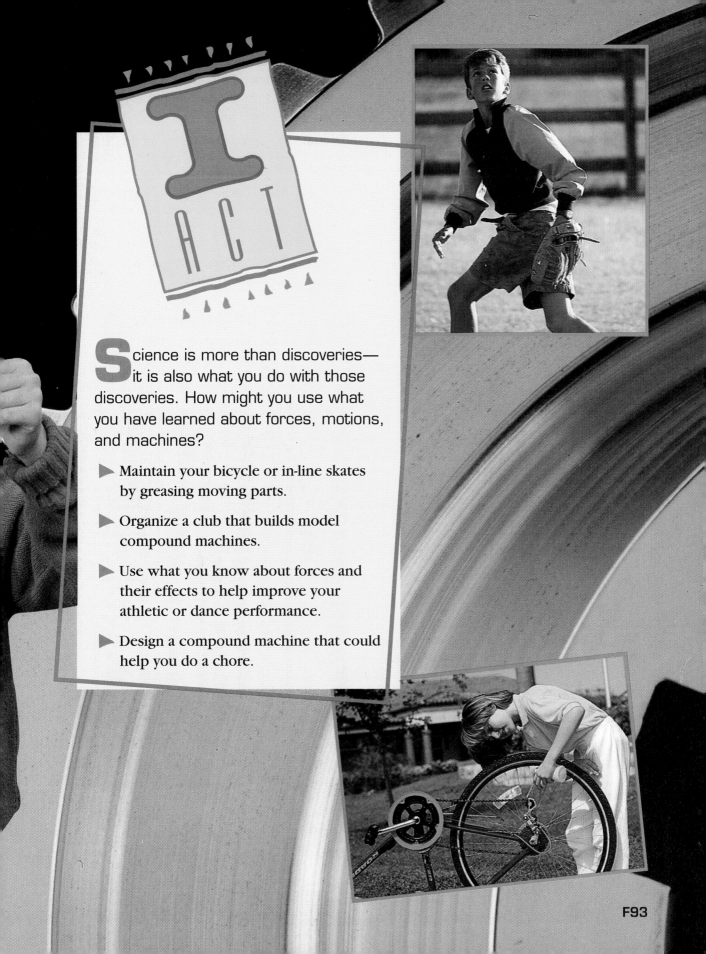

I ACT

Science is more than discoveries—it is also what you do with those discoveries. How might you use what you have learned about forces, motions, and machines?

▶ Maintain your bicycle or in-line skates by greasing moving parts.

▶ Organize a club that builds model compound machines.

▶ Use what you know about forces and their effects to help improve your athletic or dance performance.

▶ Design a compound machine that could help you do a chore.

THE LANGUAGE OF SCIENCE

The language of science helps people communicate clearly when they talk about forces, motions, and machines. Here are some vocabulary words you can use when you talk about forces, motions, and machines with friends, family, and others.

acceleration — rate of change in speed or direction. An object that speeds up, slows down, or changes direction is accelerating. Slowing down is also called *deceleration.* **(F22)**

energy — the ability to cause change. **(F24)**

force — a push or pull that gives objects energy. Balanced forces are equal forces that are applied in opposite directions and result in no change in velocity. Unbalanced forces are forces that are not equal and opposite, and they result in a change in velocity. **(F35)**

frame of reference — an object or a background that is not moving and is used to determine the movement of another object. **(F14)**

friction — the force that resists motion when one surface moves over another. An object with a large, rough surface experiences greater friction than one with a small, smooth surface. *Sliding friction* is the force that is produced when one object slides on another. *Rolling friction* is produced by wheels. *Fluid friction* is produced when objects move through gases and liquids. **(F55)**

gravity — the force that pulls all objects in the universe toward one another. Objects on Earth are pulled toward Earth's center by gravity. **(F38)**

▲ **The force of gravity causes the roller coaster to speed up as it goes downhill.**

inertia — resistance to a force. Inertia causes objects to resist changes in velocity. The more mass an object has, the greater its inertia. **(F36)**

kinetic energy — the energy of a moving object. A roller coaster racing down a hill has kinetic energy. **(F24)**

machine — any device that makes work easier or faster. *Simple machines* are levers, inclined planes, wedges, screws, wheels and axles, and pulleys. *Compound machines* are made up of two or more simple machines. **(F74)**

mass — the amount of matter in an object. **(F38)**

MACHINES

▼ **lever**

▼ **screw**

▼ **wedge and lever**

▲ **inclined plane**

▲ **wheel and axle**

▲ **pulley**

potential energy—the energy an object has because of its position. Objects that can compress, bend, or stretch and then return to their original positions have *elastic potential energy*. A rubber band has elastic potential energy. An object that has the ability to fall has *gravitational potential energy*. **(F24)**

power—the amount of work done in a certain period of time. A runner who finishes a race in 3 minutes 6 seconds is more powerful than one who finishes in 3 minutes 7 seconds. **(F73)**

velocity—the speed of an object in a certain direction. When direction changes, velocity changes, even if the moving object does not change speed. **(F19)**

weight—the force of gravity's pull on an object. Weight varies, depending on location. The closer to the center of the Earth you are, the more you weigh. **(F41)**

work—the force used to move something in the direction of the force. If you hold a box, no work is being done on the box. If you drag the box, work is being done. **(F71)**

This person weighs more on the beach than on top of the mountain because the beach is closer to the center of Earth.

REFERENCE HANDBOOK

Safety in the Classroom

Doing activities in science can be fun, but you need to be sure you do them safely. It is up to you, your teacher, and your classmates to make your classroom a safe place for science activities.

Think about what causes most accidents in everyday life—being careless, not paying attention, and showing off. The same kinds of behavior cause accidents in the science classroom.

Here are some ways to make your classroom a safe place.

THINK AHEAD.
Study the steps of the activity so you know what to expect. If you have any questions about the steps, ask your teacher to explain. Be sure you understand any safety symbols that are shown in the activity.

WATCH YOUR EYES.
Wear safety goggles anytime you are directed to do so. If you should ever get any substance in your eyes, tell your teacher right away.

BE NEAT.
Keep your work area clean. If you have long hair, pull it back so it doesn't get in the way. If you have long sleeves, roll them or push them up to keep them away from your experiment.

OOPS!
If you should have an accident that causes a spill or breaks something, or if you get cut, tell your teacher right away.

YUCK!
Never eat or drink anything during a science activity unless you are told to do so by your teacher.

KEEP IT CLEAN.
Always clean up when you have finished your activity. Put everything away and wipe your work area. Last of all, wash your hands.

DON'T GET SHOCKED.
Sometimes you need to use electric appliances, such as lamps, in an activity. You always need to be careful around electricity. Be sure that electric cords are in a safe place where you can't trip over them. Don't ever pull a plug out of an outlet by pulling on the cord.

Safety Symbols

In some activities, you will see a symbol that stands for what you need to do to stay safe. Do what the symbol stands for.

 This is a general symbol that tells you to be careful. Reading the steps of the activity will tell you exactly what you need to do to be safe.

 You will need to protect your eyes if you see this symbol. Put on safety goggles and leave them on for the entire activity.

 This symbol tells you that you will be using something sharp in the activity. Be careful not to cut or poke yourself or others.

 This symbol tells you something hot will be used in the activity. Be careful not to get burned or to cause someone else to get burned.

 This symbol tells you to put on an apron to protect your clothing.

 Don't touch! This symbol tells you that you will need to touch something that is hot. Use a thermal mitt to protect your hand.

 This symbol tells you that you will be using electric equipment. Use proper safety procedures.

Using a Hand Lens

A hand lens magnifies objects, or makes them look larger than they are.

▲ This object is not in focus.

Sometimes objects are too small for you to see easily without some help. You might want to see details that you cannot see with your eyes alone. When this happens, you can use a hand lens.

To use a hand lens, first place the object you want to look at on a flat surface, such as a table. Next, hold the hand lens over the object. At first, the object may appear blurry, like the object in **A**. Move the hand lens toward or away from the object until the object comes into sharp focus, as shown in **B**.

▲ This object is focused clearly.

Making a Water-Drop Lens

There may be times when you want to use a hand lens but there isn't one around. If that happens, you can make a water-drop lens to help you in the same way a hand lens does. A water-drop lens is best used to make flat objects, such as pieces of paper and leaves, seem larger.

MATERIALS
- **sheet of acetate**
- **2 rectangular rubber erasers**
- **water**
- **dropper**

DO THIS

1 Place the object to be magnified on a table between two identical erasers.

2 Place a sheet of acetate on top of the erasers so that the sheet of acetate is about 1 cm above the object.

3 Use the dropper to place one drop of water on the surface of the sheet over the object. Don't make the drop too large or it will make things look bent.

▶ A water-drop lens can magnify objects.

Caring For and Using a Microscope

A microscope, like a hand lens, magnifies objects. However, a microscope can increase the detail you see by increasing the number of times an object is magnified.

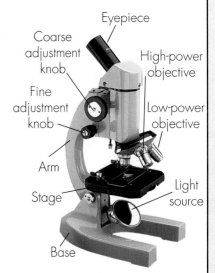

▲ **Light microscope**

CARING FOR A MICROSCOPE

- Always use two hands when you carry a microscope.
- Never touch any of the lenses of the microscope with your fingers.

USING A MICROSCOPE

1 Raise the eyepiece as far as you can using the coarse-adjustment knob. Place the slide you wish to view on the stage.

2 Always start by using the lowest power. The lowest-power lens is usually the shortest. Start with the lens in the lowest position it can go without touching the slide.

3 Look through the eyepiece and begin adjusting the eyepiece upward with the coarse-adjustment knob. When the slide is close to being in focus, use the fine-adjustment knob.

4 When you want to use the higher-power lens, first focus the slide under low power. Then, watching carefully to make sure that the lens will not hit the slide, turn the higher-power lens into place. Use only the fine-adjustment knob when looking through the higher-power lens.

Some of you may use a Brock microscope. This is a sturdy microscope that has only one lens.

1 Place the object to be viewed on the stage. Move the long tube, containing the lens, close to the stage.

2 Put your eye on the eyepiece, and begin raising the tube until the object comes into focus.

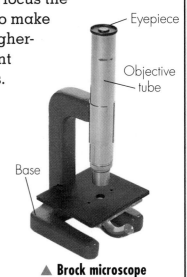

▲ **Brock microscope**

Using a Dropper

Use a dropper when you need to add small amounts of a liquid to another material.

A dropper has two main parts. One is a large empty part called a *bulb*. You hold the bulb and squeeze it to use the dropper. The other part of a dropper is long and narrow and is called a *tube*.

Droppers measure liquids one drop at a time. You might need to figure out how much liquid is in one drop. To do that, you can count the number of drops in 1 mL and divide. For example, if there are about 10 drops in 1 mL, you know that each drop is equal to about 0.1 mL. Follow the directions below to measure a liquid by using a dropper.

DO THIS

1 Use a clean dropper for each liquid you measure.

2 With the dropper out of the liquid, squeeze the bulb and keep it squeezed. Then dip the end of the tube into the liquid.

3 Release the pressure on the bulb. As you do so, you will see the liquid enter the tube.

4 Take the dropper from the liquid, and move it to the place you want to put the liquid. If you are putting the liquid into another liquid, do not let the dropper touch the surface of the second liquid.

5 Gently squeeze the bulb until one drop comes out of the tube. Repeat slowly until you have measured out the right number of drops.

▲ Using a dropper correctly

▲ Using a dropper incorrectly

Measuring Liquids

Use a beaker, a measuring cup, or a graduated cylinder to measure liquids accurately.

Containers for measuring liquids are made of clear or translucent materials so that you can see the liquid inside them. On the outside of each of these measuring tools, you will see lines and numbers that make up a scale. On most of the containers used by scientists, the scale is in milliliters (mL).

DO THIS

1 Pour the liquid you want to measure into one of the measuring containers. Make sure your measuring container is on a flat, stable surface, with the measuring scale facing you.

2 Look at the liquid through the container. Move so that your eyes are even with the surface of the liquid in the container.

3 To read the volume of the liquid, find the scale line that is even with the top of the liquid. In narrow containers, the surface of the liquid may look curved. Take your reading at the lowest point of the curve.

4 Sometimes the surface of the liquid may not be exactly even with a line. In that case, you will need to estimate the volume of the liquid. Decide which line the liquid is closer to, and use that number.

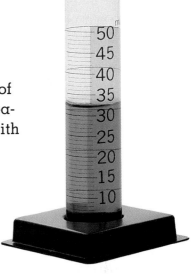

▲ There are 32 mL of liquid in this graduated cylinder.

▲ There are 27 mL of liquid in this beaker.

Using a Thermometer

Determine temperature readings of the air and most liquids by using a thermometer with a standard scale.

Most thermometers are thin tubes of glass that are filled with a red or silver liquid. As the temperature goes up, the liquid in the tube rises. As the temperature goes down, the liquid sinks. The tube is marked with lines and numbers that provide a temperature scale in degrees. Scientists use the Celsius scale to measure temperature. A temperature reading of 27 degrees Celsius is written 27°C.

DO THIS

1 Place the thermometer in the liquid whose temperature you want to record, but don't rest the bulb of the thermometer on the bottom or side of the container. If you are measuring the temperature of the air, make sure that the thermometer is not in direct sunlight or in line with a direct light source.

2 Move so that your eyes are even with the liquid in the thermometer.

3 If you are measuring a material that is not being heated or cooled, wait about two minutes for the reading to become stable. Find the scale line that meets the top of the liquid in the thermometer, and read the temperature.

4 If the material you are measuring is being heated or cooled, you will not be able to wait before taking your measurements. Measure as quickly as you can.

▶ The temperature of this liquid is 27°C.

Making a Thermometer

If you don't have a thermometer, you can make a simple one easily. The simple thermometer won't give you an exact temperature reading, but you can use it to tell if the temperature is going up or going down.

DO THIS

1 Add colored water to the jar until it is nearly full.

2 Place the straw in the jar. Finish filling the jar with water, but leave about 1 cm of space at the top.

3 Lift the straw until 10 cm of it stick up out of the jar. Use the clay to seal the mouth of the jar.

4 Use the dropper to add colored water to the straw until the straw is at least half full.

5 On the straw, mark the level of the water. "S" stands for *start*.

6 To get an idea of how your thermometer works, place the jar in a bowl of ice. Wait several minutes, and then mark the new water level on the straw. This new water level should be marked C for *cold*.

7 Take the jar out of the bowl of ice, and let it return to room temperature. Next, place the jar in a bowl of warm water. Wait several minutes, and then mark the new water level on the straw. This level can be labeled W for *warm*.

— W

— S

— C

▶ You can use a thermometer like this to decide if the temperature of a liquid or the air is going up or down.

Using a Balance

Use a balance to measure an object's mass. Mass is the amount of matter an object has.

Most balances look like the one shown. They have two pans. In one pan, you place the object you want to measure. In the other pan, you place standard masses. Standard masses are objects that have a known mass. Grams are the units used to measure mass for most scientific activities.

DO THIS

❶ First, make certain the empty pans are balanced. They are in balance if the pointer is at the middle mark on the base. If the pointer is not at this mark, move the slider to the right or left. Your teacher will help if you cannot balance the pans.

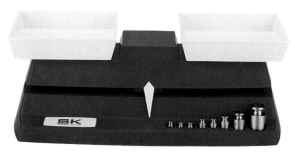

◀ **These pans are balanced and ready to be used to find the mass of an object.**

❷ Place the object you wish to measure in one pan. The pointer will move toward the pan without the object in it.

❸ Add the standard masses to the other pan. As you add masses, you should see the pointer begin to move. When the pointer is at the middle mark again, the pans are balanced.

❹ Add the numbers on the masses you used. The total is the mass of the object you measured.

▶ **These pans are unbalanced.**

Making a Balance

If you do not have a balance, you can make one. A balance requires only a few simple materials. You can use nonstandard masses such as paper clips or nickels. This type of balance is best for measuring small masses.

DO THIS

1 If the ruler has holes in it, tie the string through the center hole. If it does not have holes, tie the string around the middle of the ruler.

2 Tape the other end of the string to a table. Allow the ruler to hang down from the side of the table. Adjust the ruler so that it is level.

3 Unbend the end of each paper clip slightly. Push these ends through the paper cups as shown. Attach each cup to the ruler by using the paper clips.

4 Adjust the cups until the ruler is level again.

MATERIALS
- 1 sturdy plastic or wooden ruler
- string
- transparent tape
- 2 paper cups
- 2 large paper clips

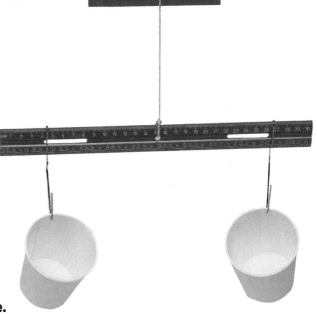

▶ **This balance is ready for use.**

Using a Spring Scale

A spring scale is a tool you use to measure the force of gravity on objects. You find the weight of the objects and use newtons as the unit of measurement for the force of gravity. You also use the spring scale and newtons to measure other forces.

A spring scale has two main parts. One part is a spring with a hook on the end. The hook is used to connect an object to the spring scale. The other part is a scale with numbers that tell you how many newtons of force are acting on the object.

DO THIS

With an Object at Rest

❶ With the object resting on the table, hook the spring scale to it. Do not stretch the spring at this point.

❷ Lift the scale and object with a smooth motion. Do not jerk them upward.

❸ Wait until any motion in the spring comes to a stop. Then read the number of newtons from the scale.

With an Object in Motion

❶ With the object resting on the table, hook the spring scale to it. Do not stretch the spring.

❷ Pull the object smoothly across the table. Do not jerk the object. If you pull with a jerky motion, the spring scale will wiggle too much for you to get a good reading.

❸ As you are pulling, read the number of newtons you are using to pull the object.

Making a Spring Scale

If you do not have a spring scale, you can make one by following the directions below.

DO THIS

1 Staple one end of the rubber band (the part with the sharp curve) to the middle of one end of the cardboard so that the rubber band hangs down the length of the cardboard. Color the loose end of the rubber band with a marker to make it easy to see.

2 Bend the paper clip so that it is slightly open and forms a hook. Hang the paper clip by its unopened end from the rubber band.

3 Put the narrow paper strip across the rubber band, and staple the strip to the cardboard. The rubber band and hook must be able to move easily.

4 While holding the cardboard upright, hang one 100-g mass from the hook. Allow the mass to come to rest, and mark the position of the bottom of the rubber band on the cardboard. Label this position on the cardboard 1 N. Add another 100-g mass for a total of 200 g.

5 Continue to add masses and mark the cardboard. Each 100-g mass adds a force of about 1 N.

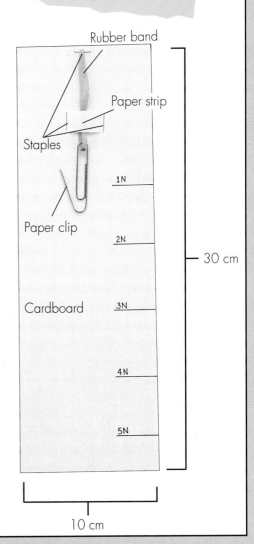

Rubber band

Paper strip

Staples

1N

Paper clip

2N

Cardboard

3N

4N

5N

30 cm

10 cm

Working Like a Scientist
How Clean Is Clean?

In science class, Rachel and Rodney had learned about bacteria and how fast they multiply. They learned that some bacteria are helpful, that most are not harmful to people, and that some can cause diseases.

Rachel and Rodney had learned that disinfectants kill bacteria. They had also found out that there are many different kinds of disinfectants. Each type of disinfectant works a little differently. They wondered, "How can you know which disinfectant will work best for what you want it to do?"

DO THIS

Ask a question.

Form a hypothesis.

Design a test. Do the test.

Record what happened.

Draw a conclusion.

Rachel and Rodney thought about this problem for a while. They put together what they already knew about disinfectants and then came up with a question that they wanted to answer. Rachel and Rodney asked, "Which type of disinfectant kills the most bacteria?"

Often, solving a problem in science starts with reviewing what you already know and *asking a question* about something you want to know. When you review what you already know, you are putting together information and finding out where the gaps are in your knowledge. When you find out what you don't know, you can ask your question. In this case, Rachel and Rodney already knew some things about disinfectants, but they did not know what seemed most important—which disinfectant is most effective.

Rachel and Rodney knew that the next step in their investigation was to suggest an answer to the question. Rachel asked her father for four kinds of disinfectants. She explained that she wanted to find out how effective they are at killing germs. Her father let her look at the bottles but told her that he would send the disinfectants to the school, where Rachel and Rodney would be working on the investigation. Disinfectants are strong chemicals that must be handled with caution.

Rachel looked at the labels on the bottles, but they all said similar kinds of things. One label claimed, "Kills any germ it touches." The ingredients in all of the bottles were different, and Rachel couldn't even read the names of most of them. She knew she couldn't figure out how each chemical worked.

Because Rachel did not know how the chemicals worked, she did not know which one would be most effective. She didn't see any reason why they all wouldn't work equally well. Rachel's suggested answer, or hypothesis, to her question was that all of the disinfectants would work equally well to kill bacteria.

The next day at school, Rachel shared her information with Rodney. He agreed with her reasoning, and they decided to use the four disinfectants Rachel's father had sent in.

DO THIS

Ask a question.
Form a hypothesis.
Design a test. Do the test.
Record what happened.
Draw a conclusion.

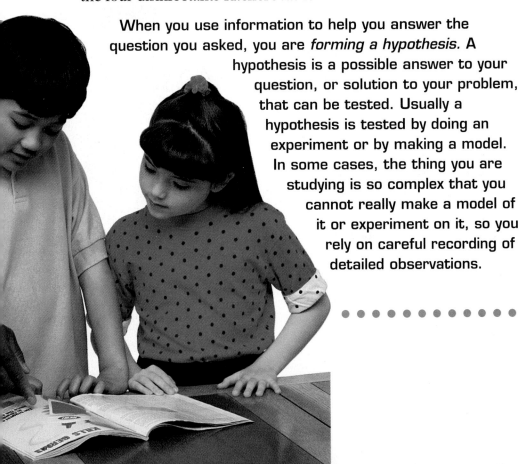

When you use information to help you answer the question you asked, you are *forming a hypothesis.* A hypothesis is a possible answer to your question, or solution to your problem, that can be tested. Usually a hypothesis is tested by doing an experiment or by making a model. In some cases, the thing you are studying is so complex that you cannot really make a model of it or experiment on it, so you rely on careful recording of detailed observations.

After you have asked a question and formed a hypothesis, you must somehow test the hypothesis. One of the most common types of test is an *experiment*. It is important to remember that a single experiment does not prove that a hypothesis is right. However, a single experiment may be enough to show that a hypothesis is not right and needs to be changed. The most important thing to remember when you are designing an experiment is that it must be focused on the question. For example, it is not useful to do an experiment that measures the pollutants in the air each day if you want to know how air pressure affects rainfall.

Rachel and Rodney worked with their teacher, Mr. Gormand, to design an experiment. They decided to grow bacteria in five dishes. Four of the dishes would be treated with different disinfectants. One of the dishes would be untreated.

Rachel and Rodney knew that it was important in any good experiment to have a control. A *control* is a sample or setup in which you don't change any variables. So the dish that was not treated with a disinfectant was their control. For any good experiment, you compare the results from your control to the results from your other samples to see if there is any difference. If there is no difference between the control and a sample, then the treatment you gave the sample had no effect.

Mr. Gormand showed Rachel and Rodney five dishes containing a substance that looked like beige gelatin. Mr. Gormand explained that the gelatinlike material was food for bacteria. He also explained that bacteria were added to the food substance before it was poured into the dishes. Then Mr. Gormand showed them four small disks made of absorbent paper. Each disk was soaked in a different disinfectant. Mr. Gormand placed a treated disk in each of four dishes. In the fifth dish, the control, Mr. Gormand placed an untreated paper disk. Mr. Gormand told Rachel and Rodney what to look for in each dish. As the bacteria multiply, they form colonies that are visible as little dots. As the bacteria increase in number, the colonies grow larger. Mr. Gormand told Rachel and Rodney that if a disinfectant killed the bacteria, a clear area— no colonies—would be found around the disk. The larger the clear area, the more effective the disinfectant. Each day, Rachel and Rodney would measure the width of the clear area from the edge of the dish to where the bacterial colonies started. They would measure the clear areas every day for five days.

Because it is very dangerous to work with live bacteria, Mr. Gormand did all of the treatments. He allowed Rachel and Rodney to handle the dishes only after the dishes were sealed, and he instructed them to wash their hands very carefully after recording their information for the day.

When you do an experiment, you must collect information. Another word for the information you collect is *data*. When you collect data, you are *recording your observations* and the results of your experiment so that someone else can understand what happened. You must not only record the information but also organize it. Organization is important if you want people to understand what you have discovered. There are many different ways to organize data. Two of the more common ways are making tables and making graphs.

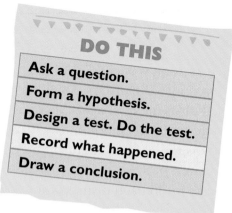

DO THIS

Ask a question.
Form a hypothesis.
Design a test. Do the test.
Record what happened.
Draw a conclusion.

Each day, Rachel and Rodney measured the clear area around each treated paper disk. They also observed the disk that was left untreated. Why did they need to look at the untreated disk? They recorded their measurements in a table each day. They then used the information in their table to make a line graph.

Often, information in a table is hard to read and understand. A graph is a good summary for many types of data.

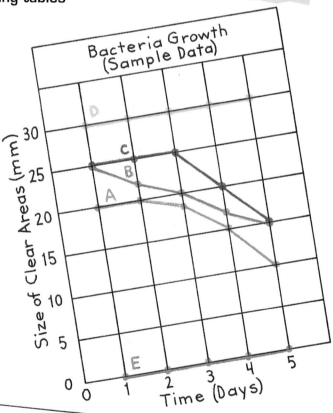

Growth of Bacteria (Sample Data)
Size of Clear Areas (mm)

	A	B	C	D	E(Control)
Day 1	20	25	25	30	0
Day 2	20	22	25	30	0
Day 3	19	20	25	30	0
Day 4	15	17	21	30	0
Day 5	10	15	15	30	0

Once all of your information is collected, you must use that information to *draw a conclusion.* One thing you are looking for when you draw a conclusion is to see if your hypothesis is supported. If your hypothesis is not supported by the results of the experiment, then it is most likely incorrect.

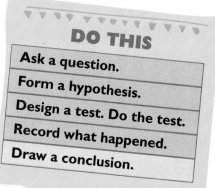

DO THIS

Ask a question.

Form a hypothesis.

Design a test. Do the test.

Record what happened.

Draw a conclusion.

Remember, an incorrect hypothesis is not a failure! Not at all. An incorrect hypothesis helps you eliminate one possible answer to a question. You can then design experiments to focus on other possible answers. Also remember that if the experiment does support your hypothesis, that does not mean your hypothesis is proven. You may have to change your hypothesis a little as a result of your experiment.

You've already seen Rachel and Rodney's data. Look back at their hypothesis. Was their hypothesis supported by the data?

Rachel and Rodney concluded that their hypothesis was not supported. What they saw in the experiment clearly showed that some disinfectants worked far better than others. They concluded that the reason some disinfectants were better was that the chemicals in the disinfectants were different.

Rachel and Rodney still did not know how the chemicals killed the bacteria. And because each bottle had many different kinds of chemicals, they did not even know which of the chemicals was the disinfectant.

Rachel and Rodney concluded that they knew that disinfectants differed in their ability to control bacteria, but they did not know why this was so. Rachel suggested that they might continue their experiments by testing two very similar disinfectants. They could compare the actions of the two mixtures and then decide what contributed most to the disinfectant.

Often conclusions in experiments will raise other questions for which you might want to find answers. The solutions to problems often raise new problems to solve. This is one way in which progress is made in science.

INDEX

Note: Page numbers in italics indicate illustrations.

Ulna, *B44*
Ultraviolet waves, *C84*
Unbalanced forces, F53
United States Agency for
    International Development,
    B72
U. S. Food and Drug Administration
    (FDA), D61
Universal gravitation, law of, C21, C95
    See also Gravity
Universe, size of, C36
Updike, John, D35
Uranus, *C39, C51*
    appearance of, C51
    discovery of, C49
Urethra, *B46*
Urinary bladder, *B46*
Ursa Major (Big Dipper), *C59*
Uterus, *B48*

Vaccination, B67, *B69*
Vacuoles, B27
Vagina, *B48*
Valles Marineris, *C44*
Valves, heart, B43
Vas deferens, B48
Veins, *B42, B43, B47*
Velocity, *F19*
    defined, F19, F96
Vena cava, *B42*
Ventricle(s), *B42*
Venus, *C38, V41*
Vertebral column, B44
Viking Landers, C44
Virtual reality
    and body defense systems,
        B66–B68
    and cell exploration, B16–B17
    and circulatory system, B42–B43
    and levels of organization,
        B31–B33
    and microorganisms, B55–B57
Virus, *B57*
    diseases caused by, B55
    reproducing, *B60–B61*
Visible-light photograph, C75, *C84*
Vitale, Christina, C62
Vitamins, D53
Vitamins and Minerals (Silverstein/
    Silverstein/Silverstein), D9
Voice That Beautifies the Land, The
    ("Twelfth Song of the
    Thunder"), A50
Volcano(es), on moon, C34, C35
Volume
    activity, D29
    defined, D27, D95
    units of, D27

Voyager space craft, C72
    and photographs of Jupiter,
        C46–C47
    and Saturn discoveries, *C48*
*Voyager: An Adventure to the Edge
    of the Solar System* (Ride/
    O'Shaughnessy), C9

Warm front, *A37, A95*
Warner, Charles Dudley, A13
Wastes, E72, E83
Water
    activities, A25
    in the air, A25–A33
    and cells, B22
    and climate, *A79–A80*
    Earth's C42
    erosion, *E41*
    on Mars, C44
    molecule, *D40*
    phases of, D89
    and soil formation, E39
    and sweating, B19
Water cycle, *A26–A27*
    defined, A26, A95
    and rain drop, *A32, A33*
Water drop, life of, A33
Water-drop lens, making, R4
Water pollution, activity, E72–E73, E84
Water treatment plant, *B6*
Waterworks, activity, E81
Watterson, Bill, *x*
Weather
    activities, A18, A20, A42–A43
    balloons, A17
    and climate, A73–A75, A74
    predicting, A15, A42–A43
Weather (Farndon), A9
Weather diorama, A6
Weathering, E37
Weather instruments, *A16–A17*
Weather map, *A45*
Weather patterns, Earth's, C42
Weather sayings, activity, A13
Weather show, A6
Weather stations
    home, *A17*
    shipboard, *A17*
Weather talk, A13–A17
    activities, A13, A14
Weather vane, *A30, A42–A43*
Wedge, *F88, F95*
    activity, F81
    defined, F81, F95
    See also Inclined plane
Weight, *F96*
    defined, D28, D95, F41, F96
    unit of, D28
Weiner, Eric, D14–D18
Westerlies, A24
Wheel and axle, *F83, F84, F89, F95*
    activity, F83
    defined, F84, F95

Wheels at Work (Zubrowski), F9
Whirl–a–Gig, *F26*
White blood cells, B34
    defense by, B67
    described, *B39*
White dwarf (star), C89, C96
White ovals, of Jupiter, C47
*Why Can't You Unscramble an Egg?
    And Other NotSuch Dumb
    Questions About Matter*
    (Cobb), D9
Whyman, Kathryn, D9
Wiewandt, Thomas, E62
Wild Horse Family Book, The (Kalas),
    E9
Willow ptarmigan, E58
Wind(s), *A22–A24*
    and climate, *A88–A89*
    local, A22, A95
    names for, A23–A24
    prevailing, A24
    and storm of century, A70
Wind Cave National Park (SD), E20
Wind erosion, *E41*
Wind friction, activity, *F58*
Windpipe, *B66*
Windsor Court Hotel, New Orleans,
    LA, D85
*Wings: The Last Book of the
    Bromeliad* (Pratchett), C8
Winter solstice, C28
Wolves, E46
Work, *F71, F75*
    activities, F72, F75
    defined, F71, F96
    and machines, F70–F89
    measuring, F71
    and power, F71–F73
Work input, *F75, F76*
Work output, *F75, F76*

X–rays, *C84*
X–ray technician, B6

Yeast, B57
Yellow star, *C88–C89*
Yerkes Observatory, Williams Bay,
    WI, C67

*Zekmet the Stone Carver: A Tale of
    Ancient Egypt* (Stolz), F9
Zodiac, *C61*
Zonda (wind), A23

ACKNOWLEDGMENTS

For permission to reprint copyrighted material, grateful acknowledgment is made to the following sources:

Career World® Magazine: "So, You Wanna Be a Chef? Be Prepared . . . to Train Like an Athlete" by Joanne Koch from *Career World®* Magazine, May 1992. Text copyright © 1992 by Weekly Reader Corporation. Published by Weekly Reader Corporation.

Carolrhoda Books, Inc., Minneapolis, MN: Cover photograph by Cheryl Walsh Bellville from *American Bison* by Ruth Berman. Photograph copyright © 1992 by Cheryl Walsh Bellville. Cover illustration by Peter J. Thornton from *Everybody Cooks Rice* by Norah Dooley. Copyright © 1991 by Carolrhoda Books, Inc.

Children's Television Workshop, New York, NY: "The Inside Story: A Fantastic Voyage Through the Human Body" by Beth Chayet from *3-2-1 Contact* Magazine, June 1992. Text copyright 1992 by Children's Television Workshop. "Incredible Edibles: Unusual Food from Around the World" by Elizabeth Keyishian from *3-2-1 Contact* Magazine, June 1989. Text copyright 1989 by Children's Television Workshop. "Do Me a Flavor! Scientists Cook Up New Tastes" by Eric Weiner from *3-2-1 Contact* Magazine, May 1989. Text copyright 1989 by Children's Television Workshop.

Clarion Books, a Houghton Mifflin Company imprint: Cover illustration by Alix Berenzy from *The Princess in the Pigpen* by Jane Resh Thomas. Illustration © 1989 by Alix Berenzy.

Crown Publishers, Inc.: Cover photograph from *Voyager: An Adventure to the Edge of the Solar System* by Sally Ride and Tam O'Shaughnessy. Photograph © 1991 by Roger Ressmeyer/Starlight.

Current Health 1® Magazine: "Food Additives: A Closer Look at Labels" from *Current Health 1®* Magazine, February 1989. Text copyright © 1989 by Weekly Reader Corporation. "Preserving the Prairie—A Return to Tallgrass" from *Current Health 1®* Magazine, December 1993. Text copyright © 1993 by Weekly Reader Corporation. From "Stop That Germ!" in *Current Health 1®* Magazine, October 1993. Text copyright © 1993 by Weekly Reader Corporation. *Current Health 1®* Magazine is published by Weekly Reader Corporation.

Delacorte Press, a division of Bantam Doubleday Dell Publishing Group, Inc.: Cover illustration by Neal McPheeters from *Wings: The Last Book of the Bromeliad* by Terry Pratchett. Illustration copyright © 1991 by Neal McPheeters.

Dorling Kindersley, Inc.: Cover illustration from *Weather* by John Farndon. Copyright © 1992 by Dorling Kindersley Ltd., London.

Aileen Fisher: "Clouds" by Aileen Fisher from *In the Woods, in the Meadow, in the Sky.* Text copyright © 1965 by Scribner's, New York.

David R. Godine, Publisher, Inc.: Cover illustration by Jonathan Allen from *Burton & Stanley* by Frank O'Rourke. Illustration copyright © 1993 by Jonathan Allen.

Greenwillow Books, a division of William Morrow & Company, Inc.: "No, I Won't Turn Orange" from *The New Kid on the Block* by Jack Prelutsky. Text copyright © 1984 by Jack Prelutsky.

Peggy Guthart: "Ready for Spaghetti" by Peggy Guthart. Text copyright 1991 by Peggy Guthart.

Harcourt Brace & Company: Cover illustration by William Noonan from *The Place of Lions* by Eric Campbell. Copyright © 1991, 1990 by Eric Campbell.

Holt, Rinehart and Winston, Inc.: From "David Powless, Conservationist" in *Holt Life Science.* Text copyright © 1994 by Holt, Rinehart and Winston, Inc.

Dean Kennedy: Cover illustration by Dean Kennedy from *Burton's Zoom Zoom Va-ROOM Machine* by Dorothy Haas. Illustration copyright © 1990 by Dean Kennedy.

Alfred A. Knopf, Inc.: "January" from *A Child's Calendar* by John Updike. Text copyright © 1965 by John Updike; text copyright renewed 1993 by John Updike.

Lodestar Books, an affiliate of Dutton Children's Books, a division of Penguin Books USA Inc.: Cover illustration by Ted Enik from *Why Can't You Unscramble an Egg?* by Vicki Cobb. Illustration copyright © 1990 by Ted Enik.

The Millbrook Press: Cover illustration by Sal Murdocca from *EUREKA! It's an Automobile!* by Jeanne Bendick. Illustration copyright © 1992 by Sal Murdocca.

National Geographic WORLD: "The Great Flood of 1993" by Barbara Brownell from *National Geographic WORLD* Magazine, October 1993. Text copyright 1993 by National Geographic Society. "Surviving Andrew, 1992's Biggest Hurricane!" by Judith E. Rinard from *National Geographic WORLD* Magazine, April 1993. Text copyright 1993 by National Geographic Society. From "Seeing Stars" by Judith E. Rinard in *National Geographic WORLD* Magazine, July 1993. Text copyright 1993 by National Geographic Society. "Chute for the (Sports) Stars" from *National Geographic WORLD* Magazine, July 1993. Text copyright 1993 by National Geographic Society.

National Wildlife Federation: "I Spy on Prairie Dogs" by Mark Hoogland, as told to Gary Turbak from *Ranger Rick* Magazine, September 1988. Text copyright 1988 by the National Wildlife Federation. "Lightning" by Robert Irby from *Ranger Rick* Magazine, August 1983. Text copyright 1983 by the National Wildlife Federation.

Scholastic Inc.: "Cell Theory Rap" by Karen McNulty from *SCIENCE WORLD,* October 1990. Text copyright © 1990 by Scholastic Inc.

Steck-Vaughn Company: Cover design from *Facing the Future: Choosing Health* by Alan Collinson.

University of Nebraska Press: From p. 95 in *Dust Bowl Diary* by Ann Marie Low. Text copyright 1984 by the University of Nebraska Press.

Franklin Watts, Inc., New York: From *Lyme Disease* (Retitled: "The Puzzle") by Elaine Landau. Text copyright © 1990 by Elaine Landau.

PHOTOGRAPHY CREDITS:

Key: (t)top, (b)bottom, (l)left, (r)right, (c)center, (bg)background

Front Cover, Harcourt Brace & Company Photographs: (tl), (tr), (b), Greg Leary.
Front Cover, All Other Photographs: (c), Terje Rakke/The Image Bank; (cr), Ewing Galloway.
Back Cover, All Other Photographs: (tl), Biophoto Assoc./Science Source/Photo Researchers; (tr), Phil Degginger/Bruce Coleman, Inc.; (b), Antony Miles/Bruce Coleman, Inc.
To The Student, Harcourt Brace & Company Photographs: iv(br), v(tl), Terry D. Sinclair; vii(tr), Weronica Anakarorn; vii(br), viii(b), Terry D. Sinclair; ix(tl), Weronica Anakarorn; xi(b), xiii, xvi(l), Terry D. Sinclair.
To The Student, All Other Photographs: iv(tl), Photri; iv(tr), Runk/Schoenberger/Grant Heilman; iv(bl), Peter Menzel; v(tr), David A. Wagner/PHOTOTAKE; v(bl), NIBSC/SPL/Photo Researchers; v(br), Peter Menzel; vi(tl), Roger Ressmeyer/Starlight; vi(tr), Giraudon/Art Resource; vi(b), NASA/JSC/Starlight; vii(tl), David R. Frazier Photolibrary; vii(bl), First LIght; viii(tl), L.L. Rue, Jr./Bruce Coleman, Inc.; viii(tr), Amy Etra/PhotoEdit; viii-ix(b), Lefever/Grushow/Grant Heilman Photography; ix(tr), Ann Purcell/Photo Researchers, ix(br) Mike Khansa/The Image Bank; x, xi(t), David Young-Wolff/PhotoEdit; xii, The Stock Market; xiv(l), Bob Daemmrich Photography; xiv(r), Myrleen Ferguson/PhotoEdit; xv(l), David Young-Wolff/PhotoEdit; xv(b), Comstock; xvi(r), David Young-Wolff/PhotoEdit.
Unit A, Harcourt Brace & Company Photographs: A4-A5, A6(t), A6(c), A6(b), Terry D. Sinclair; A8, A9, Weronica Ankarorn; A10-A11, Terry D. Sinclair; A14, Weronica Ankarorn; A14(bg), A15, A18, A20(t), A20(b), A21, A28, Terry D. Sinclair; A29(t), Weronica Ankarorn; A36, A38, Terry D. Sinclair; A39(bg), Weronica Ankarorn; A39, A40(t), A41(t), A42, A44-A45, Terry D. Sinclair; A44, Maria Paraskevas; A47, A49, A53, A54, A55, A60, A63, A66-A67, A73(bg), A73, Terry D. Sinclair; A75, Weronica Ankarorn; A77(t), A77(b), A82, A84, A90-A91(inset), A91(tr), A92-A93(bg); A92(t), A92-A93(inset), Terry D. Sinclair; A93(t), Weronica Ankarorn.
Unit A, All Other Photographs: Unit Divider Page, Peter Menzel; A1, A2-A3, Tony Freeman/PhotoEdit; A3, F.K. Smith; A7, Mike Morris/Unicorn Stock Photos; A12(border), A12, Johnny Autery; A12(inset), M. Antman/The Image Works; A13, Jan Halaska/Photo Researchers; A14(inset), Bill Horsman/Stock, Boston; A16(tl), M. Antman/The Image Works; A16(c), John Elk III/Stock, Boston; A16(bl), Jeff Greenberg/Unicorn Stock Photos; A16(r), Courtesy Thermometer Corp. of America/Color-Pic; A17(tl), David R. Frazier/The Stock Solution; A17(tr), The Granger Collection, New York; A17(b), Tom Pantages; A23, Kent & Donna Dannen/Photo Researchers; A23 (inset), Bob Daemmrich/The Image Works; A25, Charles Krebs/The Stock Market; A26, E.R. Degginger/Color-Pic; A28(bg), Richard Pasley/Stock, Boston; A29(ct), Myrleen Ferguson Cate/PhotoEdit; A29(cb), Bob Daemmrich/Stock, Boston; A29(b), Kees Van Den Berg/Photo Researchers; A30-A31(bg), Myrleen Ferguson Cate/PhotoEdit; A30, Joyce Photographics/Photo Researchers; A30(inset), Richard Pasley/Stock, Boston; A31(l), Kees Van Den Berg/Photo Researchers; A31(r), E.R. Degginger; A32-A33, The Stock Solution; A33, Tom McCarthy/Unicorn Stock Photos; A34(t), Lee Rentz/Bruce Coleman, Inc.; A34(c), E.R. Degginger/Color-Pic; A34(b), E.R. Degginger/Color-Pic; A35(tl), Nancy L. Simmerman/Bruce Coleman, Inc.; A35(tr), E.R. Degginger/Color-Pic; A35(b), Phil Degginger/Color-Pic; A40-A41(bg), Kees Van Den Berg/Photo Researchers; A40(b), Runk/Schoenberger/Grant Heilman Photography; A42-A43(bg), E.R. Degginger/Color-Pic; A42-A43(inset), Tony Freeman/PhotoEdit; A46(border), Larry West/Bruce Coleman, Inc.; A46, Timothy Schultz/Bruce Coleman, Inc.; A46(inset), Photri; A48, Phil Degginger/Color-Pic; A49(bg), H. Bluestein/Photo Researchers; A50-A51, Peter Menzel; A54-A55(bg), Tony Freeman/PhotoEdit; A56-A57, Nawrocki Stock Photo; A57, Ralf-Finn Hestoft/SABA; A58-A59, Susan Poa/Times Picayune/AP/Wide World Photos; A59, Phil Degginger/Color-Pic; A61(all), Howard B. Bluestein/Photo Researchers; A62, University of Southern

Indiana Special Collections; A64, Edward Slater/Southern Stock Photo Agency; A65, Raymond K. Gehman; A67(t), Lynne Sladky/Ap/Wide World Photos; A68-A69(bg), Charles Krupa/AP/Wide World Photos; A69, Gaston DeCardenas/AP/Wide World Photos; A71, John M. Discher/AP/Wide World Photos; A72(border), E.R. Degginger/Color-Pic; A72(t), John Shaw/Bruce Coleman, Inc.; A72(inset), Peter Southwick/Stock, Boston; A74-A75, Dan Sudia/Photo Researchers; A74, Chris Sorensen; A76(l), Rod Planck/Photo Researchers; A76(c), Thomas R. Fletcher/Stock, Boston; A76(r), Dr. Eckart Pott/Bruce Coleman, Inc.; A79, Kunio Owaki/The Stock Market; A80, Tom Brakefield/Bruce Coleman, Inc.; A81, The Bettmann Archive; A82(bg), The Bettmann Archive; A83(l), Tony Freeman/PhotoEdit; A83(r), Randall Hyman/Stock, Boston; A86(t), Robert Caputo/Stock, Boston; A86(c), Carl Frank/Photo Researchers; A86(b), James A. Sugar/Black Star; A87(t), Robert Caputo/Stock, Boston; A87(c), A87(b), James A. Sugar/Black Star; A90-A91(bg), A. & J. Verkaik/The Stock Market; A91(tl), Van Bucher/Photo Researchers; A93(b), Mary Kate Denny/PhotoEdit; A94(t), Lee Rentz/Bruce Coleman, Inc.; A94(c), E.R. Degginger/Color-Pic; A94(b), Phil Degginger/Color-Pic.

Unit B, Harcourt Brace & Company Photographs: B4-B5, B6(c), B7(t), B7(c), B7(b), Terry D. Sinclair; B8, B9, Weronica Ankarorn; B10-B11, B12 (inset), Terry D. Sinclair; B13, Charlie Burton; B18(bg), B19, B20-21(bg), B20, B21, B22(all), B23, B26, B28, B29(bg), B37, B40, B41, B49, B50, B51, B52(t), B52-53(b), B54, B59, B70(bg), B70, B73, B74, B75(tl), B76(t), B76(c), Terry D. Sinclair; B77(t), Weronica Ankarorn; B77(b), B79(c), Terry D. Sinclair; B79(b), Weronica Ankarorn.

Unit B, All Other Photographs: Unit Divider Page, Professors P.M. Motta & T. Fujita/SPL/Photo Researchers; B1, B2-B3, Bob Gossington/Bruce Coleman, Inc.; B3 (inset), NIBSC/Science Photo Library; B6(t), Franken/Stock, Boston; B6(b), Bob Daemmrich/Stock, Boston; B12(border), Ed Reschke/Peter Arnold, Inc.; B12, Michael Abbey/Photo Researchers; B14(t), Stepanowicz/Bruce Coleman, Inc.; B14(b), The Granger Collection, New York; B15(t), H. Reinhard/Bruce Coleman, Inc.; B15(ct), E.R. Degginger/Photo Researchers; B15(c), David Scharf/Peter Arnold, Inc.; B15(cb), David Madison/Bruce Coleman, Inc.; B15(b), Farrell Grehan/Photo Researchers; B16(b), Peter Menzel; B16-B17, Biophoto Assoc./Science Source/Photo Researchers; B18(t), Barry L. Runk/Grant Heilman Photography; B18(b), Runk/Schoenberger/Grant Heilman Photography; B24(all), M. Abbey/Photo Researchers; B25(t), Petit Format/Nestle/Science Source/Photo Researchers; B25(ct), C.J. Allen/Stock, Boston; B25(cb), Richard Hutchings/Photo Researchers; B25(b), David Madison/Bruce Coleman, Inc.; B28 (border), E.R. Degginger/Bruce Coleman, Inc.; B28 (inset), M Abbey/Photo Researchers; B29, Biology Media/Photo Researchers; B30(t), Biomedical Communications/Bruce Coleman, Inc.; B30(c), Biophoto Assoc./Science Source/Photo Researchers; B30(b), E.R. Degginger/Bruce Coleman, Inc.; B31(t), Ed Reschke/Peter Arnold, Inc.; B31(c), Ed Reschke/Peter Arnold, Inc.; B31(b), David A. Wagner/Phototake; B32(t), M. Abbey/Photo Researchers; B32(c), M. Abbey/Photo Researchers; B32(b), Martin Rotker/Phototake; B34, B35(t), B35(c), B35(b), B36(t), B36(b), Lennart Nilsson, THE INCREDIBLE MACHINE, National Geographic Society; B38, Bruce Iverson/SPL/Photo Researchers; B39(t), Professors P.M. Motta & T. Fujita/SPL/Photo Researchers; B39(c), CNRI/SPL/Photo Researchers; B39(b), Manfred Kage/Peter Arnold, Inc.; B43, Peter Menzel; B50(border), CDC/Peter Arnold, Inc.; B50 (inset), B52(t),(br),B53(tl,r), NCI/Science Source/Photo Researchers; B54(bg), David Scharf/Peter Arnold, Inc., B55, David Wagner/Phototake; B56(t), David M. Phillips/Photo Researchers; 56(b), M.I. Walker/Photo Researchers; B57(t), Manfred Kage/Peter Arnold, Inc.; B57(bl), Omikron/Science Source/Photo Researchers; B57(bcl), Dr. Tony Brain/SPL/Photo Researchers; B57(bcr), David Phillips/Photo Researchers; B57(br), Manfred Kage/Peter Arnold, Inc.; B58(bl), A.B. Dowsett/SPL/Photo Researchers; B58(bc), Omikron/Science Source/Photo Researchers; B58(br), A.B. Dowsett/SPL/Photo Researchers; B61, Chuck Savage/The Stock Market; B62(t), Thomas Fletcher/Stock, Boston; B62(c), M.I. Walker/Science Source/Photo Researchers; B62(b), M. Abbey/Photo Researchers; B63(t), Alfred Pasieka/Peter Arnold, Inc.; B63(ct), C.C. Duncan/Medical Images; B63(c), Manfred Kage/Peter Arnold, Inc.; B63(cb), Martin Dohrn/Photo Researchers; B63(b), E. Gueho-CNRI/SPL/Photo Researchers; B64, Scott Camazine/Photo Researchers; B65, Kent Wood/Peter Arnold, Inc.; B66, Prof. P. Motta/Dept. of Anatomy/Univ. of "La Sapienza", Rome/SPL/Photo Researchers; B67(t), Biophoto Assoc./Photo Researchers; B67(b), B68, Peter Menzel; B69, The Granger Collection, New York; B71, The Bettmann Archive; B72(t), HRW Photo; B72(b), HRW Photo; B74-B75(bg), Omikron/Science Source/Photo Researchers; B75(tr), Manfred Kage/Peter Arnold, Inc.; B76-77(bg), Phil Degginger/Bruce Coleman, Inc.; B79(t), C.C. Duncan/Medical Images.

Unit C, Harcourt Brace & Company Photographs: C4-C5, C6(c), C6(b), Terry D. Sinclair; C7(t inset) Maria Paraskevas; C7(b), Terry D. Sinclair; C8, C9, Weronica Ankarorn; C10-C11, C13, C14, C17(t), C17(b), C19, C21(t), C22, C27, C37(b), C40, Terry D. Sinclair; C50, Weronica Ankarorn; C55, Terry D. Sinclair; C58, Weronica Ankarorn; C60, C65, C66, C70, C78, C80, C85(tl), C90-C91, C91(tl), C91(tr), C92(t), C93(t), C93(b), Terry D. Sinclair.

Unit C, All Other Photographs: Unit Divider Page, NASA; C1, C2-C3, Dr. Jean Lorre/SPL/Photo Researchers; C3, JPL/NASA; C6(t), J. Hester/Arizona State University/NASA; C7(t), Photo by P. Hollembeak, Courtesy Department of Library Services, American Museum of Natural History; C12(border), Comstock; C12, NASA; C12(inset), Luis Vilotta/The Stock Market; C14(bg),

NASA/JSC/Starlight; C15(l), Art Resource; C15(r), Ron Watts/First Light; C16, Archiv fur Kunst und Geschichte; C18(t), NASA/JSC/ Starlight; C18(b), NASA; C19(bg), NASA; C20(bg), Michael Freeman; C20, Bridgeman Art Library/Art Resource, NY; C22(bg), Dennis DiCiccio/Peter Arnold, Inc.; C22(b), Roger Ressmeyer/Starlight; C23(t), Dennis DiCiccio/Peter Arnold, Inc.; C23(b), Roger Ressmeyer/Starlight; C24-C25, G. Petersen/First Light; C25(tl), Mary Evans Picture Library; C25(tr), M Timothy O'Keefe/Tom Stack & Assoc.; C25(c), Jack Parsons; C25(b), Giraudon/Art Resource, NY; C26-C27(bg), Comstock; C29(t), Thomas Kitchin/Tom Stack & Assoc.; C29(b) Thomas Kitchin/Tom Stack & Assoc.; C30(all photos) Hansen Planetarium; C32, NASA; C33(l), M. Mendillo/Boston University; C33(r), NASA; C34(t), Hansen Planetarium; C34-C35, NASA; C35(tl), NASA; C35(tr), Hale Observatories, Polomar Mountain California; C36, JPL/NASA; C36(inset), JPL/NASA; C36(border), NASA; C-37(t), U.S.S.S. Flagstaff Arizona/Starlight; C41(t), JPL/NASA; C41(c), Edmond Scientific Company/NASA; C41(b), U.S.S.S./Starlight; C42, NASA/JSC Starlight; C43(bg), Mark Lawrence/The Stock Market; C43, NASA; C44(c), NASA/JPL; C44(r), NASA; C44(c), NASA/JPL; C44(bg), U.S.S.S. Flagstaff Arizona/Starlight; C45(t), JPL/NASA; C45(b), Michael Freeman; C46(all photos) JPL/NASA; C47(bg), NASA; C47, Peter Arnold, Inc.; C48(t), STSI/NASA; C48(b), NASA; C49(t), The Bettman Archive; C49(b), Michael Freeman; C50(bg), Roger Ressmeyer/Starlight; C51(tl), JPL/NASA; C51(c), C51(b), STSI/NASA; C53, Dennis Milon/Hansen Planetarium; C54, The Arecibo Observatory is part of the National Astronomy and Ionosphere Center which is operated by Cornell University under a cooperative agreement with the National Science Foundation; C55(bg), Roger Ressmeyer/Starlight; C56(border), Roger Ressmeyer/Starlight; C56, Courtesy/Royal Observatory Edinburgh, Photographed by David Malin; C56(inset), Vaughn/Tom Stack & Assoc.; C62-C63(all photos), Ian Howarth; C64(l), Scala/Art Resource; C64(r), The Bettman Archive; C66(bg), Michael Freeman; C67(b), Ressmeyer/Starlight; C67(all other photos), Roger Ressmeyer/Starlight; C68(t), NASA/The Image Works; C68(bl), STSI/NASA; C68(br), STSI/NASA; C69, Frank Rossotto/Tom Stack & Assoc.; C72(tl), Courtesy/Anglo Australian Observatory, Photographed by David Malin; C72(r), Hansen Planetarium; C72(bl), JPL; C73, Courtesy/Anglo Australian Observatory, Photographed by David Malin; C74(border), First Light; C74, Stocktrek Photo Agency/JPL/Tom Stack & Assoc.; C74(inset), Roger Ressmeyer/Starlight; C75(tl), Frank Rossotto/Tom Stack & Assoc.; C75(tr), NASA; C75(bl), Kim Gordon/SPL/ Photo Researchers; C75(br), NASA/JPL; C78(bg), Hale Observatories/Science Photo Library/Photo Researchers; C81, John Sandford/Science Photo Library/Photo Researchers; C83, Geoff Williams & Howard Metcalf/Science Photo Library/Photo Researchers; C84(tl), Hank Morgan/Rainbow; C84(tlc), David R. Frazier Photolibrary; C84(trc), M. Siluk/The Image Works; C84(tr), Williamson/Edwards/The Image Bank; C84(bl), NASA; C84(blc), J. Heap/Goddard Space Flight Center/NASA; C84(brc), Courtesy/Royal Observatory Edinburgh, Photographed by David Malin; C84(br), NRAO/AUI/Science Photo Library/Photo Researchers; C85(tlc), First Light; C85(trc), Steve Krongard/The Image Bank; C85(tr), Ian Satley & Michael Merrill/NOAO/Starlight; C85(bl), Roger Ressmeyer/Starlight; C85(br), Ray Nelson/Phototake; C86, Roger Ressmeyer/Starlight; C90-C91(bg), STSI/NASA; C91(c), Walzenbach/The Stock Market; C92-C93(bg), Craig Aurness/First Light; C93(bg,b), Bob Abraham/The Stock Market; C94, W. Hille/Leo de Wys, Inc.; C95(tl), Hansen Planetarium/NASA Photo; C95(tr), Bernie Rokeach/The Image Bank; C95(bl), Roger Ressmeyer/Starlight; C96, Hansen Planetarium.

Unit D, Harcourt Brace & Company Photographs: D4-D5, D6(t), D6(c), D6(b), D7(c), Terry D. Sinclair; D7(b), Greg Leary; D8, Weronica Ankarorn; D9, Maria Paraskevas; D10-D11, Terry D. Sinclair; D12(bg), Weronica Ankarorn; D13, Maria Paraskevas; D15(t), Terry D. Sinclair; D16(t), Weronica Ankarorn; D19(bg), D19, D20(bg), D20, D21, Terry D. Sinclair; D24(t), Weronica Ankarorn; D24(b), D25(t), Maria Paraskevas; D25(c), Terry D. Sinclair; D25(b), Maria Paraskevas; D27, D28(b), Terry D. Sinclair; D29, Maria Paraskevas; D30(bl), D31, Terry D. Sinclair; D32, Maria Paraskevas; D33, Terry D. Sinclair; D34(tl), D34(tc), D34(bl), Weronica Ankarorn; D34(br), Terry D. Sinclair; D36 (border), D36, D36 (inset), D37, Weronica Ankarorn; D38, Maria Paraskevas; D39, Terry D. Sinclair; D41, D42(t), D42(b), Weronica Ankarorn; D43(bg), D43, D44(t), Terry D. Sinclair; D44(b), Maria Paraskevas; D45, D46, D47, D48 (bg), D48, Terry D. Sinclair; D49, Weronica Ankarorn; D50, Terry D. Sinclair; D51(br), Weronica Ankarorn; D52, D57, Terry D. Sinclair; D58, Maria Paraskevas; D62, Terry D. Sinclair; D63, Maria Paraskevas; D64(bg), D66, Terry D. Sinclair; D66 (border), Maria Paraskevas; D67, D68-D69(bg), D68, D69, D70(t), Terry D. Sinclair; D70(b), Weronica Ankarorn; D72(t), D77(bg), D77, D79, D81, D88(c), D89, D90-D91(bg), D90-D91(t), Terry D. Sinclair; D90(b), Weronica Ankarorn; D91, Terry D. Sinclair; D92-D93(b), D93(t), D93(b), D94(b), D95(tl), D95(bl), Terry D. Sinclair; D95(tcr),(tr), Maria Paraskevas.

Unit D, All Other Photographs: Unit Divider Page, First Light; D1, D2-D3, Michael Skott; D3, Richard Embery/FPG International; D7(t), Brian King/Leo de Wys, Inc.; D12, Dan Lecca/FPG International; D12(inset), David R. Frazier/Photolibrary; D14, Courtesy of International Flavors & Fragrances, John Olson, photographer; D16(b), Thomas Kitchin/First Light; D17-D18, Courtesy of International Flavors & Fragrances, John Olson, photographer; D23, Alexander Marshack; D28(l), NASA; D28(tr), John Bova/ Photo Researchers; D30(bg), Tony Freeman/PhotoEdit; D34(tr), Terje Rakke/The Image Bank; D35, Rod Planck/Photo Researchers; D40, Steve Short/First Light;

R32